JONATHAN LETHEM

The Ecstasy of Influence

Nonfictions, etc.

VINTAGE BOOKS
London

Published by Vintage 2013

2 4 6 8 10 9 7 5 3 1

First published in Great Britain in 2012 by
Jonathan Cape

Vintage
Random House, 20 Vauxhall Bridge Road,
London SW1V 2SA

www.vintage-books.co.uk

Addresses for companies within The Random House Group Limited
can be found at: www.randomhouse.co.uk/offices.htm

The Random House Group Limited Reg. No. 954009

A CIP catalogue record for this book
is available from the British Library

ISBN 9780099563433

The Random House Group Limited supports The Forest Stewardship
Council (FSC®), the leading international forest certification
organisation. Our books carrying the FSC label are printed on FSC®
certified paper. FSC is the only forest certification scheme endorsed
by the leading environmental organisations, including Greenpeace.
Our paper procurement policy can be found at:
www.randomhouse.co.uk/environment

MIX
Paper from
responsible sources
FSC
www.fsc.org   FSC C016897

Printed and bound in Great Britain by Clays Ltd, St Ives PLC

For Richard Parks

The Artist's sense of truth. Regarding truths, the artist has a weaker morality than the thinker. He definitely does not want to be deprived of the splendid and profound interpretations of life, and he resists sober, simple methods and results. Apparently he fights for the higher dignity and significance of man; in truth, he does not want to give up the most effective presuppositions of his art: the fantastic, mythical, uncertain, extreme, the sense of the symbolic, the overestimation of the person, the faith in some miraculous element in the genius. Thus he considers the continued existence of his kind of creation more important than scientific devotion to the truth in every form, however plain.

—FRIEDRICH NIETZSCHE, *Human, All Too Human*

The idea of art as an expensive hunk of well-regulated area, both logical and magical, sits heavily over the talent of every modern painter . . .

—MANNY FARBER, "White Elephant vs. Termite Art"

You must have made inconceivable promises, unsupportable by facts, in your ardor, and that counted for something, and were you asked to hold to them, or were you not?

—ANDER MONSON, "The Essay Vanishes"

Contents

VII: Dylan, Brown, and Others

VIII: Working the Room

IX: The Mad Brooklynite

x: WHAT REMAINS OF MY PLAN

Preface

1. Undressing "Me," Addressing "You"

Somewhere—I can't find it now—there's a book with a preface in which a writer of fiction admitted he couldn't write the preface to the book "you now hold in your hands" until he'd conceived of the preface as a story about a writer of fiction writing a preface; only then could he begin. Saying this, the reader of said preface was presumably drawn into an awareness that the voices in so-called "nonfictions" were themselves artful impostures, arrangements of sentences (and of the implications residing behind the sentences) that mimicked the presence of a human being offering sincerely intended and honestly useful guidance into this or that complicated area of human thought or experience. According to this belief, even an auto manual or cookbook possessed an "implied author."

Sure, you say, tell me something I don't know. But let's keep in mind that the opposite belief flourishes—i.e., that we all possess the capacity and therefore also the responsibility to testify out of some unmediatedly *true self*. Or, if mediation goes on, that it's of as little importance as the jotting hand of various forgotten human scribes who happened to capture God's words when they authored the Bible. This belief is clung to with a ferocity that suggests something immense might be at stake.

But I've introduced a confusion, even at the outset of this long test of your patience. That writer I mention isn't me, or even "me." He's—I just remembered this—an American science-fiction writer named Robert Sheckley (1928–2005). Sheckley's description works for me, though. I've never managed a routine book review, let alone an essay I thought worth reprinting, without first having to invent a character who'd be issuing the remarks the essay would subsequently record, and also figuring out what motivations this guy—call him "Lethem"—would have for working his thoughts into language. *By practical necessity I'm firmly in the doubting-nonfiction-is-exactly-possible camp*, Lethem typed insouciantly.

The reader of the preface is a fiction, too. No, no, wait, I don't for crissakes mean *you*, dear fleshly friend, semi-loyal eyeball. Hey, I clasp your hand. ("A knowledge that people live close by is, / I think, enough. And even if only first names are ever exchanged / The people who own them seem rock-true and marvelously self-sufficient."—John Ashbery, "The Ongoing Story") I'm not looking to try to persuade you that you're a cyborg, mosaic, site, interface, or any other post-human thing. My point is more that you're *pre*human, actually: I'm addressing you before you've been quite willing to appear, pretending you've arrived in order to have someone to gab with until you get here, painting your portrait to find out what you look like—only sometimes, often, you won't sit still.

Example: The odd fact is that naming Sheckley as a science-fiction writer cost me some discomfort, but an extremely familiar and tolerable form of discomfort, one I routinely self-inflict for the useful friction it generates in the conversation into which I've tossed the term. You, postulated readers: Aren't you now divided into two teams, those appalled with me for being dodgy about Sheckley and his affiliations, and those disgruntled because they didn't know, or want to know, his name? Have a look at yourselves, on either side of the room, like tweens at a dance party: Shouldn't one or the other gender be exiting the floor about now? But stay.

Please do stay.

2. Self-Consciousness, Objections To

No one is obligated to care that writers sometimes, or often, think such self-conscious stuff as the above. There're onslaughts of evidence that mention of these matters annoy the hell out of some readers. Many people prefer artists to make statements along the lines of: "I don't know what I'm doing, I just go into a small, badly furnished room and out come these stories," "The songs write themselves," "The paint tells me where it wants to go," etc. Even readers with an appetite for the dynamic curlicues of intellection so typical of the prose of forthrightly self-conscious, ontology-obsessed writers (John Barth being a perfect example) can suddenly grow nauseated by a disproportion of the stuff over time (hence Barth's terrifying decline in popularity). David Foster Wallace deserves to be remembered as a great writer not because he was capable of doing PhD-level philosophical speculation as well as shunting fictional characters (slowly) through a well-described room but because he mastered a certain area of human sensation totally: intricate self-conscious remorse *at the fact of* self-consciousness. Wallace's way of loading up this indistinct area with scrupulous depiction made a lot of people feel less lonely; meanwhile, the possibility that being the depicter made Wallace feel *more* lonely has become a widely circulated armchair-shrink's allegory for the non-usefulness of self-consciousness. Because it *doesn't help.* Doesn't help the depressed person feel undepressed, doesn't help the storyteller tell the story. **Just Do It!**: the top-to-bottom scream of our culture, and a good anthem for skippers not only of prefaces to books but of entire collections of occasional pieces by those who ought to have the grace to stick to storytelling. Never mind where that slippery slope might get you, or how the attitude shears toward the same anti-intellectual currents in American life that would shovel reading novels per se into a trench along with a lot of other things you hold dear, if you're still with me at this point. Bias spoiler alert: I think I'm an intellectual, and I think you are, too, whether you like it or not. I can't help thinking so.

All of these thoughts fall into the category of things I can't help thinking, despite having sometimes tried not to, thinking it was my duty to do so. It turns out I can't help being the self-conscious kind of artist, one who pits himself compulsively against bogus valorizing of notions of originality, authenticity, or naturalism in the arts. This is where a certain political implication comes out of hiding, and it's a political implication very dear to me. For if we consent that what appears natural in art is actually constructed from a series of hidden postures, decisions, and influences, etc., we make ourselves eligible to weigh the notion that what's taken as natural in our experience of everyday life could actually be a construction as well.

That's to say, if we pass time getting dreamy by reading stories about things that didn't really happen, set in worlds that aren't precisely our own, while acknowledging that such self-into-elsewhere dreams *are enacted by conscious means*, by acts of intention and craft (on the part of the readers as well as by the writers), it might suggest an analogous getting-from-here-to-there process: from this world, to a different one. Dreams of making real alterations in our relations to our selves and others (as well as to the systems that everywhere instill in us a dreadful foreboding that such alterations are highly unlikely) are for many people embarrassing, even rude to mention. Others grow enraged. *To comfort the disturbed, and disturb the comfortable*: what presumption, on the part of the storyteller, taking this assignment!

Yet I've got no choice, for I *am* the disturbed I seek to comfort, and also the comfortable I seek to disturb.

3. This Way to the Giant Abstract Octopus

Talking about what I'm doing, about how it feels to write the books published under Lethem's name, has become a habit. It's a second career, conducted within the Kabuki formalities of book touring, both privileged and burdensome. I don't mean to complain. I'm aware that having this bloggish book issued in boards by a major corporate publisher in 2011 is, precisely, a measure of the aristocratic privilege accorded me by the novelist's role, akin to being borne aloft in a chair like a conquistador over mountain terrain everyone else is made to traverse barefoot and with supplies on their backs. Yet it's often weird what the polite novelist lately *isn't* supposed to say aloud. We're not meant to refute critics (though fiendish questions are devised to test our adherence to this principle). Nor should we acknowledge Internet discourse about our books—that Morlockian subverse isn't fit for mention. No, we've renounced, after a brief misguided sally, entering our names on search engines. We don't rank ourselves among our contemporaries, or attack other polite novelists for being overrated or even completely full of shit (such admissions are reserved for self-loathing grumbles between novelists, by e-mail). We don't know why we do what we do, but we're not *too* amazed with ourselves for being the lucky keepers of this universal flame. That we're modest goes without saying. Influence is semiconscious, not something to delineate too extensively, except when we've patterned our latest book on a literary monument of the past, at least a half-century old, by a master with whom we'd never dare compare ourselves, only hope to be "worthy of." We don't speak of our own career's arc, let alone of crises encountered therein, because we'd never think of what we're doing in crass terms of a career. Rather, blinkered devotionally, we "serve the needs of the book at hand," and besides are permanent amateurs, born anew each time we start writing (which I suppose means we die each time we publish, but that's a downer). We're always so honored to have been invited onto your radio show.

Thanks for having me. Thanks for having me. Thank God in all his mercy that *you* were willing to *have me*.

Though like any properly fame-hungry American of my generation I spent years imaginatively yearning to know what it would be like to be interviewed, I dread reading or listening to the interviews that resulted now that I've given hundreds, because I know they're riddled with such obediences. Here, I'll try not to be obedient. I want to bite the hand that feeds me, even if that hand is sometimes yours, reader.

"I'm completely in print, so we're all stuck with me and stuck with my books." The words are Kurt Vonnegut's, making bitter rejoinder to critics he believed wished to see him evaporate from the literary landscape. Vonnegut spoke them in an interview he later collected in a book called *Palm Sunday* (subtitled *An Autobiographical Collage*; perhaps not too terrible a term for what I'm doing here). I could say the same, though if I did I'd speak more in wonder than in bitterness—and I don't mean that as a Kabuki gesture of modesty. Really, most of my heroes are partly or entirely out of print, as I always expected and am surely destined to be (as is Vonnegut, too). After all, I've written a lot of short, strange books. That even a very small number of grown men and women in 2011 might still be interested in *Amnesia Moon*—a novel a nineteen-year-old began composing in 1983—well, that's a situation that can't sustain itself forever. It isn't meant to. In the sea of words, the *in print* is foam, surf bubbles riding the top. And it's a dark sea, and deep, where divers need lights on their helmets and would perish at the lower depths.

But I lie. I have one out-of-print book. A few years ago my friend Christopher Sorrentino and I co-authored the pseudonymous *Believeniks: The Year We Wrote a Book About the Mets*. As genuine (therefore, tormented) Mets fans, our book was sincere, and a real account of the 2005 season in progress, but since the listed authors weren't Lethem and Sorrentino, but Harris Conklin and Ivan Felt, two Flaubertian buffoons we'd invented (Conklin billed himself as "America's foremost neglected poet"; Felt was a disaffected academic), the book was a fiction, too: a nonfiction written by fictional characters. It parodied Stephen King and Stewart O'Nan's (accidentally triumphalist) account of the Boston Red Sox curse-breaking championship season of 2004, and paid homage to Don DeLillo's *Amazons*, a pseudonymous faux-memoir of the first woman to play in the National Hockey League (you could look it up).

The world was as taken with *Believeniks* as it was by the achievements of the 2005 New York Mets, minus a paid attendance of two-and-some-odd million. No paperback, no translations into any language, and we couldn't get the team to let us throw out the first pitch at a game. You'd be justified in thinking that writing a fannish account of a real baseball season in the voices of two (disagreeable) fictional characters was an act on par with painting an abstract composition in oils, titling it *Giant Octopus*, then hanging it on the wall of a public aquarium and standing to one side to chortle as schoolchildren are ushered in for viewings. Well, reserve your brickbats: We did no chortling, as no schoolchildren arrived.

My point? The book in your hands wouldn't be published if I offered it under my Believenik name, Harris Conklin. "Jonathan Lethem," at least for this tiny blip in literary eternity, gets the cookie. I may seem, in places herein, exasperated with how the power of the novelist in twenty-first-century culture is circumscribed, but I grant that it does consist of power. Vonnegut wasn't feeling powerful when he made his bitter remark about being in print, but his ability to enshrine the remark in hardcovers and keep it in circulation shows he was wrong. (The pretense-of-no-power is a symptom I want to examine, not exhibit.) Then again, if you want to drive a person mad in a fame culture, offer him only a little fame, the very least amount you can scrape up. This happens every day, but it happens in slow motion to novelists. We're like the guy who gets voted off first on *Survivor*, except instead of departing the island we walk its beaches forever, muttering.

All writing, no matter how avowedly naturalistic or pellucid, consists of artifice, of conjuration, of the manipulation of symbols rather than the "opening of a window onto life." Abstract paintings of a giant octopus are all we have to put on view in my city's aquarium. We writers aren't sculpting in DNA, or even clay or mud, but words, sentences, paragraphs, syntax, voice; materials issued by tongue or fingertips but which upon release dissolve into the atmosphere, into cloud, confection, specter. Language, as a vehicle, is a lemon, a hot rod painted with thrilling flames but crazily erratic to drive, riddled with bugs like innate self-consciousness, embedded metaphors and symbols, helpless intertextuality, and so forth. Despite being regularly driven on prosaic errands (interoffice memos, supermarket receipts, etc.), it tends to veer on its misaligned chassis into the ditch of abstraction, of dream.

None of this disqualifies my sense of passionate urgency at the task of making the giant octopus in *my* mind's eye visible to *yours*. It doesn't make the attempt any less fundamentally human, delicate, or crucial. It makes it more so. That's because another name for the giant octopus I have in mind is *negotiating selfhood in a world of other selves*—the permanent trouble of being alive. Our language has no choice but to be self-conscious if it is to be conscious in the first place.

4. Models for My Behavior Who Are Not to Be Blamed for What Transpires (and One Who Is)

In the cause of transparency, I'll mention that while writing the newest pieces here I've been reading essays by Seymour Krim, Renata Adler, Ander Monson, Kathleen Fitzpatrick, Mark McGurl, Sianne Ngai, David Foster Wallace, Randall Jarrell, and Leonard Michaels. At any given instant these present infatuations made an influence in which my own loyalties and certainties dissolved, only to re-form somewhat altered when I recovered my senses. That, against an unavoidable backdrop of my own *usual suspects* list, Vivian Gornick, David Shields, Phillip Lopate, George W. S. Trow, Geoff Dyer, Samuel Delany, Geoffrey O'Brien, Annie Dillard, and Greil Marcus, those who first made me want to try writing essays and set the standard to reach for when I tried, even as their more abiding commitment to the form keeps me humble by comparison (but hey, I could kick each of their asses up and down the novel-writing block, except Delany). I'm also indebted to Manny Farber, whose original formulation of the opposition between "White Elephant Art" (big, ungainly, awards-season stuff) and "Termite Art" (prestige-immune routes of curiosity through the cultural woodwork) has proven so versatile and stimulating, to me and others, that it's in danger of floating free of Farber's first rigorous uses. Sorry.

Now, all exalted name-dropping aside, let me confess that one particular book hovers uneasily over my effort: Norman Mailer's *Advertisements for Myself*. I'll save defense of Mailer as a writer, or self-exculpation for my own fascination with him, for later, saying here just that I discovered that book at age fifteen, and have read it—or read around in it, since it's unbearable to read cover to cover—dozens of times since then. If I browse in my mental library for examples of behavior by novelists-doing-other-than-writing-novels (and the difficulties attaching thereupon), I find Mailer's *Advertisements* everywhere I turn. It's the template for throwing fiction, poetry, letters, etc. into the same collection, along with so much preening apparatus. *Advertisements* stands for the simultaneous invention, summit, and dead end of its category, and Mailer for the perfect example of the kind of writer we're defiantly happy not to suffer in our midst anymore. He's the paradigm for a novelist's willful abuse of his credibility with readers, and a White Elephant par excellence. Yet he's also a father with whom I'm enmeshed, a Big Other I feel watching me work. Disclosure: My editor had to ask me not to subtitle this book *Advertisements for Norman Mailer*. What I never even told him was that at one point I wanted it for the title.

5. Some Termite Ways to Read This White Elephant Book

Mailer offered two tables of contents, charting alternate paths through his impossible book. He also offered a list of what he considered the best pieces in the book (though nearly anyone would disagree about a couple). I won't do either, exactly. Yet even figuring anyone's sure to browse and skip, let me suggest a couple of organizing patterns not alluded to in my table of contents. A few preliminary termite holes I've bored in my edifice, to get you started on your own.

First, in my own defense: I left things out. There are pieces I liked that didn't fit, just as some pieces that seemed in themselves pretty weak went in because they *did* fit. This is that sort of book. I excluded enough belletristic work (introductions and reviews, that is) to fill another volume. On the whole, I've gathered here maybe a quarter of my "uncollected" writings, if you include fiction.

"The Ecstasy of Influence" is the eye of this particular storm. Like the essay, this book's full of other voices: epigraphs, quotes in the bodies of reviews, the utterances of musicians in the two profiles, and what I've called "plagiarisms"—i.e., lifts both acknowledged and unacknowledged, both conscious and (surely) unconscious. You could, if you wanted, take this as a kind of commonplace book, or as a list of books to read after reading mine or instead of reading mine. If this somehow were to become the last example of what a book was, left to the bemused assessment of tentacled archaeologists, it might be a lucky selection simply for being ultra-informative, for having gnawed at and disgorged so much of its own context, just as, if Ian Dury's "Reasons to Be Cheerful (Part 3)" were our culture's last surviving song, it would be a lucky selection because it name-checks "Elvis and Scotty," "Good Golly, Miss Molly," "Dali," "Harpo, Groucho, Chico," "John Coltrane," "the Bolshoi Ballet," and so on. That's how I regard this fate of ours, drowning in a cultural sea: reasons to be cheerful.

This preface, the title essay, and several of the newer ones ("Against 'Pop' Culture," "White Elephant and Termite Postures," "Advertisements for Norman Mailer," "Postmodernism as Liberty Valance," "My Disappointment Critic/On Bad Faith," "Rushmore Versus Abundance," and some of the interstitial remarks) make a sporadic argument about the contemporary intellectual situation for fiction's writers and readers, but with implications, I hope, for other kinds of public thinking and talking. They're more tendentious than the rest. If you're in no mood to see me skirmish with injustices less ultimately urgent than hunger, disease, and discrimination you might just want to skip them. (*Now he tells us.*) There's plenty else.

Conversely, many sections conclude with a brief piece, usually written headlong and heedlessly, in a mode I'd call "ecstastic." There are others of these, too, not at the ends of sections—you'll find them if you look. These were often commissioned pieces, for a journal or website I felt unable to refuse, with the small size of the readership guaranteed. (Harry Cohn: "Miss Stein, what is your secret?" Gertrude Stein: "Small audiences.") Some were written in annoyance, as I hurried back to my "real" work, to something destined for a book or for a periodical with *New York* in its name, something with a bigger readership guaranteed. (Perhaps something tendentious.) Anyway, while ecstasy isn't the guaranteed result on such occasions, it can happen. These are accidental darlings. They read in retrospect as if I'd gulped a lungful of helium, then burbled out the paragraphs before the delirious vocal effect wore off. Putting these samples on a par with the "bigger work," giving them a second life that is practically their first, is for me reason enough for this book.

THE
ECSTASY *of*
INFLUENCE

I

My Plan to Begin With

Twist away the gates of steel
Unlock the secret voice—

—DEVO, "Gates of Steel"

Every book conceals a book.

—RICHARD G. STERN

My Plan to Begin With, Part One

I came from dropping out; the only thing I knew at the start was to quit before they could fire me. My mother left college in favor of the counterculture. In the legend of Judith Lethem it was a brilliant move with no regrets, though I recall her discussing a matchbook offer from Empire State College, which awarded degrees for life experience—hers would have been for protest, encounter groups, social work, drugs. My father, a Fulbright scholar, studied painting at Columbia and in Paris, but threw over a tenure-track gig for work as a cabinetmaker, and commercial Manhattan galleries for cooperative Brooklyn ones. You ran away to make a world. Vanished into a garret and emerged with pages Prometheanly aflame. Thumbed to San Francisco. The Beat generation script sank into my deep layers even as I tired—fast—of Kerouac's novels. Your parents are the first memo to come across your desk, on a page so large you can't see past its edges. At least half of the known universe had done without higher education. In the legend of Judith Lethem (which likely lived only in my head) that half was "the smart one," our home bookshelves her word palace (later I'd notice how many of the volumes actually had *Richard Lethem, Columbia University* jotted on their flyleaves).

I still receive congratulations for having "evaded the MFA mill," unlike my generational cohort. At those moments I really ought to offer a blanket defense of those in the poignant and terrifying situation of trying to become a writer, by whatever means available; the dedication of MFA students often moves me to tears when I speak before them. Instead, I'm usually silent, embarrassed to explain that I was too drunk on a script at least fifty years out-of-date to even notice what had become the new template for becoming a writer. The system was invisible to me until it was too late. After all, didn't every novelist work as a clerk in a bookstore until they'd published their first book?

The Used Bookshop Stories

OPENING THE SHOP

At fifteen I graduated from sweeping up the painted wooden floor-boards and neatening the stock on the erratic, slapped-together wooden shelves and running to Steve's Restaurant for coffee ("light," in paper cups with the Parthenon on the side) and for corn muffins scorched on the grill, to opening the shop by myself. Saturday and Sunday mornings on Atlantic Avenue, in the little bookstore next to Kalfian Carpets and across the street from the tire shop, nothing doing here—our eccentric little bookshop was twenty or thirty years too early for gentrification, if it ever stood a chance.

Michael didn't really like to get up in the morning, and as the months went by he liked less and less to preside over the empty store. I was his solution, the local kid who'd be thrilled just to get credit with adults for "working" when what I was really doing was reading, putter-ing in the stacks, playing God of Books in this almost wholly private realm. I'd take home my "pay" in books alone, was always gathering a stack of goods in the back corridor that I'd shift into my knapsack when I'd earned them. And inside a glass-fronted case were our rare books, including a couple I coveted and saved months to earn: Henry Miller and Michael Fraenkel's *Hamlet* with a red-ribbon binding and uncut pages, and an autographed copy of Bernard Wolfe's mysterious *Limbo*. (I still own the Wolfe, but can't recall where and when I let go of the Miller-Fraenkel.)

I'd roll up the gate at eleven (having bought myself not coffee but tea and the grilled corn muffin from Steve's), pull the cart of stealable cheapo books to the sidewalk in front of the window, and plant myself at the old wooden desk to the right of the door—a sentry position, against the risk of thievery—waiting for the first customer of the day, sometimes an hour before anyone wandered in. The place had no heat, and in cold months I'd be in scarf and hat, rubbing gloved fingers together, waiting for the sun to hit the window and warm the storefront. We kept change in a cigar box in the top drawer, and the only time I ever left the desk for even a minute the box was scooped clean by some clever bandit, my fault, but Michael knew thievery was the neighborhood's nature and just shook his head. It counted not against me but against him sticking around Brooklyn, and soon enough the little shop moved up to a basement storefront on East Eighty-fourth Street in Manhattan—half the size of the Atlantic Avenue storefront and a hundred times more viable.

Paloma Picasso

My roommate was the night man at the shop on Broadway and Eightieth, a high narrow shop with a central staircase to a rare-book level upstairs, and used records in a bin beneath the stairs. I was the night man's backup, closing the place alone on Friday and Sunday nights. The store buzzed between seven and ten on weekend nights, full of couples strolling after movies or dinner, the cash register whirring. The last hour, eleven to midnight, was pretty dead, especially on a Sunday. This night, reading as usual at the counter, I was alone there apart from a long-necked beauty in haute couture who amassed a mighty pile of art and photo books, making several trips up to the counter to drop off her accumulation, then returning to her browsing. I grew mildly curious as the expensive pile swelled, feeling a faint sexy complicity between us. Then, as in a television commercial famous at the time, she revealed her identity to me wordlessly, by paying with a credit card.

Chris Butler

The hole-in-the-wall used bookshop on Bergen Street lasted probably about six months, and when the owners, a sultry hippie couple (I had a crush on her), decided to close it, I considered buying the shop and living in it as my apartment in order to make it sustainable, and life in New York, affordable. I imagined myself sitting in the open shop all day, writing—it was certainly quiet enough. Instead I moved to California, where I would live for a decade after. The shop, barely bigger than a walk-in closet, became a video store, then a hot-dog joint.

My two memories of the long empty afternoons there: I was at the counter listening to WBAI the day that the jazz drummer Philly Joe Jones died. Bizarrely, another jazz drummer, named Johnny Joe Jones, died within the same twenty-four hours. The disc jockey played examples of the music of both "Joe Joneses," his tone soberly memorial, never dwelling on the absurd coincidence of their names. I'd not heard of either man before that day.

And: One day Chris Butler, the songwriter-auteur of the Waitresses, came in and struck up a conversation. I don't know how it was he revealed himself to me, but I must have been gregarious—desperate, really, for the sort of hipster customer he appeared to be.

Imperious Memoirist

An imperious middle-aged memoirist came into the store on Solano Avenue in Berkeley one afternoon. This was a vast commercial space, four used-book-lined walls stretching into a deep storefront full of tables of remainders and new books, bins of used records, and a long magazine rack high enough that it required a mirror for us to patrol shoplifters. Four or five of us manned the floor at any given time, usually two of us at the counter behind the registers.

She had a train of courtiers with her—reverential local guides, perhaps a literary escort or two. They asked us whether we had any of her books. The staff began to find their sense of privilege funny; mere clerks drawing pay, the store nonetheless belonged to us, and we judged those who entered our space. One of us spoke rudely to the imperious memoirist. The phrase "Do you know who you're talking to?" was uttered on her behalf.

It was at this same store that we had to fend off persistent inquiries by spies for ASCAP, men and women who carried clipboards and dressed like Mormons. They wanted us to pay performance royalties on the used records we borrowed from the store's bins and played on the turntable behind the counter. The music was of course audible throughout the store, but we argued with straight faces that it was for the private enjoyment of the clerks, and, further, that the customers usually only complained about the music, which was true. When they'd leave we'd titter behind our hands, amazed at the impoverished lives of bureaucratic stiffs.

Lovecraft in the Basement

The store on Livingston Street in Brooklyn had been in operation since sometime in the '30s or early '40s, no one was sure—it had been taken over by our present boss in the '70s, and he was a man who hated books. The place was a ramshackle disaster—ancient books of neglected quality layered behind decades of dubious acquisitions. Our boss offset the uncertainties—and, to him, the mysteries—of the used-book trade by offering new editions of the Bible, books on dream interpretation, and guides to civil service tests (some guys came in and bought the test book for "Fireman" and then, after they failed, switched to "Sanitation Worker" or "Jail Guard"), and crates of used copies of *Playboy* and *Penthouse*. The store was deep and high and narrow, with ladders to reach the obscure stuff fifteen or twenty feet in the air. It also had a rank and moldy basement, at all times kept locked, and rumored to be full of treasure abandoned by the former owners, including a large collection of rare books acquired from the estate of H. P. Lovecraft.

The boss hired clerks who knew more about books than he did—he couldn't help that—and then distrusted them, fearing that they'd gather items of neglected value and ferret them from the store, out from under his nose. We would. He had strict and absurd policies in place: No employee was allowed to buy more than two books a week, even at full face value. This forced me to use friends as shills: They'd come in, pretending not to know me, and I'd put items in their hands that I wished them to buy for me. We were also strictly forbidden to linger in the basement for more than a minute or two. The boss would send us down there for a specific item—lightbulbs or a box of paper bags, not books—and then nervously wring his hands and, if we took too long, begin yelling. He feared we were trying to excavate treasure from the labyrinthine, impossible dark shelves in the basement—books whose value he could only guess at, but we might know. We were. He never left us alone in the store, not for more than a few minutes.

One morning another clerk and I (the same guy who became my roommate and was the night man at the Broadway store) got up at seven in the morning and used our keys to get inside the store and explore the basement privately and thoroughly, before opening hours and the boss's arrival. For our efforts we found maybe five or six items of interest, nothing special, and certainly no sign of the Lovecraft hoard. We each quit the store within a few weeks.

Conlon Nancarrow

A stooped and frail man with an elegant goatee browsed the record bins at the Solano store, guided deferentially by a local fellow we knew as a slightly preening, semi-famous experimental musician. When with trembling hand the elder man filled out a check to pay for the records he'd picked out, the name on the check was Conlon Nancarrow, the legendary exiled avant-gardist, who'd spent decades in Mexico punching out player-piano rolls, composing music too rapid for any human performer. I exclaimed at meeting him, and called our record buyer out of his hiding place in the back of the store. We luckily had a supply of Conlon Nancarrow LPs, a remainder item, and he signed their jackets for us with a silver marker.

Book Thieves

Word circulated among the several Berkeley stores: A ring of book thieves was plundering expensive art books and reselling them, a quick and easy racket. Our books had been identified by other clerks at other stores—and we'd been accidentally guilty of buying stock filched from our neighbor stores. The description of the thieves went out—seedy, eccentric, and gay—and we clerks at the Solano Avenue store put ourselves on high alert.

Soon enough came the day when they were detected in the store, three of them, two men and a woman, idling in the back aisles. We quietly assembled a posse of four or five clerks and, buzzing on our own outrage and adrenaline, asked them to step into the back of the store. Caught, the thieves glumly unloaded six or seven coffee-table books from under jackets and inside satchels, an astounding and brazen volume of material. We confronted them stammeringly, made insensate with fury: How could anyone bohemian, anyone who valued books, force us clerks into the role of cops? Wasn't that a breach of some bargain? Better if the book thieves had looked like the ASCAP Mormons. These thieves were awkward mirrors of ourselves, gormless, shaggy, hip—clerklike. We banished them and congratulated ourselves uneasily. I've never worked in a bookstore where the clerks didn't sometimes help themselves to the books, where we didn't feel that the wares belonged more to us than to the paying customers. And one of the best and purest and most dedicated clerks I ever worked with later ended up in a federal prison, convicted of rescuing deaccessioned antiquarian books and papers from a university library with what a judge considered excessive zeal.

Eldridge Cleaver, Greg Bear, Joseph McBride

At another Berkeley store—the grandest, in the middle of the campus strip on Telegraph Avenue, a four-story palace created in the '60s by one of the legends of Californian used-book selling—famous faces among the clientele were nothing terribly special. The store tended to attract any visitor to the campus, notable scholars who'd lose themselves in the deep third-floor humanities sections, while the rare-book room and art-book shop on the top floor were host to a stream of artists, photographers, and elite collectors. We were famous ourselves, in a way, famous for our clerkly arrogance. In friendly California, we dared to sniff and snap like New York bookstore clerks. Our totemic founding father was still present in the store, usually at the front counter, looming like Pere Ubu, spitting cigar-flavored droplets as he frowned and swore at the inferior wares offered to him at the store's buying counter, eating dim sum with his stained fingers and wearing hot sauce on his chin and collar for the rest of the afternoon. Among the rather desperate Bay Area characters who would regularly appear with a few miserable books to try to sell to the store was Eldridge Cleaver, in the last years before his death. When his books were rejected, Cleaver would only mumble and lower his eyes, wholly stripped of pride.

One quiet day the science-fiction writer Greg Bear, a large and kingly man, and at that time the president of the Science Fiction Writers of America, came to the counter to make a purchase. I recognized him—as usual, from his name on his credit card. Feeling sly, I told him that I was in fact a dues-paying member of his organization—I'd at that time sold three or four stories to science-fiction magazines, but there was no chance he'd know my name. At that, Greg Bear widened his eyes and threw open his arms (offering a Greg Bear Hug), seemingly recipient of a Socialist epiphany: Little men everywhere, even the clerk at a bookstore he'd wandered into, could be encompassed in Science Fiction's legions.

Another night, working alone at that counter on a Friday, a bearded man descended from the third floor, in the company of a woman. They'd been browsing the film section, and now presented a Paloma Picassoesque stack of out-of-print film books. The man's checkbook revealed him as Joseph McBride, biographer of John Ford, Orson Welles, and Frank Capra, a man I knew had spent long afternoons talking and hanging out on the set with Welles and Howard Hawks, among others. I blurted out: "Are you *the* Joseph McBride?" Before McBride could reply to me, the woman raised her eyebrows and deadpanned perfectly: "That's the first time I've ever heard anyone put it quite that way."

Closing the Shop

Closing the shop on Telegraph was a lot of work. We'd have to visit each of the four floors and the mezzanine—did I mention the mezzanine? that place was a kind of stadium—and flush out the recalcitrant browsers and homeless people who'd lodged in the store for the evening, ignoring our warning shouts up the stairwell that we were about to close. Eventually we'd switch off the banks of lights, one at a time, in a sequence designed to chase people toward the exits, like the exit lights along the floor of an airplane. Invariably we'd get guff from people who'd made a home in one section or another, and who felt outraged to be informed that it was in fact a bookstore and that it was closing. One night a man in the grip of rage at being exiled from the third floor called me an "effete rich boy" when I turned off the lights on him (I had long hair at that time). The insult was such a non sequitur—I was a clerk!—that I found myself laughing. But I understood later that what he'd reached for in his inchoate slur was a version of the same class defiance that clerks themselves felt: The bookstore belongs to *me*, because I love it more than you.

Closing on Solano Avenue, a suburban quadrant of Berkeley, was

more peaceful. I'd make the announcement—"We're closing in five
minutes"—and then drop the needle on the last track of Bob Dylan's
Bringing It All Back Home, which begins with the words:

> *You must leave now, take what you need, you think will last*
> *But whatever you wish to keep, you better grab it fast . . .*

—*New and Used*, 2006

The Books They Read

The Hippie Parents weren't, for all their distraction and funk, for their love triangles and LPs and antiwar demonstrations, illiterates. There might have been a few of the "back to the land" variety who subsisted on the *Whole Earth Catalog* and *Possum Living*, perhaps an oil-stained VW repair manual, but the city kind, they read books, they did. You'd find the books in the downstairs bathroom, or on their bedside tables, or maybe see them unwrapped at holidays as gifts, a cherished revelation passed from one to another, shared like a joint: *Love's Body* by Norman O. Brown, *Couples* by John Updike, *I'm OK, You're OK* by Thomas Harris, *Another Roadside Attraction* by Tom Robbins, *Knots* by R. D. Laing. *The Hite Report.* Marshall McLuhan, Timothy Leary, Carlos Castaneda, Theodore Roszak, Anaïs Nin, Philip Slater, Buckminster Fuller. The day's best sellers, books which made their world as Malcolm Gladwell, say, and Deepak Chopra, Mitch Albom, *The Lovely Bones, American Psycho,* and *The Rules* made ours. In retrospect the titles are motley, contradictory, as variable as the songs on a given decade's top-ten list or a list of its top-grossing movies. But boy, they were *seekers'* books, weren't they? Those people, they weren't retrenching, they had little fear of the unknown. Give them that. They were open not only to expansions of their cultural or social selves, their bodies and their arts and their families, but also to a bigger inside, a bigger *within*. The collective brain had more labyrinths back then. To reanimate the world of the Hippie Parents in any form deeper than a paisley cartoon would mean doing an archaeological reconstruction of those shelves, and then devoting ourselves to them as readers, to do justice to the world-mind that's now sunk in a sea of time like the *Titanic*. An outright impossibility. The Hippie Parents, floating far past the wreck on that sea's surface, couldn't do it themselves. The books, if they haven't been tossed into boxes and moved to the basement, or long since donated to thrift stores that couldn't move them, are ciphers, tiny headstones. We Hippie Children remember them as prospects, promises, opaque and threatening talismans. Now, after all, we were right. The books of the Hippie Parents have been returned to mystery. The Hippie Parents have forgotten them, if they ever really read them in the first place, and by the time we could penetrate their books, we had our own.

—Amazon.com, 2006

This next piece irks me. Predating my grasp of what the personal essay is for, it sticks at the layer of anecdote, never opens any door. Like hitchhiking itself, the journey is a little overrated—a destination would be nice. Yet the self-portraiture is honest, even in the inadvertent sense of a photograph which captures its subject ducking for cover behind his own charm.

Going Under in Wendover

I'm a black dot in the desert, a period crawling across a straight line drawn on a vast white page, sweating literally and metaphorically, regretting everything, at ground zero in midsummer 1984. I'll ask you to picture this: The highway patrol on Route 80 outside of Wendover, Nevada, had directed me to walk a mile of desert landscape, *back to Utah*, in noon's blazing sun—but to get you there, to help you understand how I could have been in that position, I have to convey what I'd misunderstood about the difference between hitchhiking in New England and hitchhiking across the deserts and mountains of the West. To do the tale justice I need to rewind, to a back road near Chatham, New York, a few weeks earlier, to a ride hitched from a hippie named Melvin in an orange Volkswagen Bug.

It was the summer after freshman year. My friend Eliot and I had each taken "leaves of absence"—Eliot's from the University of Chicago, mine from Bennington. After shrugging off college we'd run aground at Eliot's family home in upstate New York. There we contracted with Eliot's mom to prep and paint the exterior of their large house in exchange for room and board, and in our desultory way were following through—though the paint we applied would soon flake away like psoriasis, due to unfortunate shortcuts in our notion of *prep*. Each day, after sleeping in until Eliot's mother was out of the house, we got stoned, stacked the player with vinyl—James Brown, the Minutemen, and Little Feat were in heavy rotation—ascended the scaffolding, killed hornets in the eaves, and dreamed escape.

I'd left a girlfriend behind in Vermont, and one June day, horny, sick of fumes, out of dope, I defected from the paint job and hitch-hiked to Bennington to see her. That one-hour drive could usually be hitched in three. This was the reliable ratio for jaunts between the small towns that dot the New England map. You stuck out your thumb and strung together ten or fifteen short hops: bored salesmen in pickups, kindly dads, daydreaming, harmless gays, and, most of all, students from Hampshire or Bard in Toyota Corollas, who could be counted on to get you high during your ten minutes in their car. Hitchhiking was low-impact, low-commitment. You made small talk and put a few towns behind you.

Melvin was thirtyish, bearded, intense. He stopped his Bug for me somewhere just out of Chatham, and within a few miles I was, yes, stoned, and letting him fish for my story. I laid it out: girlfriend, paint job, cabin fever. Eliot and I hoped to jaunt out West to visit his crazy uncle in Berkeley, I explained, but we needed a car.

"Well, I need to get this VW back to Colorado," he said, and explained something about driving back with a girlfriend. It was too easy. By the end of the ride we'd struck a deal, exchanged phone numbers and Eliot's address. A week later, at an appointed hour, he dropped the Bug at Eliot's and vanished.

I want to say: *We drove that car as far as we could, abandoned it out West*, and we did—amid a thousand jokes about how the hollow surfaces were likely packed with a million dollars in cocaine, we drove it precisely as far as Golden, Colorado, where we found a giant "M" carved into a mountain and a pizzeria with a whole stuffed moose spread around the four walls—head, hide, and hooves. It was farther west than I'd been and it was where Melvin lived and it was where Eliot and I realized we hadn't considered how to cross the last third of this great land, hadn't even broached the subject.

We fooled around for three days in Colorado, at one point going to the Denver airport to try to cadge a lift on a mail plane, a useless notion we'd picked up who knows where. Then we found a ride board at the university in Boulder and scored Eliot a ride to Berkeley in a two-seater convertible driven by a reputedly beautiful girl—I never did lay eyes on her. That was the sole ride offered and so I volunteered to *hitchhike* to Berkeley, which I'd been daring myself to do for days. I knew how to hitchhike, right?

This was an *error of scale*. Route 80 between Cheyenne, Wyoming, and San Francisco is a vast wasteland of desert and mountain dotted with a minimum of battened-down outposts offering gas, food, and gambling. Salt Lake City and Reno are the only hubs for a thousand miles; the rest is Little America and Elko, names you'd know only if you'd stopped there to repair a tire or wolf a hoagie. Hitchhiking in this Martian zone, where anyone who stops has per se volunteered to spend forty-five minutes to two hours with you—unless they mean to leave you somewhere *between* towns, and let's not think about that, please—is a different proposition from hitchhiking in New England.

In fact it stands in relation somewhat as facing major-league pitching does to swatting at a Wiffle ball. I offer this with equilibrium now. But when the insight came to find me, which it did roughly fifty miles out of Cheyenne, between the ride with the Christian who'd warned me extensively about accepting rides from the lawless wildcat oilmen in western Wyoming, and the next ride—for which I waited an hour—in a pickup truck full of what were unmistakably lawless wildcat oilmen, with rifles and open beers in the cab, well, when that insight first came over me it felt like getting diagnosed with a fatal illness.

See me: hair growing back from a buzz, Elvis Costello nerd glasses, plaid shorts, Chuck Taylors, discernibly Jewish features (for anyone who'd seen those before), and with preparations for the desert consisting of a Meat Puppets T-shirt. Had I considered where I might spend the nights? No. Mothers, quake for your sons. I was not a stupid boy. I showed no particular signs. I did my homework and got into college and then one day stepped out onto Route 80 in August without any sunscreen.

I remember every ride. I remember a ride with a Chinese shopkeeper inexplicably delivering a vanload of soda ninety miles through Nevada, and I remember a ride in a rig with a trucker who had a sleeping baby on the bedroll in back and wanted me to sit and make sure the baby didn't roll off, and I remember a ride with a daredevil salesman, a professional speeder with radar and a CB radio who advanced me a hundred miles in under an hour. I remember them all but the story I want to tell is of Wendover, on the Utah-Nevada border.

The ride that got me out of Utah—*I thought*—was with a guy who booked rock acts at one of the two large casinos in Wendover, Nevada, just over the line. The town is a speck in the Great Salt Lake Desert, the easternmost place to gamble on Route 80. He picked me up at four on a Friday for the two-hour ride into Wendover. We listened to Neil Young's *Everybody's Rockin'* and I soaked in his air-conditioning and stared out the window at the marvelous, impossible salt flats, where lovers had trod off the highway to spell out their names in rocks now shining like black eyes against the white. The booker told me he'd been Three Dog Night's road manager in his glory days. He was friendly, but after gauging my naïveté he mentioned casually that all rooms in the casinos were likely to be booked, then gently drew a line in the salt: After he dropped me off on the highway outside of Wendover, I was not to look him up and ask him for favors. He'd see the last of me on Route 80. No hard feelings.

I waved off this weirdly prescient ultimatum, saying I meant to keep moving tonight, to push toward Reno. The sky had begun to glow when he deposited me on the off-ramp outside of town, a mile or so into Nevada. Oh, how I'd come soon to loathe that spot! I waited an hour at least, hungry and exhausted, gazing at the twinkle of Wendover across the highway, and at the expanse of waste that surrounded it and me. There's nothing to stretch time like sticking your thumb out as darkness gathers in the desert, and that spot, on a Friday night when each car was packed with weekending Mormons, was the next thing to a hitchhiker's worst nightmare.

The nightmare itself strolled along at around seven: a drifter with a walking stick and Charles Manson eyes. He appraised me in one hungry glance.

"Tough spot for a ride, huh?"

Impossible, I thought, with *you* standing anywhere in sight. "Yeah," I said.

"Well, if you can't get a lift and you want to crash, I've got a little camp . . ." He pointed past the highway, over a barren, scrubby hill.

"I'm moving on." Now more than ever.

"Well, if you *can't* . . ."

"I'd probably just go get a room in town—" I stopped, but not before painting a bull's-eye on my forehead.

"Right . . . okay."

His posture said: *I can take this kid.*

"In fact," I said, "I think I'll just go in now." And, feeling the drifter watch my back, I walked the semicircle of ramp, into Wendover.

There isn't a town in America without a cheap motel, right? No cheap motel. Wendover was two things: a pair of glossy, booked-up casinos full of clean-cut couples and Mormon families, and a sprawl of shanties and trailers which housed the suspicious, hard-bitten croupiers and security guards and maids who serviced the casinos. I walked toward the neon, my skin alive with fear. Now I understood the booker's admonition. If he hadn't given it I'd absolutely be on his doorstep.

I went into the Stateline Casino. You've seen a giant neon cowboy with a rising-and-sinking neon gun arm: that's it. They'd been booked full for this weekend long ago. The woman at reception stared at me, with my sunburn and knapsack and stink. I asked if there was a deadline for cancellations.

"Eight o'clock. Sometimes a room or two opens up. No guarantees."

Get lost! screamed her look. She couldn't know I was measuring her hostility against the wolfish eyes of the drifter, a contest she couldn't win. I camped in the lobby, eavesdropping for clues, watching her watch me. A young couple asked and got the same reply, and when I saw they were sticking around I went and stood righteously at the desk, marking my precedence. It was a quarter to eight.

The couple queued behind me. I overheard their whispers. Somehow I was transparent here.

She: "If there's only one room we could let him spend the night in our car."

Yes, I thought. I had maybe ninety dollars left. The cheapest rooms were seventy.

He: (long pause) "I don't think so."

I *hoped* there was only one room. They deserved it. I think they got a room. I only remember my flood of relief as I handed over sweat-soaked cash for a key. I'd meant to put this creepy town behind me; now coughing up my nest egg for a night inside the castle walls was a triumph. Upstairs I cranked the air, showered for the first time in two days, and donned my good shirt. On the bedspread was a complimentary roll of quarters, to ensure that road-weary voyagers to Reno drop at least a bit of boodle here first. I figured I'd spend it on dinner and went downstairs.

That night's still my only night in a Nevada casino. I'm in the black:

I took that ten-dollar roll of quarters to a slot machine and *turned it into fifteen dollars.* Then I quit, bought a shrimp salad with my winnings, and retired to a movie on cable: Farrah Fawcett and Charles Grodin in *Sunburn.* The next morning I checked out of the Stateline and walked back to my spot on the off-ramp, headed west.

That's when it got silly. I stood there in the sun from nine to noon. I counted cars, promised God I'd never hitchhike, and counted cars again. One hundred more, I decided. The hundred passed and I had no alternative but to clear the score and start again. Three times that morning I was cruised by the highway patrol, but I didn't think much of it. I'd been searched and questioned once in Wyoming and survived. Anyway, I was still worried the drifter would reappear. Cops were my friends.

Sometime after noon, when I'd begun to wonder if I was doomed to Wendover forever, they pulled over for a talk. Did I know hitchhiking was illegal in Nevada?

No, I told them, I didn't. "I'm just trying to get out of your town, sir, I'll be gone as soon as I can." This line had played in Wyoming, but it didn't play here.

It's illegal, they explained. You can hitch in Utah, but not here.

I just came from Utah, I explained. I'm headed *west*.

Too bad, they explained. Utah was a mile *that-a-away*—east—and I ought to walk back there, with my thumb down, please, so I wouldn't be in violation of the law.

But I'll only be coming back this way, I pleaded.

But you won't be committing a crime in Nevada.

So I became a speck on a page, a token moved in an absurd symbolic action across a cartographic line in real space. I trudged under slow-crawling police escort along the shoulder in midday sun through a stretch of desert until reaching a road sign which read WELCOME TO UTAH!

Follow: Westbound, Wendover was the first stop on that road in hours. Follow: Every car would stop for at least gas and a piss. Follow: I could stand there forever and die. No one would pick up *two minutes before pulling in for a rest stop.* I'd already failed for hours standing on the other side, the right side. The instant the Nevada police abandoned me to Utah, I turned and walked back in. I didn't pause at the spot I'd worn on the off-ramp, the drifter spot, the counting spot, the death spot. I slogged past it, went into town as far as the nearest gas station. I was humbled, ready to beg, to make intimate appeal to drivers filling their tanks. Up close I'd persuade someone, anyone, to get me a mile or two west and break the jinx.

I approached the attendant, to make him understand I was harmless, to get him on my side. He was an ancient Negro (I feel certain this is the word he'd have applied to himself), the first black face I'd seen in days. In a film he'd have been played by Scatman Crothers. In a film it would be hackneyed and in a certain sense even a borderline-racist gesture, to cast this first black person as my angel in a paleface-gambling-Mormon nightmare, but this was what happened. He listened to my story and he laughed and he spoke in a patois so thick I could barely make it out.

"You want to wait for me to get off work, I'll get you to the next town going west," he said, or words to that effect.

"I'll wait."

"You can sit back there."

I sat and waited and when the time came I climbed into the attendant's battered Reliant, to share space with his dog, whom the attendant explained he'd rescued from the road and taken in, likely, according to the corny script I'd begun playing in, so I'd understand I was truly a stray, a whelpling, a pup. And then the attendant got me out of Wendover before I *went under*. Or at least before going under for a third and final and famously fatal time.

Eliot still doesn't believe me, and neither, I trust, do you.

—*Rolling Stone,* 2000

Zelig of Notoriety:
Bret, Donna, and Some Others

What "The Used Bookshop Stories" elides in smash-cutting from New York to California is the same thing "Going Under in Wendover" skates over with the glib phrase "shrugging off college": Leaving Bennington was costly, but I didn't let myself feel the cost for years. Eventually I contended with it in an essay called "Defending the Searchers." That piece cut a lot deeper than "Going Under in Wendover," enough to key a cycle of self-exfoliating essays, which made up a book called *The Disappointment Artist*. Yet I still hadn't made full accounting of my throes at the little private arts college in Vermont.

Bennington was under my skin before I could define myself against it. Having made it through high school insulated from the facts of class by my parents' bohemianism, on arrival at Bennington I was in for a shock. I projected the place as the emblem of all unfair privilege in the world of the arts; this was a grudge on behalf of my father, really, but held as if it had injured my own chances before I'd begun. Later my grudge was modulated by the sense that Bennington was an innocent outpost of a system I deplored, rather than some pernicious headquarters. It was then that the assorted generosities I'd thrown over as if in a juvenile fit began to be apparent to me, and with them the sickening possibility that I'd injured my own chances more than a little by running away. In 2005 I went back to Bennington to give the commencement address. I'm not sure how much my speech could have meant to the students; I kept it deliberately wry and undeep, told jokes, riffed on the irony of their having invited back a "sophomore on leave." I've never struggled not to weep in public in such a sustained way, yet I didn't weep.

What's still left out is Bret and Donna. It was already overdetermined that my first brush with private school was at the (then) most expensive college in the country, an art school gone decadently haywire, and soon to suffer a well-publicized purge of the scandal-plagued faculty and renunciation of its cocaine days. That as a naïve teenage wannabe I should have been a classmate of Bret Easton Ellis and Donna Tartt, emblematic prodigal royalty of a glittering instant in the history of publishing, was too much, too on the nose. There were others there in those years who'd write and publish: Jill Eisenstadt, Reggie Shepard, Lawrence David, Joseph Clarke. But according to the deep law of charisma, the "story" of that time, whenever I'm asked about Bennington by others, is always Bret-and-Donna. When Bret's first book was published I'd already fled across the country, though I preferred to claim I'd scampered (see: "Going Under in Wendover"). By the time Donna's Secret History came out I was a clerk, handling copies of her book. I sold plenty of both of their books.

The college was tiny. You knew everyone. At nineteen both Bret and Donna were brilliantly formed, complete, and charismatic as Oscar Wilde or Andy Warhol. I wasn't as vivid a persona, but I was briefly true friends with Donna and spent time in Bret's company, too. Bret stood perfectly for what outraged me at that school, and terrified me, too, the blithe conversion of privilege into artistic fame. It was inconvenient that I liked him. He'd read and watched and listened to everything. I remember most a humbling talk about movies, which I considered my forte since I'd seen Hitchcock, Godard, and Nashville. Bret at nineteen had weary capsule takes on Altman films I'd never heard of—A Wedding was a masterpiece, HealtH vapid—opinions that still persuade me. Bret's reading was current and fashionable, mine was trapped in countercultural/used-bookshop amber where Richard Brautigan remained an important American novelist. Bret was close with Joan Didion's daughter and had, at the insistence of a Bennington professor, an agent. At that school at that moment I was not so much out of my depth as I was out of someone else's. Anyway, I was surely out of it.

Donna was among the first friends I made at college, in the scant

weeks before my disenchantment. My roommate Mark and I helped
her move an ancient and gigantic trunk from the maintenance building to her room, as if she'd arrived in Vermont on a steamship. She and
I spoke across a temporal gap: none of her cultural references newer
than J. M. Barrie, none of mine older than Foghorn Leghorn (the only
Southern accent I knew). I exaggerate: Donna was a transfer student,
had enjoyed the mentorship of Willie Morris and Barry Hannah, just
as I'd recently enjoyed smoking pot with my high-school math teacher,
who sometimes like to declaim passages from Frazer's *The Golden
Bough*. But Donna really could converse in perfect wistful epigrams,
seemingly pointed at posterity. With her, as with others in that first
flush, I passed through a dazzlingly quick intimacy, to violent disagree-
ment, then silence. What compels me now is that in each of these cases
the friend was another like myself: a financial-aid case there, stranded
amid the heirs to various American fortunes and the shah of Iran's
daughter (who'd brought her bodyguards). At the time I couldn't have
allowed myself to notice this, and so blamed the falling-out on personality defects in the lost friend.

In friendship Donna had a rarefied talent for secrecy and fantasy,
exactly as her books suggest. We began by passing furtive notes to each
other in a classroom of only seven or eight students, flash parodies of
our professor's sonorous wisdoms. Even casual strolls to Bennington's
"End of the World," a green slope at the foot of the commons lawn,
were occasion for Donna's mock-formal notes of invitation in my campus mailbox. She once arranged a tea party for me at an undisclosed
location off campus, to which I was led as if to a secret garden, or an
execution. I relished sharing Donna's trancelike aura until the star of
our friendship suddenly fell, and then I became paranoid, so positive
Donna was dangerous to me that I discounted my own obnoxious tan-
trums. I missed how Donna's airs of belonging were on-the-spot inventions, born as much of need as my own airs of not-belonging.

There's a peculiar spirit of abjection to my situation in Berkeley,
stranded what seemed a lifetime's distance from my glimpse of the
action in Vermont, working on my fourth unpublished novel in my off-
hours, shelving and stickering and gift-wrapping Bret's and Donna's
books at the shop while mostly not wanting to admit I'd known the
two of them. They were part of so much I couldn't think straight about
for a very long time. Perhaps you could say I was jealous and refused to
be jealous, which left silence. Yet when *American Psycho* came along I

found myself defending Bret at the shop, not only from customers but from other clerks who wanted to fall in with the censoring frenzy and bar his book from the store. I'm a free-speech absolutist, I've learned, though this was yet another of the endless series of lessons that arrived backward for me, thanks to the prevailing background of my upbringing—wait, I'd think: Others actually don't see the vindication of *Tropic of Cancer* and *Lolita* as a permanent and self-evident triumph of reason over nonsense? The argument's still open? I felt outraged (and still am) by anyone interested in books who'd condemn one they hadn't read. I took it, therefore, as my duty to read *American Psycho*, the first time I'd more than skimmed one of Bret's. It was a satirical bludgeon: stultifying, cruel, hilarious, worth defending. But my secret was that I felt I defended a friend, though I had no reason then to know whether Bret would remember my name if he heard it aloud.

Donna's scandal was another brand. No one had ever seen a first novel hoisted past reviewers into legend by a publicity machine, or if they had, they'd forgotten. David Bowman told me: "When that book was rolled out the sense of occasion was so large I remember thinking: I wish *I* had a novel out. Then I remembered I *did*." This phenomenon wasn't a cause to defend, which was just as well, since my response to Donna's book was as murky to me as the unexamined loss of our friendship. Every person I recalled from our time at Bennington seemed reworked in her pages, except I saw no spot for myself—unless, as I joked to my girlfriend, it was as the murdered Vermont farmer, a character so beneath the regard of the book's characters that he barely registers as human. Between me and myself it wasn't a joke. I felt certain I was the farmer. I should have been uniquely positioned to savor Donna's elegant ironies, but either they were wasted on me or I credited them to myself.

By the time I crawled out of obscurity I'd find myself congratulated for being part of a generation of writers who'd helped put a corruptly oversold Brat Pack safely in the rearview mirror—though really I was Bret and Donna's contemporary (as were Wallace, Eugenides, Moody, others seen as coming "next"). As with the kudos for skirting an MFA, I could only consent to this praise in bad faith. My old classmates and I had loads of cultural stuff in common, and also tended to similar commitments (to traditional narrative, to genre, perhaps also to a dubious melancholy) in our work. Possibly the only clear thing I'd gathered from my richly confusing hours in their company was that both were completely serious about their work. This should be the simplest thing to point out: No writer is equivalent to his or her publicity, his or her photograph, his or her flap copy, even less to your uncomfortable feelings about it (your resentment at being *sold* things, generally), however much you're entitled to those feelings. Yet neither Bret, with his Warholian flippancy, nor Donna, with her near-Salingerian silence, has ever much altered the cartoon overreaction to their arrival. Bret's resorted, in his last two novels, to writing into the teeth of it. I think of him as a child star, in the King Tut or Bob Dylan sense of being locked into a public identity before he could possibly have formed a resilient interior life. Lou Reed called it "growing up in public."

Notoriety is the only true form of postwar American literary fame. Not regard among readers, but real fame, of the household-name variety. I find this thought pretty persuasive, though I can't remember whether to credit it to someone else or myself. Consider Miller (censorship), Nabokov (ditto), Mailer (knives, etc.), Vidal (feuds, homosexuality), Capote (ditto), Rushdie (fatwa), on through Bret and his "Brat" cohort. So it was that, with new notorieties eclipsing the old ones, I began to kid myself that I at last knew what my early acquaintance with Bret and Donna was for: I'd been specially appointed to be the Zelig to literary notoriety in my generation, the extra guy in the photograph. This was after I fell in with Dave Eggers, in San Francisco, before McSweeney's and his memoir. I attended Dave's ambitiously odd, charged parties, heard him hatch conceptual-art publishing schemes, then watched him grow mired in grotesque fame and need to fight through. Dave's pixilated munificence was strengthened by the battle not to inhabit the cartoon—his superpower was to draw vitality from his enemies, who grew squalid, Gollumesque. I also knew Jonathan Franzen, pre-*Corrections*. (I'd been a bookseller handling Jonathan's debut, too, ten years before.) Now, with a mutual friend, the painter Julia Jacquette, who'd met Jonathan at Yaddo, we ate Italian cookies and played Scrabble—at which Franzen cleaned my clock. Then I sent him a copy of *As She Climbed Across the Table*, which he acknowledged pretty kindly, saying he thought I'd picked a healthy approach in writing short novels and publishing often. The remark might have seemed mercenary if it hadn't sounded depressed; I detected in it the cost to him of saying even that much, at a time when Jonathan feared he'd vanished in the interval between his second and third books. I felt I knew Franzen, and sympathized when he later tested an unworkable sincerity in the prime-time arena. His fame, then and now, had a Chauncey Gardiner quality, seeming called into being by a novelist-shaped vacancy on the cover of *Time* (see: "Rushmore Versus Abundance"). These later brushes could be complicated for me, as they'd be for any writer with an ego, but were never as unfathomable as the earlier ones. I had the Zelig's advantage: present in the photograph, but free to disappear from it as well, the next time you glanced.

Bret and I had one more odd fate to share. I'd gotten to know him again in Manhattan in the '90s. Our friendship, though ostensibly between two working novelists, seemed less to overwrite our college acquaintance than to extend it against a new backdrop of ersatz grown-ups. Every encounter was on his terms. I revisited my Bennington role, the reverse-slumming Brooklyn kid slipping out for dinner at Baltha-zar, Bret's regular place. Afterward we'd go to a party bankrolled by a publisher or magazine, which still happened frequently then. We did drugs. It's one of Zelig's traits, a weakness that is also a capacity, that he melts agreeably into nearly any milieu, at least briefly. There might be an element of Stockholm syndrome in the way I could still be lured by Bret's glum magnetism, and that I still found him a figure of sympathy, like rooting for Jose Canseco or Barry Bonds—something I also did.

The fate: Bret and I were out on the town on Monday, September 10, 2001, well into the early hours of the following day. We began at Baltha-zar, then moved to a party at a concocted "speakeasy" behind Ratner's Deli, called Lansky's Lounge. If you need a symbol of pre-9/11 excess, I offer my whereabouts that night in the spirit of disclosure to the pros-ecution. I'd been sleeping off a hangover in my Brooklyn bed when I was woken by the eruption of an airplane against the building across the river, less than a mile away—the sound of the fireball, a tremor in my floor. I'd later give testimony in the *Times* (see: "Nine Failures of the Imagination"), but I left the Bret part out of it.

We've lost touch. Bret was kind to me, in the ways he knows how, in two distinct parts of my life, but both are vanished. Likely it was inevitable that when I mentioned to a friend that I'd begun writing about Bret that my friend should draw my attention to a recent inter-view where Bret claims—peevishly I'd say—to have hardly known me. Inevitable because I think that Bret, in his Andy Warhol way, has no equipment for believing anyone outside his most immediate and present circle could consider him a friend. This slight cast me, for an instant, into my old Bennington shame, the sulky outsider denied. Yet it was a gift. My Stockholm syndrome burst like a soap bubble. Why go on about Bret, Bret, Bret? This whole essay, I thought, should be about Donna—amazing, strange, sad, lost (well, lost to me) Donna. Yet that friendship remained frozen in its ruined moment, two nineteen-year-olds who'd forged a meaningless grandiose enmity.

Or not meaningless. Maybe our disaffection had a subject. In three semesters at Bennington I kept switching work-study jobs, looking for one that fit to hide my shame. It wasn't that I thought work was in itself shameful, but the fact that I worked while other students didn't— mostly, they didn't—was syllogism for the cloud of egalitarian delusion from which I'd fallen, or kept continuously falling, still waiting to learn what the impact would feel like when I landed. For a while I found a sanctuary in the ceramics department, a zone abandoned between classes. There I worked mixing clay and dusting out kilns, my only company the agreeably stoned and hippieish ceramics instructor, with whom I debated the comparative merits of Robert Heinlein and Arthur C. Clarke. Later I'd hide out as the projectionist at the school's movie theater, a bat in a belfry—suitable employment for an aspiring novelist hoping to project his reels into waiting brains. But my first work-study job, probably the only one available to a new freshman, was on the front lines of my secret class war: I served food at the dining hall to my fellow students, stuck on the wrong side of the counter with the Vermont locals, those whom we elsewhere snubbed as if they were Cro-Magnons taking up space on our Homo sapiens campus, subhuman like that farmer-victim of *Secret History*'s murderous classicists. Is it hallucination that among my fellow student-workers there, those of us in paper aprons and possibly paper hats as well, holding outsized food-service ladles dripping with gunk, at least for a shift or two, was Donna? The possibility came flooding into recollection just now, as the sympathy I'd been spending on Bret found a different home. I have no way to confirm it. The image may be a fantasy: Perhaps I only recall serving Donna food from across that counter. If it is a fantasy, it was surely induced by rereading the brilliant first pages of Donna's novel, where her narrator describes filling out his application to "Hampden" College: "Would you like to receive information on Financial Aid? Yes." As any crime writer knows, if you want to hide a clue, bury it at the start of a book.

Clerk

I *was* what I would be if I wasn't a writer: a clerk in a used bookstore. No other possibility. I worked in eight bookstores in fifteen years, five years during high school and college, then ten years straight after that. Shelving, running registers, re-alphabetizing sections, learning the arcana. I was bitter, intense, typical, holding myself superior to customers who could afford the best items I could only cherish in passing, part of a great clerkly tradition. I was certainly aware of the tradition. I still repair broken alphabetical runs and straighten piles on tables, absently, despite myself, whenever I'm in stores. It calms me during book tours. The last five years I worked at one of the best stores in the country. I was becoming an expert in the books I cared about most, modern first editions and rare paperbacks. In, say, another fifteen years of apprenticeship—a trifle in antiquariania, as with any serious guild—I might have been one of the top rare-lit men in the world.

Or it might have all gone south. Some clerks never make it, end up burned out, start stealing books, like cops gone bad. They get hooked on tea, next thing they know they end up in a card game. Then a craps game. Then they wake up in a pool hall. Then this big Mexican lady drags them off to Philadelphia. They get a job as a "before" in a Charles Atlas ad. Then the big Mexican lady burns the house down and the next thing they know they're in Omaha. They move in with a high-school teacher who does a little plumbing on the side, who's not much to look at but who's built a special kind of refrigerator that can turn newspaper into lettuce. Then these clerks settle in, start scheming. Using the high-school teacher's know-how they begin printing up samizdat Gold Medal paperback originals by fake noir authors with names like Orphus Blurt and Crash Burnstein and Walter Girlfriend. You see those books come floating across the buying counter and you just grin: You know a haywire clerk's out there, flaming like a shred of Korean barbecue. I think that's probably the type of clerk I would've become, after a while.

—*Brick*, 2004

II

DICK, CALVINO, BALLARD: SF AND POSTMODERNISM

Through no fault of my own I'm in a sticky situation
I'm suffering the consequences of a bad education

—BLUE ORCHIDS, "Bad Education"

My Plan to Begin With, Part Two

The project of self-exile wasn't halfway complete. The geographical genius of the Bay Area made a good start (Berkeley an island-nation decorated by my parents' counterculture, America's Amsterdam), but I needed to detach from the literary mainland, too. I'd beam my signal down from space instead. I mapped an orbit, a willfully eccentric course I couldn't prove was navigable but had to try. Japan had Kobo Abe; Poland, Stanislaw Lem; Italy, Calvino. The U.K. had J. G. Ballard. These writers were fabulators and world literary figures, in the Nobel conversation. Behind them, the inarguable weight of Kafka, Borges, Cortázar. Ursula Le Guin called Philip K. Dick "our own homegrown Borges," but I knew he didn't cut that ice, not completely. Maybe I could. This was a stupid idea. Nobody wanted it done. If Vonnegut had needed to fudge his origins, if Samuel Delany's or Tom Disch's or Le Guin's writing still didn't qualify for graduation day, I should notice the structural resistance in the barrier I wanted to break down—resistance from both sides. My difficulty persuading writing teachers of the worth of my secret pantheon was only equaled by the shrug of most science-fiction people when I suggested DeLillo and Barthelme should interest them. I'd taken the logic of Borges's essay—"Kafka and His Precursors," in which a writer creates a private lineage for himself by the act of appearing—as being equivalent to a literary-political cause: Unite the divided realms! But my private myth didn't translate.

Those postmodernists, Barthelme and Co., whom I'd been reading with excitement, and cribbing from wildly, could have suggested a home for my leanings. There was even an official headquarters, Brown University, where Robert Coover kept the flame lit. My thrill at disenfranchisement demanded more, though. I needed to come from Pulpland and then be sanctified, an underdog script someone should have talked me out of. I'd carry my heroes on my back, prove that Patricia Highsmith and Charles Willeford and especially Philip K. Dick ("our homegrown Borges" was then out of print, not in the Library of America) were the exact same thing as Faulkner or Pynchon. My ego would reorganize institutions, bookstores, canons. What this script mostly guaranteed was that I'd appear to SF partisans (if you love Cyril Kornbluth, wave your hands in the air) as a caddish betrayer of an honorably self-sustaining subculture. Meanwhile, to sentinels of literature (nearly any editor or reviewer over the age of thirty-five), I'd look to have arrived at the dance in concrete overshoes.

If my early novels should triangulate between DeLillo and Lem, or Steve Erickson and Ballard, I took it as given I'd also pen bushels of jargon-drunk surrealist tales connecting the dots between Borges, R. A. Lafferty, and Kenneth Koch. I managed a few before my project got gunked up with mimetic texture, sentimental references to myself, to Brooklyn, to certain songs and sandwiches I admired. Later I'd see Ben Marcus's or George Saunders's stories and feel a pang, as though they'd become the writer I hadn't gotten around to being, but still reserved the right to be.

Holidays

New Year's Eve

Dress the cat in bags and break out the plankton sandwiches! Another year is come and gone.

The first child born after the toll of midnight will frequently bear miniature antlers. They recede in the first six months and rarely re-appear.

Tocog

Tocog (or "Gocot") celebrates the arrival of the meat-loaf clans. They come to the table dressed to the nines in their formal jacket of glazed pastry or glistening aspic. Who will be named the unrivaled queen of the traditional mixtures?

Saint Sebastian's Day

There are explanations for the association of Saint Sebastian's Day with gunplay. I am afraid no single explanation will be sufficient. It is inadvisable to go outdoors during Saint Sebastian's Day.

April Fools' Day

April fools are no worse than October or March fools, yet we hang them in effigy from lampposts, and children construct tissue-paper voodoo dolls of April fools to flush down the toilet. As recently as the 1930s living fools were still being lynched in maddened towns in isolated parts of the Midwest.

The Death of Toyland

Toyland was America's first utopian community. The characteristic spires and gazebos of Toyland are now taken very much for granted but were unprecedented in their day, and struck some observers as profound, others as terrifying. Surrounded on three sides by hostile savages, isolated from other settlers by their strange beliefs and unusual practices, the citizens of Toyland took to the sea in rafts in 1822 and were never seen again. Though the Toylanders are little missed, the gradual death of Toyland was an inevitable consequence of their disappearance. Toyland was declared dead in 1956.

Auteurs' Day

Directors are recognized as the true authors of films on Auteurs' Day.

Arbor Day

George Washington Arbor and Jonathan Livingston Appleseed fought their famous duel on Arbor Day, in 1875. Arbor's words echo wherever lies are told. "I cannot tell the truth," he said. "I hated the man who died beneath the tree, but it was not my bullet that killed him."

Phone Day

Do you have any idea how many phone calls I make on any given morning? I have no need of Phone Day.

Easter

Each year the warm-blooded species hold a weeklong festival to honor the passing of the giant lizards who ruled the earth for so many thousands of years. Voles and raccoons attack nested eggs in a reenactment of the original trauma. Will our guilt ever be appeased?

The proponents of Ash Wednesday offer an alternate theory, asserting that it was a gigantic volcanic eruption that exterminated the dinosaurs. In my view this belief is an indulgence.

Halloween

When the children appear at my door I invite them inside. I offer them plankton sandwiches and glasses of tea. Most of them leave quickly, but a few are still living with me, quiet as cats. They sleep in the loft rafters, and sometimes share in the housework and gardening.

Zeno's Day

Zeno's Day grows shorter every year, but it will never completely disappear.

Thankstaking

The vacuum cleaner has replaced the cornucopia in most traditional Thankstaking ceremonies.

Horizon

For seven nights the beehives are moved inside the house. The youngest child will be responsible for asking the bees the ritual questions, the eldest for hiding the honey. No fax machines are to be operated during the week of Horizon.

Christmas

Christmas holds us in its deathly grip. The dictionary defines it as "the state of one who has committed an offense, esp. consciously," but I do not believe small children who experience Christmas are aware of their culpability. I ask, at what point does Christmas truly live in us? Is it when the men burst in to smother the flaming tree? Is it during the shaping and dressing of the tar baby? No one knows.

We all tremble in the grasp of Christmas. It is unsafe and unfair. We should not have to endure it. There should be a single Christmas, held at a previously agreed location, by a family of actors. It could be broadcast, safely mediated by the information handlers. Christmas ought to be enacted by astronauts, on the moon, or deep under the sea.

Perhaps the men who don the Santa suit understand Christmas, but they are never permitted inside the house. They gather in tribes under bridges and highways to build fires and eat plankton sandwiches, and their laughter stops whenever anyone comes close enough to hear.

—Crank, 1996

Crazy Friend

1.

There's a street corner in Brooklyn, Seventh Avenue and Flatbush, a place I associate with—well, I associate it with plenty of things. In my mind this corner hinges Park Slope and the neighborhoods on Flatbush's far side: Prospect Heights and Fort Greene, which were, for various complicated reasons over which I've wrung my hands elsewhere, racially intimidating to me. As a white kid, I'd charted the safe hours and itineraries nearer to home, and forged a few vital truces, but in these Flatbush-north territories I'd have been without passport or compass. Park Slope intimidated me, too, but differently. As with Carroll Gardens, that other far border of my personal Brooklyn: the white Irish or Italian precincts had their own way of making me feel mocked, socially disjointed, or even physically endangered. Yet there was another trail to follow in Park Slope in the '70s, the sons and daughters of book editors and psychotherapists who'd fashioned there a less qualified, less bohemian, more posh, and tree-lined version of the gentrification that made my own home turf so varied, enthralling, and treacherous. If I could crack this group of teenagers—they were a group, the Slopies—I'd find untold alliances. My disadvantage was that I went to public school, and the way in was through cliques joined at the various private academies, or at Catholic school.

And then, almost as suddenly as I knew I wanted it, I did find a way in. But this was loaded, too: a pair of girls a bit older than I was (and all girls are older than all boys at the ages we were at, and I was especially young), and brilliant, and attractive to me, and well integrated into the Slopies' network of influence and high-level flirtation, play, and art-making. They might be curious about me, but they didn't need me the way I needed them. These girls, Deena and Laurene, were dancers, musicians, painters, writers—it wasn't obvious which, yet, but they might have their choice. They were crazily verbal, crazily charismatic, crazy with talent. They sang songs they'd written themselves, parodic and brilliant, like a private language: I memorized them, as I would in those days memorize a record by the Residents or Frank Zappa.

These weren't like my earlier friendships, found spilling outdoors onto the sidewalks, nor did they clarify in the way my friendships with male schoolmates did. I couldn't seem to get these girls on the phone. Months would pass. I'd change, or feel I'd changed, sexually, socially, artistically, somehow, and want desperately for them to notice, to get word of it. But I wasn't on their radar, it seemed, except when we were directly hanging out. And then, if I caught up with Deena and Laurene, they were changed, too. I had to learn about the new black or Puerto Rican boyfriend, the new favorite band or other infatuation, and everything I'd studied in them previously had become old currency, not even fit to trade for the new. I had to remember not to mention what they'd left behind for fear I'd be next. These girls blew hot, and could be mockingly affectionate or even briefly lusty in my direction, but in their willingness to show disdain, to crush unworthiness like a bug, they were fundamentally cool, cool, cool. I had a lot to learn, and I put my own enthusiasms and provenances on the table very carefully, or so it felt to me. They had a name for what they despised, "green," a word which seemed to encapsulate being lame, unenlightened, feeble, corny, overreaching or straining for effect, and much else. I lived in fear of being cast in that shade.

The corner of Seventh and Flatbush was a meeting point, a place I'd have to walk to get to their zone, if only because the crow-flies direction took me through too many bad patches. Most crucially, past Sarah J. Hale High School, which might as well have been a city block of pure quicksand. So I drew a triangle, up Flatbush to that corner, then south, as if walking into their neighborhood meant opening up Brooklyn like a door and slipping through. The subway stopped on Seventh and Flatbush, too, so if the girls were going to sweep me up to Manhattan, as they sometimes did, the portal was there. The corner also featured a movie theater, a first-run palace called the Plaza, one safe enough to attend at night, unlike those in downtown Brooklyn. The theater marked the corner as a site of some first experiences to come. It throbbed with potential for "a date." In fact, in my mind, the intersection was the Brooklyn equivalent of the Rolling Stones' lyric, from "Dance (Part 1)": Mick Jagger's sleazy, cursory intonation, "Hey, what am I doing standing here on the corner of West Eighth Street and Sixth Avenue and . . . / Ah, skip it. / Nothing. Keith! Watcha, watcha doing?" The corner knew something about what I wanted to get over as, but couldn't yet.

So it was that standing there one day, under wider circumstances I could no better reconstruct than the tatters of some former civilization, one of these girls made a random taunt that struck me as a meaningful bolt from the blue, and which I've never forgotten but never completely understood, either. I'd said I had to go meet a friend, I think, but left the friend unnamed, whether out of shame or awkwardness or some combination of the two. Deena, the verbally wilder and more freely hostile of the two, said, sneering in bogus accusation, "Who—*Eldridge Palmer*?" Deena didn't mean anything important by it, was just amusing herself, I think, by acting as if I was hiding something. It might provoke something funny along the lines of defensiveness from me— couldn't hurt to try.

The name Deena had plucked up from thin air seemed—if one was reasonable—to be a riff on Eldridge Cleaver, and therefore on the fact of my parents' radical political affiliations, or on the fact that a lot of my friends from my other world, away from Park Slope, were black. But I didn't hear it that way. The latest sensation in my life, the revolution in my cultural appetite and worldview, one I'd have probably been unable to coherently share with these two under even the best of circumstances, was for science fiction generally and for Philip K. Dick specifically. I'd just weeks before read, with tumultuous, revolutionary excitement, *A Maze of Death*, *Ubik*, and *The Three Stigmata of Palmer Eldritch*. Each book depicts the infiltration of reality by an intoxicatingly malignant death force. In *Three Stigmata*, that force is Palmer Eldritch, a man who's become a monstrous god, a kind of living drug or cancer. In the end, everyone and everything shows Palmer Eldritch's face, like evil DNA. Now my friend had seemed to name him by accident. Only it couldn't be an accident. Palmer Eldritch *was* everywhere, the novel was merely testament to cosmic conditions! I began trying to describe this. Gibbering, I'm sure it seemed from the perspective of the girls.

"Of all the possible names, how'd you pick that one?" I demanded. "It can't be a coincidence!"

She immediately scorned my excitement. "Who cares?" she said. "What did I even say? Eldridge Hoover? Elron Seaver? Whatever!"

I'm guessing here, but I must have gone on trying to explain, ever more pedantically, grinding my axles into a morass of embarrassment. Science fiction, it turned out, was *green*.

You never forget the site of a schooling in shame.

2.

Where Philip K. Dick had come from, for me, was my best friend Jake's dad, Harry. Harry was younger than Jake's mom, and when they divorced, as everyone's parents seemingly did, Jake's mom retained the family home and maintained the upstanding parental postures—in fact, she was one of the most reliable parents around if, in those prodigious slippery days in our unreliable neck of the woods, you were looking for someone to chide or encourage you or to make you a sandwich, as if you were still a younger child. We counted on her for that. Harry, though, became like Jake's erratic and brilliant older brother, or his crazy grown-up friend. He slipped back toward adolescent enthusiasms, and took Jake along for the ride. Jake got to see all the Pink Panther movies, for instance, and *Kentucky Fried Movie* and *Groove Tube*, too. Harry took Jake out to Junior's Restaurant, the legendary Brooklyn cheesecake palace, for dinners consisting of little more than shrimp cocktail and an egg cream. And, seeing Jake's enthusiasm for comics, Harry started bringing around his own just-read copies of mass-market paperback science fiction. This wasn't the old "classic" '50s-vintage stuff I'd discovered on my mother's shelves, Ray Bradbury and Isaac Asimov, but the latest hip, psychedelically packaged material: Roger Zelazny, Harlan Ellison, and fatefully for me, Philip K. Dick. The first of Dick's books I laid eyes on was *A Scanner Darkly*, from 1977; the second might have been *The Zap Gun* or *Clans of the Alphane Moon*.

From Jake's shelves I also recall *The Golden Man*, though this would have been a bit later, since that book wasn't published until 1980. A collection of Dick's stories selected by a young editor named Mark Hurst, *The Golden Man* was prefaced by Dick with a famous—at least to me—personal reminiscence called "The Lucky Dog Pet Shop." There, Dick defines his sense of his own status, the artist-as-depraved-outsider, knocking helplessly on the windows of "serious" literature, reduced to batting out pulp tales while eating horse meat intended for dogs—acquired at the pet shop of the essay's title—because he couldn't afford human food.

Jake cared more for Zelazny, whose fantasies of superpower and martyrdom better dovetailed with the '70s Marvel Comics we both adored. And, though I was alive to something in the presentation, I didn't plunge into reading Dick, not immediately. I circled the books, soaking in random vibrations they gave off. My reading began a year or so later, though it felt like a lifetime's distance from Jake's comics-lair bedroom, when I scored used copies of *Ubik* and *A Maze of Death* and *The Three Stigmata of Palmer Eldritch*, matching black Bantam paperbacks, less zany-looking, more enticingly ominous, than the books that Jake's father had delivered to our attention. Reading these three, I made Dick my own, forging a relationship into which I'd pour vast personal capital over the decades that followed. But if I'm honest with myself about provenance, Jake's too-fun dad hovered oddly in the background of the affair.

3.

I had a girlfriend by the last year of high school, Lorna. Time-wise, we're talking about a scattering of fifteen or twenty months from the scene of the kid who stood at Seventh and Flatbush trying so earnestly to explain to the Slopie girls who Palmer Eldritch was, but in the time-lapse nature footage of childhood memory, this is a lifetime's distance. For one thing, I'd somehow, absurdly, consumed another twenty or so Philip K. Dick novels in that interval, taken the author into my body like wine and wafer. If, previously, I was alerted to Palmer Eldritch's presence all around me, now I was Palmer Eldritch. And I liked it. Also I had a girlfriend. That poor kid a year and a half ago didn't.

I've written about Lorna elsewhere. She's the girl I pathetically stalked home from the subway station in an essay called "Speak, Hoyt-

Schermerhorn." Teenagers who'd figured out how to fuck should, you'd think, enjoy themselves, but in fact Lorna and I had a neurotic and tempestuous romance, full of elaborate betrayals and pleading arguments. The summer of 1982, the summer between high school and college, the year Philip K. Dick died, Lorna and I broke up three times, and we were in an extended fight that sweltering June afternoon when I took her with me to see *Blade Runner*, which had opened a day or two before. Of course we walked up Flatbush Avenue to Seventh, to see the film at the Plaza.

I was in a funk, angry at her, angry at myself for reasons I couldn't admit or articulate. My expectations for the film were a tormented muddle—I'd heard it committed injustices to the book, and that it wasn't going over well with those who lately rooted for science-fiction movies to take over Hollywood. After *Star Wars* and *Close Encounters of the Third Kind*, this film wasn't about to find any comfortable place in the culture. Worse, I was crossed up in the opposite direction, too: Much like a fan who resents seeing his favorite underground band sign with a major label, I worried Dick was being stolen from my exclusive purview. I'd been planning to make a pilgrimage to California to meet Dick, and then learned he'd died, in February that year. Absurd as it was to take his death personally, I did.

So, victim to all this and our native bile, Lorna and I fought outside the theater, right there at my thorny intersection, in sight of all the avenues crisscrossing through my past and future. I threw a sweaty little tantrum because we'd arrived late, pedantically asserting how crucial this viewing was to me, and how badly I hated being late to movies. Of course by the time I'd settled myself down and we purchased our tickets and went inside, the trailer reel had just finished. We were exactly as late as the duration of my tantrum.

I watched *Blade Runner* with a grudge in several directions. Lorna's only reaction was to find the violence upsetting, and we left the theater in a worse funk yet. I couldn't defend the film against her distaste, nor adopt her rejection of it as an adequate response for myself. I'd sat tabulating the film's failings against the book, not grasping what was sensationally vivid and original in the experience. I thought the hard-boiled voice-over embarrassing and derivative, totally *green*. I revere the film now, have seen it in its various versions at least a dozen times, but I still dislike that voice-over.

Six weeks later I was in college in Vermont, self-exiled from my unresolved dilemmas at Flatbush and Seventh. Lorna, and the Slopie girls, remained with me in ways I could and couldn't acknowledge. I'd become an early member of the Philip K. Dick Society, the grassroots posterity-boosting coalition lead by the rock critic Paul Williams. A society newsletter was among the first mail I ever received at my campus mailbox, and I stared at the return address dreamily, already plotting some more decisive evasion or exile, a leap to get me onto Philip K. Dick's map and off my own. Dick might be dead, but I could still make a pilgrimage to the Lucky Dog Pet Shop.

4.

I wrote to Paul Williams to introduce myself, my pretext an interest in adapting Dick's *Confessions of a Crap Artist* into a screenplay. An absurdist domestic tragedy set in '50s California, *Confessions*, in my dream, could become a script an Altman or Hal Ashby might shoot, a class-conscious period melodrama. The urge to bring one of Dick's realist novels to light as a major film—I envisioned several Oscars— was a glimmer of my yearning to rehabilitate him for traditional literary taste, rather than leave him to the sub(cult)ure where I'd found him. Advertising Dick as a writer per se, installing him in a shame-free canon, reflected the wish to join my own weird enthusiasms to my aspirations as a legitimate artist, but also to repair the shame I'd learned to feel on Seventh and Flatbush, or any subsequent instant when I was reminded, and I was constantly reminded, that science fiction was a "subliterary" pursuit.

But I wasn't a filmmaker, or screenwriter, or any kind of writer yet. I also didn't have any way of securing the adaptation rights Paul was obligated to protect for the interests of Dick's heirs, so my request was foolish. Paul treated it kindly. The exchange of letters between us, anyway, put a more definite image in my mind, a shape for my defection to California.

5.

It took two years to carry out that defection, to manifest the self-exiling urge to work from what would appear to others, and myself, as a margin, a position of disenfranchised minority. Dick's margin, science fiction, was a working proposition I could use. Other writers I now relished operated from inside that exile zone, that quarantine: Disch, Delany, Ballard. Science fiction was a literary Brooklyn for me.

I introduced myself to Paul Williams at the Claremont Hotel in Oakland, at a science-fiction convention called SerCon One. Every name I'd spent teenage years reading seemed to be there in human form, from Delany to Terry Carr and Ian Watson. I'd known two novelists growing up, Stanley Ellin and L. J. Davis. I'd met Bernard Malamud and John Ashbery at Bennington, but hadn't declared myself, just skulked, sniffing like a hound. Here, the hotel held a literary universe, weird wizened men who still recalled L. Ron Hubbard as an irritating colleague; William Gibson, mellow prescient icon, calm in the inflamed ranks of the Cyberpunk Politburo. I had reservations: The science-fiction world looked like a cultural cul-de-sac, detached from all I was otherwise immersed in, in my life with my friends. Then Paul appeared wearing a Meat Puppets T-shirt—at that time I called them my favorite band— and I decided it might be all right.

Paul and I wandered from the hotel, down Ashby Avenue, and we got a soda and talked. I announced my various schemes and intentions and by the end of the day was crowned third-in-command at the Philip K. Dick Society. This effectively meant I could join in and sometimes even host the "mailing parties" for the newsletter. We'd gather in my living room in Berkeley and listen to music and seal envelopes and elicit from Paul tales of time spent in Dick's company, and about halfway through, when we'd gotten organized—there was a vast complication involving "bulk mail" having to be ordered by Zip Code in order to get a favorable rate from the post office—we'd smoke a big joint and everything would get wonderfully confusing. This was a fair distance from Bernard Malamud. I'd located my margin, oh yeah.

6.

My first five or six "published" critical pieces appeared in the pages of the society newsletter. They're agony, stiff as a freshman term paper, arch as an anonymous notice in the *Times Literary Supplement*, circa 1954. Label this style "Overcompensating Autodidact." Here's the last, published in *PKDS Newsletter #24*, dated 1990. It's probably the most revealing, and the least awkward (though I can't swear I'll be able to resist massaging some of the clenched syntax as I retype the thing):

Two Dickian Novels

What do we mean when we call a work "Dickian"?

The novels of Philip K. Dick show the influence of science fiction published in the '40s and '50s. From Frederik Pohl and Cyril Kornbluth, Dick borrowed a satirical, dystopian near-future setting. From A. E. van Vogt a predilection for reality disjunctions. From Robert Heinlein a measure of solipsism and paranoia. Yet searching the works of these authors for a reading experience that is essentially Dickian is frustrating. Similarly, many of the newer writers in SF—I'm thinking of K. W. Jeter, Rudy Rucker, and Tim Powers, among others—profess an admiration for Dick's work, and often employ Dickian elements in their own. But the "Dickian" effect is rarely, if ever, central; these writers are appropriately busy with their own themes and motifs.

There are, however, instances of fiction that are more fundamentally Dickian; works that, rather than evoking Dick's milieu, reproduce—in many cases unknowingly—the signature disruptive effects of a novel by Dick.

Let me describe a novel I've just read. The book's main character is, without his knowledge, murdered in the first chapter. He proceeds to enter a bizarre and shadowy mirror-world, and experiences there a bewildering array of "impossible" events. He spends most of the novel in pursuit of an elusive policeman, who is supposed to possess the ability to enlighten the protagonist in his confusion. Mysterious signs of this policeman are everywhere. In the end, the protagonist learns he is dead, only to have this awareness immediately stripped from him. The novel ends with our character back where we first found him: newly murdered, on the verge of the events of the novel we've just finished reading.

The novel is *The Third Policeman*, written in 1940 by an Irish journalist who published fiction under the name Flann O'Brien. Though I can't do it justice in this short space, the book is wildly funny, linguistically brilliant, and highly Dickian. Specifically, a sibling to *Ubik* and *A Maze of Death*. It also conveys a strong flavor of Lewis Carroll, a thread I'll pick up again in a moment.

The chances of Dick having read *The Third Policeman* (and not mentioning it anywhere) are slim. It's almost certainly an instance of parallel development. What's remarkable is how perfectly distilled the *Dick Effect* is in O'Brien's novel. Freed of Dickian trappings (the so-called "junk" elements that Stanislaw Lem identified), *The Third Policeman* is nonetheless unmistakably Dickian. This is not to say anything against, just for instance, talking robot taxicabs. I'm personally fond of talking robot taxicabs. The crucial point (which Dick himself proves in *The Transmigration of Timothy Archer*) is that talking robot taxicabs aren't strictly necessary.

Now take *Memories of Amnesia*, by Lawrence Shainberg, published in 1988 yet showing no direct influence, or even knowledge, of Dick's work. Again, the futuristic settings and artifacts familiar to Dick's readers are absent. In the case of *Memories of Amnesia* even the Dickian plotline, still on view in *The Third Policeman*, is missing. Nonetheless, the Dickian essence survives. Dick perceived reality as a paradoxical, distorted, and even dysfunctional thing, and he sought, through his writings, a variety of possible explanations; political, religious, philosophical, psychological, even pharmacological. One of the very few he didn't pursue was a neurological explanation. (Since his death biographers have to some extent explored that possibility for him; indeed, the proposed diagnosis of temporal lobe epilepsy is a fascinating lens through which to consider his life and work.) Shainberg, the author of *Brain Surgeon: An Intimate View of His World*, has in *Memories of Amnesia* relentlessly explored Dickian themes in the fascinating and rich language of neurology.

His book is the first-person account of a neurosurgeon who begins to experience symptoms of brain damage; in the middle of delicate surgery he bursts out singing "Oh, Susannah." He experiences these symptoms as an exhilarating taste of freedom from the constraints of rationality. The narrator is simultaneously doctor and patient—recalling *A Scanner Darkly*'s Bob

Arctor, who's both drug abuser and narc—and the distinctions between illness and health, sanity and madness, illusion and reality, quickly blur. The result is a deliriously unsettling excursion. The introspective, insistently questioning, and highly self-absorbed texture of this narrative resembles *Valis* and *Radio Free Albemuth* in particular. Perhaps needless to say, the novel ends on a note of almost unbearably unresolved tension.

Shainberg, like O'Brien, has been compared to Lewis Carroll. (Shainberg makes the connection explicit, taking an epigraph from *Alice in Wonderland*.) Borges and Pirandello, two of the great international writers commonly cited as relevant comparisons to Dick, are often compared to Carroll. Baseline adjectives like *dreamlike*, *menacing*, and *surreal* apply equally to Dick and Carroll. Yet in searching the indexes of various critical works on Dick I don't find reference to Carroll.

Two questions, then: Might Lewis Carroll be an important and unrecognized common denominator for some of Dick's themes and motifs? And might an inquiry into what we call the *Dick Effect* begin not with Dick's companions in the pulp SF of the '50s, but instead with an exploration of the history of "strangeness" (or, "cognitive estrangement") in fiction per se?

"Two Dickian Novels" is a fledgling effort in my gentrification campaign, that which culminates, twenty years on, with my chaperoning Dick into the Library of America. With a nakedness that's halfway endearing, the young critic scurries to carpet his hero's bare floor in quality-lit signifiers: Carroll, Borges, etc. (I planned a follow-up to "Two Dickian Novels," with more examples from outside SF's ghastly precincts—Iris Murdoch's *The Black Prince* was one; others I've forgotten.) If you're feeling generous, say I'm carving out a zone for my own future operation, arrayed with useful precedents, as in Borges's "Kafka and His Precursors." If you're feeling less generous, diagnose it as a case of contamination anxiety working itself out in (barely) public view. I wanted to woodshed with Dick and some other writers condemned to an SF ghetto, but I didn't want to live there. If I could drag Dick out in advance, he'd be my stalking horse, maybe. There's a line running straight from this effort through my rather discombobulated *Village Voice* essay "The Squandered Promise of Science Fiction" in 1998; the question is whether incompletely acknowledged personal necessities, projected onto writers besides myself, render these "critical" efforts disingenuous. The same judgment could probably extend to describe the piece you're reading now. Am I green? No? Maybe? What about now?

7.

By mentioning in the essay K. W. Jeter and Tim Powers, two writers who'd as young men had the luck of showing up on Philip K. Dick's doorstep and gaining his friendship, I might also have been negotiating my disappointment that I couldn't duplicate their trick. I'd run out of time, so my own jaunt west could only be to posthumous Dickland. I'd have to make do with Paul and other residual traces. Suggesting Jeter and Powers weren't especially "Dickian," I left a possibility open, that another literary heir might arrive soon, one who'd more persuasively step into the great man's boot prints—never mind if he never got to sit at the great man's knees.

8.

I was so proud I'd written about a contemporary writer that I took the trouble of photocopying the piece and sending it to Lawrence Shainberg, care of his publisher. Years later, Larry and I became friends. He admitted he was baffled by the piece, had never heard of Philip K. Dick, and that when he tried reading *Valis*, found it impossibly bad.

9.

That same Chestnut Street one-bedroom apartment in the Berkeley flats where the society gathered to stuff newsletters into envelopes, and where I wrote my first thirty-odd stories and three novels, happened to be three blocks from the small Francisco Street two-bedroom house where Dick lived from 1950 to '58, and where he wrote his first fifty-odd stories and six or seven novels. That also put me two or three blocks from the Lucky Dog Pet Shop and a number of other Dick "landmarks." It was with Paul that I first walked over to gaze at the Francisco Street house, a stroll that became a ritual of my daylight writing hours.

Though the house divulged no secrets, there was something eerie and monastic in tracing the path from one negligible address to another on streets where no one ever walked, where barely anyone drove. I also once veered past the Dick house at four in the morning, tripping on Ecstasy, but at that moment I was more enthralled by the live human at my side than with my dead crazy friend Phil, and I gave the place barely a nod.

I did visit Lucky Dog, too, and try to get the clerk to admit that the shop knew its place in Philip K. Dick's personal mythos. Did they know a great man once bought horse meat here? Yes, they agreed, someone had mentioned an article like that once, and had promised to bring it in and show it to them. But that person never returned. I promised I'd bring it in and show it to them, and then I, too, never returned. I made another unsatisfying pilgrimage to Tupper & Reed, one of the two music shops where Dick worked before making the perilous leap into life as a full-time freelance short-story writer. Art Music, the other, had closed. But Tupper & Reed divulged no secrets, either. It was Art Music that had been the really important site for Phil, Art Music whose owner had been the model for so many lovable, tyrannical father-boss figures in Dick's fiction, like Leo Bulero from *The Three Stigmata of Palmer Eldritch*. (I bought my then-wife an electric guitar at Tupper & Reed. Imported into our apartment the guitar exuded no Dickian essence, but we each learned three or four chords; I could play Bob Dylan's "Tangled Up in Blue," while she could play Elvis Costello's "Two Little Hitlers," and did, ominously often if you considered the lyrics. Eventually, a photograph of myself beside this guitar would appear on the jacket of my arguably least-Dickian novel, *You Don't Love Me Yet*.) Phil Dick's Berkeley, everywhere I tried to pin it down, evaporated like the locations in *Time Out of Joint*, to be replaced with thin strips of paper labeled with the names of the missing items: *Pet Shop*, *Music Store*, *Two-Story House*.

I impetuously went into a tattoo parlor and had the spray-can logo from the first American edition of *Ubik* tattooed on my left upper arm. Well, half impetuously: The day before, my then-wife and my sister had gotten tattoos at that same parlor, so it was familial peer pressure that made this decision for me. I wasn't certain I wanted a tattoo, actually, but if I was going to have one I was certain what tattoo I wanted. My then-wife was tattooed with an ampersand (still her trademark), my sister with a plate of green eggs and ham from the Dr. Seuss book of the same name, a tattoo which has become widely photographed because my sister wears sleeveless shirts. I echoed my sister's choice by selecting a gooey fictional substance that gives title to the book in which it appears—I challenge you to find another example.* I never wear sleeveless shirts, but word of my tattoo has circulated, slightly, a viral rider on my moderate fame, and I'm occasionally called on by sly interlocutors to sheepishly exhibit it while signing at a bookstore. In two decades I've watched my spray can swell, shrink, and grow slack with the changing contours of my arm, gain hairs, survive mosquito bites. The simple colors haven't faded badly, but the blue outline has blurred, victim of the entropy the spray-product Ubik was supposed to combat. Dick ensured Ubik's immortality; I've ensured its mortality.

Perhaps the tattoo helped, but in any case I quit wandering over to Francisco Street. The action I required, the essence I sought, wasn't located on the exterior of that building but in the interior of my own— and just as anyone wandering past the Francisco Street house in 1956 would have no notion what was being hatched inside that drab façade, no one passing Chestnut Street could have known what I was up to, typing up on a Selectric typewriter in quiet, ignominious joy draft after draft of novels with working titles like *Apes in the Plan*, *White Lines*, *Fractal Days*, and *Satisfying Lack*.

10.

Also short stories, in many instances more nakedly derivative of Dick's work even than the novels, though my own material kept leaking through. Most went unpublished; a few slipped into print in science-fiction magazines or poetry journals; all precede "The Happy Man," the story which I chose to open my first story collection, and so have been essentially excluded as juvenilia from my "collected works" (except for four which were absorbed into *Amnesia Moon*). I'll include two here, both circa 1990, not for their lasting quality but for light shed, however mortifying. Here's "Ad Man," a pat little fable in which I labor to update Dick's typical satire of advertising with the then-fashionable motif of nanotechnology.

*Tono-Bungay, by H. G. Wells.

Ad Man

"Look here, man. Closer."

The two men bent in together over the magnifying glass, their shoulders hunched, their breath held. The detail of the painting blurred at the edges of the lens. What they examined now was nothing more than a single brushstroke, magnified tremendously.

As they watched, both trembling, the painted line slowly began to move, to thicken, and change direction. Then the artist's breath misted over the lens.

"Crap." They both stood up, abruptly. The artist put his hand to his forehead, and looked at the other man for reaction.

The other man pocketed the glass and said: "Advertising. I'm sorry, man. The painting's definitely infected."

"Infected," said the artist flatly. "What the fuck does that mean?"

The other man smiled sadly and gestured towards the table in the corner of the artist's ramshackle house. The artist nodded, and they went together and sat there. But when the man reached out for the Mason jar of water on the table the artist said: "No. That's for cleaning with. It's no good for drinking."

It was a lie. The water in the mason jar was fine. The artist just wasn't in the mood to share it with the stranger.

The man smiled and said: "Never mind. I've stopped making the distinction." He tipped the jar back and took a long drink, then lifted the jar as if for a toast.

The artist made a sour face. "What's happening to my painting?" he said.

"Microprocessors," said the man, wiping his lips. He put the jar down. "Little invisible robots, with tiny little hands, and tiny little tools in their tiny little hands. They run around rearranging things at a level we can't see."

"What? Like the medical things?"

"Exactly. Only this is another type, not medical. Commercial. Something the Americans were fooling around with just before the war. We didn't think it had crossed over here, at first. Now it's turning up everywhere."

"Commercial." The artist narrowed his eyes. "What does that mean?"

"Corporations manufactured them. They're programmed to redesign existing artworks into advertising. The companies got tired of waiting for talent to sell out, I guess. And the costs are lower."

The artist couldn't believe his ears. "You're saying my painting is being transformed into an *advertisement*? For some American product that doesn't even fucking exist anymore?"

The man nodded.

"Well, that's ridiculous!" blustered the artist. "Advertising— for what?"

"We'll have to see how it comes out, won't we?"

"Shit!"

"It takes days to finish," said the man. "But we'll be able to tell before that. There's two main companies involved in the outbreak here. Fazz and White Walnut, two drinks. White Walnut has the classier campaign, a couple of white-suited pimplike guys reclining on a tropical beach. Fazz has this manic clown-donkey thing, with big pinwheel eyes . . ."

The artist groaned.

"Anyway, they're easy to tell apart. I'll know in half an hour."

"How did this happen?" asked the artist incredulously.

"Imported records, I think. The first outbreak was a radio station playing American hits. All the songs started to evolve towards the Fazz theme:

Fazz!
Nothing as good as
Fazz!

"Or else the White Walnut music, this thing with coconuts dropping onto drums, and Hawaiian guitar. Whoever was singing on the record, they'd suddenly be pushing this product. We burnt the station's whole collection. But the things had already escaped, I guess." The man smiled to himself. "They got to some films. We had Jay Gatsby drowning his sorrows in Fazz, then so cheered by the stuff that he got up and did a little song and dance."

"Is mine the first painting?"

"Oh no. I saw this big Hieronymus Bosch thing, hundreds of characters on a gigantic landscape, and both products had gotten to it. They were competing, trying to wrest away control of this sort of battlefield in the painting, and the characters were all divided up into two armies, the Walnuts versus the Fazzians—"

"Jesus! How did you become the big expert?"

"I was a technician in a hospital. I worked with the bloodstream ones. I recognized this other type when it turned up, that's all."

"It's such a fucking joke," said the artist. "Their whole culture was fucking leveled."

"Yes," said the man cheerily. "I may never have the pleasure of tasting a Fazz." He pointed over the artist's shoulder. "Look."

The artist turned and looked at his painting.

His radiation sunset had grown donkey ears. And out of the swirling orange underneath, features were beginning to resolve. Cartoon eyes, and a gigantic grin.

"The Fazz donkey," said the man.

"Oh god." The artist's head fell into his hands. "It's horrible."

"I wonder how it got all the way out here," said the man, getting up from the table. "Have you shown this painting?"

"No," said the artist. "It isn't even finished. I took some others to Sydney last week, though—"

The artist saw the man glance quickly over at the racks against the wall.

"You aren't saying—" The artist jumped up, but not before the man had walked over and pulled a painting from the rack. It showed the Fazz donkey, in full splendor across the landscape, a bubbling, frosty glass in hand, his eyes dazzling op-art pinwheels, and over the artist's sky a word balloon:

SEX AND FAZZ
AND ROCK AND ROLL!

The artist flipped frantically through the rack. Each image was different, but each featured the leering donkey and plastic bottles of the green drink.

"Everything's ruined!" wailed the artist.

The man knelt and squinted closely at the canvases, but didn't say anything.

"I can't ever paint in here again, can I? It'll all come out Fazz."

"Until we eliminate the microprocessors, yes," said the man musingly.

"Is there a way?"

"It wouldn't be easy, with so little technology at our disposal anymore. They're programmed to defend themselves. But I've had an idea . . . If it worked, we might even be able to reclaim your artwork."

"Tell me."

"The surgeon micros. They work by assuming the expertise of the doctor, by recording a version of his brain into their own programming. In essence they become miniaturized copies of the human surgeon. If we could have them instead record your impulse, towards protecting these paintings . . ."

"What does that involve?"

"It's simple if you're not squeamish. I inject a vial of blank medical micros into your bloodstream. They'll work their way to your brain, and document, in place of further medical skills, your painting expertise. If I'm guessing right they'll also pick up your care for these works, and your dislike for the Fazz micros swarming over them. Then, once they've reproduced sufficiently, you touch them to the painting. With luck they'll become your little avenging angels . . ."

"I'm game," said the artist grimly. "I've got nothing to lose. My work is all I have."

"Who knows," said the man. "We may invent a new art form. You may get to put your brushes into storage. If your micros get strong enough they can go transforming all the old moldering advertising into your imagery. Hah! Then we'll have you to deal with."

"A good deal more sightly than this crap," muttered the artist. "When can we start?"

"I've got the stuff in my car," admitted the man. "I packed it up when your friend called and told me about your painting. I'd been hoping for this chance."

"You haven't tried it before?"

"No."

"But there's no danger?"

"None except failure. The medical micros might not adapt. But they're used quite routinely by now."

They stepped out onto the porch together. By coincidence it was sunset, and the colors in the sky were incredible. They stopped and stared together. The visitor hadn't much taste for painting, but he could see how this recent development in sunsets would make a fit subject.

When it was over he went to the car and unpacked the medical equipment.

Once the vial was injected the artist went downstairs and brought up more of the good water, for celebration. On sudden impulse he brought up two of his last remaining beers as well. "Here," he said, tossing one to the man. "This won't interfere, will it?"

"What, the alcohol? No." The man laughed. "The medical micros can fend for themselves; that's the whole point." He pried open the bottle and took a sip. "God, that's nice. It's been months."

The artist didn't say anything. The two men sat together in the twilight, savoring the beer, waiting. After an hour had passed the visitor said: "Try touching your hand to the painting. If they're ready they'll crawl out through your pores and go to work."

The artist shuddered, then did as he was told. No immediate effect was visible.

"Don't worry," said the man. "They'll have jumped. I just hope they understand the assignment."

They went back to the table, though the beer was now long gone. The artist got out a checkerboard and the men played. It was hard, though, to keep from looking over constantly at the painting, and neither man resisted much. In the dim light it was too easy to imagine change that hadn't actually occurred. After a while the visitor went over and took out his magnifying glass.

"I don't know," he said. "The lines of the donkey are still thickening."

"What do you mean? Are you saying it didn't work?"

"Let's hope your little soldiers are still marshalling their forces, surveying the enemies' positions. They certainly haven't attacked yet. The advertisement is still taking shape."

The artist paced the room angrily, while the man continued to pore over the canvas with the glass.

"When—"

"Be patient," said the man. "This is a new process. It's probably still too soon. In the meantime, I'm exhausted. Is there a place I can lie down?"

The artist scowled. He went over to the painting and lifted it from the top. "Sure, sure," he said. "I'll unfold the cot—Ow!" He dropped the painting and held up his hand, wincing.

"What's the matter?"

"It stung me! Look at this!"

The man hurried over. The artist's palm was dotted with tiny incisions, all beading with blood.

"What did it do? What's going to happen?"

The man sighed. "It's a failure, worse than I expected. The Fazz micros must have defeated the medical ones, and, what's more, appropriated their skills. All we've done is add to their arsenal, I'm afraid. They've got the talents of a million tiny surgeons at their disposal now. The nip you took was just a warning. Hands off. They're protecting their territory."

"You mean I can't even touch my own paintings?" said the artist, incredulous.

"They're not your paintings anymore," the man pointed out. "They're the work of Fazz."

"Fuck the work of Fazz," said the artist. "I want to destroy them. I don't even want to see this ugly face again. I don't care, I'll give up painting if I have to."

"It's probably better," agreed the man sadly. "We shouldn't let these new surgical ones spread. That's nasty what they did to your hand."

The two men spent the better part of the night loading the paintings into a pile on the lawn, then lighting the pile into a bonfire. At the end they staggered back into the house, exhausted, faces streaked with sweat and ash.

"I'll get out the cot," said the artist. "You shouldn't have to drive back like this, before you've slept."

"That's good of you, man. It's been quite a night." The man paused. "You know, you ought to come back to the city with me in the morning, get your mind off this thing for a few days. Your friend was asking about you—" The man stopped, his jaw hanging open, and stared at the artist's forehead.

"What?" said the artist.

"Your flesh," said the man, dumfounded. "Your head." The artist reached up and felt his head. At first he thought he'd put on a hat. But no. Whatever the knobby protrusions were, they were sprouting right out of the skin.

What's interesting (and uninteresting) here is mostly plain, but I'll mention that the aggression of pop culture on the fine arts—on a painter of oils on canvas specifically—rehearses my own creative paternity. After all, I'm a painter's kid. On the one hand, I've given my dad's artistic medium the high moral ground; on the other, I've fated it to drown in banality or be thrown on a pyre. The story glances ahead to my interest in notions of artistic influence, and the propagation of cultural stuff by automatic or viral processes. The story's not completely un-germane to "The Ecstasy of Influence," it just isn't good. But here's another.

Walking the Moons

"Look," says the mother of The Man Who Is Walking Around The Moons Of Jupiter, "he's going so fast." She snickers to herself and scuttles around the journalist to a table littered with wiring tools and fragmented mechanisms. She loops a long, tangled cord over her son's intravenous tube and plugs one end into his headset, jostling him momentarily as she works it into the socket. His stride on the treadmill never falters. She runs the cord back to a modified four-track recorder sitting in the dust of the garage floor, then picks up the recorder's microphone and switches it on.

"Good morning, Mission Commander," she says.

"Yes," grunts The Man Who, his slack jaw moving beneath the massive headset. It startles the journalist to hear the voice of The Man Who boom out into the tiny garage.

"Interview time, Eddie."

"Who?"

"Mr. Kaffey. *Systems Magazine*, remember?"

"O.K.," says Eddie, The Man Who. His weakened, pallid body trudges forward. He is clothed only in jockey undershorts and orthopedic sandals, and the journalist can see his heart beat beneath the skin of his chest.

The Mother Of smiles artificially and hands the journalist the microphone. "I'll leave you boys alone," she says. "If you need anything, just yodel."

She steps past the journalist, over the cord, and out into the sunlight, pulling the door shut behind her.

The journalist turns to the man on the treadmill.

"Uh, Eddie?"

"Yeah."

"Uh, I'm Ron Kaffey. Is this O.K.? Can you talk?"

"Mr. Kaffey, I've got nothing but time." The Man Who smacks his lips and tightens his grip on the railing before him. The tread rolls away steadily beneath his feet, taking him nowhere.

The journalist covers the mike with the palm of his hand and clears his throat, then begins again. "So you're out there now. On Io. Walking."

"Mr. Kaffey, I'm currently broadcasting my replies to your questions from a valley on the northwestern quadrant of Io, yes. You're coming in loud and clear. No need to raise your voice. We're fortunate in having a pretty good connection, a good Earth-to-Io hookup, so to speak." The journalist watches as The Man Who moistens his lips, then dangles his tongue in the open air. "Please feel free to shoot with the questions, Mr. Kaffey. This is pretty uneventful landscape even by Io standards and I'm just hanging on your every word."

"Explain to me," says the journalist, "what you're doing."

"Ah. Well, I designed the rig myself. Took pixel satellite photographs and fed them into my simulator, which gives me a steadily unfolding virtual-space landscape." He reaches up and taps at his headset. "I log the equivalent mileage at the appropriate gravity on my treadmill and pretty soon I've had the same experience an astronaut would have. If we could afford to send them up anymore. Heh." He scratches violently at his ribs, until they flush pink. "Ask me questions," he says. "I'm ready at this end. You want me to describe what I'm seeing?"

"Describe what you're seeing."

"The desert, Mr. Kaffey. God, I'm so goddamned bored of the desert. That's all there is, you know. There isn't any atmosphere. We'd hope for some atmosphere, we had some hopes, but it didn't turn out that way. Nope. The dust all lays flat here, because of that. I try kicking it up, but there isn't any wind." The Man Who scuffs in his Dr. Scholl's sandals at the surface of the treadmill, booting imaginary pebbles, stirring up nonexistent dust. "You probably know I can't see Jupiter right now. I'm on the other side, so I'm pretty much out here alone under the stars. There isn't any point in my describing that to you."

The Man Who scratches again, this time at the patch where the intravenous tube intersects his arm, and the journalist is afraid he'll tear it off. "Bored?" asks the journalist.

"Yeah. Next time I think I'll walk across a gassy planet. What do you think of that? Or across the Pacific Ocean. On the bottom, I mean. 'Cause they're mapping it with ultrasound. Feed it into the simulator. Take me a couple of weeks. Nothing like this shit.

"I'm thinking more in terms of smaller scale walks from here on in, actually. Get back down to earth, find ways to make it count for more. You know what I mean? Maybe even the ocean isn't such a good idea, actually. Maybe my fans can't really identify with my off-world walks, maybe they're feeling, who knows, a little, uh, alienated by this Io thing. I know I am. I feel out of touch, Mr. Kaffey. Maybe I ought to walk across the corn belt or the sunbelt or something. A few people in cars whizzing past, waving at me, and farmers' wives making me picnic lunches, because they've heard I'm passing through. I could program that. I could have every goddamn Mayor from Pinole to Akron give me the key to their goddamn city."

"Sounds O.K., Eddie."

"Sounds O.K.," echoes The Man Who. "But maybe even that's a little much. Maybe I ought to walk across the street to the drugstore for a pack of gum. You don't happen to have a stick of gum in your pocket, Mr. Journalist? I'll just open my mouth and you stick it in. I trust you. We don't have to tell my mother. If you hear her coming you just let me know, and I'll swallow it. You won't get in any trouble."

"I don't have any," says the journalist.

"Ah well."

The Man Who walks on, undaunted. Only now something is wrong. There's a hiss of escaping liquid, and the journalist is certain that The Man Who's nutrient serum is leaking from his arm. Then he smells the urine, and sees the undershorts of The Man Who staining dark, and adhering to the cave-white flesh of his thigh.

"What's the matter, Kaffey? No more questions?"

"You've wet yourself," says the journalist.

"Oh, damn. Uh, you better call my mom."

But The Mother Of has already sensed that something is amiss. She steps now back into the garage, smoking a cigarette and squinting into the darkness at her son. She frowns as she discerns the stain, and takes a long drag on her cigarette, closing her eyes.

"I guess you're thinking that there might not be a story here," says The Man Who. "Least not the story you had in mind."

"Oh no, I wouldn't say that," says the journalist quickly. He's not sure if he hasn't detected a note of sarcasm in the voice of The Man Who by now. "I'm sure we can work something up."

"Work something up," parrots The Man Who. The Mother Of has his shorts down now, and she's swabbing his damp flank with a paper towel. The Man Who sets his mouth in a grim smile and trudges forward. He's not here really. He's out on Io, making tracks. He's going to be in the Guinness Book of World Records.

The journalist sets the microphone back down in the dust and packs his bag. As he walks the scrubby driveway back to the street he hears The Man Who Is Walking Around The Moons Of Jupiter, inside the garage, coughing on cigarette fumes.

Okay, that's a little better. I liked the mood and voice of this piece when I wrote it, and still do, despite the blatant failings: the slipshod, second-hand misogyny—an unwelcome influence from Dick—and the hint of body-horror, as though a trickle of urine disqualifies anyone's dignity (the writer of this story obviously hadn't yet changed a diaper). The Man Who recalls Dick's shambling-sacrificial antiheroes, like Mercer in *Do Androids Dream of Electric Sheep?*, or Molinari in *Now Wait for Last Year*, but he's enough my own, enough a product of observation and self-inspection, that I can take pleasure in him, especially when he requests the chewing gum.

What interests me most, though, is how the relationship between the callow journalist and The Man Who now looks like an early, guilty allegory of my own attempts to enlist Philip K. Dick or any other "crazy friend" for my lucid artistic purposes—an unconscious warm-up to what I'd later pursue in a couple of short stories from *Men and Cartoons*: "Planet Big Zero" and "Interview with the Crab." The relationship even forecasts the betrayal enacted between object-friend and subject-friend in *The Fortress of Solitude*. This short story hangs in there for me, finally, because in it I see myself knocking on my own door (Chestnut Street), not just Dick's (Francisco Street).

11.

Believing I'd written a breakthrough piece and knowing what manner of breakthrough would mean the most to me, I sent "Walking the Moons" to Gordon Lish at *The Quarterly*. He rejected it flamboyantly. I sent it to Howard Junker at *ZYZZYVA*; he teasingly subjected the story to two rounds of edits before rejecting it. When the story was published in a tiny SF magazine out of Austin, Texas, called *New Pathways*—Junker's edits intact—it was picked up for *The Year's Best Science Fiction*. Whether this was vindication or epitaph for my literary aspirations, I couldn't say. Self-marginalization was well under way; self-gentrification would wait.

12.

Ten years and several personal revolutions later I sat in a sushi restaurant in Brooklyn with Hampton Fancher, the screenwriter of *Blade Runner*, who wanted to persuade me to let him adapt and direct a version of my Dick-meets-Chandler first novel, *Gun, with Occasional Music*. Hearing Hampton's description of how deeply he'd responded to the book, tabulating details that had electrified him, I had to laugh: Loads of what he described was *Blade Runner*'s direct influence on my novel, of course. Hampton and I were trapped in a circular influential mirror, admiring our own distorted reflections. And each of us shadowed by another, a face like Palmer Eldritch's seeping through.

Hampton, like Paul Williams, like Jeter and Powers, had enjoyed the opportunity denied me: to know Philip K. Dick personally. But unlike those others, who claimed friendship with my paranoid, prickly hero, Hampton Fancher—who'd appeared out of nowhere as a new crazy friend for me, a patchouli-reeking flamenco-dancing Hollywood hipster, boyfriend of starlets, who'd endear himself to me again and again with his shambolic frankness—stated flatly, "Dick didn't like me." The remark, so simple and indisputable, entered my body as a decades-delayed electric shock: Why should I ever have assumed Dick would have liked *me*? Our kinship, presumed since I was fourteen years old, was a one-way street, an imposition of my desire.

By this time I'd become a serial ambassador for Dick's work, defending it to serious readers in essays, introductions, panel discussions, and so forth. More than once I'd joked that Dick's gentrification was possible only after death had cleared the awkwardness of his personal presence (his defensive vanity about his literary status, his persecution complex at being appropriated for theories or causes) from the landscape. If he'd stuck around, Dick surely would have found a way to dishearten and derail his would-be enshriners. Yet had I bothered to consider that Dick might have loathed me, and renounced my striving on his behalf?

13.

When I was ten or eleven I made a friend in school, a kid who'd been saddled with the nickname *Aardvark*, whether by his family or by other friends, I don't know. Aardvark had long hair, longer even than mine; an asymmetrical, loping gait; a plan to become a puppeteer like his hero, Jim Henson; and a strange, shy confidence. I fell in love. I brought Aardvark home after school one day, to present to my mother, and in front of her I called him, with open admiration, "*really weird.*" I don't remember how Aardvark and I spent that afternoon. There weren't many like it. Soon Aardvark had grown out of his nickname, and loped on to interests beyond Muppets and me. Under another assumed name Aardvark became one of New York City's celebrated graffiti writers. For a time, he was King of the A-Train. He shifted into legend, so I went on knowing of him after our brief friendship.

What I recall about that day was my mother's reprimand, after Aardvark had gone home. Barely a reprimand, really, just some food for thought: Was I so certain my friend liked being dubbed "weird"? Maybe

I should hesitate before making friends self-conscious of their eccentricities, locking them into cute roles. I was shamed but also confused by my mother's censure. I associated the open celebration of bizarre behaviors specifically with my parents, and my mother was known for awarding baroque nicknames ("Captain Vague," "Jerry Cheesecake," etc.), monikers etching this or that personal episode into legend. I thought it was obvious how adoring my use of *weird* had been. For what it's worth, I've never completely shed my sense that *weird* or *crazy* were typical hallmarks of quality, of the characters and artifacts I'd spend my life relishing and collecting and, if I was lucky, originating, crazy books, crazy movies, crazy thoughts. To have a crazy friend was to have waded into the crazy world and given it a soul kiss. For wasn't it a crazy world?

14.

I've had so many opportunities to talk to Philip K. Dick without him talking back: Time works that way. I've built a few of my palaces on his shambles, and no one can ever tell me I shouldn't have. There are days, though, when I wonder whether I'm like Gordon Lish to Dick's Raymond Carver—Lish, so sly and urbane, forcibly enlisting "the natural man" Carver in his editorial schemes, dressing him up like a pet bear. Or (speaking of bears) maybe I'm like Werner Herzog, editing the dead naturalist Timothy Treadwell's footage into *Grizzly Man*, then puzzling over the marionette I've got up on his feet and dancing—his aspect so remarkable, his private face still and forever hidden from view. But Lish and Herzog, they're crazy, too, even if they're better at getting through days, better at talking on a telephone or balancing a checkbook, than Carver and Treadwell. They're crazy with love, for one thing, even if it is love of a colonizing, acquisitive variety.

15.

Sometimes, also, I think I hate Philip K. Dick for not loving Hampton Fancher. How could you be so *small*?

16.

Dick often gave his characters powerful but unsteady father figures who resembled Dick's boss at Art Music, Herb Hollis: bullying and

charismatic, generous and treacherous. The motif is familiar from
Orson Welles's movies, the "big father" often played by Welles himself,
as Falstaff, or Kane, or Quinlan. I've fooled with this motif myself, in
Motherless Brooklyn's Frank Minna. More often, though, my character
pairs are like siblings, or friends, linked by bonds of guilt, yearning,
and mutual betrayal. Maybe this is a typical difference between the
postwar generation of Dick and his peers—those whose parents were
toughened by the Depression and World War II—and my generation,
we who got the questing, self-revising boomers as parents. For myself
and Jake, at times our parents were less like parents and more like crazy
friends. So our friendships involved a measure of mutual parenting or,
since mutual parenting was really impossible, the impulse to rescue
each other from our parents' squishy legacies (see: *The Fortress of Solitude*). And for all my reverence, I never really looked at Philip K. Dick
as a literary father, more like a brilliant older brother whose brave and
also half-assed forays charted wild paths for me to follow.

17.

Dick's old cadre of readers bristle at hearing him called "crazy," or at
the rehearsals of his human frailties, his drugs and divorces, which tend
to accompany the laurels the larger culture lately keeps draping on his
tomb. I've never understood the problem. Apart from the pointlessness
of the question—was Melville crazy? was Malcolm Lowry? Kafka?—
I suppose I'm residually inclined to hear the word as a shred of beatnik
exultation: "That's *crazy*, man!" I'm still looking for the crazy wherever
I can find it. It's hard enough to kick against the plastic Victorianisms
of our culture, the social sarcophagus of daily life. Even attempting it
can make you crazy, let alone succeeding as well as Dick did. I *like* helpless braggarts, obsessive fools, angry people. My ears prick up at the
word "pretentious"—that's usually the movie I want to see, the book I
want to read, the scene I want to make. Nearly anyone I've found worth
knowing was difficult enough, vivid enough, to qualify at some point
as my crazy friend.

   The Slopie girls are women now. I'm never out of touch with Laurene. I could write a hundred pages about stone-dependable friendship;
this isn't it. Deena, meanwhile, is still out there raging, shaming me
with flippant satires of my passionate greenness, wrecking our friend-

ship as often as not, forcing me (it seems to me) to wreck it in return. We've gone many months, and once nearly a decade, in the dark, not knowing whether we'll speak again. I'm furious at her now, but writing this as a valentine, I'd like to think: Come back, crazy friend. I'm big enough for you still. I've got what it costs to know you, and though I may seem reluctant to spend it all in one place, I'd hate to die with it in my pocket.

What I Learned at the Science-Fiction Convention

Through the magic portal, in print and nominated for a Nebula Award, I found a seat waiting for me on a dais in an endlessly resumed panel discussion, in a floating opera that touched down for weekends at Radissons, Hyatt Regencys, Ramadas, to the bewildered amusement of the hotel staff and the permanent obliviousness of anyone else. (There may be one being enacted down the street as you read these words.) I embraced the science-fiction community instinctively, out of my long responsiveness to countercultures that judge themselves sufficient worlds, pocket universes in permanent abreaction to what lies outside their boundary. Like hippies. The situation reworked the confusion of my upbringing (wait, the '60s failed, and will be treated as a reversible mistake?). Now I wasn't the fall guy in the story. My eccentrically insatiable reading made me an expert on the lands beyond the science-fiction redoubt. I knew more about contemporary writing than anyone else in the joint. Since the name of the never-ending panel discussion was "Science Fiction and the Mainstream," my private grail quest took on a recursive quality, my (yearning) trajectory distilled in the field's: born in pulp shame, then vindicated as relevant to every contemporary experience.

After Pynchon, Joseph McElroy, DeLillo, and others had made ready use of the technological NOW that had swallowed the future, after Doris Lessing and Stanley Kubrick and Haruki Murakami, after

Delany, Ballard, Angela Carter, Thomas Disch, Russell Hoban, James Tiptree Jr., and others had etched their beauties into literary history, what did the quarantine mean to any thinking reader? My idealism, though, turned out to be grit in the gears of a gorgeous antiquated machine that had glanced once in the direction of the ivory tower then chosen instead to trudge across its own moon valley forever. On the other side of the barrier, I'd underestimated the undertow of reaction against opening "literary fiction" to present realities: technology, jargon, vernacular cultural stuff. Or "the fantastic," even if the gothic imagination was as fundamental to human literature as Shakespeare's *Tempest* and so forth; you'd go mad trying to point out something so obvious to a roomful of people who'd begun nodding before you began speaking. (The nervous readers, imperious critics, benighted booksellers, and tut-tutting librarians, all so invested in the quarantine, were nowhere within hearing range.) And so that was what the many brilliant and underestimated writers did when they sat on the never-ending panel titled "Science Fiction and the Mainstream": go briefly mad. And then they'd move to the hotel bar and, defending against pain, gossip about conventions they'd attended five and ten and fifty years before.

The irony was, the writers in the bar had vacated a hotel conference room full of what many writers fear can't really exist: devoted readers who weren't themselves aspiring writers, and who savored their work, collected their editions, and were conversant in literary-critical context. Of course, this was a paraliterary context, full of names from an alternate twentieth-century canon: Weinbaum, Simak, Effinger. The readers could not only trace a given story's inner workings but could quote the reaction to it in the letters column of *Galaxy* from May 1951. The Radisson was a magical arena of sublime reverence for acts of the literary imagination and scrupulous regard for the results. Yet for the writers, with few exceptions, this couldn't salve their self-perpetuating injuries.

These were matters of class, hierarchy, caste; things Americans like to deny, or acknowledge only in others, as if observing from some pleasantly egalitarian aerie—the enlightened middle class to which we must certainly belong. I'd write "These were obviously matters of class, etc.," except that for all my attempts I've never made it obvious to anyone besides myself. For me the insight is definitive, which probably makes this a confession of some agonized caste posture I'm not aware I've assumed (it feels like I'm walking upright, I swear). The idea that status-anxious guardians of literary culture require a designated underclass to revile: That's never seemed too exotic a diagnosis. More curious to me was the entrenched and defiant injustice-collecting of those who'd been informed they'd contracted writing cooties. Twenty years later critics like Mark McGurl and Kathleen Fitzpatrick helped me grasp the operations of "identity politics" in the late-twentieth-century literary marketplace: the huge currency of authentic "outsider" roles, and the baroque operations left to those without a simple claim by gender, race, orientation. At that point the tribal sulks and credential inspections within the science-fiction caste began to make a lot more sense. I'd surely been enacting my own inversion of privilege by insisting on my genre scars: I'd be an outer-borough kid who'd taken the subway to the big literary city, and had possibly also hopped the turnstiles on his way.

Before knowing any of this I'd made lifelong friends in the bar of the Radisson.

When I published stories in science-fiction magazines I played fly-in-the-cyber-ointment, if anyone cared. I tended to write against the notion of cheap and effective transcendence—to write fantasy stories against fantasy, that is. There was a tremendous oversupply of digital transcendence on the market in that particular time and place, the '80s Bay Area. Everyone suddenly worked for *Wired* magazine (at a San Francisco industrial loft which at the time seemed a futurist hive, the Google campus of its time) or was starting up Salon.com or some other site now taken for granted. Others were secret agents for *Mondo 2000*, or Donna "Manifesto for Cyborgs" Haraway's grad students, busy espousing (in text) the notion that we were right on the verge of leaving not only text but also our human bodies in the dust, in favor of polymorphic virtual interfaces which wouldn't so much replace sex and art as combine the two into something much more interesting (never mind that nothing is more interesting). The whole Bay Area was the Radisson now, only it was harder to find the bar where the malcontents hung out, since here it was those who'd drunk the most Kool-Aid, rather than the dissenters, who wore black and talked about the Velvet Underground. At a party for *Future Sex* magazine I overheard a woman whisper to her friend, "If the future of sex is bald guys with ponytails, I want no part of it." Jaron Lanier, one of the architects of virtuality, sat alone at the *Future Sex* party's bar, unapproachable in a field of awe, hunched like Miles Davis.

My dour stories worked the "57 Channels (and Nothin' On)" vein. I specialized in deflation: Digitized boredom was still boredom; pixel kitsch still kitsch; amnesia didn't actually make the past go away; new stuff gets adapted to the same old impulses, high and low. (Another deflation narrative lay ahead of me: Superheroes don't solve much.) The abiding human prospect—exalted, tragic, ridiculous, or all of the above—ground on. It was as though no cybernauts had glanced at the rhetorics surrounding the onset of cinema, or radio. Each revolutionary medium changed everything and nothing, killed all known precedents and left them perplexingly alive. I have magazines and radios and a fax machine in my book-lined house. An awful lot of what anyone does with their hours in polymorphic cyberville is read and write, gather in epistolary mobs, gossip about books or about theater they've attended, or watch brief movies, like those in Edison's cinematographic viewing boxes, while petting their obstinately prehistoric genitals.

In New York in the '90s, it was as though I'd retreated in time. Nobody had informed the Old World of its due date, or that anyone but pirates wore piercings and tattoos. There was no middle, apparently, between the realms; you chose a team, Cybersexual or Luddite, and the Luddites ran New York. Forget examples like Pynchon or DeLillo: for some of the rearguard critics, it seemed, to put a technology into a piece of fiction, even with an air of skepticism, might be as dubious as advocating for the colonization of Saturn. The Empire City waited a decade or more, for the collapse of somebody's favorite magazine, maybe *Newsweek* or *Gourmet*, for the Bay Area's memo to land. By the time it did, corporatism had humbled the utopian dreamers and made them billionaires. They couldn't beat late capitalism, but they could own it. Culturally speaking, all that was left to do was panic, or so dictated the pundits overly impressed by their own crumbling perches. The conversation that ensued had less than nothing to do with the experience—and refused to learn anything from the on-the-ground reports—of actual human artists of any type. This retrenchment, as exasperating and ahistorical as the hype, doomed us to a cycle of Nostalgic Fulminators versus Comments Section Goon-Futurists. Again, the middle was gone. The middle only happened to be where everyone dwelled. The penitent Jaron Lanier of 2010 wasn't so different from the transformationalist Lanier of 1986: Both overrated the future. As for novelists, whether you wanted to change the world you were born to or merely to describe it as you found it, shouldn't you find it first? That started with noticing that the past exists (but not living *there*, either).

The mental room tone of the Radisson is Genius Asperger's (which is not to presume a diagnosis of any of its actual occupants): cognitively astonishing accounts of living in a world to which one does not fully belong, the terms of which one cannot fully discern or trust. This aura prevails in the conversation as much as it defines the contents of the writing. The protagonist in science fiction analogizes not to the writer but to the reader, plunged into a world organized according to hidden operations, full of codes to crack, and of the affective feedback of people taking for granted what you're puzzling to grasp. This stance feels important for its resemblance to science, philosophy, or what the academics call "theory"; to experience it is to feel consciousness as a never-ending stream of epiphanies—*Wait, they use a fork to consume this substance, but this other they lift to their mouths with their bare hands? Fascinating!* At its best, unpolluted by too many compensatory power fantasies, it *is* important, if you grant that examining the invisible systems that organize everyday life might be worthwhile. And science fiction is hardly the only kind of fiction eligible for being polluted by compensatory power fantasies, though in other publishing categories they aren't usually advertised with helpless blatancy on the dust jackets.

The peculiarity of the quarantine is that Genius Asperger's may be the defining artistic room tone of our time, speaking as it does to the bewilderments attaching to the confluence of global corporatism, late-twentieth-century technological revolutions, the information ecology, and so forth. From the works of creators as seminally "postmodern" as Kubrick, John Ashbery, Andy Warhol, Jean-Luc Godard, Laurie Anderson, David Byrne and Brian Eno ("This is not my beautiful house"), Antonioni, David Lynch, Lydia Davis, Guided by Voices ("I am a scientist, I seek to understand me"), to the writings of the Pynchon-DeLillo-Wallace continuum and newer works by Shelley Jackson and Tom McCarthy (not to presume a diagnosis of any of the actual creators), you might grasp the outlines of a consensus approach to the matter of negotiating selfhood, these days: embracingly curious while affectively challenged. The emphasis might be on abreaction (the sickness unto death of solipsism, paranoia, finding no way outside the maze of corporate imperatives) or adaptation (becoming an eager termite boring holes through the edifice, or a DJ recombinantly repurposing the stuff piling up), or both. The underlying air of disassociation isn't so far removed, I think, from the fact that after a day or two at a science-fiction convention it can not only be surprisingly challenging to enact the unspoken protocols for getting in and out of a crowded elevator (a difficulty that's rampant at the Radisson) but it can seem both fascinating and urgent to consider that such protocols exist in the first place, and then to attempt to describe them, to consider how they formed and were taken unassumingly into our bodies. Please believe me: This can happen to you.

The Internet's only a much more complex (and crowded) elevator.

I'm not terribly interested in whether real, brain-chemically-defined Asperger's is over- or underdiagnosed, or whether it exists at all except as a metaphor. I'm interested in how vital the description feels lately. Is there any chance the Aspergerian retreat from affective risk, in favor of making one's way into the world in the role of alienated scientist-observer, might be an increasingly "popular" coping stance in a world where corporations, machines, and products flourish within their own ungovernable systems? If so, finding such a stance human itself—finding it *more* human, rather than less—might be one of the imperatives of our art. If there's anything to this at all, you'd have to agree that the science-fiction people are not only canaries but that they sensed before anyone else that we'd entered a coal mine.

You'll catch an echo in the first line—was it Philip K. Dick's death I took personally, or Italo Calvino's? This made two in a row: living writers I'd declared my favorite who then died just as I set out to meet them in person. I should quit doing that.

The Best of Calvino: Against Completism

I took Italo Calvino's death—twenty years ago as I write—personally. He didn't know it, but he'd broken a date. One of the greatest European writers of the twentieth century, and among the only Italian writers, with Moravia, Pirandello, and Eco, to have penetrated our translation-retardant literary culture, Calvino had been about to visit the United States to deliver a series of lectures at Harvard, when, only sixty-two, he suffered a cerebral hemorrhage and, weeks later, died. On top of the Harvard commitment, Calvino had agreed to a small American book tour, which would take him as far as Cody's Books in Berkeley. I was scheduled to be seated in the front row, breathlessly. Instead, I learned of Calvino's death by reading a notice taped to Cody's doors on the night when he would have read.

Calvino was more than simply one of my favorite writers. Gore Vidal, in the *New York Review of Books*, wrote that "Europe regarded Calvino's death as a calamity for culture." Selfishly, I took it as my own calamity, feeling deprived of a chance to announce myself to the one living writer who effortlessly straddled the contradictions that my own (inchoate) writerly impulses presented. Calvino, it seemed to me, had managed effortlessly what no author in English could quite claim: His novels and stories and fables were both classically modern and giddily postmodern, at once conceptual and humane, intimate and mythic. With his frequent referencing of comics and folktales and film, and in his droll probing of contemporary scientific and philosophical theory, Calvino encompassed motifs associated with brows both high and low in a lucid style wholly his own. As comfortable mingling with the Oulipo group in Paris (Georges Perec, Harry Mathews, Raymond Queneau, and others, who spliced the DNA of literature with surrealist games) as he was explicating his love for and debt to Hemingway, Stevenson, and the Brothers Grimm, Calvino seemed to never have compromised in his elegant explorations of whatever made him curious in nature, art, or his own sensory life (like women's calves). His prose was ambassadorial, his work a living bridge between Pliny the Elder, Franz Kafka, and Italian neorealist cinema. And—I intuited then, I know now—he was a kind and generous person, colleague, teacher, friend. Had he lived a couple more months, Calvino would have likely tolerated my effort to waste a few of his shrinking hours on earth by making him listen as I bragged of how much he'd influenced my unwritten works.

I worry a little about the state of Calvino's shelf, twenty years later. Not that any of his books are out of print; the opposite. Calvino's two U.S. publishers have been scrupulous in presenting every one of his titles in elegant trade paperback editions (most of these in an appealing uniform sequence from Harcourt Brace). I'm using the word "titles" advisedly: Gore Vidal's 1974 essay, introducing Calvino to readers in English, was called "Calvino's Novels," yet Calvino stakes out a curious distance from the tradition of "the novel." Only *The Baron in the Trees* claims a novel's typical form and proportion; most of his books are arrangements or sequences of stories, fables, fragments, or fugues, linked by common characters, by symbols or motifs, or by some elaborate frame. Beyond that, it's useless to generalize about them. *Marcovaldo* and *Mr. Palomar* feature lead characters, author/reader-surrogate types, who observe the city, countryside, and universe; *The Castle of Crossed Destinies* and *Invisible Cities* are matrices of interwoven fables and meditations; *If on a Winter's Night a Traveler* is a metafictional antinovel made of first chapters; the two collections *Cosmicomics* and *t zero* feature (mostly) another bemused witness, this time of evolution: His name is always Qfwfq, but he takes alternating form as a mote of cosmic dust, a dinosaur, a seashell, a caveman, and others. (Someone teach these books in Kansas, please—Darwin's foes would evaporate in a cloud of epiphanies.)

To make things more complicated, some of Calvino's best work is scattered in other collections, *Difficult Loves*, *Numbers in the Dark*, *Under the Jaguar Sun*, and *The Watcher*. There are two great novellas, published together as *The Nonexistent Knight and The Cloven Viscount*. Throw onto the pile three volumes of essays and lectures, and the problem emerges: This completist's heaven is a browser's purgatory.

I say this as an admitted completist, but also as a former bookstore clerk, one who Calvinoishly watched other readers as they chose books. With too many uniformly lavish editions, the novice reader, wading in, is at the mercy of dumb luck. This happens a lot. Steerforth Press, meaning well, has made it as likely that a reader curious about Dawn Powell will come out of a bookstore clutching the glum early volumes set in Ohio or the misfiring *The Happy Island*, as that they'll snag *Turn, Magic Wheel* or *The Locusts Have No King*. Will that reader try twice? Behind the gorgeous jackets, flawed books jostle beside the masterpieces.

Italo Calvino never wrote a bad book. But his greatness is like a mist cloud, without a single, encompassing magnum opus to make a beginner's entry point, or to shove into the time capsule of posterity. Is it sacrilegious to propose a fat volume called *The Best of Calvino*? Or call it *Tales*, or *Sixty Stories*. It isn't as though the individual volumes need to go out of print to make room for the omnibus I'm envisioning. Maybe it's outrageous to do violence to a structure as organically perfect as *Invisible Cities*. Fine: Include the whole thing, the way *The Thurber Carnival* made room for *My Life and Hard Times*.

When Knopf, in 1980, honored Ray Bradbury with *The Stories of Ray Bradbury*, the editors broke into linked sequences of stories like *The Martian Chronicles* and *The Illustrated Man* (the dedication reads: " . . . for Nancy Nicholas and Robert Gottlieb, whose argument about favorites put this book together"). Similarly, the someday compiler of *The Selected Stories of John Updike* will have to pillage the Maples and Bech sequences. "Greatest Hits" collections have their place in literary history. Before Leon Edel came along, Henry James's "The Figure in the Carpet" was part of a volume called *Embarrassment*. Trust me, only hard-core Jamesians would recognize the other titles on the contents page. For them, *The Complete Stories of Henry James* floats on, available in libraries and used bookstores. Arguments about favorites are energizing things, and they honor reputations as beautifully as do uniform sets of Complete Works. Italo Calvino, in his long-but-too-short career, scattered his treasures. Sure, he deserves readers who'll savor them in their original formats, but he also could use a treasury.

—*The New York Times Book Review*, 2005

Postmodernism as Liberty Valance

Notes on a Ritual Killing

1. Spoiler alert. John Ford's *The Man Who Shot Liberty Valance* is an allegorical Western that I am now going to totally pretzel into an allegory for something else entirely. Actually I'll reverse it: The original allegorizes the taming of the western frontier, the coming of modernity in the form of the lawbooks and the locomotive, and memorializes what was lost (a loss the film sees as inevitable). My version allegorizes the holding at bay, for the special province of literary fiction, of contemporary experience in all its dismaying or exhilarating particulars, as well as a weird persistent denial of a terrific number of artistic strategies for illuminating that experience. The avoidance, that's to say, of any forthright address of what's called postmodernity, and what's lost in avoiding it (a sacrifice I see as at best pointless, an empty rehearsal of anxieties, and at worst hugely detrimental for fiction).

2. The chewy center of *TMWSLV* is a gunfight. A man stands in the main street of a western town and (apparently) kills another man. The victim—for this is, technically, murder—represents chaos and anxiety and fear to all who know him, and has been regarded as unkillable, almost in the manner of a monster or zombie from another movie genre; his dispatch is regarded by the local population with astonished relief and gratitude, such that they will shower the killer with regard (he's destined to become his party's nominee for vice president of the

United States). The secret the movie reveals: The killer was not the man in the street, but another.

3. The three persons in *TMWSLV*: James Stewart a.k.a. "Ransom Stoddard," the upstanding, even priggish young lawyer from the east, defined by his naïve sincerity and dedication to the rule of law; John Wayne a.k.a. "Tom Doniphon," cynical veteran of the frontier, who tends to an isolationist-libertarian approach toward civilization but is essentially lovable and will become heartbreaking by film's end; and Lee Marvin a.k.a. "Liberty Valance," a sadistic, amoral thug who delights in sowing chaos and exposing the fragility of social convention (by terrorizing family restaurants, newspaper offices, elections, etc.).

4. Stewart/Stoddard believes he's "the man who killed Liberty Valance" (he stood, after all, in the center of town, visible to all, with a gun in his hand). More important, the witnesses believe he's the one. In fact, it was Wayne/Doniphon who did the deed, while hidden in a shadowy alley, after having elaborately conspired to goad the helpless and pacifistic Stewart/Stoddard into his public role as a gun-toting defender of public peace against the savage anarchy of Marvin/Valance.

5. Liberty Valance, i.e., "Free Persuasion"—what an absurd, obvious, Pynchonian name! But then, the characters in Dickens and Henry James have odd names, too.

6. "Venturing back in time isn't the only option for novelists loath to address the mass media that most Americans marinate in. There are also those populations cut off from the mainstream for cultural reasons, such as recent immigrants and their families. And then there are those at the geographical margins . . . It's remarkable how many recent American literary novels and short stories are set on ranches . . . The American novelist is buffeted by two increasingly contradictory imperatives. The first comes as the directive to depict 'The Way We Live Now' . . . Cliché it may be, but the notion that no one is better suited

to explain the dilemmas of contemporary life than the novelist persists . . . [The] other designated special province of the literary novelist: museum-quality depth. The further literature is driven to the outskirts of the culture, the more it is cherished as a sanctuary from everything coarse, shallow and meretricious in that culture. If these two missions seem incompatible, that's because they are. To encompass both . . . you must persuade your readers that you have given them what they want by presenting them with what they were trying to get away from when they came to you in the first place."

—Laura Miller, *The Guardian*

7. Let's wade into the unpleasantness around the term "postmodernism": Nobody agrees on its definition, but in literary conversations the word is often used as finger-pointing to a really vast number of things that might be seen as threatening to canonical culture: author-killing theories generated by French critics, collapsings of high and low cultural preserves into a value-neutral fog, excessive reference to various other media and/or mediums, especially electronic ones (ironically, even a Luddishly denunciatory take on certain media and/or mediums may be suspect merely for displaying an excess of familiarity with same), an enthusiasm for "metafiction" (a word that ought to be reserved for a specific thing that starts with Cervantes, but isn't), for antinarrative, for pop-culture references or generic forms, for overt (as opposed to politely passive) "intertextuality," for unreliable narration, for surrealism or magic realism or hysterical realism or some other brand of "opposed-to-realism" affiliation, for "irony" (another term that's been abused out of its effective contour and function, and its abusers have fewer excuses than do those of postmodernism), etc. etc. etc. Now, any writer espousing, let alone employing, all of the above things would be a gorgon-headed monster, surely deserving rapid assassination for the safety of the literary community in general. (Or maybe not, maybe they'd be splendid.) But—and I present this as axiomatic—such a person, and such writing, is impossible to consider seriously because all of the modes denounced under the banner of "postmodernist" are incompatible: You can't, just for instance, exalt disreputable genres like the crime story and also want to do away with narrative.

8. The reverse person, a literary person inclined toward or at least compelled by none of the above-named modes or gestures—and I present this not as axiomatic but as an obnoxious opinion—would be dull beyond belief. They basically would have declined the entire twentieth century (and interesting parts of several others). *You've read our entire menu, sir? And nothing was of interest? Really,* nothing?

9. " . . . as a phenomenon, postmodernism is either specifically aesthetic or more generally cultural; it is either revolutionary or reactionary; it is either the end of ideology or the inescapable conclusion of ideology . . . It is expressed in architecture, art, literature, the media, science, religion and fashion, and at the same time it is equivalent to none of these. It is both a continuation and intensification of what has gone before and a radical break with all traces of the past. It is, above all, simultaneously critical and complicit."

—Kathleen Fitzpatrick, *The Anxiety of Obsolescence*

"Critical debates about postmodernism constitute postmodernism itself."

—Stephen Connor, *Postmodernist Culture*

10. I suggested that abusers of the word "postmodernism" had excuses. I offer the above quotes as exculpatory evidence. The serious use of the term manifestly propagates bewilderment. But the quotes are also a reminder that the term has serious uses. It means more than "art I don't like."

11. What postmodernism really needs is a new name—or three of them.

12. The first "postmodernism" that requires a new name is our sense— I'm taking it for granted that you share it—that the world, as presently defined by the advent of global techno-capitalism, the McLuhanesque effects of electronic media, and the long historical postludes of the

transformative theories, movements, and traumas of the twentieth century, isn't a coherent or congenial home for human psyches. Chuck Klosterman details this suspicion in his essay on the Unabomber, called "FAIL" (though it might as well be called "Sympathy for Theodore Kaczynski"). His conclusion, basically, is that in the teeth of contemporary reality we'd all be a little bit crazy *not* to sometimes wish to kill that sort of postmodernism. I speak here as one who's spent loads of his own good faith hurling tiny word-bombs at the rolling edifice of the triumphalist Now. This postmodernism we'll call Kaczynski's Bad Dream.

13. The second substitute term I'll offer is for the avowed, self-declared postmodernist school of U.S. fiction writers: Robert Coover, John Barth, Donald Barthelme, Stanley Elkin, William Gass, John Hawkes, a few others, many of them one another's friends, and many of them influential teachers. A few non-teachers—Pynchon, of course (unless he was teaching high-school social studies or geometry somewhere). This clan, when Barth and Pynchon were scooping up major prizes, rode high enough that they seemed worth knocking down. This is the epoch John Gardner tilted against in *On Moral Fiction*. True, this tribe once had the effrontery to imagine itself the center of interest in U.S. fiction, but if you still hold that grudge your memory for effrontery is too long. To go on potshotting at these gentlemen is not so much shooting fish in a barrel as it is shooting novelists who rode a barrel over Niagara Falls twenty or thirty years ago. Or the equivalent of the Republican Party running its presidential candidates against the memory of George McGovern. (Of course, both are done, routinely.) We'll call these guys Those Guys.

14. Last, the "postmodernism" consisting simply of what aesthetic means and opportunities modernism and an ascendant popular culture left in their wake (or not their wake, since both, or at least popular culture, are still around). By "means and opportunities" I am alluding to the vastly expanded and recombinant toolbox of strategies, tones, traditions, genres, and forms that a legacy of modernist-style experimentation, as well as a general disintegration of boundaries (between traditions, tones, etc.), has made available to a writer, or to any kind of

artist. Luc Menand made this very simple in an essay on how Donald Barthelme's stories go on stubbornly regenerating their uses and interest for new generations of readers; he suggested that postmodernism, as an artistic movement, represents the democratization of modernism's impulses and methods. We'll call this third principle, for the sake of my allegory, Liberty Valance.

15. I'd like to suggest that the killing of Liberty Valance in order to preserve safety and order in the literary town is a recurrent ritual, a ritual convulsion of literary-critical convention. The chastening of Those Guys, and the replacement of their irresponsible use of Free Power with a more modest and morally serious minimalist aesthetic sometime in the late '70s, was a kind of Gunfight at the O.K. Corral, a point of inception for the ritual. Who first played the role of Stewart/ Stoddard, the true-of-heart citizen shoved into the street to take on the menacing intruder? Was it Raymond Carver? I think Raymond Carver might have been the original Man Who Shot Liberty Valance. Who's played the role recently? A few: Alice Munro, William Trevor, Cormac McCarthy, Marilynne Robinson, Jonathan Franzen.

16. The worth, or the intentions, of the writer propped up on Main Street as the killer of postmodernism is not the point. The person (or book) in the street is a surrogate. The Wayne/Doniphon figure is the critic in the shadows, maneuvering the writer in question in a contest of the critic's devising (excepting, I suppose, the John Gardner or Tom Wolfe scenario of self-appointment, where both roles are played by the same actor). According to the critic's presentation the writer has, at last, killed Liberty Valance on behalf of the terrified populace. Yet the terrified populace is probably a straw man, too, a projection of the critic's own fear of disreputability or disorder.

17. The persistence of the ritual disproves the ostensible result: Liberty Valance is shot, but never dies. ("Leopards break into the temple and drink the sacrificial chalices dry; this occurs repeatedly, again and again; finally it can be reckoned upon beforehand and becomes part of the ceremony."—Kafka.) Books don't kill other books, nor do liter-

ary stances or methods kill, or disqualify, differing sorts, and those—stances and methods—don't actually originate from moral positions per se. A given book elaborates its own terms, then succeeds or fails according to them, including on the level of morals. None of this ensures the accomplishment of any writer working in any methodology (whether consciously or in merry obliviousness to the range of options available). A book as full of misrule, as seemingly heedless to ethical consequence as Marvin/Valance in John Ford's film, might be as sacred as any other.

18. The reason postmodernism doesn't die isn't that the man in the shadows has a peashooter instead of a weapon. Critics do kill things: books frequently, careers from time to time (just ask Those Guys). The reason postmodernism doesn't die is that postmodernism isn't the figure in the black hat standing out in the street squaring off against the earnest and law-abiding "realist" novel against which it is being opposed. Postmodernism is the street. Postmodernism is the town. It's where we live, the result of the effects of Liberty Valance's stubborn versatility and appeal, and the fact of Kaczynski's Bad Dream.

19. Yet Liberty Valance and Kaczynski's Bad Dream aren't the same "postmodernism." The freedom and persuasiveness of the full array of contemporary stances and practices available to the literary artist aren't something to renounce even if the Full Now makes us anxious to the verge of nervous breakdown. At its best, one is a tool for surviving the other—the most advanced radiation suit yet devised for wandering into the toxic future.

20. Changing metaphors entirely at the last minute: Both Kabuki and Noh theater began as fluid popular forms, licensed to depict their own contemporary reality, before sealing themselves within sacralized pools of approved forms, metaphors, and references. And in the history of twentieth-century popular music there's a name for the school of jazz that glanced at the innovations of bebop and all the implications and possibilities of what lay beyond, but declined to respond. The name for that school is Dixieland.

The Claim of Time

By the time J. G. Ballard died, talk of his years-long struggle with cancer should have prepared his followers ("fans" is too pale a word for the devotion Ballard aroused), yet the news still struck us as a shock. Ballard was, unmistakably, a literary futurist, at ease in the cold ruins of the millennium a lifetime sooner than the rest of us; his passing registered as a disorienting claim of time upon the timeless. Whether you embrace or reject on his behalf the label "science-fiction writer" will indicate whether you regard it as praiseful or damning, but no one reading Ballard could doubt the tidal gravity of his intellect, or the stark visionary consistency of the motifs which earned him that rarest of literary awards, an adjective: Ballardian. Now, and not a moment too soon, comes *The Complete Stories of J. G. Ballard*, a staggering 1,200-page compendium of a lifetime's labors in the medium in which Ballard was perhaps most at home.

Each of Ballard's ninety-two short stories is like a dream more perfectly realized than any of your own. His personal vocabulary of scenarios imprints itself from the very first, each image with the quality of a newly minted archetype. Ballard was the poet of desolate landscapes marked by signs of a withdrawn human presence: drained swimming pools, abandoned lots littered with consumer goods, ruined space stations, sites of forgotten military or vehicular tragedies. Himself trained in medicine, Ballard created protagonists and narrators who are frequently doctors or scientists, yet expertise never spares them from the fates they see overtaking others. If Ballard's view of the human presence in his landscapes is grimly diagnostic, his scalpel is wielded with tenderness, his bedside manner both dispassionate and abiding.

Here, the panorama set before one such observer, from 1966's "The Day of Forever":

> Despite the almost static light, fixed at this unending dusk, the drained bed of the river seemed to flow with colours. As the sand spilled from the banks, uncovering the veins of quartz and the concrete caissons of the embankment, the evening would flare briefly, illuminated from within like a lava sea. Beyond the dunes the spires of old water towers and the half-completed apartment blocks near the Roman ruins at Leptis Magna emerged from the darkness. To the south, as Halliday followed the winding course of the river, the darkness gave way to the deep indigo tracts of the irrigation project, the lines of canals forming an exquisite bonelike gridwork.

Ballard in a grain of sand: the visual poetry of ruin; a syntax scientifically precise yet surreally oversaturated; and the convergence of the technological and the natural worlds into a stage where human life flits as a violent, temporary shadow. Yet Ballard at his best never seems to load the dice against humanity. He merely rolls them.

Every bit as striking as Ballard's feeling for entropy is his fictional engagement with neighbor arts from which literary writing too often seems quarantined: music, sculpture, painting, architecture. Ballard evokes art-creation with the passion of an exile for a lost kingdom. Like his scientific characters, Ballard's overreaching artists glimpse seeds of doom at the heart of their endeavors. And, in perhaps his most famous vision, the novel *Crash*, technology, sculpture, sex, and death recede to the same vanishing point: the permanently contemporary site of the car crash.

Returning the favor, the neighbor arts relished Ballard. From the Comsat Angels, a rock band named for a 1968 story, to Radiohead, David Cronenberg, Wim Wenders, Simon Critchley, Alexis Rockman, John Gray, Joy Division, Gary Panter, and countless others, Ballard probably inspired more rock musicians, philosophers, painters, and filmmakers than fiction writers. Reversing the notion of the "writer's writer," he's less esteemed in literary culture than in the wider sphere. His presence is also far stronger in the U.K. than in the United States. *The Complete Stories* ought to alter both these imbalances.

My own favorite of Ballard's stories is 1964's "The Drowned Giant." This tale of a vast carcass awash on an English beach is as elegant and devastating as any of Kafka's or Calvino's fantasies, simply asking: What happens when Gulliver drifts home?

Equally perfect, "The Secret Autobiography of J.G.B.," posthumously published in *The New Yorker* and the penultimate story in the collection, gently inserts the writer himself into an emptied-out version of his beloved London suburb of Shepperton, there to discover himself at an endpoint that is also a beginning. With his more celebrated role as a social critic of modernity, Ballard was also a poet of infinite regress, gnawing at the Zeno's paradox of our place in the cosmos with the rigor of an Escher or Bach.

Not to take away from his verdict on the twentieth century: Ballard's a bard of techno-anomie, of late-capitalist disaffection, and his writings are just the tonic if your local cloverleaf traffic jam or gated community or global-warming harbinger has got you feeling out of sorts. But it's precisely his grounding in deeper undercurrents of cosmic-existentialist wonder that give that tonic its fizz. His is the voice reminding you not to take the postmodern hangover too personally: It was always going to happen this way.

A writer viewed as radical is rarely also so entrenched in formal reserve as was Ballard. Much of the energy in his fiction comes from the pull of his prophecy against the dutiful, typically middle-class English politesse of his characters, the unradicalism of their attitudes toward one another and themselves. In the *Vermilion Sands* stories, which scatter through his first two decades, much of the dialogue might be taken from a Barbara Pym novel, if instead of small-town vicarages Pym's milieu had been a crumbling desert resort inhabited by aging celebrities.

Ultimately, Ballard is simply a master short-story writer, if by this we mean to describe a maker of unforgettable artifacts in words, each as absolute and perplexing as sculptures unviewable from a single perspective. In this book of ninety-two stories are at least thirty that you can spend a lifetime returning to, to wander and wonder around. The measure of the lesser pieces is that they support rather than diminish the masterworks—and that Ballard's hand is always unmistakable.

Taking measure of a writer's life's work can be intimidating, yet I hope this book will not only be purchased but read. Ballard's sensibility not only rewards immersion but thrives there. He may have written both an autobiographical diptych of novels (*Empire of the Sun* and *The Kindness of Women*) and an autobiography, but these stories form another version of autobiography: one inadvertent, oracular, and deeply telling.

I should add that I'm no Ballard "expert." I quit keeping up with his novels after 1988's *Running Wild*, never to return, and though I believed myself well schooled in his short fiction there were dozens here I'd never read before; in fact, my prime years reading him are a quarter-century behind me. Yet very few writers I've encountered, even those I've devoted myself to, have burrowed so deeply into my outlook, and in my work, where I find myself recapitulating Ballardian patterns not for their beauty, though they are beautiful, but for their tremendous *aptness* in attempting to confront the dying world before me, and inside me.

Consider this, then, a late-to-press elegy for perhaps the most profoundly elegiac writer in literature—and like all who mourn, Ballard had first to love.

—*The New York Times Book Review*, 2009

Give Up

Dear E(arth),

I am writing to tell you to give up. You may already be a winner, the kind of winner who wins by losing, rolling onto your back and showing me your soft parts, letting me tickle and lap and snort at your supplicant vitals. Perhaps I should put this more forcefully: GIVE UP. You stand no chance. Resistance is futile, futility is resistant, reluctance is flirtatious, relinquishment is freedom. I love you and I am better than you in every way, grander, greater, glossier, more glorious, more ridiculous, energetic, faster in footraces and Internet dial-up speed, hungrier, more full of sex and fire, better equipped with wit and weaponry. I'm taller than you and can encircle you with my lascivious tongue. Admit this and admit me. By opening this envelope you've been selected from among the billions upon trillions of amoebic entities, you're plucked up from the galaxy's beach like a seashell by a god, something in you sparkled for a moment, terribly unlikely it means anything much in the scheme of things, improbable that taking notice of you squeezed onto the agenda of one such as me, but I was amused, don't ask me why, it's practically random like a lottery (yet you'll never be able to spend the wealth of my love, to run through it and waste it like the hapless lottery winner you are, though you may try, you'd never spend it in a dozen profligate lifetimes). My eyes settled on you in a weak moment (and you'll never see another, no, I'm an edifice, an enigma, to one such as you my science is like magic). Don't delay, act now, give up, you've been selected by a higher being from another realm to be plucked from your impoverished species to join me, to be seated in the empty throne beside me (only because I'd never troubled to glance to one side before to notice a seat existed there; not, somehow, until my gaze lit on you) where none of your lowly cringing fellows has ever resided, you're unworthy but will be made worthy by the acclaim of my notice. I say again, I'm superior to you, you're tinsel, static, a daisy, a bubble of champagne that went to my head and popped, and I don't even know why I want you and you'd better not give me the chance to think twice. You'll find I've anticipated your responses and attached them below (see attachments, below); they're feeble and funny, helpless and endearing, and you've already blurted yes take me yes how can I resist yes I give up yes. So do as I say now, you've already done it, you're in my arms like an infant, a ward, a swan. Give up, you gave up already, you're mine.

Love,
M(ars)

—*The Walrus,* 2008

III

Plagiarisms

At present Mickey is everybody's god, so that even members of the Film Society cease despising their fellow members when he appears. But gods are not immortal. There was an Egyptian called Bes, who was once quite as gay, and Brer Rabbit and Felix the Cat have been forgotten too, and Ganesh is being forgotten . . .

—E. M. FORSTER, "Our Diversions" (1934)

The Ecstasy of Influence

A plagiarism

> *All mankind is of one author, and is one volume; when one man*
> *dies, one chapter is not torn out of the book, but translated into*
> *a better language; and every chapter must be so translated . . .*

—JOHN DONNE

LOVE AND THEFT

Consider this tale: A cultivated man of middle age looks back on the
story of an *amour fou*, one beginning when, traveling abroad, he takes
a room as a lodger. The moment he sees the daughter of the house, he
is lost. She is a preteen, whose charms instantly enslave him. Heedless
of her age, he becomes intimate with her. In the end she dies, and the
narrator—marked by her forever—remains alone. The name of the girl
supplies the title of the story: Lolita.

The author of the story I've described, Heinz von Lichberg, published his tale of Lolita in 1916, forty years before Vladimir Nabokov's
novel. Lichberg later became a prominent journalist in the Nazi era,
and his youthful works faded from view. Did Nabokov, who remained
in Berlin until 1937, adopt Lichberg's tale consciously? Or did the earlier
tale exist for Nabokov as a hidden, unacknowledged memory? The history of literature is not without examples of this phenomenon, called

cryptomnesia. Another hypothesis is that Nabokov, knowing Lichberg's tale perfectly well, had set himself to that art of quotation that Thomas Mann, himself a master of it, called "higher cribbing." Literature has always been a crucible in which familiar themes are continually recast. Little of what we admire in Nabokov's *Lolita* is to be found in its predecessor; the former is in no way deducible from the latter. Still: Did Nabokov consciously borrow and quote?

"When you live outside the law, you have to eliminate dishonesty." The line comes from Don Siegel's 1958 film noir, *The Lineup*, written by Stirling Silliphant. The film still haunts revival houses, likely thanks to Eli Wallach's blazing portrayal of a sociopathic hit man and to Siegel's long, sturdy auteurist career. Yet what were those words worth—to Siegel, or Silliphant, or their audience—in 1958? And again: What was the line worth when Bob Dylan heard it (presumably in some Greenwich Village repertory cinema), cleaned it up a little, and inserted it into "Absolutely Sweet Marie"? What are they worth now, to the culture at large?

Appropriation has always played a key role in Dylan's music. The songwriter has grabbed not only from a panoply of vintage Hollywood films but from Shakespeare and F. Scott Fitzgerald and Junichi Saga's *Confessions of a Yakuza*. He also nabbed the title of Eric Lott's study of minstrelsy for his 2001 album *Love and Theft*. One imagines Dylan liked the general resonance of the title, in which emotional misdemeanors stalk the sweetness of love, as they do so often in Dylan's songs. Lott's title is, of course, itself a riff on Leslie Fiedler's *Love and Death in the American Novel*, which famously identifies the literary motif of the interdependence of a white man and a dark man, like Huck and Jim or Ishmael and Queequeg—a series of nested references to Dylan's own appropriating, minstrel-boy self. Dylan's art offers a paradox: While it famously urges us not to look back, it also encodes a knowledge of past sources that might otherwise have little home in contemporary culture, like the Civil War poetry of the Confederate bard Henry Timrod, resuscitated in lyrics on Dylan's *Modern Times*. Dylan's originality and his appropriations are as one.

The same might be said of *all* art. I realized this forcefully when one day I went looking for the John Donne passage quoted above. I know the lines, I confess, not from a college course but from the movie version of *84 Charing Cross Road* with Anthony Hopkins and Anne Bancroft. I checked out 84, *Charing Cross Road* from the library in the hope of finding the Donne passage, but it wasn't in the book. It's alluded to in the play that was adapted from the book, but it isn't reprinted. So I rented the movie again, and there was the passage, read in voice-over by Anthony Hopkins but without attribution. Unfortunately, the line was also abridged, so that, when I finally turned to the Web, I found myself searching for the line "all mankind is of one volume" instead of "all mankind is of one author, and is one volume."

My Internet search was initially no more successful than my library search. I had thought that summoning books from the vasty deep was a matter of a few keystrokes, but when I visited the website of the Yale library, I found that most of its books don't yet exist as computer text. As a last-ditch effort I searched the seemingly more obscure phrase "every chapter must be so translated." The passage I wanted finally came to me, as it turns out, not as part of a scholarly library collection but simply because someone who loves Donne had posted it on his homepage. The lines I sought were from Meditation 17 in *Devotions upon Emergent Occasions*, which happens to be the most famous thing Donne ever wrote, containing as it does the line "never send to know for whom the bell tolls; it tolls for thee." My search had led me from a movie to a book to a play to a website and back to a book. Then again, those words may be as famous as they are only because Hemingway lifted them for his book title.

Literature has been in a plundered, fragmentary state for a long time. When I was thirteen I purchased an anthology of Beat writing. Immediately, and to my very great excitement, I discovered one William S. Burroughs, author of something called *Naked Lunch*, excerpted there in all its coruscating brilliance. Burroughs was then as radical a literary man as the world had to offer. Nothing, in all my experience of literature since, has ever had as strong an effect on my sense of the sheer possibilities of writing. Later, attempting to understand this impact, I discovered that Burroughs had incorporated snippets of other writers' texts into his work, an action I knew my teachers would have called plagiarism. Some of these borrowings had been lifted from American science fiction of the '40s and '50s, adding a secondary shock of recognition for me. By then I knew that this "cut-up method," as Burroughs called it, was central to whatever he thought he was doing, and that he quite literally believed it to be akin to magic. When he wrote about his process, the hairs on my neck stood up, so palpable was the excitement. Burroughs was interrogating the universe with scissors and a pastepot, and the least imitative of authors was no plagiarist at all.

CONTAMINATION ANXIETY

In 1941, on his front porch, Muddy Waters recorded a song for the folklorist Alan Lomax. After singing the song, which he told Lomax was titled "Country Blues," Waters described how he came to write it. "I made it on about the eighth of October '38," Waters said. "I was fixin' a puncture on a car. I had been mistreated by a girl. I just felt blue, and the song fell into my mind and it come to me just like that and I started singing." Then Lomax, who knew of the Robert Johnson recording called "Walkin' Blues," asked Waters if there were any other songs that used the same tune. "There's been some blues played like that," Waters replied. "This song comes from the cotton field and a boy once put a record out—Robert Johnson. He put it out as named 'Walkin' Blues.' I heard the tune before I heard it on the record. I learned it from Son House." In nearly one breath, Waters offers five accounts: his own active authorship: he "made it" on a specific date. Then the "passive" explanation: "it come to me just like that." After Lomax raises the question of influence, Waters, without shame, misgivings, or trepidation, says that he heard a version by Johnson, but that his mentor, Son House, taught it to him. In the middle of that complex genealogy, Waters declares: "This song comes from the cotton field."

Blues and jazz musicians have long been enabled by an "open source" culture, in which preexisting melodic fragments and larger musical frameworks are freely reworked. Technology has only multiplied the possibilities; musicians have gained the power to *duplicate* sounds literally rather than simply approximate them through allusion. In '70s Jamaica, King Tubby and Lee "Scratch" Perry deconstructed recorded music, using astonishingly primitive pre-digital hardware, creating what they called "versions." The recombinant nature of their means of production quickly spread to DJs in New York and London. Today an endless, gloriously impure, and fundamentally social process generates countless hours of music.

Visual, sound, and text collage—which for many centuries were relatively fugitive traditions (a cento here, a folk pastiche there)—became explosively central to a series of movements in the twentieth century:

futurism, cubism, Dada, musique concrète, situationism, pop art, and appropriationism. In fact, collage, the common denominator in that list, might be called *the* art form of the twentieth century, never mind the twenty-first. But forget, for the moment, chronologies, schools, or even centuries. As examples accumulate—Igor Stravinsky's music and Daniel Johnston's, Francis Bacon's paintings and Henry Darger's, the novels of the Oulipo group and of Hannah Crafts (the author who pillaged Dickens's *Bleak House* to write *The Bondwoman's Narrative*), as well as cherished texts that become troubling to their admirers after the discovery of their "plagiarized" elements, like Richard Condon's novels or Martin Luther King Jr.'s sermons—it becomes apparent that appropriation, mimicry, quotation, allusion, and sublimated collaboration consist of a sine qua non of the creative act, cutting across all forms and genres in the realm of cultural production.

In a courtroom scene from *The Simpsons* that has since entered into the television canon, an argument over the ownership of the animated characters Itchy and Scratchy rapidly escalates into an existential debate on the very nature of cartoons. "Animation is built on plagiarism!" declares the show's hot-tempered cartoon-producer-within-a-cartoon, Roger Meyers Jr. "You take away our right to steal ideas, where are they going to come from?" If nostalgic cartoonists had never borrowed from *Fritz the Cat*, there would be no *Ren & Stimpy Show*; without the Rankin/Bass and Charlie Brown Christmas specials, there would be no *South Park*; and without *The Flintstones*—more or less *The Honeymooners* in cartoon loincloths—*The Simpsons* would cease to exist. If those don't strike you as essential losses, then consider the remarkable series of "plagiarisms" that link Ovid's "Pyramus and Thisbe". with Shakespeare's *Romeo and Juliet* and Leonard Bernstein's *West Side Story*, or Shakespeare's description of Cleopatra, copied nearly verbatim from Plutarch's life of Mark Antony and also later nicked by T. S. Eliot for *The Waste Land*. If these are examples of plagiarism, then we want more plagiarism.

Most artists are brought to their vocation when their own nascent gifts are awakened by the work of a master. That is to say, most artists are converted to art by art itself. Finding one's voice isn't just an emptying and purifying of oneself of the words of others but an adopting and embracing of filiations, communities, and discourses. Inspiration could be called inhaling the memory of an act never experienced. Invention, it must be humbly admitted, does not consist in creating out of void but out of chaos. Any artist knows these truths, no matter how deeply he or she submerges that knowing.

What happens when an allusion goes unrecognized? A closer look at *The Waste Land* may help make this point. The body of Eliot's poem is a vertiginous mélange of quotation, allusion, and "original" writing. When Eliot alludes to Edmund Spenser's "Prothalamion" with the line "Sweet Thames, run softly, till I end my song," what of readers to whom the poem, never one of Spenser's most popular, is unfamiliar? (Indeed, the Spenser is now known largely because of Eliot's use of it.) Two responses are possible: grant the line to Eliot, or later discover the source and understand the line as plagiarism. Eliot evidenced no small anxiety about these matters; the notes he so carefully added to *The Waste Land* can be read as a symptom of modernism's contamination anxiety. Taken from this angle, what exactly is postmodernism, except modernism without the anxiety?

SURROUNDED BY SIGNS

The surrealists believed that objects in the world possess a certain but unspecifiable intensity that had been dulled by everyday use and utility. They meant to reanimate this dormant intensity, to bring their minds once again into close contact with the matter that made up their world. André Breton's maxim "Beautiful as the chance encounter of a sewing machine and an umbrella on an operating table" is an expression of the belief that simply placing objects in an unexpected context reinvigorates their mysterious qualities.

This "crisis" the surrealists identified was being simultaneously diagnosed by others. Martin Heidegger held that the essence of modernity was found in a certain technological orientation he called "enframing." This tendency encourages us to see the objects in our world only in terms of how they can serve us or be used by us. The task he identified was to find ways to resituate ourselves vis-à-vis these "objects," so that we may see them as "things" pulled into relief against the ground of their functionality. Heidegger believed that art had the great potential to reveal the "thingness" of objects.

The surrealists understood that photography and cinema could carry out this reanimating process automatically; the process of framing objects in a lens was often enough to create the charge they sought. Describing the effect, Walter Benjamin drew a comparison between the photographic apparatus and Freud's psychoanalytic methods. Just as Freud's theories "isolated and made analyzable things which had heretofore floated along unnoticed in the broad stream of perception," the photographic apparatus focuses on "hidden details of familiar objects," revealing "entirely new structural formations of the subject."

It's worth noting, then, that early in the history of photography a series of judicial decisions could well have changed the course of that art: Courts were asked whether the photographer, amateur or professional, required permission before he could capture and print an image. Was the photographer *stealing* from the person or building whose photograph he shot, pirating something of private and certifiable value? Those early decisions went in favor of the pirates. Just as Walt Disney could take inspiration from Buster Keaton's *Steamboat Bill, Jr.*, the Brothers Grimm, or the existence of real mice, the photographer should be free to capture an image without compensating the source. The world that meets our eye through the lens of a camera was judged to be, with minor exceptions, a sort of public commons, where a cat may look at a king.

Novelists may glance at the stuff of the world, too, but we sometimes get called to task for it. For those whose ganglia were formed pre-TV, the mimetic deployment of pop-culture icons seems at best an annoying tic and at worst a dangerous vapidity that compromises fiction's seriousness by dating it out of the Platonic Always, where it ought to reside. In a graduate workshop I briefly passed through, a certain gray eminence tried to convince us that a literary story should always eschew "any feature which serves to date it" because "serious fiction must be Timeless." When we protested that, in his own well-known work, characters moved about electrically lit rooms, drove cars, and spoke not Anglo-Saxon but postwar English—and further, that fiction he'd himself ratified as great, such as Dickens, was liberally strewn with innately topical, commercial, and time-bound references—he impatiently amended his proscription to those explicit references that would date a story in the "frivolous Now." When pressed, he said of course he meant the "trendy mass-popular-media" reference. Here, transgenerational discourse broke down.

I was born in 1964; I grew up watching Captain Kangaroo, moon landings, zillions of TV ads, the Banana Splits, *M*A*S*H*, and *The Mary Tyler Moore Show*. I was born with words in my mouth—"Band-Aid," "Q-tip," "Xerox"—object-names as fixed and eternal in my logosphere as "taxicab" and "toothbrush." The world is a home littered with pop-culture products and their emblems. I also came of age swamped by parodies that stood for originals yet mysterious to me—I knew Monkees before Beatles, Belmondo before Bogart, and "remember" the movie *Summer of '42* from a *Mad* magazine satire, though I've still never seen the film itself. I'm not alone in having been born backward into an incoherent realm of texts, products, and images, the commercial and cultural environment with which we've both supplemented and blotted out our natural world. I can no more claim it as "mine" than the sidewalks and forests of the world, yet I do dwell in it, and for me to stand a chance as either artist or citizen, I'd probably better be permitted to name it.

Consider Walker Percy's *The Moviegoer*: "Other people, so I have read, treasure memorable moments in their lives: the time one climbed the Parthenon at sunrise, the summer night one met a lonely girl in Central Park and achieved with her a sweet and natural relationship, as they say in books. I too once met a girl in Central Park, but it is not much to remember. What I remember is the time John Wayne killed three men with a carbine as he was falling to the dusty street in *Stagecoach*, and the time the kitten found Orson Welles in the doorway in *The Third Man*." Today, when we can eat Tex-Mex with chopsticks while listening to reggae and watching a YouTube rebroadcast of the Berlin Wall's fall—i.e., when damn near *everything* presents itself as familiar—it's not a surprise that some of today's most ambitious art is going about trying to *make the familiar strange*. In so doing, in reimagining what human life might truly be like over there across the chasms of illusion, mediation, demographics, marketing, imago, and appearance, artists are paradoxically trying to restore what's taken for "real" to three whole dimensions, to reconstruct a univocally round world out of disparate streams of flat sights.

Whatever charge of tastelessness or trademark violation may be attached to the artistic appropriation of the media environment in which we swim, the alternative—to flinch, or tiptoe away into some ivory tower of irrelevance—is far worse. We're surrounded by signs; our imperative is to ignore none of them.

USEMONOPOLY

The idea that culture can be property—*intellectual* property—is used to justify everything from attempts to force the Girl Scouts to pay royalties for singing songs around campfires to the infringement suit brought by the estate of Margaret Mitchell against the publishers of Alice Randall's *The Wind Done Gone*. Corporations like Celera Genomics have filed for patents for human genes, while the Recording Industry Association of America has sued music downloaders for copyright infringement, reaching out-of-court settlements for thousands of dollars with defendants as young as twelve. ASCAP bleeds fees from shop owners who play background music in their stores; students and scholars are shamed from placing texts facedown on photocopy machines. At the same time, copyright is revered by most established writers and artists as a birthright and bulwark, the source of nurture for their infinitely fragile practices in a rapacious world. Plagiarism and piracy, after all, are the monsters we working artists are taught to dread, as they roam the woods surrounding our tiny preserves of regard and remuneration.

A time is marked not so much by ideas that are argued about as by ideas that are taken for granted. The character of an era hangs upon what needs no defense. In this regard, few of us question the contemporary construction of copyright. It is taken as a law, both in the sense of a universally recognizable moral absolute, like the law against murder, and as naturally inherent in our world, like the law of gravity. In fact, it is neither. Rather, copyright is an ongoing social negotiation, tenuously forged, endlessly revised, and imperfect in its every incarnation.

Thomas Jefferson, for one, considered copyright a necessary evil: He favored providing just enough incentive to create, nothing more, and thereafter allowing ideas to flow freely, as nature intended. His conception of copyright was enshrined in the Constitution, which gives Congress the authority to "promote the Progress of Science and useful Arts, by securing for limited Times to Authors and Inventors the exclusive Right to their respective Writings and Discoveries." This was a balancing act between creators and society as a whole; second comers might do a much better job than the originator with the original idea.

But Jefferson's vision has not fared well, has in fact been steadily eroded by those who view the culture as a market in which everything of value should be owned by someone or other. The distinctive feature of modern American copyright law is its almost limitless bloating—its expansion in both scope and duration. With no registration requirement, every creative act in a tangible medium is now subject to copyright protection: your e-mail to your child or your child's finger painting, both are automatically protected. The first Congress to grant copyright gave authors an initial term of fourteen years, which could be renewed for another fourteen if the author still lived. The current term is the life of the author plus seventy years. It's only a slight exaggeration to say that each time Mickey Mouse is about to fall into the public domain, the mouse's copyright term is extended.

Even as the law becomes more restrictive, technology is exposing those restrictions as bizarre and arbitrary. When old laws fixed on reproduction as the compensable (or actionable) unit, it wasn't because there was anything fundamentally invasive of an author's rights in the making of a copy. Rather it was because copies were once easy to find and count, so they made a useful benchmark for deciding when an owner's rights had been invaded. In the contemporary world, though, the act of "copying" is in no meaningful sense equivalent to an infringement—we make a copy every time we accept an e-mailed text, or send or forward one—and is impossible to regulate or even describe anymore.

At the movies, my entertainment is sometimes lately preceded by a dire trailer, produced by the lobbying group called the Motion Picture Association of America, in which the purchasing of a bootleg copy of a Hollywood film is compared to the theft of a car or a handbag—and, as the bullying supertitles remind us, "You wouldn't steal a handbag!" This conflation forms an incitement to quit thinking. If I were to tell you that pirating DVDs or downloading music is in no way different from loaning a friend a book, my own arguments would be as ethically bankrupt as the MPAA's. The truth lies somewhere in the vast gray area between these two overstated positions. For a car or a handbag, once stolen, no longer is available to its owner, while the appropriation of an article of "intellectual property" leaves the original untouched. As Jefferson wrote, "He who receives an idea from me, receives instruction himself without lessening mine; as he who lights his taper at mine, receives light without darkening me."

Yet industries of cultural capital, who profit not from creating but from distributing, see the sale of culture as a zero-sum game. The piano-roll publishers fear the record companies, who fear the cassette-tape manufacturers, who fear the online vendors, who fear whoever else is next in line to profit most quickly from the intangible and infinitely reproducible fruits of an artist's labor. It has been the same in every industry and with every technological innovation. Jack Valenti, speaking for the MPAA: "I say to you that the VCR is to the American film producer and the American public as the Boston Strangler is to the woman home alone."

Thinking clearly sometimes requires unbraiding our language. The word "copyright" may eventually seem as dubious in its embedded purposes as "family values," "globalization," and, sure, "intellectual property." Copyright is a "right" in no absolute sense; it is a government-granted monopoly on the use of creative results. So let's try calling it that—not a right but a *monopoly on use*, a "usemonopoly"—and then consider how the rapacious expansion of monopoly rights has always been counter to the public interest, no matter if it is Andrew Carnegie controlling the price of steel or Walt Disney managing the fate of his mouse. Whether the monopolizing beneficiary is a living artist or some artist's heirs or some corporation's shareholders, the loser is the community, including living artists who might make splendid use of a healthy public domain.

THE BEAUTY OF SECOND USE

A few years ago someone brought me a strange gift, purchased at MoMA's downtown design store: a copy of my own first novel, *Gun, with Occasional Music*, expertly cut into the contours of a pistol. The object was the work of Robert The, an artist whose specialty is the reincarnation of everyday materials. I regard my first book as an old friend, one who never fails to remind me of the spirit with which I entered into this game of art and commerce—that to be allowed to insert the materials of my imagination onto the shelves of bookstores and into the minds of readers (if only a handful) was a wild privilege. I was paid $6,000 for three years of writing, but at the time I'd have happily published the results for nothing. Now my old friend had come home in a new form, one I was unlikely to have imagined for it myself. The gun-book wasn't readable, exactly, but I couldn't take offense at that. The fertile spirit of stray connection this appropriated object conveyed back to me—the strange beauty of its second use—was a reward for being a published writer I could never have fathomed in advance. And the world makes room for both my novel and Robert The's gunbook. There's no need to choose between the two.

In the first life of creative property, if the creator is lucky, the content is sold. After the commercial life has ended, our tradition supports a second life as well. A newspaper is delivered to a doorstep, and the next day wraps fish or builds an archive. Most books fall out of print after one year, yet even within that period they can be sold in used bookstores and stored in libraries, quoted in reviews, parodied in magazines, described in conversations, and plundered for costumes for kids to wear on Halloween. The demarcation between various possible uses is beautifully graded and hard to define, the more so as artifacts distill into and repercuss through the realm of culture into which they've been entered, the more so as they engage the receptive minds for whom they were presumably intended.

Active reading is an impertinent raid on the literary preserve. Readers are like nomads, poaching their way across fields they do not own—artists are no more able to control the imaginations of their audiences than the culture industry is able to control second uses of its artifacts. In the children's classic *The Velveteen Rabbit*, the old Skin Horse offers the Rabbit a lecture on the practice of textual poaching. The value of a new toy lies not in its material qualities (not "having things that buzz inside you and a stick-out handle"), the Skin Horse explains, but rather in how the toy is used. "Real isn't how you are made . . . It's a thing that happens to you. When a child loves you for a long, long time, not just to play with, but REALLY loves you, then you become Real." The Rabbit is fearful, recognizing that consumer goods don't become "real" without being actively reworked: "Does it hurt?" Reassuring him, the Skin Horse says, "It doesn't happen all at once . . . You become. It takes a long time . . . Generally, by the time you are Real, most of your hair has been loved off, and your eyes drop out and you get loose in the joints and very shabby." Seen from the perspective of the toymaker, the Velveteen Rabbit's loose joints and missing eyes represent vandalism, signs of misuse and rough treatment; for others, these are marks of its loving use.

Artists and their surrogates who fall into the trap of seeking recompense for every possible second use end up attacking their own best audience members for the crime of exalting and enshrining their work. The Recording Industry Association of America prosecuting their own record-buying public makes as little sense as the novelists who bristle at autographing used copies of their books for collectors. And artists, or their heirs, who fall into the trap of attacking the collagists and satirists and digital samplers of their work are attacking the next generation of creators for the crime of being influenced, for the crime of responding with the same mixture of intoxication, resentment, lust, and glee that characterizes all artistic successors. By doing so they make the world smaller, betraying what seems to me the primary motivation for participating in the world of culture in the first place: to make the world larger.

SOURCE HYPOCRISY, OR, DISNIAL

The Walt Disney Company has drawn an astonishing catalog from the work of others: *Snow White and the Seven Dwarfs, Fantasia, Pinocchio, Dumbo, Bambi, Song of the South, Cinderella, Alice in Wonderland, Robin Hood, Peter Pan, Lady and the Tramp, Mulan, Sleeping Beauty, The Sword in the Stone, The Jungle Book*, and, alas, *Treasure Planet*— a legacy of cultural sampling that Shakespeare, or De La Soul, could get behind. Yet Disney's protectorate of lobbyists has policed the resulting cache of cultural materials as vigilantly as if it were Fort Knox— threatening legal action, for instance, against the artist Dennis Oppenheim for the use of Disney characters in a sculpture, and prohibiting the scholar Holly Crawford from using any Disney-related images (including artwork by Lichtenstein, Warhol, Oldenburg, and others)— in her monograph *Attached to the Mouse: Disney and Contemporary Art*.

This peculiar and specific act—the enclosure of commonwealth culture for the benefit of a sole or corporate owner—is close kin to what could be called *imperial plagiarism*, the free use of third-world or "primitive" artworks and styles by more privileged (and better-paid) artists. Think of Picasso's *Les Demoiselles d'Avignon*, or some of the albums of Paul Simon or David Byrne: Even without violating copyright, those creators have sometimes come in for a certain skepticism when the extent of their outsourcing became evident. And, as when Led Zeppelin found themselves sued for back royalties by the bluesman Willie Dixon, the act can occasionally be an expensive one. *To live outside the law, you must be honest*: Perhaps it was this, in part, that spurred David Byrne and Brian Eno to recently launch a "remix" website, where anyone can download easily disassembled versions of two songs from *My Life in the Bush of Ghosts*, an album reliant on vernacular speech sampled from a host of sources. Perhaps it also explains why Bob Dylan has never refused a request for a sample.

Kenneth Koch once said, "I'm a writer who likes to be influenced." It was a charming confession, and a rare one. For so many artists, the act of creativity is intended as a Napoleonic imposition of one's uniqueness upon the universe—*après moi le déluge* of copycats! And for every James Joyce or Woody Guthrie or Martin Luther King Jr. or Walt Disney who gathered a constellation of voices in his work, there may seem to be some corporation or literary estate eager to stopper the bottle: Cultural debts flow in, but they don't flow out. We might call this tendency "source hypocrisy." Or we could name it after the most pernicious source hypocrites of all time: Disnial.

YOU CAN'T STEAL A GIFT

My reader may, understandably, be on the verge of crying, "Communist!" A large, diverse society cannot survive without property; a large, diverse, and modern society cannot flourish without some form of intellectual property. But it takes little reflection to grasp that there is ample value that the term "property" doesn't capture. And works of art exist simultaneously in two economies: a market economy and a *gift economy*.

The cardinal difference between gift and commodity exchange is that a gift establishes a feeling-bond between two people, whereas the sale of a commodity leaves no necessary connection. I go into a hardware store, pay the man for a hacksaw blade, and walk out. I may never see him again. The disconnectedness is, in fact, a virtue of the commodity mode. We don't want to be bothered, and if the clerk always wants to chat about the family, I'll shop elsewhere. I just want a hacksaw blade. But a gift makes a connection. There are many examples, the candy or cigarette offered to a stranger who shares a seat on the plane, the few words that indicate goodwill between passengers on the late-night bus. These tokens establish the simplest bonds of social life, but the model they offer may be extended to the most complicated of unions— marriage, parenthood, mentorship. If a value is placed on these (often essentially unequal) exchanges, they degenerate into something else.

Yet one of the more difficult things to comprehend is that the gift economies—like those that sustain open-source software—coexist so naturally with the market. It is precisely this doubleness in art practices that we must identify, ratify, and enshrine in our lives as participants in culture, either as "producers" or "consumers." Art that matters to us—which moves the heart, or revives the soul, or delights the senses, or offers courage for living, however we choose to describe the experience—is received as a gift is received. Even if we've paid a fee at the door of the museum or concert hall, when we are touched by a work of art something comes to us that has nothing to do with the price. The daily commerce of our lives proceeds at its own constant level, but a gift conveys an uncommodifiable surplus of inspiration.

The way we treat a thing can change its nature, though. Religions often prohibit the sale of sacred objects, the implication being that their sanctity is lost if they are bought and sold. We consider it unacceptable to sell sex, babies, body organs, legal rights, and votes. The idea that something should never be commodified is generally known as *inalienability* or *unalienability*—a concept most famously expressed by Thomas Jefferson in the phrase "endowed by their Creator with certain unalienable Rights." A work of art seems to be a hardier breed; it can be sold in the market and still emerge a work of art. But if it is true that in the essential commerce of art a gift is carried by the work from the artist to his audience, if I am right to say that where there is no gift there is no art, then it may be possible to destroy a work of art by converting it into a pure commodity. I don't maintain that art can't be bought and sold, but that the gift portion of the work places a constraint upon our merchandising. This is the reason why even a really beautiful, ingenious, powerful ad (of which there are a lot) can never be any kind of real art: An ad has no status as gift; i.e., it's never really *for* the person it's directed at.

The power of a gift economy remains difficult for the empiricists of our market culture to understand. In our times, the rhetoric of the market presumes that everything should be and can be appropriately bought, sold, and owned—a tide of alienation lapping daily at the dwindling redoubt of the unalienable. In free-market theory, an intervention to halt propertization is considered "paternalistic" because it inhibits the free action of the citizen, now reposited as a "potential entrepreneur." Of course, in the real world, we know that child-rearing, family life, education, socialization, sexuality, political life, and many other basic human activities require insulation from market forces. In fact, paying for many of these things can ruin them. We may be willing to peek at *Who Wants to Marry a Multimillionaire?* or an eBay auction of the ova of fashion models, but only to reassure ourselves that some things are still beneath our standards of dignity.

What's remarkable about gift economies is that they can flourish in the most unlikely places—in run-down neighborhoods, on the

Internet, in scientific communities, and among members of Alcoholics Anonymous. A classic example is commercial blood systems, which generally produce blood supplies of lower safety, purity, and potency than volunteer systems. A gift economy may be superior when it comes to maintaining a group's commitment to certain extra-market values.

THE COMMONS

Another way of understanding the presence of gift economies—which dwell like ghosts in the commercial machine—is in the sense of a *public commons*. A commons, of course, is anything like the streets over which we drive, the skies through which we pilot airplanes, or the public parks or beaches on which we dally. A commons belongs to everyone and no one, and its use is controlled only by common consent. A commons describes resources like the body of ancient music drawn on by composers and folk musicians alike, rather than the commodities, like "Happy Birthday to You," for which ASCAP, 114 years after it was written, continues to collect a fee. Einstein's theory of relativity is a commons. Writings in the public domain are a commons. Gossip about celebrities is a commons. The silence in a movie theater is a transitory commons, impossibly fragile, treasured by those who crave it and constructed as a mutual gift by those who compose it.

The world of art and culture is a vast commons, one that is salted through with zones of utter commerce yet remains splendidly immune to any overall commodification. The closest resemblance is to the commons of a *language*: altered by every contributor, expanded by even the most passive user. That a language is a commons doesn't mean that the community owns it; rather it belongs between people, possessed by no one, not even by society as a whole.

Nearly any commons, though, can be encroached upon, partitioned, enclosed. The American commons include tangible assets such as public forests and minerals, intangible wealth such as copyrights and patents, critical infrastructures such as the Internet and government research, and cultural resources such as the broadcast airwaves and public spaces. They include resources we've paid for as taxpayers and inherited from previous generations. They're not just an inventory of marketable assets; they're social institutions and cultural traditions that define us as Americans and enliven us as human beings. Some invasions of the commons are sanctioned because we can no longer muster a spirited commitment to the public sector. The abuse goes unnoticed because the theft of the commons is seen in glimpses, not in panorama. We may occasionally see a former wetland paved; we may hear about the breakthrough cancer drug that tax dollars helped develop, the rights to which pharmaceutical companies acquired for a song. The larger movement goes too much unremarked. The notion of a *commons of cultural materials* goes more or less unnamed.

Honoring the commons is not a matter of moral exhortation. It is a practical necessity. We in Western society are going through a period of intensifying belief in private ownership, to the detriment of the public good. We have to remain constantly vigilant to prevent raids by those who would selfishly exploit our common heritage for their private gain. Such raids on our natural resources are not examples of enterprise and initiative. They are attempts to take from all the people just for the benefit of a few.

UNDISCOVERED PUBLIC KNOWLEDGE

Artists and intellectuals despondent over the prospects for originality can take heart from a phenomenon identified about twenty years ago by Don Swanson, a library scientist at the University of Chicago. He called it "undiscovered public knowledge." Swanson showed that standing problems in medical research may be significantly addressed, perhaps even solved, simply by systematically surveying the scientific literature. Left to its own devices, research tends to become more specialized and abstracted from the real-world problems that motivated it and to which it remains relevant. This suggests that such a problem may be tackled effectively not by commissioning more research but by assuming that most or all of the solution can already be found in various scientific journals, waiting to be assembled by someone willing to read across specialties. Swanson himself did this in the case of Raynaud's syndrome, a disease that causes the fingers of young women to become numb. His finding is especially striking—perhaps even scandalous— because it happened in the ever-expanding biomedical sciences.

Undiscovered public knowledge emboldens us to question the extreme claims to originality made in press releases and publishers' notices: Is an intellectual or creative offering truly novel, or have we just forgotten a worthy precursor? Does solving certain scientific problems really require massive additional funding, or could a computerized search engine, creatively deployed, do the same job more quickly and cheaply? Lastly, does our appetite for creative vitality require the violence and exasperation of another avant-garde, with its wearisome killing-the-father imperatives, or might we be better off ratifying the *ecstasy of influence*—and deepening our willingness to understand the commonality and timelessness of the methods and motifs available to artists?

GIVE ALL

A few years ago, the Film Society of Lincoln Center announced a retrospective of the works of Dariush Mehrjui, then a fresh enthusiasm of mine. Mehrjui is one of Iran's finest filmmakers, and the only one whose subject was personal relationships among the upper-middle-class intelligentsia. Needless to say, opportunities to view his films were—and remain—rare indeed. I headed uptown for one, an adaptation of J. D. Salinger's *Franny and Zooey*, titled *Pari*, only to discover at the door of the Walter Reade Theater that the screening had been canceled: Its announcement had brought threat of a lawsuit down on the Film Society. True, these were Salinger's rights under the law. Yet why would he care that some obscure Iranian filmmaker had paid him homage with a meditation on his heroine? Would it have damaged his book or robbed him of some crucial remuneration had the screening been permitted? The fertile spirit of stray connection—one stretching across what is presently seen as the direst of international breaches—had in this case been snuffed out. The cold, undead hand of one of my childhood literary heroes had reached out from its New Hampshire redoubt to arrest my present-day curiosity.

A few assertions, then:

Any text that has infiltrated the common mind to the extent of *Gone With the Wind* or *Lolita* or *Ulysses* inexorably joins the language of culture. A map-turned-to-landscape, it has moved to a place beyond enclosure or control. The authors and their heirs should consider the subsequent parodies, refractions, quotations, and revisions an honor, or at least the price of a rare success.

A corporation that has imposed an inescapable notion—Mickey Mouse, Band-Aid—on the cultural language should pay a similar price.

The primary objective of copyright is not to reward the labor of authors but "to promote the Progress of Science and useful Arts." To this end, copyright assures authors the right to their original expression but encourages others to build freely upon the ideas and information conveyed by a work. This result is neither unfair nor unfortunate.

Copyright, trademark, and patent law is presently corrupted. The case for perpetual copyright is a denial of the essential gift-aspect of the creative act. Arguments in its favor are as un-American as those for the repeal of the estate tax.

Art is sourced. Apprentices graze in the field of culture.

Digital sampling is an art method like any other, neutral in itself.

Despite hand-wringing at each technological turn—radio, the Internet—the future will be much like the past. Artists will sell some things but also give some things away. Change may be troubling for those who crave less ambiguity, but the life of an artist has never been filled with certainty.

The dream of a perfect systematic remuneration is nonsense. I pay rent with the price my words bring when published in glossy magazines and at the same moment offer them for almost nothing to impoverished literary quarterlies, or speak them for free into the air in a radio interview. So what are they worth? What would they be worth if some future Dylan worked them into a song? Should I care to make such a thing impossible?

Any text is woven entirely with citations, references, echoes, cultural languages, which cut across it through and through in a vast stereophony. The citations that go to make up a text are anonymous, untraceable, and yet *already read*; they are quotations without inverted commas. The kernel, the soul—let us go further and say the substance, the bulk, the actual and valuable material of all human utterances—is plagiarism. For substantially all ideas are secondhand, consciously and unconsciously drawn from a million outside sources, and daily used by the garnerer with a pride and satisfaction born of the superstition that he originated them; whereas there is not a rag of originality about them anywhere except the little discoloration they get from his mental and moral caliber and his temperament, and which is revealed in characteristics of phrasing. Old and new make the warp and woof of every moment. There is no thread that is not a twist of these two strands. By necessity, by proclivity, and by delight, we all quote. Neurological study has lately shown that memory, imagination, and consciousness itself are stitched, quilted, pastiched. If we cut-and-paste our selves, might we not forgive it of our artworks?

Artists and writers—and our advocates, our guilds and agents—too often subscribe to implicit claims of originality that do injury to these truths. And we too often, as hucksters and bean counters in the tiny enterprises of our selves, act to spite the gift portion of our privileged roles. People live differently who treat a portion of their wealth as a gift. If we devalue and obscure the gift-economy function of our art practices, we turn our works into nothing more than advertisements for themselves. We may console ourselves that our lust for subsidiary rights in virtual perpetuity is some heroic counter to rapacious corporate interests. But the truth is that with artists pulling on one side and corporations pulling on the other, the loser is the collective public imagination from which we were nourished in the first place, and whose existence as the ultimate repository of our offerings makes the work worth doing in the first place.

As a novelist, I'm a cork on the ocean of story, a leaf on a windy day. Pretty soon I'll be blown away. For the moment I'm grateful to be making a living, and so must ask that for a limited time (in the Thomas Jefferson sense) you please respect my small, treasured usemonopolies. Don't pirate my editions; do plunder my visions. The name of the game is Give All. You, reader, are welcome to my stories. They were never mine in the first place, but I gave them to you. If you have the inclination to pick them up, take them with my blessing.

KEY: I IS ANOTHER

This key to the preceding essay names the source of every line I stole, warped, and cobbled together as I "wrote" (except, alas, those sources I forgot along the way). First uses of a given author or speaker are highlighted in **bold**. Nearly every sentence I culled I also revised, at least slightly—for necessities of space, in order to produce a more consistent tone, or simply because I felt like it.

TITLE

The phrase "the ecstasy of influence," which embeds a rebuking play on Harold Bloom's "anxiety of influence," is lifted from spoken remarks by Professor **Richard Dienst** of Rutgers.

LOVE AND THEFT

"A cultivated man of middle age . . ." to " . . . hidden, unacknowledged memory?" These lines, with some adjustments for tone, belong to the **anonymous editor** or **assistant** who wrote the jacket-flap copy of **Michael Maar**'s *The Two Lolitas*. Of course, in my own experience, jacket-flap copy is often a collaboration between author and editor. Perhaps this was also true for Maar.

"The history of literature . . ." to " . . . borrow and quote?" comes from Maar's book itself.

"Appropriation has always . . ." to " . . . Ishmael and Queequeg . . ." This paragraph makes a hash of remarks from an interview with **Eric Lott** conducted by **David McNair** and **Jayson Whitehead**, and incorporates both interviewers' and interviewee's observations. (The text-interview form can be seen as a commonly accepted form of multivocal writing. Most interviewers prime their subjects with remarks of their own—leading the witness, so to speak—and gently refine their subjects' statements in the final printed transcript.)

"I realized this . . ." to " . . . for a long time." The anecdote is cribbed, with an elision to avoid appropriating a dead grandmother, from **Jonathan Rosen**'s *The Talmud and the Internet*. I've never seen *84 Charing Cross Road*, nor searched the Web for a Donne quote. For me it was through Rosen to Donne, Hemingway, website, et al.

"When I was thirteen . . ." to " . . . no plagiarist at all." This is from **William Gibson**'s "God's Little Toys," in *Wired* magazine. My own first encounter with William Burroughs, also at age thirteen, was less epiphanic. Having grown up with a painter father who, during family visits to galleries or museums, approvingly noted collage and appropriation techniques in the visual arts (Picasso, Claes Oldenburg, Stuart Davis), I was gratified, but not surprised, to learn that literature could encompass the same methods.

CONTAMINATION ANXIETY

"In 1941, on his front porch . . ." to " . . . declares: 'This song comes from the cotton field.'" **Siva Vaidhyanathan**, *Copyrights and Copywrongs*.

" . . . enabled by an 'open source' . . . freely reworked." **Kembrew McLeod**, *Freedom of Expression®*. In *Owning Culture*, McLeod notes that, as he was writing, he happened to be listening to a lot of old country music, and in my casual listening I noticed that *six* country songs shared *exactly* the same vocal melody, including Hank Thompson's "Wild Side of Life," the Carter Family's "I'm Thinking Tonight of My Blue Eyes," Roy Acuff's "Great Speckled Bird," Kitty Wells's "It Wasn't God Who Made Honky Tonk Angels," Reno & Smiley's "I'm Using My Bible for a Roadmap," and Townes Van Zandt's "Heavenly Houseboat Blues." . . . In his extensively researched book, *Country: The Twisted Roots of Rock 'n' Roll*, Nick Tosches documents that the melody these songs share is both "ancient and British." There were no recorded lawsuits stemming from these appropriations . . .

" . . . musicians have gained . . . through allusion." **Joanna Demers**, *Steal This Music*.

"In '70s Jamaica . . ." to " . . . hours of music." Gibson.

"Visual, sound, and text collage . . ." to " . . . realm of cultural production." This plunders, rewrites, and amplifies paragraphs from McLeod's *Owning Culture*, except for the line about collage being the art form of the twentieth and twenty-first centuries, which I heard filmmaker **Craig Baldwin** say, in defense of sampling, in the trailer for a forthcoming documentary, *Copyright Criminals*.

"In a courtroom scene . . ." to " . . . would cease to exist." **Dave Itzkoff**, the *New York Times*.

" . . . the remarkable series of 'plagiarisms' . . ." to " . . . we want more plagiarism." **Richard Posner**, combined from the *Becker-Posner Blog* and the *Atlantic Monthly*.

"Most artists are brought . . ." to " . . . by art itself." These words, and many more to follow, come from **Lewis Hyde**'s *The Gift*. Above any other book I've here plagiarized, I commend *The Gift* to your attention.

"Finding one's voice . . . filiations, communities, and discourses." Semanticist **George L. Dillon**, quoted in **Rebecca Moore Howard**'s "The New Abolitionism Comes to Plagiarism."

"Inspiration could be . . . act never experienced." **Ned Rorem**, found on several "great quotations" sites on the Internet.

"Invention, it must be humbly admitted . . . out of chaos." **Mary Shelley**, from her introduction to *Frankenstein*.

"What happens ..." to " ... contamination anxiety." **Kevin J. H. Dettmar**, from "The Illusion of Modernist Allusion and the Politics of Postmodern Plagiarism."

SURROUNDED BY SIGNS

"The surrealists believed ..." to the Walter Benjamin quote. **Christian Keathley**'s *Cinephilia and History, or the Wind in the Trees*, a book that treats fannish fetishism as the secret at the heart of film scholarship. Keathley notes, for instance, Joseph Cornell's surrealist-influenced 1936 film *Rose Hobart*, which simply records "the way in which Cornell himself watched the 1931 Hollywood potboiler *East of Borneo*, fascinated and distracted as he was by its B-grade star"—the star, of course, being Rose Hobart herself. This, I suppose, makes Cornell a father to computer-enabled fan-creator reworkings of Hollywood product, like the version of George Lucas's *The Phantom Menace* from which the noxious Jar Jar Binks character was purged; both incorporate a viewer's subjective preferences into a revision of a filmmaker's work.

" ... early in the history of photography" to " ... without compensating the source." From *Free Culture*, by **Lawrence Lessig**, the greatest of public advocates for copyright reform, and the best source if you want to get radicalized in a hurry.

"For those whose ganglia ..." to " ... discourse broke down." From **David Foster Wallace**'s essay "E Unibus Pluram," reprinted in *A Supposedly Fun Thing I'll Never Do Again*. I have no idea who Wallace's "gray eminence" is or was. I inserted the example of Dickens into the paragraph; he struck me as overlooked in the lineage of authors of "brand-name" fiction.

"I was born ... *Mary Tyler Moore Show*." These are the reminiscences of **Mark Hosler** from Negativland, a collaging musical collective that was sued by U2's record label for their appropriation of "I Still Haven't Found What I'm Looking For." Although I had to adjust the birth date, Hosler's cultural menu fits me like a glove.

"The world is a home ... pop-culture products ..." McLeod.

"Today, when we can eat ..." to " ... flat sights." Wallace.

"We're surrounded by signs, ignore none of them." This phrase, which I unfortunately rendered somewhat leaden with the word "imperative," comes from **Steve Erickson**'s novel *Our Ecstatic Days*.

USEMONOPOLY

" . . . everything from attempts . . ." to " . . . defendants as young as twelve." **Robert Boynton**, the *New York Times Magazine*, "The Tyranny of Copyright?"

"A time is marked . . ." to " . . . what needs no defense." Lessig, this time from *The Future of Ideas*.

"Thomas Jefferson, for one . . ." to " ' . . . respective Writings and Discoveries.' " Boynton.

" . . . second comers might do a much better job than the originator . . ." I found this phrase in Lessig, who is quoting Vaidhyanathan, who himself is characterizing a judgment written by **Learned Hand**.

"But Jefferson's vision . . . owned by someone or other." Boynton.

"The distinctive feature . . ." to " . . . term is extended." Lessig, again from *The Future of Ideas*.

"When old laws . . ." to " . . . had been invaded." **Jessica Litman**, *Digital Copyright*.

" 'I say to you . . . woman home alone.' " I found the Valenti quote in McLeod. Now fill in the blank: Jack Valenti is to the public domain as _____ is to _____.

THE BEAUTY OF SECOND USE

"In the first . . ." to " . . . builds an archive." Lessig.

"Most books . . . one year . . ." Lessig.

"Active reading is . . ." to " . . . they do not own . . ." This is a mashup of **Henry Jenkins**, from his *Textual Poachers: Television Fans and Participatory Culture*, and **Michel de Certeau**, whom Jenkins quotes.

"In the children's classic . . ." to " . . . its loving use." Jenkins. (Incidentally, have the holders of the copyright to *The Velveteen Rabbit* had a close look at *Toy Story*? Could be a lawsuit there.)

SOURCE HYPOCRISY, OR, DISNIAL

"The Walt Disney Company . . . alas, *Treasure Planet* . . ." Lessig.

"Imperial Plagiarism" is the title of an essay by **Marilyn Randall**.

" . . . spurred David Byrne . . . *My Life in the Bush of Ghosts* . . ." **Chris Dahlen**, *Pitchfork*—though in truth by the time I'd finished, his words were so utterly dissolved within my own that had I been an ordinary cutting-and-pasting journalist it never would have occurred to me to give Dahlen a citation. The effort of preserving another's distinctive phrases as I worked on this essay was sometimes beyond my capacities; this form of plagiarism was oddly hard work.

"Kenneth Koch . . ." to " . . . *déluge* of copycats!" **Emily Nussbaum**, the *New York Times Book Review*.

YOU CAN'T STEAL A GIFT

"You can't steal a gift." **Dizzy Gillespie**, defending another player who'd been accused of poaching Charlie Parker's style: "You can't steal a gift. Bird gave the world his music, and if you can hear it you can have it."

"A large, diverse society . . . intellectual property." Lessig.

"And works of art . . ." to " . . . marriage, parenthood, mentorship." Hyde.

"Yet one . . . so naturally with the market." **David Bollier**, *Silent Theft*.

"Art that matters . . ." to " . . . bought and sold." Hyde.

"We consider it unacceptable . . ." to " ' . . . certain unalienable Rights.' " Bollier, paraphrasing Margaret Jane Radin's *Contested Commodities*.

"A work of art . . ." to " . . . constraint upon our merchandising." Hyde.

"This is the reason . . . person it's directed at." Wallace.

"The power of a gift . . ." to " . . . certain extra-market values." Bollier, and also the sociologist **Warren O. Hagstrom**, whom Bollier is paraphrasing.

THE COMMONS

"Einstein's theory . . ." to " . . . public domain are a commons." Lessig.

"That a language is a commons . . . society as a whole." **Michael Newton**, in the *London Review of Books*, reviewing a book called *Echolalias: On the Forgetting of Language* by Daniel Heller-Roazen. The paraphrases of book reviewers are another covert form of collaborative culture; as an avid reader of reviews, I know much about books I've never read. To quote Yann Martel on how he came to be accused of imperial plagiarism in his Booker-winning novel, *Life of Pi*,

Ten or so years ago, I read a review by John Updike in the *New York Times Review of Books* [*sic*]. It was of a novel by a Brazilian writer, Moacyr Scliar. I forget the title, and John Updike did worse: he clearly thought the book as a whole was forgettable. His review—one of those that makes you suspicious by being mostly descriptive . . . oozed indifference. But one thing about it struck me: the premise . . . Oh, the wondrous things I could do with this premise.

Unfortunately, no one was ever able to locate the Updike review in question.

"The American commons . . ." to " . . . for a song." Bollier.

"Honoring the commons . . ." to " . . . practical necessity." Bollier.

"We in Western . . . public good." **John Sulston**, Nobel Prize winner and a co-mapper of the human genome.

"We have to remain . . ." to " . . . benefit of a few." **Harry S. Truman**, at the opening of the Everglades National Park. Although it may seem the height of presumption to rip off a president—I found claiming Truman's stolid advocacy as my own embarrassing in the extreme— I didn't rewrite him at all. As the poet Marianne Moore said, "If a thing had been said in the *best* way, how can you say it better?" Moore confessed her penchant for incorporating lines from others' work, explaining, "I have not yet been able to outgrow this hybrid method of composition."

UNDISCOVERED PUBLIC KNOWLEDGE

" . . . intellectuals despondent . . ." to " . . . quickly and cheaply?" **Steve Fuller**, *The Intellectual*. There's something of Borges in Fuller's insight here; the notion of a storehouse of knowledge waiting passively to be assembled by future users is suggestive of both "The Library of Babel" and "Kafka and his Precursors."

GIVE ALL

" . . . one of Iran's finest . . ." to " . . . meditation on his heroine?" **Amy Taubin**, the *Village Voice*, although it was me who was disappointed at the door of the Walter Reade Theater.

"The primary objective . . ." to " . . . unfair nor unfortunate." **Sandra Day O'Connor**, 1991.

" . . . the future will be much like the past . . ." to " . . . give some things away." Open-source film archivist **Rick Prelinger**, quoted in McLeod.

"Change may be troubling . . . with certainty." McLeod.

" . . . woven entirely . . ." to " . . . without inverted commas." **Roland Barthes**.

"The kernel, the soul . . ." to " . . . characteristics of phrasing." **Mark Twain**, from a consoling letter to Helen Keller, who had suffered distressing accusations of plagiarism (!). In fact, her work included unconsciously memorized phrases; under Keller's particular circumstances, her writing could be understood as an allegory of the "constructed" nature of artistic perception. I found the Twain quote in the aforementioned *Copyrights and Copywrongs*, by Vaidhyanathan.

"Old and new . . ." to " . . . we all quote." **Ralph Waldo Emerson**. These guys all sound alike!

"People live differently . . . wealth as a gift." Hyde.

" . . . I'm a cork . . ." to " . . . blown away." This is adapted from the Beach Boys song " 'Til I Die," written by **Brian Wilson**. My own first adventure with song-lyric permissions came when I tried to have a character in my second novel quote the lyrics "There's a world where I can go and / Tell my secrets to / In my room / In my room." After learning the likely expense, at my editor's suggestion I replaced those with "You take the high road / I'll take the low road / I'll be in Scotland before you," a lyric in the public domain. This capitulation always bugged me, and in the subsequent British publication of the same book I restored the Brian Wilson lyric, without permission. *Ocean of Story* is the title of a collection of **Christina Stead**'s short fiction.

Saul Bellow, writing to a friend who'd taken offense at Bellow's fictional use of certain personal facts, said, "The name of the game is Give All. You are welcome to all my facts. You know them, I give them to you. If you have the strength to pick them up, take them with my blessing." I couldn't bring myself to retain Bellow's "strength," which seemed presumptuous in my new context, though it is surely the more elegant phrase. On the other hand, I was pleased to invite the suggestion that the gifts in question may actually be light and easily lifted.

KEY TO THE KEY

The notion of a collage text is, of course, not original to me. **Walter Benjamin**'s incomplete Arcades Project seemingly would have featured extensive interlaced quotations. Other precedents include **Graham Rawle**'s novel *Diary of an Amateur Photographer*, its text harvested from photography magazines, and **Eduardo Paolozzi**'s collage-novel *Kex*, cobbled from crime novels and newspaper clippings. Closer to home, my efforts owe a great deal to the recent essays of **David Shields**, in which diverse quotes are made to closely intertwine and reverberate, and to conversations with editor **Sean Howe** and archivist **Pamela Jackson**. Last year **David Edelstein**, in *New York* magazine, satirized the Kaavya Viswanathan plagiarism case by creating an almost completely plagiarized column denouncing her actions. Edelstein intended to demonstrate, through ironic example, how bricolage such as his own was ipso facto facile and unworthy. Although Viswanathan's version of "creative copying" was a pitiable one, I differ with Edelstein's conclusions.

The phrase *Je est un autre*, with its deliberately awkward syntax, belongs to **Arthur Rimbaud**. It has been translated both as "I is another" and "I is someone else," as in this excerpt from Rimbaud's letters:

> For I is someone else. If brass wakes up a trumpet, it is not its fault. To me this is obvious: I witness the unfolding of my own thought: I watch it, I listen to it: I make a stroke of the bow: the symphony begins to stir in the depths, or springs on to the stage.
>
> If the old fools had not discovered only the *false* significance of the Ego, we should not now be having to sweep away those millions of skeletons which, since time immemorial, have been piling up the fruits of their one-eyed intellects, and claiming to be, themselves, the authors!

—Harper's, 2007

The Afterlife of "Ecstasy"

The previous essay roused mostly happy static for me. Lawrence Lessig wrote to *Harper's*: "I was troubled by the link between the creativity evinced in the essay and 'plagiarism'—especially troubled when I found buried in the text the only sentence I have ever written that I truly like. (Which sentence will remain a mystery here.) I was troubled because the freedom that Lethem depends upon—the freedom to integrate and build upon the work of others—does not need the license the plagiarist takes . . . it is not too much to demand that a beautiful (or ugly) borrowed sentence be wrapped in simple quotation marks." I replied: "A call for quotation marks suggests that an essay such as mine ought to be considered in the context of academic, scientific, or journalistic discourses—realms where standards of accurate citation are necessary and sensible. Perhaps my essay should be judged in that context. Yet, assembling it, I was aware of my own impulses to beguile, cajole, evoke sensation, and even to manipulate, impulses not so different from those underlying my novels and stories . . . Artists are among other things mischievous, and we should try to remember that we wish them to be. In songs, films, paintings and much poetry, allusions and even direct quotations are subsumed within the voice of the artist who claims them. Citations come afterward, if at all. There are no quotation marks around the elements in a Robert Rauschenberg collage . . ." This wasn't really contentious. Lessig's letter, as I saw it, welcomed me to the

ranks of the "Copyleft" All-Stars: hip-hop samplers, digital provoca-
teurs, and their legal defenders. And, now, one stodgy, midcareer novelist. If *Motherless Brooklyn*'s success had obligated a brief stint as Oliver
Sacks Jr., trying not to disgrace myself on the Tourette's-advocacy circuit, now I made another round of panels and conferences, playing
Robin to Lewis "The Gift" Hyde's Batman, for a minute or two. At the
height I (Mailerishly) debated Judge Richard Posner on a Chicago stage.
The Men Who Care About Borrowing Too Much are without exception
noble-intentioned, generous men, and I relished my brief days in their
vanguard, before I melted back into the novelist crowd.

Yet the essay was also a Rorschach blot. I'd tried to occupy abandoned acreage in the middle of a battlefield, between the extremes
of copyright-abolitionist anarchy and what I saw as a retrenchment
behind the romantic notion of the capital-A Artist in a Promethean
vacuum (a notion stoked behind the scenes by corporate interest, and
by a commentariat addicted to dummy cries of "plagiarist" whenever
a little cobbling-work cropped up). I'd offer the polarized zone testimony from a middling type, making his rent on copyrights and not
reliant on legally actionable (or even particularly obvious) borrowing,
who still couldn't fudge his belief that sublimated swipes—and apprenticeship in slavish imitation—were basic to writing, and nothing new.
If so, falling silent while other artists were forced to defend shrinking
turf was shabby.

But the battle depends on pretending acreage in the middle doesn't
exist (the term for this is "straw man"). The future went on being overrated by its advocates and enemies both, at the expense of noticing that
digital culture was only a focusing lens for tendencies as creaky as (at
least) Shakespeare and *Sing Out!* magazine. The essay wasn't concerned
with Internet culture in itself (which is why it barely mentions it). My
target was the reactionary backlash at what Internet and sampling culture happened to make (even more) obvious: the eternal intertextuality of cultural participation—of reading, writing, making things from
other things. Calling for playful acknowledgment of that fact didn't
equal self-proclamation as a revolutionary, but the opposite: This matter was old as the hills, which is why I'd combed the hills to find old
words to say so. I'd pitted the piece specifically against "the violence
and exasperation of another avant-garde, with its wearisome killing-
the-father imperatives," yet a critic as sharp as *n+1*'s Marco Roth could

get inflamed at what he called "the fantasy of the writer as a hip-hop DJ." Sigh. The truth was, anyway, that on close inspection "Ecstasy" contradicted itself internally, as any rhetoric conflating file-sharing pirates and Thomas Jefferson were likely to have done. To defend the words I'd drawn into conjunction from so many places was at least as silly as attacking them. The essay was now an artifact whose weird repercussions I could try to fathom as innocently as anyone else.

Somatics of Influence

If over time I felt anything lacking in the exhaustive Frankenstein's monster of "Ecstasy," it was less that I wished I'd driven intellectual pilings deeper—screw it—but rather that the whole thing was so top-down cognitive, such a dissertation. I'd said all except what might matter most: that I felt influence, and thrilled to it, with my body, and did so before I knew it had a name. The collective "I" of "Ecstasy" couldn't investigate the mystery of a boy-reader's buzz at detecting the throb of the forgotten Victorian poems parodied in Carroll's *Alice*, or how it felt to surmise the existence of Edward G. Robinson from a Bugs Bunny aside, indicating occult histories waiting to exfoliate themselves to your curiosity. Never mind the intertextual erotics of twentieth-century popular music, that vast song-with-annotations, and what a throb of quote-recognition could do to you listening alone on headphones, or in a group on a dance floor, decades before "sampling." (Dancing was itself a laboratory of free-form imitation, every quote instantaneously claimed by your body's fingerprint-inimitability.) Never mind the way your hungry eye warped inside-out seeing your hero Robert Crumb draw satires of your hero Philip Guston's paintings that themselves riffed on Crumb's earlier comics. On the other side of the argument, disgust and other bodily alarms were routinely enlisted: Plagiarized writing smelled wrong, originality gleamed—you knew it when you saw it (except when you were wrong, which was constantly, since there was always some precursor to be discovered). You'll never listen to Led Zeppelin in the same way after you'd heard the Willie Dixon songs they'd stolen: So this tale of disenchantment and censure was supposed to go. Well, actually, though they should have cut Willie Dixon a check (and eventually did), Led Zeppelin used his songs to change the way I heard everything, including Willie Dixon, and my body declared this a positive good. I couldn't want the new stuff not to exist, or to be too deferential to the old, any more than I wanted the old stuff I found myself compulsively driven to excavate backward—the songs, the books—to have been toppled or eradicated by what came next (the "weary killing-the-father imperatives"). Sometimes more is more. I'd shied from personal testimonies, wishing to test my intuitions in a communal tongue. Now, omitting the personal somatics of influence felt like neglect.

As for canons, why should it be that to valorize reuse indicated, of all things, an enmity to canons? I was a fiend for canons. Sampling was "Ancestor worship," according to D.J. Spooky. Let a million canons Bloom. Only, canons not by authoritarian fiat but out of urgent personal voyaging. Construct your own and wear it, an exoskeleton of many colors.

Or maybe I did want to spin some turntables, at least for a minute or two. My first fiction after "The Ecstasy of Influence" was this collage. Count it as one of several money-put-where-mouth-is gestures but also as a confession of the addictive qualities of the scissors and pastepot. After the bogus dissertation of "Ecstasy," this was a Rauschenberg collage, and it was a relief to let the torn paper and glue blobs be obvious.

Always Crashing in the Same Car

(A Mashup)

As soon as I was outside the city I realized night had fallen. I turned on my headlights. It seems to me that one of the strongest gratifications of night driving is precisely that you can see so little and yet at the same time see so very much. The child awakes in us once again when we drive at night, and then all those earliest sensations of fear and security begin shimmering, tingling once again inside ourselves. The car is dark, we hear lost voices, the dials glow, and simultaneously we are moving and not moving, held deep in the comfort of cushions as once we were on just such a night as this one, yet feeling even in the softness of the beige upholstery all the sickening texture of our actual travel. For night driving our eyes, too, must remove one kind of inner transparency and fit on another, because they no longer have to make an effort to distinguish among the shadows and the fading colors of the evening landscape the little speck of the distant cars which are coming toward us or preceding us, but they have to check a kind of black slate which requires a different method of reading, more precise but also simplified, since the darkness erases all the picture's details which might be distracting and underlines only the indispensable elements, the white stripes on the asphalt, the headlights' yellow glow, and the little red dots. It's a process that occurs automatically, and if I was led to reflect on it that evening it was because as the external possibilities of distraction diminished, the internal ones got the upper hand within me, and my thoughts raced on their own in a circuit of alternatives and doubts I couldn't disengage.

At first I paid no attention, then it came again, flashing across my eye, and then yet again, until at last, forced to take a closer look, I saw sunlight glinting off the hood of a car. I adjusted my mirror and thought no more of it—I was after all on a road, cars are to be expected. Yet when after a number of divagations and turns and accelerations it was still with me, I begin to pay it more heed. Can it be that I was being followed? But was it always the same car that pursued me? I could no longer say. I tried not to think too obsessively about my pursuers, but what else was I to think about? They were behind me, watching me, waiting for me to make a mistake. So far I had made no mistakes.

There seemed a figure in the driver's seat, or if not a figure perhaps only a raised headrest, the sun glinting off the dirty windshield making it difficult to say anything with certainty. The other car at first was not with me and then it was, unless it was another similar car. It was there, then was gone, then there again. I stopped for fuel and saw no car but then, driving again, there it was, behind me. That car that was chasing me was faster than mine. From time to time it became easy to believe I was not being followed, the pursuit behind, I came to believe, extremely subtle, invisible more often than visible. The car sometimes freshly washed, sometimes covered with mud, the paint such that it caught the light differently at different times of the day, making me always think, "Could that possibly be the car? Aren't I mistaken?"

In my escape I headed for the center of the city. I jockeyed for an opening in the line of cars; finally someone slowed for a tenth of a second at the yield sign and I got in. Cars shot past me at seventy and eighty miles an hour, the drivers sprawled behind their wheels, fish-eyed and hostile. I saw a gap and went for it, flooring the Cutlass and feeling the characteristic lag in the transmission. I moved the car into the slow lane as we turned around the central drum of the interchange, accelerating when we gained the open deck of the motorway, traffic speeding past us. It was a healthy decision; the pursuer was constantly behind me but we were separated by several other cars as we joined the fast westward sweep of the outer circular motorway.

Everywhere the perspectives had changed. The concrete walls of the slip road reared over us like luminous cliffs. The marker lines dividing and turning formed a maze of white snakes, writhing as they carried the wheels of the cars crossing their backs, as delighted as dolphins. The overhead route signs loomed above us like generous dive-bombers. I pressed my palms against the rim of the steering wheel, pushing the car unaided through the golden air. Two airport coaches and a truck overtook us, their revolving wheels almost motionless, as if these vehicles were pieces of stage scenery suspended from the sky. Looking around, I had the impression that all the cars on the highway were stationary, the spinning earth racing beneath them to create an illusion of movement.

We stopped at a traffic signal, in a long column. I felt definitely more hostile toward the cars that preceded me and prevented me from advancing than toward those following me, which however would make themselves declared enemies if they tried to pass me, a difficult undertaking in view of the dense jam where every car was stuck fast among the others with a minimum freedom of movement. In short, the man who was my mortal enemy was now lost among many other solid bodies where my chafing aversion and fear are also perforce distributed, just as his murderous will though directed exclusively against me was somehow scattered and deflected among a great number of intermediary objects.

Looking closely at this silent terrain, I realized that the entire zone which defined the landscape of my life was now bounded by a continuous artificial horizon, formed by the raised parapets and embankments of the motorways and their access roads and interchanges. These encircled the vehicles like the walls of a crater several miles in diameter. Here and there a driver shifted behind his steering wheel, trapped uncomfortably in the hot sunlight, and I had the sudden impression that the world had stopped. Gradually I realized what I'd seen in the rearview mirror. The car was a maroon Cutlass, identical to my own. I looked slowly to my left and saw my own face in the car next to me, glassy-eyed, mouthing words. I could read the words. They were, "Go back. Go back."

A police car sped down the descent lane of the flyover, headlamps flashing, the rotating blue light on its roof flicking at the dark air like a whip. Above me, on the crest of the ascent lane, two policemen steered the traffic streams from the nearby curb. Warning tripods set up on the pavement flashed a rhythmic "Slow . . . Slow . . . Accident . . . Accident . . ." I cranked the window down to see what it was that interrupted my way. Lines of cars moved past a circle of police spotlights.

It was a horrible smashup of forty or fifty streamlined multi-cylinder automobiles; and each of them must have been traveling well over two hundred miles an hour to achieve, even in combination, such a terrible mass of wreckage. Ambulances and policemen were all about, and so were doctors and nurses and interns. Arc lights that flared over the sites of major collisions, while firemen and police engineers worked with acetylene torches and lifting tackle to free unconscious wives trapped beside their dead husbands, or waited as a passing doctor fumbled with a dying man pinned below an inverted truck. Scores of newspapermen were there interviewing onlookers and victims and taking flashlight photos of the mess. By each wrecked automobile there must have been six or seven insurance adjusters and nine or ten lawyers. A tremendous crowd of curiosity-seekers had gathered; the thruway was blocked completely from curb to curb. There was no way, of course, of getting out behind, because even as I stopped, the traffic piled up in back of me for ten or fifteen miles.

I got out to stretch my legs. Close by, I found a mobile saloon mounted on a truck and two trailers; its personnel had rushed it to the scene, let down the sides of the trailers, and set up shop where they did a remarkable business. A crowd was gathering on the sidewalks, and on the pedestrian bridge that spanned Western Avenue the spectators leaned elbow to elbow on the metal rail. The smallest of the cars involved in the accident, a yellow Italian sports car, had been almost obliterated by a black limousine with an extended wheelbase which had skidded across the central reservation. The limousine had returned across the concrete island to its own lane and struck the steel pylon of a route indicator, crushing its radiator and nearside wheel housing, before being hit in turn by a taxi joining the flyover from the Western Avenue access road. The head-on collision into the rear end of the limousine, followed by a rollover, had crushed the taxi laterally, translating its passenger cabin and body panels through an angle of some fifteen degrees. The sports car lay on its back on the central reservation. A squad of police and firemen were jacking it onto its side, revealing two bodies still trapped inside the crushed compartment. I moved around through the crowd, inspecting the corpses and standing by different wrecks whenever I saw they were about to be photographed.

The thruway was jammed, a horizontal Christmas tree of flashing red lights. Anyone could look at their watch, but it was as if that time strapped to your right wrist or the beep beep on the radio were measuring something else—the time of those who hadn't made the blunder of trying to return to the city on the southern thruway on a Sunday afternoon and, just past the suburbs, had had to slow down to a crawl, stop, six rows of cars on either side, start the engine, move three yards, stop, talk with the two nuns in the 2CV on the right, look in the rearview mirror at the pale man driving the Caravelle, ironically envy the birdlike contentment of the couple in the Peugeot playing with their little girl, joking, and eating cheese, or suffer the exasperated outbursts of the two boys in the Simca, in front of the Peugeot. I even got out at the stops to explore, not wandering off too far (no one knew when the cars up front would start moving again, and you'd have had to run back so that those behind you wouldn't begin their battle of horn blasts and curses), and exchanged a few discouraged and mocking words with the two men traveling with the little blond boy, whose great joy at that particular moment was running his toy car over the seats and the rear ledge of the Taurus. It didn't seem the cars up ahead would budge very soon. I observed with some pity the elderly couple in the Citroën ID that looked like a big purple bathtub with the little old man and woman swimming around inside, he resting his arms on the wheel with an air of resigned fatigue, she nibbling on an apple, fastidious rather than hungry. I decided not to leave the car again and to just wait for the police to somehow dissolve the bottleneck.

At one point (it was nighttime now), some strangers came with news. The pavement had caved in around Yonkers, and five cars had overturned when their front wheels got caught in the cracks. The idea of a natural catastrophe spread all the way to the pale man, who shrugged without comment. The first to complain was the little girl in the Datsun, and the soldier and I left our cars to go with her father to get water. In front of the Simca, I found a Toyota occupied by an older woman with nervous eyes. No, she didn't have any water, but she could give me some candy for the little girl. The couple in the ID consulted each other briefly before the old woman pulled a small can of fruit juice out of her bag. I expressed my gratitude and asked if they were hungry, or if I could be of any service; the old man shook his head, but the old lady seemed to accept my offer silently. Later, the girl from the Dauphine and I explored the rows on the left, without going too far; we came back with a few pastries and gave them to the old lady in the ID, just in time to run back to our own cars under a shower of horn blasts.

The boys in the Simca pulled out inflatable beds and lay down by their car; I lowered the back of the front seat and offered the cushions to the nuns, who refused them. Before lying down for a while, I thought of the girl in the Dauphine, who was still at the wheel. Pretending it didn't make any difference, I offered to switch cars with her until dawn, but she refused, claiming that she could sleep in any position. Night would never come; the sun's vibrations on the highway and cars pushed vertigo to the edge of nausea.

Something would have to be done in the morning to get more provisions and water. The soldier went to get the leaders of the neighboring groups, who were not sleeping, either, and they discussed the problem quietly so as not to wake up the women. The leaders had spoken with the leaders of faraway groups, in a radius of about eighty or a hundred cars, and they were sure the situation was analogous everywhere. The farmer knew the region well and proposed that two or three men from each group go out at dawn to buy provisions from the neighboring farms, while I appointed drivers for the cars left unattended during the expedition. There was a coffee-and-doughnuts man threading his way through the traffic even now, but coffee was beyond my means.

Nobody kept track anymore of how much they had moved that day; the girl in the Dauphine thought that it was between eighty and two hundred yards; I was not as optimistic. In fact I couldn't remember seeing a car move recently. I never even saw a car move, just heard them. That night I'd dreamed another start-up, or perhaps it was real, a far-off flare that died before I'd even ground the sleep out of my eyes, though in the rustle of my waking thoughts it was a perfect thing, coordinated, a dance of cars shifting through the free-flowing streets. Perhaps the start-up was only a panic begun by someone warming their motor, reviving their battery. What woke me in the morning was the family up ahead cooking breakfast. They had a stove on the roof of their car and the dad was grilling something. The old lady in the Impala had given up, spent most days dozing in the backseat. Her nephew from a few blocks away came over and tinkered with her engine now and again, but it wasn't helping. It just meant the nephew was at his wheel for the start-up, another dead spot, another reason not to bother waiting to move. "Not Responsible! Park and lock it!" the loudspeakers at the tops of the poles in the vast asphalt field shouted, over and over.

Suddenly I felt gripped by a gust of enthusiasm: It was wonderful to know that freedom exists and at the same time to feel oneself surrounded and protected by a blockade of solid and impenetrable bodies, and to have no concern beyond raising the left foot from the clutch, pressing the right foot on the accelerator for an instant and immediately lowering it again on the brake, actions which above all are not decided by us but dictated by the traffic. Reality, ugly or beautiful as it may be, was something I could not change. At that moment, something unbelievable was happening five hundred, three hundred, two hundred and fifty yards away. There was a start-up, a fever of distant engines and horns honking as others signaled their excitement—a chance to move! The boy was pointing ahead and endlessly repeating the news as if to convince himself that what he was seeing was true. The elated lookout had the impression that the horizon had changed. Then we heard the rumble, as if a heavy but migratory wave were awakening from a long slumber and testing its strength.

In the morning we moved a little, enough to give hope that by afternoon the route to New York would open up. You could feel the line of cars was moving, even if only a little, even if you had to start and then slam on the breaks and never leave first gear; the dejection of again going from first to neutral, brake, hand brake, stop, and the same thing time and time again. By night, speeding up, the lanes could no longer stay parallel. From time to time, horns blew, speedometer needles climbed more and more, some lanes were going at forty-five miles an hour, others at forty, some at thirty-five, a mad race in the night among unknown cars, where no one knew anything about the others, where everyone looked straight ahead, only ahead.

We had been cruising along pretty well at twilight, my father concentrating on getting in another fifty miles before dark, when they were cut off by the big two-toned Mercury and my father had to swerve four lanes over into the far right. My parents later decided that the near-accident was the cause of my premature birth. They even managed to laugh at the incident in retrospect, but I always suspected my father pined after those lost fifty miles. In return he'd gotten a son.

When I was six I got to sit on my father's lap, hold the wheel in my hands, and "drive the car." With what great chasms of anticipation and awe did I look forward to those moments! My mother would protest feebly that I was too young. I would clamber into Dad's lap and grab the wheel. How warm it felt, how large, and how far apart I had to put my hands! The indentations on the back were too wide for my fingers, so that two of mine fit into the space meant for one adult's. My father operated the pedals and gearshift, and most of the time he kept his left hand on the wheel, too—but then he would slowly take it away and I'd be steering all by myself. My heart had beaten fast. At those moments the car had seemed so large. The promise and threat of its speed had been almost overwhelming. I knew that by a turn of the wheel I could be in the high-speed lane; even more amazingly, that I held in my hands the potential to steer us off the road, into the gully and death.

When I was seven there was a song on the radio that my mother sang to me, "We all drive on." That was my song. I sang it back to her, and my father laughed and sang it too, badly, voice hoarse and off-key, not like my mother, whose voice was sweet. "We all drive on," we sang together.

> You and me and everyone
> Never ending, just begun
> Driving, driving on.

These days I have stopped paying attention to the cars going in my direction and I keep looking at those coming toward me which for me consist only in a double star of headlights that dilates until it sweeps the darkness from my field of vision then suddenly disappears behind me, dragging a kind of underwater luminescence after it. How, I began to wonder after a few lifetimes of this constant circling, traveling from country to country, never stopping except to sleep briefly in the car before going on again, my mind increasingly distracted, nerves increasingly unstrung, how can one ever be certain of anything? Once you start driving, how can you ever stop? A perverse idea hit me: Maybe it was only the pressure of our dead traditions that kept people glued to their westward course. Suddenly twelve lanes, which had seemed a whole world to me all my life, shrank to the merest thread. Who could say what Eastbound might be? Who could predict how much better men had done for themselves there? Maybe it was the Eastbounders who had built the roads, who had created the defenses and myths that kept us all penned in filthy Nashes, rolling west. What if I crashed across the twelve lanes of Westbound to the Median, the beginning of no-man's-land? Beyond that, where those distant lights swept by in their retrograde motion—what?

I am always moving. I am forever transporting myself somewhere else. I am never exactly where I am. Tonight, for instance, we are traveling one road but also many, as if we cannot take a single step without discovering five of our own footprints already ahead of us. Now we are traveling as if inside a clock the shape of a bullet, seated as if stationary among tight springs. And we have a full tank of fuel, and tires hardly a month old.

Every chance that I take, I take it on the road. Do not ask me to slow down. Hands off the wheel. It is too late. After all, at 149 kilometers per hour on a country road in the darkest quarter of the night, surely it is obvious that your slightest effort to wrench away the wheel will pitch us into the toneless world of highway tragedy even more quickly than I have planned. And you will not believe it, but we are still accelerating.

At least you are in the hands of an expert driver.

—Bowie, Hawkes, Evenson, Calvino, Kessel, Finney, Cortázar, Shiner, Ballard, Lethem

—*Conjunctions*, 2007

Against "Pop" Culture

In the termite phase of my career the term "pop culture" made sense to me. It seemed an approximate cover for loose bushels of enthusiasms: rock and roll, movies, comics, science fiction, and crime writing. Once I got lashed to the mast of my private canon, the word "pop" looked squishier and squishier to me, and lately I seem to want to blow it up whenever it's offered to me.

Pop music or pop art: fair enough. These seemed specific enough to matter. But "pop culture" seemed like a password to a clubhouse (for those who identified) and a term of quarantine (for those championing what they believed remained outside—or above—the radioactive area). The snobbish grudge against pop culture was that those who cared for it cared for all of it equally, and the problem was that this grudge was too often justified in the values-suspended vale of fandom. Having admitted to seeing *Star Wars* too many times as a thirteen-year-old, should I have to subsequently pretend I thought the movie was much good, once a decade of Kurosawa, Hawks, Kubrick, and Lang had straightened out my thinking? Couldn't I talk about comics as an intoxicant while expressing exhaustion at the measly narrative or visual chops in the '70s comics that had intoxicated me?

Well, I could try, but I wouldn't necessarily be heard. The superb critic John Leonard (as much a personal hero of my teenage years as Leonard Nimoy), acting precisely in the role of the notorious "gray eminence" from David Foster Wallace's "E Unibus Pluram" essay, spanked my cumulative life's work in the *New York Review of Books* for being uncritically pegged on iconography he found wearisome. The same month another man named John Leonard devoted his television column in *New York* magazine to defending the '70s television program *Kojak* against the insult of an inferior remake. Except it was the same John Leonard. *My Fetishes, Okay, Yours, Not So Okay.*

Another lie "pop culture" embeds: pop-as-in POPular. I usually preferred Unpop: comics canceled for lack of readers, bands sans career, paperback-original novelists who'd filled word counts behind interchangeable covers. I began to resent on the behalf of these losers (in whose company I wishfully numbered myself) the canard that they were tainted by commerce. The science-fiction writers I knew functioned like poets, mining for tribal rewards, names unknown elsewhere, and no thought of quitting their day jobs—yet you'd still hear literary novelists slight "commercial writing." At least poets (and literary novelists) could chase tenure. Anyway, the creators I adored tended to want to claw their way out, whether they succeeded in their lifetimes like Chandler and Ballard or flopped like Highsmith and Dick. I was a tormented snob dressed in PopCult garb because it made the nearest-to-hand defense of what I loved, but it wasn't *my* defense, and vast continents of category fiction and television didn't stir me at all. I felt dubious from all sides, in a Jews for Jesus or Log Cabin Republican kind of way. Even in the Radisson bar no one was certain where I stood, while out in the main convention hall the pop-culture revelers guiltlessly browsed Telly Savalas figurines. In this jumbled zone, the line "pop culture" drew wasn't worth the time spent erasing it.

Anyway, wasn't the novel itself once upon a time a suspiciously "pop" form? I liked "vernacular culture" better, if only because it wasn't automatic—it raised questions, instead of shutting them down. Just so long as you noticed that vernaculars (film, jazz, and the novel) are routinely shanghaied for ivory towers. Within a year of my discovering Philip K. Dick, his "pulp" context evaporated, overwritten by native kinship with Franz Kafka, Talking Heads, and Giorgio de Chirico—at least in the fantasia of my curiosity. Was this really an interest in "pop"? Couldn't we just say *culture*?

Pynchon V. Pym/The Fallacy of Lateral Influence/
My Hideous Formality

Writers' memoirs are supposed to wear you out with: *And Then I Wrote.*
I wanted to wear you down with: *And Then I Read.* Certain names,
though, seemed impossible to get into the conversation—was I embarrassed to say I'd rather be stuck on a desert island with the collected
works of Barbara Pym than those of Thomas Pynchon? (And was I
totally crazy to suspect Pynchon would say the same?) Or was it that
when I pointed to certain of my enthusiasms tape recorders broke
down out of boredom? Anthony Burgess, Anthony Powell, Iris Murdoch, Penelope Fitzgerald, J. B. Priestley, Anita Brookner, Elizabeth
Bowen, L. P. Hartley, George Gissing, Muriel Spark—for whatever
reason, I'd located a century of not-exactly-high-modernist U.K. fiction that I couldn't quit reading, and that formed my sense of what
novels should feel like when I set out to write them. I felt fashionable
being asked about Pynchon and DeLillo, and was awed enough when
I read them to gladly flatter myself claiming them as totems, but really
had already gleaned what I'd need of political paranoia from Graham
Greene (as well as from Iron Curtain dystopias by Orwell, Lem, the
brothers Strugatsky), and it was Greene's sense of form, of how a novel
was proportioned and how to present a character, that seeped into my
writing muscles. I first thought I never wanted to write a long novel
at all; when I changed my mind, I modeled on none of the modernist or postmodernist versions of amplitude, but on *Great Expectations*
and *Another Country.* I'd grooved to the postures of the Beats—what
bookish-hippieish kid of my generation wouldn't have?—but was
seduced, embarrassingly enough, much more by the writing of the
Angry Young Men. I still prefer Kingsley to Martin, and, if I live awhile,
stand a chance to be the last human to know the difference between
John Wain and John Braine.

My writing isn't experimental. When I've nodded to the repertoire
of avant-garde effects, I took it for granted that the experiments in
question were conducted by others, in the past. Now they're part of
the palette. A literary critic who puts the word "experimental" within
a mile of my stuff is either in bad faith or ill-informed about a century
including Oulipo, Language poetry, and, well, surrealism. Even lamer,
the Fallacy of Contemporary Influence, in which generations of writ-

ers work miraculously in concert. It shouldn't be too hard to figure out that Michael Chabon and I really weren't formative influences on each other. It's math, literally. Look for common denominators instead.

Likely every writer with the luck of being reviewed or interviewed undergoes a similar time-lost sensation, of being made by stuff that's no longer fashionable or even legible by the time their own work emerges. Mine was aggravated by the used-bookstore lag I've described elsewhere, and by what may have been a compensatory crush on mandarin, rather than outlaw, dialects. I sometimes think that Raymond Chandler made so much sense to me for the English boarding-school diction underneath the hard-boiled slang. No wonder that when I first tried, my criticism sounded like ersatz G. K. Chesterton. Much as I exalted Seymour Krim and Lester Bangs, I didn't have access to that informality—my defaults were highfalutin'. I sounded a lot less hip than writers decades older than I was. For instance, John Leonard.

Furniture

However appalling to consider, however tedious to enact, every novel requires furniture, whether it is to be named or unnamed, for the characters will be unable to remain in standing positions for the whole duration of the story. For that matter, when night falls—whether it is depicted or occurs between chapters—characters must be permitted to sleep in beds, to rinse their faces in sinks, to glance into mirrors, and so on. (It is widely believed that after Borges mirrors are forbidden as symbols in novels. However, it is cruel to deny the characters in a novel sight of their own faces; hence mirrors must be provided.) These rules attend no matter how tangential the novel's commitment to so-called "realism," no matter how avant-garde or capricious, no matter how revolutionary or bourgeois. Furniture may be explicit or implicit, visible or invisible; may bear the duty of conveying social and economic detail or be merely cursorily functional; may be stolen or purchased, borrowed, destroyed, replaced; may be sprinkled with crumbs of food or splashed with drink; may remain immaculate; may be transformed into artworks by aspiring bohemians; may be inherited by characters from uncles who die before the action of the novel begins; may reward careful inspection of the cushions and seams for loose change that has fallen from pockets; may be collapsible, portable; may even be dragged into the house from the beach where it properly belongs—but, in any event, it must absolutely exist. Anything less is cruelty.

—*The Novelist's Lexicon*, 2010

IV

FILM AND COMICS

I offer a merciful break, for a section or two, from self-advertisements, and from the claustrophobia of the novelist worrying about novels. Instead, other people's work, in other mediums. (A cynical fly on my studio wall buzzes: "But your brush still moves like a self-portraitist's. And you haven't put the mirror in the closet.")

First, three exultant riffs on the superhero-as-private-cargo cult. Which is, pretty obviously, how I prefer them.

Supermen!: An Introduction

So answer the question, even if only in the privacy of your mind: *Who was your first?* No, go further back even than your "official" first— recollect, if you can, not the first superhero with whom you consummated your curiosities but the first who gave you an inkling, the first to stir the curiosities you hadn't known you possessed, the first human outline in a cape flashing through your dawning gaze. Was it Adam West's Batman? A tattered five-year-old issue of *The Silver Surfer*, in some godlike prodigal older brother's dorm? A *Mad* magazine parody? *Underdog*? Some kid on your summer beach who clutched a towel to either side of his neck and leaped yelping off a dune and then looked at you like you were stupid for not getting the reference that burned so powerfully in *his* mind?

If you're approximately of my generation, things untangled themselves pretty quickly after that first disordered flush of infatuation. Superheroes, when you looked into the subject, appeared to spring from a few stolid figures and then to degenerate into a fractious and enthralling rabble. That's to say, I'm forty-five years old, and for me, Superman and Batman were pretty much like my parents. The anchor DC characters were heartening to have around, and good in a crunch, and sometimes, with their long histories, still surprising when you dug their old photographs out of the trunk—you hung out with people that looked like *that*? You dated *him*? But, increasingly, dull and taken for granted.

(Wonder Woman, Flash, and Aquaman were your aunts and uncles, familiar without being vivid.) Marvel's first-order characters were pretty established, too, but they still had the alluring scent of their fresh invention over them. They were something like cool kids who'd lived on your block in the decade before you started playing on the street and now were off at college or in the army, but their legend persisted. I'd put Thor and the other Avengers in that range, and the Fantastic Four, and Hulk, and Dr. Strange. Spider-Man was your older brother, of course— a great guy, an idol, but he didn't belong to you. What was wholly yours were your contemporaries, the oddities launching themselves before your eyes: Ghost Rider and Warlock and Luke Cage and Deadman and Ragman and Omega the Unknown, or nutty gangs like the Guardians of the Galaxy and the Defenders. These were as thrilling and unreliable as new friends in the schoolyard, and they lived in a world your parents, or Superman, would never even begin to understand. Beyond them lie even more antiheroic antiheroes, the Watchmen and Invisibles needed to gratify our recomplicating appetites.

It may be latent in human psychology to model the world on a fall from innocence, since we each go through one. I can't know because I speak as an American, and I do know that as a culture we're disastrously addicted to easy fantasies of a halcyon past, one always just fading from view, a land where things were more orderly and simple. (The model is doubly useful, open equally to our patronizing dismissals of the past and to our maudlin comparisons to a corrupted present.) For that reason, so many really smashing cultural investigations open up a window onto the truly disordered and frequently degenerate origins of things we've sentimentalized as pure and whole and pat.

A collection like *Supermen!* works like a reverse neutron bomb to assumptions about the birth of the superhero image: It tears down the orderly structures of theory and history and leaves the figures standing in full view, staring back at us in all their defiant disorienting particularity, their blazing strangeness. Like Luc Sante's *Low Life* or Michael Lesy's *Wisconsin Death Trip*, in place of generalizations about the vanished past it offers a revelatory nightmare of evidence that the place we came from is as deep and strange as any place we might have been ourselves, or might imagine we are on the way to going. Just as the drug slang and hippie argot or jive talk that struck me as so characteristic of the '70s where I encountered it so often turned out to be rooted in '20s and '30s jazz-hipster vernacular, just as Pre-Code Hollywood films can so often seem shockingly advanced, so, too, motifs and gestures we might believe typical of our own postmodern comics era are rooted in earlier explorations.

That's not to say this isn't primitive stuff (or that much of the pleasure it imparts isn't in its crudity and naïveté), only that the primitive stuff, when you turn your eyes to it, is so rich and singular, so jam-packed with curdled or mangled sophistications borrowed from other mediums and forms, that it verges on precognitive sight in its total blindness. And, that the primitive stuff can make you consider how primitive the sophisticated stuff of the present might be, too, in ways we can barely know. Beyond that, my own generalizations turn useless: One turns to the catalog of marvels within: the oblique id on display in the tendency of these artists to instinctively side with their sneering, cackling villains, so much more like cartoonists than the heroes, thus displaying a howling self-loathing—the Flame, being flogged in silhouette, and his seeming readiness to undress in the long panel in which he contemplates his seductive rescuer ("Only one thing can stop them," she teases him: "Fire!"); the Basil Wolverton science-fiction comics, each panel like some uncanny rebus, all surfaces stirring from beneath with some incompletely disclosed or acknowledged emotional disquiet, a barely sublimated mystical Freudian dream; Sub-Zero's absurd masochistic fracas with Professor X, who in his lumpen brown armor comes as near as any comics villain ever did to embodying SHITMAN (Sub-Zero even punishes him with a shower at the finish, adding, "make it hot!"); the insane verbal and visual poetry of Fletcher Hanks, who can smash your mind merely with the force of his unexpected hyphenization ("IF I CAN DOMINATE THOSE VULTURES UP THERE, I'LL BE ABLE TO CON-QUER THE EARTH!"); Rex Dexter's rocket ships and robots plainly cribbed from the pulp-science-fiction magazine covers of Virgil Finlay and Frank R. Paul; Jack Cole's hysterical and frenzied battle between the intrepid proto–Plastic Man Daredevil and the towering racist monstrosity the Claw. To give yourself to the pages in which these supermen appear is to helplessly rediscover the magnetic force of a totally opaque and infinitely awkward and versatile iconography, to recover the seed of mystery at the heart of superhero love to begin with—like learning a foreign language that turns out to be the only tongue you've ever spoken.

—book introduction, 2009

Top-Five Depressed Superheroes

1. Black Bolt. Black Bolt isn't allowed to speak because his voice is so horribly destructive that it might demolish the world. His wings resemble accordions, the most harmless and charming of instruments (apart from the kazoo), mocking the cataclysmic potential of his speaking voice. He never learned sign language, and it can be infuriating waiting for him to scribble a note, or while he attempts to indicate his thoughts with a scowl or pout. In restaurants it takes Black Bolt hours to decide on the simplest order. Ostensibly many other superheroes look up to him for leadership, but if you really pay any attention to his band of followers, you perceive immediately that they are all freaks, with lousy powers. His dog is ugly.

2. The Vision. The Vision has red skin and a synthetic body which oscillates from ethereal to super-dense. Neither state, however, serves as a satisfying expression of the feelings inside him. The Vision is obsessed with his traumatic past: An evil android created him for dark purposes. This sort of hurt can be difficult to get over, and most other superheroes have always steered a respectful berth around the Vision. In 1973 the Vision quite unexpectedly got married, to another superhero, the Scarlet Witch. They were divorced in 1997. In her memoir, published last year, the Scarlet Witch revealed that a substitute android had been created to fulfill a majority of the Vision's requests for public appear-

ances, and claimed that toward the end of the marriage she had found it difficult to tell the two apart. The Scarlet Witch has recently been linked in British tabloids with Liam Gallagher of Oasis.

3. Deadman. Deadman's problem is worn on the sleeve of his name: He's dead. He handles it pretty gracefully, having been a circus acrobat in his former life. Deadman rarely bothers to dress as a civilian, since his secret identity is a corpse. His skin is red. It probably ought to be green, but the Spectre's skin is green. This is only one of several ways in which the Spectre appears to occupy turf which probably ought to have been Deadman's. In earlier days Deadman regarded himself as the Spectre's protégé. However, the Spectre never proposed Deadman for membership in the Justice League of America. Deadman doesn't know how to raise the subject with the Spectre, so he never calls him anymore.

Deadman has a nagging feeling that in his trench coat he resembles a flasher. At least this much is true: He feels naked without it.

4. Ragman. Ragman was given his powers by the electrocution of five failed Jewish immigrants who had been sitting in an alley complaining about their failed businesses—a knife sharpener, a pawnbroker, a hat blocker, a mohel, and a tenement owner who was ruined when the *Village Voice* listed him as one of the city's Top Ten Slumlords in 1976. All the strength of the five men flowed into the body of a homeless man picking through a garbage can nearby, who became Ragman. Ragman is the poverty superhero, unable to afford a costume other than a big pile of rags. He never fights villains who can afford costumes. Instead he rescues starving kittens and breaks up three-card monte games. Ragman keeps himself in White Castle hamburgers by buying cartons of cigarettes and selling singles for a nickel apiece. During the Giuliani mayoralty Ragman was discreetly paid off to move to Baltimore, where he remains.

5. Omega the Unknown. Like Black Bolt, he never spoke. Energy beams came out of his hands, not always at his command. He might be considered Superman's depressed cousin, since he'd come from a

destroyed planet. Unlike Superboy, Supergirl, or Superdog, Superman has never acknowledged Omega. Omega's priorities were very unclear, and so he had the power to depress others, as well as himself. Omega's comic book was so punishingly dull that Marvel began to put the Hulk and Spiderman on the cover, and once, in a measure of striking desperation, Scrooge McDuck made a guest appearance. After ten issues the title was canceled anyway. After cancellation, Marvel was contacted by attorneys from Omega's home planet, which turned out not to be destroyed at all. This resulted in the first recall of the entire run of a published comic book in the industry's history. Until a successful appeal of the court's order in 1996, Marvel was still required to refund the full cover price of any issue of Omega the Unknown returned by a consumer, as well as the cost of return postage.

Shout, 2002

I got this larkish thing, based on painter Scott Alden's imaginary super-hero, into Playboy. *This was a secret victory, since I'd had several stories rejected on the basis that "Hef has a policy against any mention of mas-turbation." I suppose they figured he wouldn't know what* le petit mort *meant.*

The Epiphany

The Epiphany, 2009, Scott Alden

The Epiphany, Earth's subtlest, secretest, most selfless superhero, may perish at any instant. That every waking second is a matter of life and death is, for *The Epiphany*, a way of life, mortality his middle name. In fact, he's roused himself from ordinary sleep to find he's been strapped to *The Chair of Death* by his nemesis, the snide, jaded, and callous French Supervillain, *Le Petit Mort!*

Yet, as always seems to be the case, there is plenty of time, while secured to *The Chair of Death*, for *The Epiphany*'s life to flash before his eyes. For *The Epiphany*, this happens in reverse:

His "golden" years, semiretirement, laurel-resting, award-accepting, fan-mail answering, reenactments of his greatest adventures in television docudramas, clasped to the First Lady's bosom during visits to the White House of a president whose policies he finds bankrupt and manner he regards as repugnant, always feeling the charlatan, the ersatz-hero, dolled up in his *Epiphany* suit yet not actually detecting any throb of his powers, forever playing the part of himself, chasing ghosts of defeated enemies he now misses as if they were friends, though god knows he hated them heartily enough at the time.

Those years of meandering exile in the transparent invisible timeless extra-dimensional *Precinct of Snoredom*, in the hapless company of *The Boneless Men*, from where it seemed he'd never return.

His triumphant rescue of *The Polymorphs* from their captivity in the nefarious tendrils of *Stockholm Syndrome* and *Capitulator*, really the last fine moment he could call his own.

That momentous final battle with his mocking midcareer nemesis *Déjà Vu*, in *The Forest of Trees Falling*, which no one actually ever heard about but *The Epiphany* vows he will never permit himself to forget.

Those long disillusioned years attempting to hold together a Supergroup with his fellow heroes *Eureka!*, *Tour de Force*, and *Non Sequitur*, in order to do mortal combat with the repulsive and unsettling group of Supervillains *Le Petit Mort* had for a time assembled around him in the cause of World Conquest—*Freudian Slip*, *Wandering Eye*, and *Senior Moment*—and the terrible lonely realization that he and the others could never hope to coordinate their schedules, that like him they mostly failed to control or even predict the marvelous onset of their powers—that sudden eclipsing of their civilian identities by their heroic ones—and therefore that the life of *The Epiphany* was to be a solitary and lonely one, at last and forever, and that his covert feelings of attraction to *Non Sequitur* could never hope to find an appropriate moment to be confessed.

His first shocking encounters with *Le Petit Mort*, who presented himself to *The Epiphany* as a boon companion, a long-lost brother—only to discover that time spent in *Le Petit Mort*'s company gave way to staggering sensations of emptiness, self-loathing, and doubt, days when he couldn't even crawl from beneath the bedcovers let alone fumble his way to the chest of drawers where his costumes lay folded or balled, waiting for him to resume his Heroism, to reassert himself, where they indeed lay in drawers smelling of mustiness and mothballs, probably he should take them all to the Chinese Laundromat and have them fumigated, or then again possibly instead build a bonfire in his backyard and quietly incinerate the costumes and scatter the ashes, his whole superheroic career a momentary whim taken seriously for far too long—but no! The infernal and insidious *Le Petit Mort* had snuck up on him again!

And above all, his Origin Story, still an artifact of wonder and mystery even to himself. Other superheroes find their points of origin in outward action and reaction, colorful tales of being irradiated in space or bitten by an animal or experimented upon by some government or villain, bright anecdotes easily distilled into legend and swapped around as keepsakes: Superheroes aren't born, they're made! Not so for *The Epiphany*. He, apparently, *was* born, though unknown to himself, mistaking his life for ordinary until that moment in late adolescence when, awake at night in bed watching headlights flicker long across the ceiling plaster, his parents having quit murmuring through the wall beside him, alone awake in that ordinary house in the ordinary suburbs in which he'd to this point taken himself to be an ordinary child within a perfectly ordinary family, he'd with a sensation of ineffable unquantifiable yet unmistakable intensity *discovered himself*, hidden up to that point in plain sight. Felt the powers in him all at once go from inchoate to manifest, with a thrill of self-understanding as complete and all-encompassing as it was quick to shudder from him and vanish: These were the very first moments of the existence of *The Epiphany*, facing no villain yet apart from doubt and fear and time itself hurtling so precipitously into the future. Tasting that which would bring him so much joy and sorrow through his lifetime, the ineluctable inception and quick termination of his recurring Interludes of Power. And it was this that he most feared his enemies discovering: It was only during the Interludes that *The Epiphany* was any kind of superhero at all. In the long stretches between he was as vulnerable as any hostage or bystander, as some extra face tucked into a crowded comic-book panel pointing to the skies and crying for help from some costumed Person of Wonder.

It is at this exact instant of self-recollection that *The Epiphany* knows that he has fallen again into the oldest and simplest trap of all; that the life flashing before his eyes is a premonition of the future, not a vision of the past; that *The Chair of Death* is only the chair in his breakfast nook, where he sits at the start of each day; that he has survived another brush with *Le Petit Mort* and stands on the verge of his whole life, again or for the first time, impossible to say which. For *The Epiphany* the beginning is always also the end, every villain ahead of and behind him at once, the day starting anew. This is precisely the nature of his powers: life always flashing before him, life always waiting for him to resume in its interrupted course. He has only to get out of his chair. In fact, *The Epiphany* is already wearing his costume, rather than his civilian clothes (not that anyone besides *The Epiphany* would notice the difference between the two, his costume is so subtle, so slight). He must have put it on without thinking, when he first got out of bed.

—*Playboy*, 2009

*Right around when I began regularly boasting of my interest in them,
superheroes took over the world. These weren't my grubby, self-loathing,
thwarted friends, though. They were full of sparkly vicarious juice, and
they packed theaters. I weighed in twice: at the start, when I could still be
a little proud of* Spider-Man's *ascension, and seven years later, when* The
Dark Knight *struck me as the wretched emblem of a bankrupt civilization.
Maybe I was just having a bad September. In the years between, though,
I'd quit even trying to explain what you see me intuit in "Izations": that
not only are superhero movies no genre at all, not, at least, in the sense
that a devotee of Westerns, screwball, or film noir might find such definitions splendid, but that the mysterious "reading protocols"—the panels
and gutters, the disjunctive gaps and leaps and silences, the shifts from
verbal to visual, the static assertion of motion—that made comics a real
medium were instantly and uncannily destroyed by adaptation to film.
What's left doesn't strike me as much.*

Izations

An overnight success in the making for nearly forty years, *Spider-Man*
had been in the making in the mind of the child seated behind me
(at an eleven o'clock show at a multiplex in Brooklyn on May 3, the
earliest possible viewing as a member of the general public) for several
months before the film's opening, at least. Perhaps six years old, the
child's murmured comments showed a burnished precognition of the
film's various plot points, key character arcs, and, at least once, with a
precise line of dialogue. I guess these had been gleaned and rehearsed
from advertising sources, but also from some highly accurate comic-
book- or picture-book-ization of the movie—an advertising source in
an only slightly subtler sense. *"It's always like that for him,"* the child
mused when, in the film's opening sequence, Peter Parker, Spider-

Man's "real" teenage self, missed the bus for school. In that one remark the child encapsulated instantly what the director and producers had gotten so right in casting Tobey Maguire as the misfit character, and in their overall gentle, persistent faithfulness to the homely tone of the '60s Spider-Man comics. "I can't wait until Aunt May says, 'You're not Superman, you know,'" the child stage-whispered a bit later (Aunt May being the parentless Peter Parker's sweetly feeble guardian, who speaks this admonitory line in ignorance of Parker's superheroic secret), and again it was evident how deeply programmed the "Marvel Style" had been into the advertising campaign.

I couldn't begrudge this flow of ingenuous utterances, for the child seated behind me was one of the silentest in a very boisterous room. The audience alternated compulsive chatter with breathless silence, and with three or four midfilm bouts of spontaneous, delighted applause. Myself, I shed an awkward tear at several points, mourning my own lost innocence as glimpsed through the double lens of the film and the crowd's response to it, and overwhelmed by the simple power of an overwhelming collective experience you've anticipated for decades, as when one's mostly losing local sports team nails a championship. I was completely beguiled from my cynicism. You may now safely consider me to have overrated the movie.

But spontaneous applause by an auditorium full of children is not a thing to be cynical about—especially, I must risk saying, when that audience is eighty percent inner-city blacks, as this one was. That they knew that Spider-Man was *for them*—the film was free of black faces—probably speaks to many things. At least one of these is a key element of Spider-Man's myth: No matter how blandly central and popular this character becomes, and no matter how whitewashed of ethnicity the name "Parker" has always been, Parker-Spider-Man is always an "other." Spider-Man's official creator (more on authorship controversies below) Stan Lee (typically, for his generation of showmen, a de-Judaized "Stanley Lieber") has boasted, "Spider-Man's costume covers every inch of his body . . . any reader, of any race, in any part of the world, can imagine himself under that costume . . ." But, quite satisfyingly, Parker doesn't don that costume until after sixty-five minutes of the film's running time (my own informal measure, by wristwatch). His white skin is thoroughly on view. No, it's the preexisting backdrop of Superman's and Batman's deep whiteness which establishes Spider-Man's metaphoric blackness. Clark Kent and Bruce Wayne live in palaces of privilege and operate from fantasy cities, Gotham and Metropolis, while working-class Spider-Man is a bridge-and-tunnel person, from Queens, in the real New York. Spider-Man's good intentions get misrepresented in the media, and he gnaws over this injustice, wondering why he ought to help anyone when he's never been given a hand up himself. Spider-Man is always short of a buck, Spider-Man don't get no respect, etcetera. ("*It's always like that for him.*") Furthermore, Spider-Man, as a dashiki-wearing instructor at a Brooklyn day-care center once explained to me and a group of other (multihued) children, wasn't actually invented by white people at all, but in fact derived from an African legend of a spider-demon of the jungle, a trickster figure. *Everyone* knew this, it was as basic as Elvis Presley's music having originated in black sources. I listened, that day, and believed. It may have been nonsense, or only coincidence, but the fact that it needed to be claimed was poignant. It is also perhaps instructive in understanding why, for such an apparently simple and popular character, Spider-Man ("the original wall-crawling, web-slinging white nigger," Jeff Winbush proclaimed in the *Comics Journal* in 1995) took so long to be given a flattened and universalized Hollywood rendering. Or why, now that he *has* been given that treatment, so many forty- or thirtysomething men of a certain type (I mean, like *myself*) are bearing down with such emotional intensity on the results. Like Colin Wilson's *Outsider* or A. E. van Vogt's *Slan*, Spider-Man was a wunderkind-outcast identification available to anyone who'd mixed teenage grandiosity with even the mildest persecution complex, let alone real persecution. Matt Groening once proposed a magazine called "Sullen Teen." Long before trench-coat mafia, *The Amazing Spider-Man* was that magazine.

Spider-Man was also the first superhero whose civilian identity would be a likely reader of comic books. The truth, though, is that when, at age twelve, we began seriously reading them (Marvel's were the only good ones, unmistakably), my friend Karl and I disliked and distrusted the omnipresent Spider-Man. This was in 1976, three or four years since the lecture from the day-care instructor, and Spider-Man, African trickster or not, was resting on his laurels. Even in the '60s, *The Amazing Spider-Man* wasn't the most interesting of the Marvel titles (that would have been *The Fantastic Four*), just the most archetypally non-archetypal, and the one with which the company as a whole was most identified. By the mid-'70s Spider-Man's great plotlines—the Death of Gwen Stacy (Peter Parker's ethereal blond girlfriend, who would haunt him like Kim Novak in *Vertigo*); the Unmasking of Green Goblins #1, #2, and #3 (a shock each time); the Marriage of Aunt May to Doctor Octopus (an odious villain)—were well behind him. And Peter Parker had settled for what seemed to us a second-best girlfriend, the dark-haired "girl next door," Mary Jane Watson, a mere glass of beer—the champagne of Gwen Stacy was not for the likes of us. So Karl and I resented Spider-Man like we resented the Beatles, for being such lavish evidence we'd been born too late. The '70s adventures were full of clues to the great history we'd missed. Worse, the character had developed an irritating tendency to invade other stories—Marvel had discovered that Spider-Man's presence on a front cover jacked up sales, so he'd guest-star in weaker-selling books.

Spider-Man had become a logo, in other words, like Superman before him. Karl and I were more interested in the mysterious depth of newer and less popular characters: the Vision, Black Bolt, Omega the Unknown, Warlock, Ghost Rider, Son of Satan, all of whom were brooding, tormented antiheroes, unattractive to young children. We'd caught the outsiderish, sulky Marvel scent, and wanted our own share. In these cases, it was precisely those humdrum guest appearances of the dull old web-slinger (or the Hulk, who served the same purpose) which provided the least interesting tales—and often signaled the final issue of a commercially foundering title. Ironically, in gravitating toward those Marvel characters who were not yet (nor would ever be) logos, Karl and I were recapitulating that rejection of icons in favor of darker, more amorphous figures which had been the essence of Spider-Man's earlier ascension over Superman and Batman. We were on a quest for Ever-More-Spidery-Man.

The prototype wouldn't leave us alone, however. This was mostly due to the relentless cheerleading of Stan Lee, in a venue called "Marvel Bullpen Bulletins": a page of Marvel gossip and advertising featured in every issue of every comic, written in a style which might be character-ized as high hipster—two parts Lord Buckley, one part Austin Pow-ers. Stan Lee was a writer gone Barnum, who'd abandoned new work in favor of rah-rah moguldom. He was Marvel's media liaison and their own biggest in-house fan, a schmoozer. Picture an Orson Welles who'd never bothered to direct films again after *The Lady from Shang-hai*, just bullshitted on talk shows, reliving his great moments. Like Welles's, Stan Lee's great moments were beset by authorship disputes. Lee's particular emphasis on Spider-Man as Marvel's signature creation may have had something to do with that character being the only one of the company's greatest and most popular early inventions—the Fantastic Four, the Hulk, Thor, Doctor Doom, and Silver Surfer—not largely attributable, according to almost every account, to Jack "King" Kirby. Kirby is the artist and auteur understood by cognoscenti to be the "real" creator: Keith to Stan Lee's Mick. Lee has been alleged to be a mere dialogue writer who filled in word balloons in otherwise finished pages, and to have made off like a bandit with all the official credit, the dough, and, final insult, Kirby's original artwork. Lee's "I just wanna be loved" persona has weathered decades of abuse on these grounds in fan magazines, on panels at conventions, and probably right this minute on the Internet. Kirby, by any measure a visionary, the greatest inventor in comics history, in fact subsequently showed himself to be rather icy and remote without Lee's goofy, humanizing touch, and a writer of execrable dialogue: Keith needed his Mick. But breakups are a tender subject.

Kirby didn't draw Spider-Man. The man who did is Steve Ditko, Marvel's great mystery man—a "reclusive, lifelong bachelor," according to a recent profile in the *L.A. Times*. He's also described as "heavily influenced by Ayn Rand's philosophy of Objectivism." I myself remember once finding an outré, off-brand comic, featuring a character called the Blue Beetle, which was drawn and written by Ditko: The story was a screed against modern art and beatnik nihilism, disguised as a beautifully illustrated superhero adventure. Ditko has been belatedly credited in the new film, a vindication he reportedly accepts grudgingly. He likely has as profound a creative claim on the early Spider-Man as Kirby had on the bulk of the Marvel characters, but "the J. D. Salinger of comics" has been no obstacle to Lee's attention-hogging claims of authorship in the thirty-five years since Ditko quit Marvel in a silent, Objectivist huff.

So the icon sank into our brains. As with the Beatles, bonding could occur in retrospect. We '70s kids listened to *Revolver* and *The White Album* and *Abbey Road* and fell in love, however sheepishly, with the great progression we'd just missed. Marvel reprinted their famous '60s plotlines in digests called *Marvel Tales* and *Marvel's Greatest Comics* and in a trade paperback called *Origins* (the cover of which showed Lee's hairy knuckles at a typewriter, while the best-known characters flew, fully costumed, from the platen), so we late-born could catch up. In 1980, at John Lennon's slaying, my entire high school was in mourn-

ing for "our hero"; similarly my old resentment of Spider-Man was sublimated beneath a surge of proprietary feeling when I first heard, maybe
two years ago, that "my Spidey" was finally getting his fifteen minutes.
In fact, I'd sentimentally rewritten my personal history, according to
the dictums of the "Bullpen Bulletin," so that until my research into
the movie disproved it, I could claim (in *Bookforum*, two years ago)
that "the first romantic loss for a lot of guys my age was Gwen Stacy's
death." This was a retrospective fiction, I now see. Gwen Stacy was dead
before I met her, which imparts a gnostic eeriness to our sundered love.

I've probably given full enough account of the auditorium of self
that was me, inside that larger auditorium of rooting children. Director
Sam Raimi was wise sticking to the 1963–64 version of the comic book,
rather than being tempted by the later recursions, and this Spider-Man
is fully naïve, fully Ditko. Each loss he suffers, each sacrifice he makes,
is his first. The key innovation, it turns out, is how *slightly* Marvel
darkened and sophisticated the superhero myths of an earlier era. In
his job as freelance newspaper photographer of Spider-Man's heroics,
Peter Parker parodies Clark Kent's special press access to the doings of
Superman, but with an emphasis on fetish and spectatorship—there's
something sexual in setting up remote cameras to document your
gymnastics. Slightly. There's also something adolescent-masturbatory
in Parker's closed-door explorations of his new web-goo-shooting
prowess—slightly. Raimi never allows any heavy symbolism or camp
opportunism to spoil the simpler pleasures. The emphasis is on a sweet
bungler's coping attempts to live up to great power, great responsibility.
The early comics, and this movie, are loaded with Dickensian family
drama—missing fathers, vulnerable fathers, fathers gone bad. You'd
better grow up quick, kid. The biggest deviation is that Mary Jane Watson is now the ur-girlfriend, with no sign of Gwen Stacy around. But
the halcyon past is not always what it is cracked up to be. My researches
unearthed this horrible fact—the Marvel scripters who followed Lee on
the job killed off Gwen Stacy because they found the character unwork-
ably dull, a cold fish. Red-haired Mary Jane was more approachable,
sexier, all along. If I'd known sooner I might have been spared some
pining.

Tobey Maguire brings to the film a tenderness and also a watchfulness not unlike that of Montgomery Clift in *Red River*. In that film
Clift seemed, in his hesitancy and alertness, to be simultaneously in

character and in a seat in the theater beside us, considering both the cattle drive and John Wayne as the great natural phenomena they were. Similarly, Maguire plays audience surrogate, regarding the Green Goblin and even Spider-Man with a degree of noncommittal fascination. His ability to endow lines like "Goblin, what have you done?" with introspective echoes carries the film to a deeper place in that effortless way of an actor, which no director or screenwriter can offer. A *slightly* deeper place. The most unlikely cheer from my crowd was at Spider-Man/Parker's (his mask is half off) long-delayed first kiss with Mary Jane. Maguire's vulnerability had persuaded them that he *really* might not get the girl, so it was a triumph. A slicker actor would have cued revulsion in children, but here the icky inevitability of movie clinches had been thwarted.

Less interesting: the villain's genesis; the villain's madness; the villain's cackling; his plans, explosions, momentary triumph, eventual defeat. The special effects are utter and seamless plastic, and go lengths to prove things we don't need or even want proven. As the critic A. O. Scott has written, the impulse to knit together improbable, break-neck, still-photographic comic-book panels into a flow of smoothly animated movement is a self-defeating one. The real evocation and mystery inherent in the comic form is found in the white lines of border between panels, where the imagination of the reader is energized and engaged. Comic books are all stills and jump cuts. I don't know whether this effect can ever be claimed for film, but I perversely hope not. I was happy that in this moment of digital apotheosis, with anything possible, what those kids and I wanted and got was a good movie kiss.

It all worked. Records were broken. Those are always counted in dollars, but I wonder: Did more human souls just see the same film in three days than ever before in history? I guess there's no way to measure because there's no way to correct for repeat viewers. Still, whatever exactly happened in America May 3–5, they'll want it to happen again. In the theater, preceding the movie, while I was still considering being annoyed by the garrulous child behind me, before I'd given in to the stream of commentary, we watched a trailer for the unfinished filmization of *The Incredible Hulk*. All they had yet was a short sequence showing the actor's transformation from normal man to gigantic green monster, his rapid destruction of a house, then a simple card which read "Hulk. Summer 2003." It was awesome. The parent of the child behind me snorted at seeing that the film was more than a year from release: "Summer 2003? Oh, please." It might be hard to be a parent these days. Remember, we were at the eleven o'clock Friday-morning showing. The child, though, was typically unguarded: "I think I'm a little scared of *that*." The parent replied sourly: "You'll have plenty of time to prepare yourself."

—*London Review of Books, 2002*

Everything Is Broken (Art of Darkness)

"Broken pipes, broken tools / People bending broken rules . . ." These words come from "Everything Is Broken," a 1989 Bob Dylan song. The lines happen to be set to a Ventures-style guitar riff familiar from the '60s *Batman* television show starring Adam West, my own personal ur-Batman, cheesy and harmless though he may be. By necessity I thought of Dylan's song when, last night, I marked a return to my own Gotham City—Brooklyn, domesticated and oversold as it may be—by perversely commemorating September 11 by finally seeing *The Dark Knight*, now nestling into place between *Titanic* and *Star Wars* as the second most popular film of all time. (We'll agree to set aside nonmonetary definitions of "popular.") This was after a long summer spent in the distant countryside, laboring in the salt mine of a novel in progress, far from multiplexes, and also beyond reach of a reliable wireless signal. That's to say I'd been deaf to tabloid and blog reality, had instead been gleaning the culture merely through the tinny earpiece of a daily paper (this one) that on this particular Maine peninsula is delivered by truck to local grocery stores, usually by eleven o'clock. Most days I remembered to pick up a copy.

When I parted ways with the wider data stream in early June, Bill Clinton was still a red-faced bully, "Palin" the name of my favorite member of the Monty Python ensemble, and *The Dark Knight* a would-be summer popcorn hit made awkward in advance by the tragic death of a young actor. I don't mean to play dumb: Before I switched off my sonar Heath Ledger's extraordinary physical projection into nihilistic madness as Batman's nemesis, the Joker, was already widely and disturbingly in evidence in the culture in the form of stills and You-Tube clips, a premonition of something—but of what? Three months later, *The Dark Knight* having been ratified as the movie we all desperately needed to see, we ought to understand.

Last night, coming home from the movies, I didn't. It couldn't have helped that I switched on MSNBC to find my nightly Alaskan Wildlife Atrocities coverage preempted by vintage 2001 news footage of the destruction of the World Trade Center, accompanied only by the original newscasters, caught revising their disbelief in real time. In my confusion I scurried for the shelter of Google. There I found affirmed what a certain yellow-shading-to-orange-alert panic I'd experienced in my multiplex seat had led me to fear, but I hadn't articulated for myself: *The Dark Knight*, with its taciturn and self-pitying vigilante, its scenes of rendition and torture, its elaborately leveraged choices between principles and human lives, might offer a defense of the present administration's cursory regard for human rights abroad and civil rights at home, in the cause of reply to attacks from an irrational and inhuman evil. Poor Batman, forced again and again to violate the ethics that define him, to destroy the world to save it.

A fellow novelist, Andrew Klavan, celebrated this interpretation in the *Wall Street Journal*: " . . . a paean of praise to the fortitude and moral courage that has been shown by George W. Bush in this time of terror . . ." Trace the Bat signal's outline with your finger and "it looks kind of like a 'W.' " Is it so?

In the words of critic Dave Kehr, "I'm not sure that it matters whether or not *The Dark Knight* espouses conservative values . . . it certainly expresses them . . . ideology creeps in on little cat feet, whether you want it to or not." I'd add that a popular myth or symbol as resilient, open-ended, and also somehow opaque as Batman has a tendency to collect and recapitulate meaning beyond a creator's accounting. Yet Klavan's confident partisan interpretation seemed to grant this film too little and too much at once. Perhaps I'm prone to bear down on *The Dark Knight* as the tea leaves in the dregs of a political summer's cup, but I couldn't shake the sense that a morbid incoherence was the movie's real "takeaway," chaotic form its ultimate content.

Everyone agrees that Ledger's Joker steals the show, but really, what's there to steal? The film was the Joker's to begin with. Scene after scene presents a sensual essay in taking good-guy torture and a crumbling social and economic infrastructure equally for granted. No one in this Gotham can remember a time before corruption, and the movie declines to hint at a way out, only noting that our hero's bitterness was predetermined by his failure—or was it the reverse?

Like the fogy I've become I felt brutalized as I watched, but after the tide of contradictions had receded I wasn't stirred to any feeling richer than an exhausted shrug, as when confronted by headlines reminding me that we no longer have a crane collapse or bank failure, we have the *latest* crane collapse, the *latest* bank failure. In its narrative gaps, its false depths leading nowhere in particular, its bogus grief over stakeless destruction and faked death, *The Dark Knight* echoes a civil discourse strained to helplessness by panic, overreaction, and cultivated grievance. This Batman wears his mask because he fears he's a fake—and the story of his inauthenticity, the possibility of his unmasking, is more enlivening than any hope he might deliver. The Joker, on the other hand, exhibits his real face, his only face, and his origins are irrelevant, his presence as much a given as the Second Law of Thermodynamics, or Fear Itself.

If like me you'd hoped, distantly, vaguely, probably idiotically, that the 2008 presidential contest might be a referendum on truths documented since the previous presidential election, guess again. That our invasion of Iraq was founded on opportunistic lies, that it was hungered for by its planners in advance of the enabling excuse of 9/11, is a well-delineated blot on American history. It is also one that, nonetheless, apparently cannot afford to be described within hearing of its irrational deniers (a majority of Republican voters still believe, or believe again, that Saddam Hussein was involved in the World Trade Center attack). Never mind that Barack Obama's having stood for this truth defined, once upon a time, his distance from his rivals for the Democratic nomination. He may have been free to do so only because he wasn't yet in national office. For those of us interested in a conversation about accountability it was always declared to be too soon—we remained unsure of the evidence, or too traumatized to risk fraying the national morale—until the moment when it was abruptly too late, when it became old news.

Yet I suspect it is still *the* news. While both teams are running on the premise that Washington Is Broken, I'm disinclined to disagree, only to add: Our good faith with ourselves is broken, too, a cost of silencing or at best mumbling the most crucial truths. Among these, preeminently, the fact that torture evaporates our every rational claim to justice and will likely be the signature national crime of our generation—a matter in which we are, by the very definition of democracy, complicit. (I wonder if some unconsciously hope that electing a man who was himself tortured will provide moral cover, just as the trauma of Batman losing his parents to violent crime forever renews his revenger's passport.) No wonder we crave an entertainment like *The Dark Knight*, where every topic we're unable to quit not-thinking about is whirled into a cognitively dissonant milkshake of rage, fear, and, finally, absolving confusion.

It may be possible to see the nightly news in a similar light, where any risk of uncovering the vulnerable yearnings, all the tenderness aroused by the seemingly needless death of a promising young actor or a brilliant colleague, all hope of a conversation between the paranoid Blues and the paranoid Reds, all that might bind us together is forever armored in a gleeful and cynical cartoon of spin and disinformation. Key words—*change*—are repeated until adapted out of meaning into self-canceling glyphs. Meanwhile, pigs break into the lipstick store, and we go hollering down the street after them, relieving ourselves of another hour or day or week of clear thought.

Beneath the sniping over symbols no more material to our daily selves than Danish cartoons to an Iranian's, I suppose any of us can think of a few things that lie in ruins: a corporate paradigm displaying no shred of responsibility to anyone but shareholders, yet seemingly impervious to question; a military leadership's implicit promise to its recruits and their families; a public commons commodified into channels that feed any given preacher's resentments to a self-selecting chorus. If *everything is broken* perhaps it is because for the moment we like it better that way. Unlike some others, I have no theory who Batman is—but the Joker is us.

—*The New York Times*, Op-Ed, 2008

Godfather IV

For my money, if there is to be a *Godfather IV* the series should aban-
don any notion of *sequel* or *prequel*, forsake any impulse toward *the
epic* or *the broad-canvas pageant of history.* Instead, the Godfather series
should plunge back into what we all secretly crave and fetishize: the
iconography of the original film, those sequences and set pieces which
have become, in thirty-seven short years, almost biblical in their mythological resonance and allegorical power. Depict scenes from Luca
Brasi's childhood, showing how he became the character doomed to
be garroted in an empty bar. Show us a Korean War scene—just how
did Michael earn his medals? Give us Fredo's life in Vegas. Film the
prehistory of John Marley's Hollywood studio head; show his acquisition of his prized racehorse; better yet, let us see the approach of the
Godfather's ninjalike emissaries from the horse's point of view. Please,
please let us know Sterling Hayden's corrupt Captain McCluskey in his
off-hours, meet his wife and kids, show him entering the restaurant
and using the very same toilet behind which is taped the pistol that will
murder him. The cannoli—when and by whom were they eaten? Who
baked the cannoli?

—*GQ*, 2008

Great Death Scene (*McCabe & Mrs. Miller*)

I'm walking down the street with a screenwriter friend when we duck into Video Free Brooklyn to rent Altman's *McCabe & Mrs. Miller*. "Great death scene!" my friend exclaims. I instantly agree, but it turns out we mean two different things. He's thinking of McCabe—Warren Beatty, that is—succumbing from his bullet wounds after going to ground in a snowstorm, then enveloped by swirling flakes and the elegiac tones of Leonard Cohen's "The Stranger Song." Yes, this is one of the Western's great death scenes. It completes one of the slowest and most heartrending descents in all cinema, the shattering of McCabe's dreams having come to stand for a farewell to both the Western tradition (which was practically always saying farewell from its beginning, anyway) and to the sublimely fragile idealisms of the glamorous hippies both Beatty and McCabe really were beneath gruff Western garb.

The death I had in mind comes in the middle of the film. Keith Carradine plays a gooberish cowboy who trots into town because he's heard of McCabe's fabulous whorehouse. An angel of innocent lust ("Who wants to be next?" he asks the prostitutes, and when one says, "Which one of us do you fancy?," he replies, "Aw hell, don't make no difference, I'm gonna have you all!"), the man-boy endears himself to all and then is gunned down, in an act of horrifically whimsical sadism, while trying to buy himself a pair of dry socks for the journey home. Killed on a wobbling rope bridge across a frozen river, the lanky Carradine plunges through the ice and drifts in place, while Altman's wide framing pitilessly stares, letting the viewer fill in every bit of the emotion.

The Western is a genre wealthy with death scenes, but the most characteristic are in close-up, and often quite talky, featuring last cigarettes and stoical words of forgiveness. I'm thinking of Charles Winninger in *Destry Rides Again*, Burt Lancaster in *Ulzana's Raid*, Robert Duvall in *Geronimo*, and above all, Joel McCrea in *Ride the High Country*. Altman handles his deaths differently. Nobody gets last words or smokes. The camera zooms in or out of wide shots emphasizing the victim's surrender to an indifferent natural environment, withholding any hope of an ascent into legend (these guys' last names aren't Holliday or James). *McCabe* is one of the most painterly films ever shot by an American director, and these deaths evoke Breughel's Icarus, plummeting mutely into a chilly sea. Any talk was gotten out of the way long before, practically before the film begins. (Which is good, given that you can only make out about a third of this film's dialogue, unless you hit Rewind a lot.) In a sense, my friend and I don't disagree even slightly: The entirety of *McCabe & Mrs. Miller* is a "great death scene."

—*The New York Times Magazine*, 2007

Kovacs's Gift

A warning: There's a mystery at the heart of this inquiry, one we won't really be able to penetrate here, instead only hope to define, the better to abide with it. The mystery I have in mind isn't what I like to call the Bob Hope/Lenny Bruce Perplex, though it does apply to Ernie Kovacs; i.e., why need we be given so many (predictable) life-decades of the one, such scant (mercurial) years of the other? Why couldn't a few years, *heck, even months*, have been shifted from one to the other? For me Kovacs goes with Nathanael West and Buddy Holly in the Greatest Potential Unrealized column. (Cars and airplanes have a lot to answer for.) But the Hope/Bruce thing is merely a fannish way of complaining about death, which isn't really a mystery at all, though our fear wants to call it one. Faced with someone as alive and yet as dead as Ernie Kovacs is (both more alive and more dead than ourselves, that is), we living are stuck with our fear.

Anyway, cataloging Potential Unrealized—a mug's game, in truth—shouldn't stand in the way of lavishing appreciation for the thing that *was* given, of scrupulously cherishing said gift, of raising its provider onto a pedestal commensurate with the pleasure and wonder we've drawn from said gift, and also of archiving the evidence left behind, securing it in libraries and museums, and in the annals of culture. Only in Kovacs's case we've failed utterly. How many recent geniuses—not arcane, hermetic geniuses ensconced in high modernist castle or tower,

I mean, but accessible, relevant, capricious, joyous, salt-of-the-earth, explosively generous, and even silly geniuses (are there any others who'd even rate all those adjectives besides Kovacs?)—how many are so totally erased from their right place in cultural memory? In Ernie Kovacs's case, literally erased. Taped over, for crissakes.

This goes beyond any artist's worst fears of being out of print, or of receding in mists of antiquity, or even of being a victim of the chemical time bomb of nitrate prints that have devoured century-old silent films; this is more recent and irresponsible and incredible even than that. *They taped over his work*, the fuckers. Here's Ernie Kovacs, the bridging figure, at the very least, between Groucho Marx and David Letterman; the immediate and proximate father, at the very least, of both *Monty Python's Flying Circus* and Nam June Paik; the uncle, at the very least, of *Laugh-In* and *The Tonight Show* and a thousand lesser television moments; the permissive next-door neighbor, at the very least, of Donald Barthelme and Frank Zappa. A man whose great work was accomplished in the '50s and '60s and whose widow and collaborator was alive until two years ago as of this writing is, rather than a household name, a rumor, a subliminal notion, if not strictly even a secret to which you and I have, to this point, alone been privy.

Eh? What's that I hear you say? *Who's Ernie Kovacs?*

Young person, I'm deeply disappointed in you. I thought we were together in this. And no, I'm not going to explain, let alone sell, Ernie Kovacs to you. No, with what time remains to me here I'll pretend I didn't even hear that terrible question you asked, and instead go on and degenerate into a personal accounting of a few of the peculiar things I love about Kovacs and how they came to me, and then I'll try to recollect my purpose in trying to define that mystery I mentioned to begin with.

1. Ernie Kovacs was, along with the Beatles and the Monkees, Alfred Hitchcock and Mel Brooks, Ray Bradbury and Isaac Asimov, one of the ten or so cultural things I most plainly recall my mother deliberately introducing to me. I can know, thanks to outside sources, the exact circumstances of her opportunity (in a world before the universal jukebox of the Internet): PBS, Channel Thirteen, which showed a sequence of the Kovacs "Specials" in 1977. She simply sat me down in front of our family's television (in which everything, up to and including *The Wizard of Oz*, was broadcast in the same black and white as the Kovacs

shows). She didn't need to do more than that. All of the Beatles and
Monkees, Brooks, Bradbury, Asimov, and Hitchcock were at that time
alive, so Kovacs was my introduction to dying too young. Since my
mother was about to do that herself, it's probably not surprising how
personal this feels to me.

2. The Nairobi Trio is (and I've conducted tests on my own children,
trust me) one of only two things in the entire universe with the power
to wildly delight any human being from age two to the most sophisticated (i.e., sullen, punk, tripping on drugs) teenager to adults of any age,
and not only do so on first contact but repeated to infinity. I'm certain
this effect would pertain across any imaginable cultural or linguistic
boundary, and I'd even be willing to bet that there are certain animal
species (guess) who'd likely be entertained by the trio. (The sole other
thing containing this vast power being a Buster Keaton gag in a short
called *The Scarecrow*, involving a dog chasing Keaton along the top
walls of a roofless structure. One of the last things Kovacs filmed was a
pilot for a television show called *Medicine Man*, featuring himself and
Buster Keaton. Buster Keaton, along with Jack Benny, Edward G. Robinson, Jimmy Stewart, and many others, attended Kovacs's funeral.)
The Nairobi Trio is three monkeys (who doesn't like monkeys?) playing instruments (who doesn't like monkeys playing instruments?) and
bonking one another on the head (who doesn't like monkeys playing instruments and bonking one another on the head?). But these
monkeys, really men in monkey suits (one long rumored to be Jack
Lemmon) and dressed in heavy overcoats, are also, in an uncanny conflation, wind-up figures in some infernal device. That's to say, at a level
we register semiconsciously, the Nairobi Trio are emblems of eternity,
doomed to their slow-burn enactment until the solar system implodes.

3. Poets, a fierce and suspicious lot, don't like being made fun of.
Yet every poet I know adores Percy Dovetonsils, Kovacs's affectionately
devastating charade of a cocktail-sipping, loopily lisping connoisseur
of doltish rhyme. One poet I know signs his correspondence Percy
Dovetonsils.

4. The offhand danger contained in Kovacs's work is that once his
sensibility has colonized a certain cultural matter it stands no chance
of ever being retrieved for serious purpose. I have had to take it on
faith my whole life that the song "Mack the Knife" conveys some sultry
essence of decadence or menace; for me, thanks to Kovacs's use of it as

complement to an endless series of sight gags (which are in turn exalted
into a weird aura of decadence or menace by the song), it is only like
having my arms held behind my back while I am tickled. *Swan Lake*
was always done in gorilla outfits, no? Who could ever read *Camille*
now without hearing a cough? When I first learned that an important
art-film cinematographer was named László Kovács, I had trouble
believing I wasn't being kidded, that László whoever-he-was hadn't
picked the surname sheerly as a joke.

5. Not unrelated, Ernie Kovacs wrote for *Mad* magazine. Of course
he did.

6. Ernie Kovacs wrote a novel, he claims, in thirteen days. The subject was the New York television rat race; he turned it in just before
moving to Los Angeles, and when his publisher asked when he'd do the
copyedits, he quipped, "On the first rainy day." In fact, it was a sudden
Los Angeles rain that likely caused Kovacs to crash his car the night he
died. Either that, or he was trying to light his cigar while driving in the
rain.

Enough of my morbid and sentimental list, which could go on forever. Here's the mystery I offered to frame: Putting aside how Kovacs
makes you laugh (and it should be said that much of his work is too
conceptual and deliberate and even awkward to be smoothly seductive
to the viewer's hilarity; it often presents itself as humorous while actually being only interesting and uncomfortably odd), his great claim, his
indisputable achievement, is as an excavator of a new medium's possibilities. Kovacs is to videotaped television what D. W. Griffith and
Orson Welles are to narrative in projected celluloid, what McCartney/
Lennon and George Martin are to eight-track tape-recording in pop
music, what Hank Shocklee is to digital sampling in hip-hop: one of
those artists whose personal expressivity takes the form of a series of
astonishing and playful demonstrations of what a medium's potential—and true nature—might be. If we take this as a given, and I
think it's impossible not to, on the evidence, then the mystery is how
an artist defined by his place within a medium rightly characterized
by Marshall McLuhan as "cool," and whose explorations seem in so
many ways to prove McLuhan exactly right, moving as they do in the
direction of postmodern fragmentation, of parody, of repetition, of
irony, of disruption of convention without convention's replacement
by new frameworks, instead by an increasingly rapid series of subse-

quent disruptions; if we further agree that most of Kovacs's avowed inheritors—from *Laugh-In* and Monty Python, to video art, to Carson and Letterman, and beyond—are unquestionably "cool" in temperature (elusive, ironical, uncommitted), the mystery is this: How is it that Kovacs, our human guide into this cool world, is himself such an almost unbearable figure of *warmth*? You feel you know this guy from somewhere else, and that you'd like to be inside the television *with* him, that's what's odd. Watching, you feel his anger, his ambition, his joy, his nearly violent curiosity, his impatience, his terror of screwing up all are worn right on the outermost surface of his being. Even self-amusement, usually the iciest part of a comic's persona, and therefore either carefully hidden or brandished as a fuck-you (think Groucho and Letterman again), in Kovacs is an element drawing you nearer. There are a few moments on these tapes when he breaks down and laughs for a while at something invisible to the viewer either because it lies outside the frame or because it hides somewhere inside his head, and you kind of want them to go on forever. That's it, the whole mystery I want to outline and that I don't purport to solve: how it can be that Ernie Kovacs generates such an astounding degree of *love* in the viewer, that you'd almost rather see him laugh than laugh yourself.

—*Playboy*, 2011

Marlon Brando Breaks

We know now what we could only have suspected: By the time *Rolling Stone* writer Chris Hodenfield and photographer Mary Ellen Mark cornered Marlon Brando on the Montana set of Arthur Penn's *The Missouri Breaks* it was basically over, not only for Brando as a beauty and a star but, largely, as an actor; not only for Brando in all those senses but also for the world he'd known and made; over, perhaps even for us, before we'd even begun. The year of the film's release, 1976, marked a fair horizon line for the sunset of so many radical possibilities: the end of a wide-open era of American filmmaking Brando personally catalyzed by his performances in the '50s and crowned in Coppola's *Godfather*; the end of a species of genuine risk in performance—risk of failure, that is—a species unknown to Brando's smug and calculating *Missouri Breaks* costar Jack Nicholson, who'd prove so willing to compromise with Hollywood's every shift from art to commerce; the winnowing and commodification of a vibrant alternative culture of pop and drug-based revelation; the chance that the Democratic Party could throw up anything but feeble moderation to the surging reactionary tide that has carried us to where we now live, a world in which Brando's beloved Black Panthers and American Indian Movement can only be recalled as quaint precursors to really *important* terrorism.

"He had this rule," recalls Mary Ellen Mark today. "You had to ask him first: Mr. Brando, may I take your picture? I was there for ten days and of course I didn't get anything. I said, So Marlon, I'm leaving, I don't think I got anything. He said, Well, you can photograph me now. I did it all at the end. I got about four frames. Maybe ten exposures." She adds: "That's fine, I'm a purist. Less is more. He liked it, and asked me to work on *Apocalypse Now*."

Brando looked chunky. Brando looked crazy. And when given full voice by Hodenfield's generous profile, Brando sounded heretical, paranoid, visionary, distracted, and alternately cynical and reverent about his craft, which he'd practiced not at all in the years since the polaropposite triumphs of *The Godfather* and *Last Tango in Paris*. So this was a Marlon Brando come out of the wilderness, beamed in from Tahiti, specifically, the world's greatest actor condescending not only to be interviewed but to be sighted at large on planet Earth in the first place.

As Hodenfield portrays the scene, Brando was treated with dazed awe by the professionals on the set, normally so irreverent and hard to impress. The crew waited out his enigmatic silences, wrote lines on cue cards to indulge his growing resistance to memorization, and turned a blind eye when the FBI, seeking to pin Brando to a whole series of outlaw political affiliations, arrived to interrogate the actor in his trailer. In *Breaks* Brando plays a mercurial Western serial killer, one using his role as a bounty hunter as an excuse for his nihilistic undermining of the frontier's tenuous social fabric. The part seems an ideal container for Brando's muddle of motives for even bothering to make a film at that point in his life. He delivers with Shakespearean gusto, in a wild variety of accents, like Norman Mailer running for mayor.

Yet *Missouri Breaks* is broken. The film is unable to sustain the performance and its insinuations, leaning instead to convention: Nicholson dispatches Monster Brando and gets the girl. The real showdown between the two occurs in the middle of the film, when Brando, unarmed and undressed, wreathed in a bubble bath and facing the point of Nicholson's gun, utterly dominates the younger actor simply by turning his appallingly fleshy back and rolling his eyes to the ceiling, daring Nicholson's character to shoot him in the back (or perhaps to reproduce the notorious butter scene). Nicholson, understandably, quits the stage in disgust.

What's shocking in the moment is Brando's complicity with the collapse of his masculine energies, and of all they imply for the viewer's self-image. Nicholson's reaction prefigures the audience's revulsion at the remainder of Brando's public career: revulsion for his gargantuan bulk and ugliness—the ruins of the prettiest man anyone had ever seen—and for his seeming failure to care about his art. Brando must have intuited how untenable he was as "a man of the people," as an advocate for Native Americans or a surrogate for you and me. Instead he'd become a monster and a saint, beyond the human ken. All that remained was *Apocalypse Now*, one more ludicrous embodiment of an inhuman villainy, and signature on his accomplishment. In his villainous roles of the '70s Brando planted a tombstone on the grave of individualist American manhood, where lay the rebels and martyrs of *The Wild One*, *The Fugitive Kind*, and *On the Waterfront*. The Brando of *Missouri Breaks* is a hired killer, ready to destroy more than anyone had ever asked him to. Including Marlon Brando.

—*Rolling Stone*, 2006

Missed Opportunities

Did you know that Jerry Lewis turned down the role of the killer in *Cruising*, the lead in *Being There*, and the title role in *Charly*? What's more, he turned down the Robert Shaw part in *Jaws*, and the role of Salieri in *Amadeus*. Also Peter Ustinov's part in *Logan's Run*. Can you imagine him as Humbert Humbert? Apparently he couldn't. And we will never have the privilege of knowing how he would have handled *Portnoy's Complaint*—he turned down a chance to star in and direct that film. He was also screen-tested for the Sterling Hayden role in *The Godfather* and the John Hurt role in *Alien*, though it is unclear whether he was actually offered these parts or not. How different might be the history of American film in the '70s had he actually taken the roles of the wiretapper in *The Conversation*, Popeye Doyle in *The French Connection*, or Lex Luthor in *Superman*—though I suppose we can be grateful to him, in a sense, for the opportunities given Gene Hackman, who certainly did not disappoint in these parts. Nor is it likely he could have improved on Jason Robards's portrayal of Ben Bradlee in *All the President's Men*, or on Rip Torn's performance in *The Man Who Fell to Earth*. Perhaps most frustrating for the film buff is the knowledge that Alfred Hitchcock, the Master of Suspense, died before realizing his hope of casting Lewis in a thriller. Lewis had previously turned down the Martin Balsam part in *Psycho* and the Sean Connery part in *Marnie*. Equally tantalizing is the large Lewis role trimmed out of

Nashville during last-minute edits—in interviews Lewis claims it as his masterwork. Robert Altman attempted to make it up to him, but an embittered Lewis turned down parts in Altman's next seven films. He also turned down the parts that went to Walter Matthau in both *Charley Varrick* and *King Creole*, thus missing his chance to work with veteran director Don Siegel (as well as to appear opposite Elvis Presley). He also turned down the John Lithgow part in *Blow Out* and the part that was reworked for Richard Pryor in *Blue Collar*. He refused the part Jack Lemmon played in *The China Syndrome*, though it was later pointed out that the role was developed for Lemmon and Lewis was never offered it. He also refused the role of the off-screen voice of Charlie in the hit television series *Charlie's Angels*, a role taken by John Forsythe, later of *Dynasty*. Unquestionably, *Excalibur* would have been a different film completely had Lewis not dropped out during the first week of shooting to be replaced by Nicol Williamson as Merlin. He also turned down the role of the arsonist in *Body Heat*.

Strangely, Jerry Lewis was never considered for any part by Michael Cimino.

—McSweeney's, 1999

Donald Sutherland's Buttocks
or
Sex in Movies for People Who Have Sex

"—Donald Sutherland's buttocks—" Those were the words that drew my attention from the other side of the table. My wife's friend Pauline was speaking them to my wife. What struck me most wasn't the odd specificity of the reference, nor the muddled thrill of jealousy and delight that lurches through my heart as it does anytime I gather that someone is talking of something sexual with my wife (and which ensures the instant obliteration of my attention to any topic I might have been discussing at my end of the table). What struck me then, and what strikes me now, is that I knew what Pauline was talking about, instantly. And so I leaned across and said, "*Don't Look Now.*"

No one who has ever seen it has forgotten the sex scene between Donald Sutherland and Julie Christie in Nicholas Roeg's *Don't Look Now.* The scene is characterized by a tension between Roeg's cool, artily distancing camera and the (apparent) commitment to total disclosure on the part of the unclothed actors, which has led to the legend that what was filmed was something more than a performance. The borderline-explicit sex is edited, too, in a disconcerting series of cuts, with flash-forwards to the couple dressing to go out afterward. This deepens the meaning of the sex scene, adds a note of pensiveness, even sadness. The rest of the film—a supernatural melodrama both tragic and terrifying—seems to tug at the edges of that single scene, making the sex appear in retrospect more poignant and precious. Their beautiful, disturbing, uncannily real fucking will turn out to be the only moment of reprieve for the two characters, the only moment of absolute connection. Even the film's title comes to seem a reference to the intensity of the sex scene. The result is like a brand sizzling into the viewer's sexual imagination. We feel we've learned something about sex, even as we're certain it required every bit of our own previous knowledge of sex to be in a position to receive and confirm the scene's knowingness, its completely nonverbal epiphanies. And so when I heard Pauline say "Donald Sutherland's buttocks," I felt with a shudder my memory of this scene instantly recover itself, and I was touched and frightened and turned on again. And I wanted to take my wife away from Pauline and the others and show her the scene, because unlike nearly any other scene of sex I'd ever watched, this one was like a piece of my own sexual past.

This, to put it bluntly, is what I want. Not Donald Sutherland's buttocks in and of themselves but films that install themselves this way in my sexual imagination, by making me feel that sex is a part of life, a real and prosaic and reproducible fact in the lives of the characters, as it is in my own life, and at the same time makes me feel that sex is an intoxicant, a passage to elsewhere, a jolt of the extraordinary which stands entirely outside the majority of the experiences of the characters, as it stands in relation to my own experience. Do I contradict myself? Very well, I contradict myself. I want the paradox. I want it all.

Where and how this can come to happen in cinema's future is beyond my expertise—it occurs rarely enough in cinema's past and present that I suspect it is beyond anyone's expertise, that it instead must be discovered, perhaps even scared up sideways, in the midst of operations in pursuit of other truths. (Certainly *Don't Look Now* wasn't conceived, or received, as a "sex film"—and I've recently learned that the famous scene was in fact an afterthought, shot after the script was exhausted but the director unsatisfied.) I didn't meet even a hint of it in *Closer* or *Y Tu Mamá También* or *Henry & June* or *We Don't Live Here Anymore*, but I did in the Israeli director Dover Koshashvili's *Late Marriage*, a slice-of-life drama both farcical and realistic. In *Late Marriage*, when the mama's-boy protagonist calls on his secret girlfriend, an older woman, the two unexpectedly devour each other in a long explicit scene that pinballs from annoyance to arousal to boredom and back to arousal, with a pause in the middle to sniff a used tissue for traces of bodily fluids—precisely the sort of Donald Sutherland's buttocks moment that makes a sex scene ineffable and lasting, a revelation. I met it for an instant in Preston Sturges's *The Lady Eve*, in the expression that crosses Barbara Stanwyck's face, so giddy it almost feels like an actor's lapse out of character, as she says to Henry Fonda, "Why, Hopsie . . . You ought to be kept in a cage!" (Oh, yes, I meet it often when I watch Barbara Stanwyck, and I wonder where our Barbara Stanwyck is hiding . . . might it be Maggie Gyllenhaal? On the strength of *Secretary* it seems possible . . . but then why aren't today's filmmakers making dozens of Maggie Gyllenhaal vehicles . . . what's their problem?) I met it, unexpectedly, in Miranda July's ensemble comedy *Me and You and Everyone We Know*, where several child characters are portrayed with their sexual curiosities not only intact but capable of setting up genuine erotic reverberations in the adults, with results that are not only disturbing and funny but also disconcertingly honest. (This is a matter that American films have been too fearful to take up, despite Hollywood's compulsive trafficking in child sexuality as an unacknowledged source of revenue, and as a source of energy in otherwise lifeless product.) I met it in Ralph Bakshi's pornographic animated films, a couple of times—most of all in the crude sequence of sex in a moving jalopy, set to Chuck Berry's frantic and bawdy "Maybellene." The scene somehow manages to convey a moment of sexual self-discovery in the autobiographical cartoonist character who is drawing the images, ratifying his own lust by satirizing it. I met it, of course, in Luis Buñuel's *Belle de Jour*, when Catherine Deneuve, playing a wealthy housewife slumming as a prostitute, dares herself to look into the mysterious buzzing box presented to her by the enigmatic Asian whorehouse customer. What she sees there intrigues her, and her curiosity pleases the Asian gentleman. We cut to a scene afterward, where both have been gratified by whatever it was that occupied the strange, buzzing box—we never get to see inside it ourselves. Am I calling for a return to reticence, to mystery? No. I'm calling for what I don't know to be calling for, I'm calling for surprise, for complicity delivered in an instant, I'm calling for filmic moments that lure and confuse me the way sex can, at its best. I don't want to choose between scrupulous, grainy, documentary realism (or the new and unsavory high-definition nudity I've been warned about) and fantasy, imagination, exaggeration, cartoons—I want them both. Give me prosthetics, like Marky Mark's penis extension in *Boogie Nights*—give me even more like that, give me a whole cinema of actors in fake bodies, like Cindy Sherman's prosthetic pimply butts and swollen breasts in her still photographs. Give me the sex lives of animated characters, and of rotoscoped actors, like the ones in Richard Linklater's *Waking Life* and *A Scanner Darkly*—a perfect solution to marrying glamorous and recognizable actors to explicit bodies without disturbing us or the actors by disclosing the actual bodies of actors, a perfect way to keep from rupturing the dream. Give me real bodies, too, of actors I haven't met yet, in scenarios which are stubbornly unpornlike and only half erotic, like Michael Winterbottom's *9 Songs*. Let me see what happens if Michael Winterbottom has to show his bottom, and Eliot Winterpenis his penis, and Carla Summertits her tits, and Lucius Springtesticles his testicles, and Delia Solsticeclitoris her clitoris, and so on. And, for that matter, Donald Sutherland is still among the living: Let's see how his buttocks are holding up. C'mon, show me something the mention of which will make my head turn at a dinner party thirty years from now. Try and make me blink. Try and make me keep from blinking.

—*Nerve*, 2005

The Drew Barrymore Stories

1. I was riding in an elevator in a London hotel with Alfred Hitchcock and Drew Barrymore. Alfred Hitchcock said, "Do you think he's opened the box of poisoned chocolates yet?" Though I knew it was only one of Alfred Hitchcock's deadpan jokes, I grew nervous. Drew Barrymore smiled and laughed, so infectiously that I couldn't help laughing myself. She said, "I took the poisoned chocolates out and replaced them with chocolates filled with sympathy and affection." Even Alfred Hitchcock began laughing now.

2. John Coltrane and Miles Davis and Drew Barrymore and I were backstage at a nightclub in Chicago. Miles Davis was berating John Coltrane for playing a twenty-minute solo. I was trying not to be noticed. Drew Barrymore was picking through a box of chocolates an admirer had sent backstage, biting into several of them to examine the filling. John Coltrane said, "I don't know how to stop playing." Miles Davis said, "Just take the damn horn out of your mouth." Drew Barrymore said, "Or if you wanted to you could just begin playing very softly, until you were so quiet that the others could play over you." Miles Davis said, "That would be fine too, yes."

3. Ernest Hemingway and Howard Hawks and John Coltrane and Drew Barrymore and I were in a fishing boat on the Snake River in Colorado. John Coltrane and Drew Barrymore were baiting fishhooks with whiskey-filled chocolates an admirer had sent to Hemingway. I was trying to make coffee on a Bunsen burner. Howard Hawks said to Ernest Hemingway, "I bet you I can make a good movie out of your worst book." Ernest Hemingway said, "What book is that?" Howard Hawks said, "That piece of shit known as *To Have and Have Not*." Drew Barrymore said, "Look over there!" We all turned, and Drew Barrymore pushed Howard Hawks out of the boat.

4. Gertrude Stein and Jack London and F. Scott Fitzgerald and Jack Kerouac and Truman Capote and Drew Barrymore and I were in a large outdoor hot tub in Sausalito, playing a drinking game called What's Your Secret? Gertrude Stein said, "Small audiences." Truman Capote said, "It's not your turn, Gertrude, it's Scott's." F. Scott Fitzgerald said, "There are no second acts in American lives." I started to ask him whether he meant that American lives skipped straight to the third act, but the others ignored me. Jack London said, "If you put some eggshells in with the coffee grounds it leaches the acid out of the coffee and it tastes a lot better." Jack Kerouac mumbled something nobody could make out, and Truman Capote said, "That's not writing, Kerouac, that's typing." Drew Barrymore got out of the hot tub and put on her robe and said, "Does anyone want hot chocolate instead of coffee? I don't have any eggshells, but I do have marshmallows."

5. I was running in the New York Marathon with Laurence Olivier and Dustin Hoffman and John Coltrane and Drew Barrymore, only Laurence Olivier was riding a banana-yellow moped. Drew Barrymore was accepting orange slices and Dixie cups of chocolate milk from the crowds at the police barriers and laughing infectiously, but Dustin Hoffman and John Coltrane and I were too out of breath to join in. By the time we crossed the Kosciusko Bridge into Long Island City Dustin Hoffman looked terrible and I was concerned he wouldn't be able to finish the race. Laurence Olivier said, "What's the matter?" Dustin Hoffman said, "I was up all night last night because I wanted this scene

to look realistic." Laurence Olivier said, "Why don't you try acting, my boy?" We all looked at Laurence Olivier like he was an asshole. Drew Barrymore said, "I know a shortcut." Dustin Hoffman said, "To acting?" Drew Barrymore said, "No, a shortcut," and she pointed past the police barriers at our left. We all turned our heads and when we looked back she was gone.

—*Another Magazine*, 2005

V

WALL ART

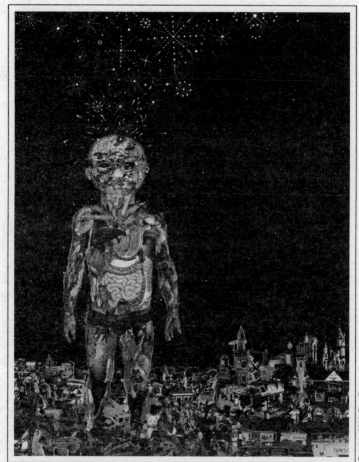

I thought I'd be a painter before I knew I'd write. The company of artists still makes sense to me, and sometimes my artist friends ask me to write about their work, a flattering and impossible request. Unlike music or film writing, which I devour, art writing mostly leaves me cold. I can't make that vocabulary my own. So I've offered artists stories instead. The artists, in return, give me pictures for my walls. Since I've always felt a little bereft of the paintings I never painted, this is a good thing.

The Collector (Fred Tomaselli)

The collector started with pennies. Or seashells. He could no longer recall. The two were opposites married in his obsessive vision. The seashells, indifferent and precultural, washed out of circulation on the shore, or came to him in tissue-paper-cushioned packages from a warehouse inventory. No two were alike, as with fingerprints or snow-flakes, yet they conformed to hierarchies of scarcity and value, made a subject for catalogs and lists. That these were also skulls, an assembly of carapaces, opened a first doorway into the morbidity of his love. Abraham Lincoln was a crazed worthless token, brown and bearded, a filthy tide of unsilver pouring from his parents' pockets, but subject to secret reorganization in embossed cardboard folders. A penny was not so much money as the DNA of money. Spotting the year and the mint signatures under Lincoln's nose was the first act of reading the secret inscriptions that underwrote the universe, a child's garden of conspiracy. Wheat-backed pennies were the essential evidence that the past was a purer land, that Americans had been expelled from a garden. The wartime aluminum cents were evidence of life on Mars.

Putting Lincoln's head upright in orderly rows was something, any-way, a sport for bleary afternoons. The staccato profile made a wedge of digits, ones-not-zeros, accumulating in an arrow moving past-to-future. Though pointing to a time when he'd jar or shelve them with his father's cavalier disdain, the precision and recursiveness of the pennies riveted him inside his present, the dawdling idle hours spent within the brackets of the blue-embossed cardboard holders. The shells were more troubling, harder to quantify. The boxes in which they were stored accumulated crumbs in the corners, evidence of dissolution, of the shells' complicity with stardust, with the antihuman ebb of entropy. One day on a visit to his grandparents' neighbor he spotted on a coffee table a hideous decorative clock from Florida ornamented with affixed shells, several valuable specimens possibly ruined with clumps of glue and glitter. Shells grew, he understood now. They were clocks themselves. They lurked in fathomless beds of frond and mud, were exuded in octopus and shark shit.

These were his first two ruined collections, early maps of shame. The hinges frayed on the gap-haunted blue cardboard penny books. Pennies from a certain mint refuse to migrate to the coast. Perhaps some doppelgänger boy elsewhere held the reverse of your collection, hoarded your missing pieces, like a game of Gin Rummy or Go Fish. Speaking of fish, the shells stunk. They delivered up not only sounds but odors from elsewhere. They refused to be decanted, were just passing through.

He began to associate the shells with the curls of yellow, calcified snot he'd accidentally archived beneath his desk.

One day his mother presented him with a bankbook containing a balance begun by the birthday check from his grandmother. She showed him paper rolls for gathering pennies, for proving their value in weekly schleps to the teller's window, then offered him the flood of crappy pennies wedged in drawers and overrunning jars everywhere. He capitulated, quit examining the coins for their pedigree, quit yanking them from circulation. They had their pitiful denomination after all. Savoring the rarity of one in a thousand was too much like staring at your feet as you walked. After a while you had to just accept that each foot flopped in front of the previous, forever, even when you took your eyes away.

He wondered if he was doomed to collect everything before he was done. He fell for the whole baseball-card thing for about five minutes, long enough to pass through mannerist, modernist, minimalist, and postmodern periods at the speed of sound. The flashy cards revealed too much, bright emblems, team trademarks smeared everywhere and disguising nothing, the pitiful, needy eyes of dying veterans and no-hope rookies, faked smiles to mortify your glance. Gray cardboard flip sides loaded with inane jokes and statistics, prehistories of minor-league struggle, and dusty with starch. Did anyone collect the gum? The cards were for statistical study—no, for flipping—no, for protecting in laminated folders—no, they were only a product, a scam, the grocery clerk annoyed that you didn't figure it out sooner and just get your dad to buy the whole carton on one visit instead of slouching around the joint bugging him for weeks.

At the end he wrecked the whole relationship in one resentful, shattering act, a spasm of appropriation and collage involving toy scissors and a bottle of Elmer's. On the inside of his notebook binder the California Angels fluttered, pinkish baseball putti, over a roaring inferno of flame-licked Reds and Dodgers. Disembodied mitts swarmed the scene like luna moths, horrified and attracted as he himself had been.

Ground zero for all collections, it seemed, was the glue bottle, the lumps of pearly translucent white that held the swirling chaos of the world in place even as they officially devastated the value of any item affixed, according to all known specialists. You were a fucking idiot to glue anything to anything else but you did it all the time. A "real" collector tolerated the slippage, the loose and therefore implicitly temporary nature of his hoard, by capturing coins and cards and shells and stamps in sheaths and slipcases, delicate frames. You glued shit to backgrounds like a maniac. You'd have sealed the books on your shelves in laminate if you could. Superglue, which was reputed to solder fingers to eyeballs, was too scary to even let into the house, knowing your propensities.

The gluing impulse was especially treacherous when it came to stamp collecting. He'd been given the albums and a head start of a million torn-off corners of envelopes by an uncle from Vegas. Here was another precise history to duplicate, every stamp ever issued in the United States, plus their dark cousins, the postage-due stamps. In fact, in two years of solid work he'd never catch up with the backlog of stamps to soak or steam off envelopes. The ideal stamp had nothing to do with this bogus labor anyway, but was clean of postmark, never licked, perhaps even in an intact block of four. These were purchased at the Collector's Counter on the eighth floor of the department store, a somber ritual, religious possibly, related to visits to the bank window, and with no overtones of the grocery-store baseball-card gum-and-garbage runs. Yet faced with a pristine stamp and its appointed place in an album, a date with destiny, how to keep from just licking the thing and pressing it into place? What the fuck was a dry mount, anyway? On a humid day they licked themselves, self-ruining, so why lose the chance? Thirty-year-old stamp glue had the titillating savor of an old wine uncorked. Who was it waiting for, if not for him?

Maybe the only thing you collected, after all, was glue itself.

Drugs and music made another set of twins. Each were like seashells or stardust you took into your body. Living where he did, in the city locked in pavement to the sea, the drugs and the music were his first chance to import nature beyond his own boundaries. They made tidy analogues for sex or the forest, possibly more satisfying than any wider exploration would ever be, certainly safer. Drugs and songs were seashells he could seek to turn into pennies. First you saw a band, absorbed the essence of live moments which like drug fumes evaporated into your organs and left no evidence apart from your altered sense of self and any bragging rights you'd risk. Then you collected their albums, all the B sides and rarities from the Denver mint. In drugs he dabbled, a ready tourist, stopping nowhere but gathering sample flavors like stamps in a passport: Quaalude, Mescaline, Amsterdam Hash. His record collection, on the other hand, was a plummet into addiction. He'd boarded a carousel of pure and infinite unsatisfaction, where solid ground whirled beneath his gaze, no chance of stepping off. He rarely listened to a song to its end anymore, perpetually upping the dose with a junkie's agitation. The connoisseur soon learned every song had "versions," which raised the stakes. Music was a kind of fractal disaster area.

The first time he put blotter acid on his tongue he thought: They printed the player's statistics directly on the gum. And the player is me. The whole team, pitcher, catcher, batter, even the third-base coach frantically signaling from his lime-drawn grass box in the foul area, touching his nose, his ear, his crotch, the bill of his cap—hey, what's he trying to say to me?

If I'm the coach, why don't I grasp the coach's signals?

If I am my own collection, why am I scattered outside of my body?

If that's my favorite band, why don't I enjoy any of their albums?

Now somebody started a band, four guys in a basement, pawnshop instruments reflecting no consensus as to whether stickers were cool or not, in a sea of amplifier wires in a concrete zone cleared in the clutter of abandoned family stuff, including, he couldn't help noticing, a pile of rotting stamp albums, lurching herky-jerky song openings with no firm conclusion in mind, except perhaps the ongoing argument certain to escalate to band-breakup level sooner or later, which would easily enough solve the problem of how to end the song. Somebody else renovated a two-story house in Culver City to make an indoor marijuana factory, sun-spectrum light fixtures, sprinkler hoses for nutrient-enriched water, rows of green plants throbbing with redolent active ingredient, flower buds rupturing, the plants' overwhelmed stalks needing support from slings, crutches, buttresses. This was a going concern, you could splice the DNA of the best weed you'd ever toked into the mother plant in the closet and like a science-fiction monster you'd rule the earth, exactly as you couldn't splice the Sex Pistols' DNA into your shitty band and were destined to rule exactly nothing.

One day a bunch of them drove down into Borrego Springs on mushrooms and it was exactly as good as Disney's *The Living Desert* and at that moment he realized that everything he loved most was a seashell. Maybe it was time to get out of the city.

Now he was a bird-watcher, with binoculars and a field guide. He walked in the woods but also sought to draw his collection to himself, magnetize his subjects like iron filings. He lured them to the edges of the house, to miniature platforms and chimney-shaped feeders mounted and hung in the trees, with piles of seed and corn and dried berries, bait for feathered creatures. He spied at them through his windows, enumerated them in his book, a reverse Peeping Tom. Sparrow, wren, cardinal, crow. The house resembled a big knocked-out cartoon head, circles of birds wreathing it as he dashed, like a lone pupil in kooky eye sockets, from window to window. He got himself a bird-watcher's clock, too, which chimed a different birdsong at each hour. On a day trip to the beach he garnered pipers who ran like tidy punctuation at the edge of surf, then was taken aback at two lumpen terns nosing for clams at the breakwater rocks. Guiltily he noted these rarities in his book. Not all birds were birds, he felt. Category errors nagged his psyche. He wanted a division between water and sky. He saw he was trying to purify, the collector's fatal mistake. Repentant, he logged the dirty-looking terns. Between birds he picked mushrooms, not psychedelic things, and at night he gazed at the stars. His military-surplus thigh pockets bulged with field guides. At night a single light brought flat moths of all sizes to his windows, self-adhering decal-souls. But he hadn't glued anything to anything else in what felt like years. Whatever he'd wish to affix was beyond reach of Elmer's nozzle.

Then came the squirrels. These anti-birds clarified things radically. They filched seed and corn, clambered along wires, defeated all measures, and, bad actors, screeched off the visiting birds. The vermin needed to be thwarted, which gave his life a new grim purpose. A war of logistics rapidly escalated: how to feed one kind and starve another. The squirrels twitched past any obstacle. Soon enough he concluded death was not only the preferred solution, it was too good for the bastards. He'd been converted into Elmer Fudd, a poker-in-holes. The wabbit kicked the bucket. The day he found his first victim curled like an ampersand in dead leaves, tiny mouth pursed in disdain, tail rigid, he understood. It wasn't really about the birds anymore. Poison was the new glue.

Years later he attended a party at the home of a wealthy big-game hunter, a man of feral leisure. The hunter had a carriage house behind his mansion, full of trophies. He'd left it open for the guests to peruse. Wandering in among a gaggle of partiers, bearing drink and ice in a plastic cup, expecting perhaps a few tattered moose heads, he was shocked instead at entering a multichambered temple of earthly death. The walls were heaped everywhere with stuffed and mounted corpses, ibex, yak, water buffalo, Scottish goats with wiry beards. Room after room, countless bodies leaped from the walls, cougars and pythons arranged in elaborate tableaux, miming attack, their frozen moments of death, perhaps an argument that the hunter had only shot in self-defense. The floor beneath guests' strolling feet was a bear's skin, then a tiger's, then a crocodile's pebbly back. Plaques accompanying the stuffed heads accounted for the dates of the kills, a regimented life's work, no time wasted in the global hopping. Photographs showed the teams of natives who'd assisted in trapping the victims, framing them for the hunter's bullet. The hunter the triumphant white face in their center, boot on a head with a lolling tongue.

Staring at the uncredited taxidermist's eyeball work, he spotted the telltale glue.

Back in the main house, they were introduced. The ruddy-faced hunter's eyes glistened with impatience at the inadequate hairless apes circulating among his kills. In that razor look the collector felt himself collected, or at least browsed. The hunter had worked out a handshake unlike any other, encircling a proffered hand in a tight ring and squeezing the line of knuckles together to produce unmistakably intentional pain. You had to grant it was an accomplishment: a handshake you'd gnaw your arm off to get free of.

"Sometimes when I see a Lincoln-head penny I still think that an uncirculated 1909 S-V.B.D. would be the ideal one."

"Remember William Burroughs in *Drugstore Cowboy*, searching through that whole bedspread covered with pharmaceuticals, just looking for one Dilaudid? He tells them the rest of their stuff is crap, that the Dilaudid was the only pill worth anything."

"When I was a kid I used to get confused about the difference between astronauts and dinosaurs. The only evidence of either one was basically just footprints. And rocks."

"Dude, what if bird-watching was not about watching lots of different birds, but watching just one. Pick a bird—not a species, but a sole, actual bird—and follow it anywhere, watch it forever. Like, vertical instead of horizontal bird-watching. That would be pretty fucking cool."

"You know those machines that smash a penny into a souvenir image of some local building or monument? I can't begin to explain how depressing I find that."

"What I find depressing is that you can pay to have your filthy name put on a star or a crater on the moon that never did anything to hurt you in the first place, never so much as glanced in your direction."

"I once put a quarter in a vise and cut it in half with a hacksaw. Then walked around with the halves in my pocket, trying to figure out if it was still money."

"Me and my brother once spent a five-dollar bill that was autographed by Muhammad Ali. We basically just needed five bucks that day."

"I heard this comedian say that he keeps his seashell collection scattered on the beaches of the world."

"I still like birds, though."

"I like birds fine, man. Just not at the expense of other things. Like, say, mammals."

His uncle, who'd lived alone in an apartment, had to be moved into a home. His father asked him to drive out to Vegas to help. In an instant, walking through the door, a lifetime's romance with his uncle's bachelorhood was shattered, a romance he hadn't noticed himself sustaining. The rope-tied newspapers and unopened mail formed a maze for a creature barely human, a rot-gnawed Habitrail space, demanding contortions just to reach the bathroom door, the toilet itself a barely visible outpost in a mouse hole carved in mountains of bathroom magazines. A sofa had been buried under what a quick inspection proved was nineteen years before, *Newsweek* with Bhopal on the cover.

When he got home he tried to flush the stamp collection down the toilet. They reeked of putridity to him now, a flaky carcass, skin of so many lost years, steamed off envelopes whose overlaid routes would describe the nervous system of the world. The plumbing choked on the stamps. He ended up plunging the toilet. The stamps, moistened a third time for their final voyage, swam on his tiles and over the bathroom's threshold, to be wrecked on the reef of the carpet. Others invested in the toilet's crannies, where he had to scour them free with a brush, one curved like the mirrors a dentist uses to get an angle on a molar. He felt by the end like a toilet-cleaner bird, picking at the porcelain mouth of a miniature hippopotamus.

These days he wondered if all the aspirins and cigarettes in circulation resembled pennies, whether they were issued from different mints, and whether their point of origin as well as their date of issue could be ascertained by examining microscopic serial-number imprints.

He began to consider the possibility of an aspirin or cigarette collection mounted into embossed cardboard holders, as with his lost penny collection.

Such a collection would of course be destined like all others for failure, the die-cut cardboard slots intended to bear the earliest and scarcest aspirins or cigarettes reproachfully empty.

He had fantasies of flash-laminating his coffee table, capturing everything on it in a plastic glob, magazine, coins, half-eaten sandwich, ashtray.

The truth was he needed to quit smoking, clean his apartment, scoop up the pennies everywhere. He'd laminate when he was dead, what was the hurry? Stuff was collecting everywhere you looked.

He'd be okay. The universe was the glue that held him together.

—*Art Review*, 2004

An Almost Perfect Day (Letter to Bonn)

October 2004

Dear Elena,

Yesterday I made a visit to an artist's studio in Williamsburg, Brooklyn. My friend Fred Tomaselli is a painter and collagist who has become notorious for using real drugs in his paintings—marijuana leaves, psychedelic mushrooms, Ecstasy tablets, as well as legal pharmaceuticals and over-the-counter remedies such as Pepto-Bismol and Bayer aspirin. He arranges the leaves and pills and other substances in beautiful arrays, much in the manner that a child builds gorgeous artifacts out of Lego blocks, or a pointillist creates illusions of shimmering color by daubing paint. He also uses tiny cut-out images from magazines and books: birds, body parts, and pictures of toys and machines. These are always placed on the canvas surface with the scrupulous attention of a surgeon or diamond cutter. His work sometimes has a resemblance to Arcimboldo, the painter who made human heads out of meats, vegetables, and books. Some of Fred's pictures are abstract and some are pictorial, but in every case a close examination reveals some unusual detail or image or object on the canvas. The result is fabulously beautiful. His work is celebratory, and I find it explosively happy even when the drugs or some of the other imagery takes on a somewhat ominous overtone. The paintings are full of love. I visited his studio because I'm going to try to write about his work soon, for a catalog to accompany an exhibition in Scotland, although I have no idea what to say. The trick will be avoiding the cliché of calling his work "transgressive"—I think Fred's become bored with that misunderstanding about his efforts. The drugs are a part of his life and the world around him that Fred became curious about collecting and reorganizing, and giving a new purpose. There's no attempt to assault or dismay the viewer, and I don't think the work is actually transgressive in any way, despite the fact that occasionally it happens to be illegal.

It was pouring rain as I approached Fred's warehouse studio, but despite the weather, after spending a while looking at his work and talking about my plans to write about it, Fred and I decided impulsively to go out for a hamburger lunch at Peter Luger's, a famous steak restaurant about a mile away, under the Williamsburg Bridge. Peter Luger's, which was opened by a German family nearly a hundred years ago, is the most famous and also the most eccentric and old-fashioned restaurant in Brooklyn—and one of the most celebrated restaurants in all of New York. They grow their own beef and have a very simple menu consisting of steaks, hamburgers, and a few simple side items like creamed spinach, scalloped potatoes, and onion rolls. The point of going there is to gorge yourself on the best cow meat available in New York, as well as to savor the atmosphere. The place looks like a German inn of the previous century, or at least a New Yorker's idea of one, with heavy wooden paneling and various decorations suggesting chivalry, hunting, the Black Forest, etcetera—shields, horns, giant brass beer steins, etcetera. The floors are covered with sawdust. The waiters are famous for their hostility and bullying, and for forcing you to order what they think is the best meal, or for sneering at you if you go outside their recommendations. This reputation is obviously something they cultivate and cherish because they know people come expecting to be given a hard time. They never fail. For instance, when Fred ordered his burger, he made the mistake of hesitating when the waiter asked if he wanted fries. You could see the waiter get a gleam in his eye. The scene went down like this:

Fred: I'll have the burger.
Waiter: Fries?
Fred: Um, just the usual burger order . . . um . . .

Waiter: (Says nothing, just scowls at Fred.)

Fred: Um . . . don't some fries come on the side with that?

Waiter: That depends on whether you say yes
    or no when I ask you if you want fries.

Fred: Um, okay, sorry, yes, I'll have the fries.

Waiter: See, now fries come with that.

The meal was incredibly satisfying—they really do have the best cows in the world hidden away somewhere, their own private supply. After eating the beef Fred and I made the somewhat self-destructive decision a person always makes after a meal at Peter Luger's. Again, the decision was made with the assistance of some serious strong-arming by the waiter. He said, "Coffee and dessert?" and we could see he'd be enraged if we said no. Dessert at Peter Luger's is just an excuse for what they like to call "schlag," which they bring in a gigantic bowl and dump all over whatever poor little piece of pie or strudel you happen to have ordered. As hard as this may be to believe, especially for you where you're reading this letter, Peter Luger's schlag is the thickest and most delicious in the world, I believe, and impossible not to eat until you are groaning. If you're smart you remember that it is permitted to order "just the schlag," because whatever is beneath it is really beside the point.

Afterward we drifted out to the street, back into Fred's car, and returned to his studio. He showed me his secret stash of raw mate-rials—drawers full of pills, and other drawers full of envelopes loaded with tiny pictures of different flowers, and birds, and human body parts, all cut very carefully out of books and magazines with an X-ACTO knife. Feeling quite jolly—and perhaps just a tiny bit transgressive—Fred showed me envelopes full of tiny photographs of penises and vaginas, all about an eighth of an inch long. Then he showed me a few rare books he'd collected, including an early issue of the *Harvard Review* with the first articles on LSD written by Timothy Leary and Richard Alpert. We talked about Fred's family, his wife, Laura, and their beautiful boy, Desi, and we talked about our friends, and we didn't talk about politics at all, not even the politics of art. We were high on beef, coffee, and schlag, and it was an almost perfect day.

Give my best to my friends in Germany, and I'll see you in Bonn.

Jonathan

The Billboard Men

Oranges on Fire, 1976, Mike Mandel and Larry Sultan

NIGHT AND THE SUBLIMINAL CITY

By night (though it was as bright at midnight as at noon) Salem and Marlboro had begun converting the billboards to better reflect the recent mood of the time-ruined city. They forged a language to describe the city's fugitive pockets of mercenary industry, those portable stalls of black-market wares that flared up and vanished at the side of the highway without warning, stalls selling items both necessary and absurd: glass doorknobs mounted on walking sticks, useless princess telephones, bundles of multihued television cable and flamboyant pre-knotted neckties, T-shirts bearing the images of forgotten cartoon stars, grapefruits and oranges permanently on fire. Though the city was painstakingly dying—and indeed Salem and Marlboro found they could travel vast miles of elevated asphalt with no visible indication of the life that still scurried on the widening avenues below—it had far from emptied entirely. The city was in fact expanding across the desert, in the manner of the galaxy itself, the bleached-bone spaces that had always underlain the vast human outcropping now rising from between the stretches of paving, between the flat-topped, sun-worn buildings, between the fields of parked or abandoned cars. Tides of commerce had long ago thrown up the improbable oasis of steel and concrete on this parched desert, had rerouted rivers and commanded the water to sustain the lives here for a time, and then time and the waters had come to a halt, the sun frozen at perihelion in the sky. Now, in this long dying, it might be the commercial impulse that would outlive the city itself.

Salem and Marlboro worked in silent tandem, the instinct and understanding quick between them, and with no fear of exposure for the period it took them to complete the alterations. Like plastic surgeons the two carved differences into the grinning faces that beckoned to the absented highways. They found it surprisingly easy to uncover the cravenness just below the surface, the subcutaneous accusations and complicity inside the seductions, as though the billboards' own self-reproach had actually ached to be freed. Elsewhere they merely echoed the non sequiturs of life in the amnesiac suburbs, making surrealist enunciation out of what no one even remembered well enough to take for granted: the maps and place-names of the defunct empire, the charts and graphs of the business elites, the textbook illustrations and dissection diagrams of the absconded natural sciences. Material was anywhere they looked. Everything they tried worked.

Returning to the billboards days and weeks after an intervention, Salem and Marlboro frequently found testament to the persuasive power still residing in the medium, and to their ability to capture and redirect it: little honorific shrines of cactus and cabbages, arranged as if gazing upward at the advertisements, or small encampments of stubbed cigarettes and crushed beer cans, where bands of rovers had stopped to contemplate or briefly worship at their results.

A BESEECHING COMES ACROSS THE SKY

Kent was lodged as usual in a tremendous traffic jam, a speck in a flotilla of cars that crept like some great windless island of kelp and plastic flotsam caught in the ocean's stream, the first time he noticed one of the billboards, the ones that seemed to have him particularly in mind.

YOU'RE LIVING ALL OVER ME. WE MAKE YOU US. EVERY GOOD REASON IS
NO LONGER ENOUGH. MY BEST FRIEND IS TRYING TO KILL ME. More and
more lately Kent seemed to live in his car, his apartment an adjunct, a
kind of garage for his driver's body, his true life and the true life of the
city actually taking place on the overpasses, the ostensible byways from
one ebbing destination or another. The value of arrival diminished
daily. What mattered were the products one could adapt to use inside
the vehicle itself, and also those items one could acquire without exiting the freeway system, at the monstrous commercial pull-offs, which
had become Potemkin villages, false fronts where life could be enacted
if one didn't examine the details too closely. Drive-thru windows were
most perfect of all, and someday, Kent envisioned, he'd be able to make
purchases without even slowing to a stop. Or was it one of the uncanny
billboards that had made that prediction? WHOSE NEWS ABUSES YOU?
Kent no longer felt clearly the difference between those insights arising
on the inner or outer surface of his mental windshield.

   YOU'RE TWO OF A KIND, the newest billboard had read, AND ONE OF
YOU MAY BE REDUNDANT. Kent found he couldn't agree more.

THE SKY WAS THE COLOR OF A TELEVISION TUNED TO THE MILLION-DOLLAR MOVIE

Vantage and Strike mostly found that the more things were ruined the
better they liked them. Perhaps the destruction enunciated something
lurking in the things themselves at the outset, but Vantage and Strike
could never have bothered with this perception: They were too deep
inside the fact of the city to parse it as a concept, or to figure any possible alternative. The city was their natural world. Perhaps it was their
irritation at the possibility of anything preceding the city that motivated their urge to shift it more deeply into a state of randomness, of an
entropy to echo cosmic ruin. In any event, their tools were cruder than
those of Salem and Marlboro, and their results more utterly violent.
Vantage and Strike worked with spray cans and crowbars, with pots
of unstable home-brewed acid concoctions and fecal smearings, but
this was only because blowtorches, bullets, and bombs were not available to them. They worked not in silence but with screams of laughter.
The things they did to the billboards sometimes rendered whole zones
unstable, and certainly struck fear in passersby. Yet they, too, were in

a conversation with the ancient marketing voices. They'd heard them their whole lives and in many senses could be seen as the children of those voices.

Vantage and Strike also attacked Salem and Marlboro's results, with gusto and glee equal to that with which they set themselves against the unaltered originals. That other presences labored at the billboards only exhilarated the younger men, but the solidarity they felt hardly precluded destruction of the older artists' works. This defacing was another conversation, a sign of life worth itself, no matter what might be obliterated in the meantime. The city around them, after all, burned. Here it was always night, and gangs roved the suburbs. More cars lay on their backs or sides than not. Vantage and Strike didn't have the luxury of Salem and Marlboro's sunburned vacancies, nor Kent's population-choked ennui. They wouldn't have known what to do if they had.

FOR YOU HAVE IT YOUR WAY WE DO IT ALL

Perhaps inevitable, Salem and Marlboro could envision an end to their work, not because it had failed but because its success reframed not only the wasted city but their own vision of their places in it. They grew in different directions until it was evident their partnership might begin slipping from them, ungrudgingly, in the manner of the desert's and the sky's widening influence. Salem had become compelled by these dawning blank spaces, the sand and sky, and so he began to contemplate billboards along vast lines, billboards to replace the sky or wrap around it, frames the viewer might be tempted to enter and be lost in. Salem contemplated the commercial power of natural history itself, the sales job implicit in Darwin's theory, each creature a refurbished model outmoding the previous on the showroom floor, the sun's irresistible advertisement for growth and mutation.

Marlboro went the other way, to the billboard as microcosm. It seemed to him that cars flashed their own little emblems and ads, the hubcaps, hood ornaments, and particularly license plates, and so Marlboro began subtly altering these last, beginning with the coastal state's vanishing moniker: CALL I'LL PHONE YA, KILL FOR NADA, CAR PORN TRIVIA. Clothing and eyewear, too, turned out when you looked to be riddled with tiny billboards, minute invasions of commerce into the subliminal life of the body. Even with eyes closed, flashbulb phosphenes burned into vision's screen by an unsetting sun might consist of a medium, one far beyond Madison Avenue's wildest dreams. Marlboro began scheming on this virgin re(tin)al estate, plotting to erect the first billboard of the inner eyelid.

UNKIND DOUGHNUTS

Kent, still in his car, began unexpectedly dreaming of his apartment. In its architectural lineaments the place was a marvelous specimen, a sixty-sixth-level floor-through with picture panes on four sides, which had once featured panoramic views of ocean at one hand and mountains on the other, while downtown's spiny tangle unfolded vertiginously below. The last time he'd been there, however, Kent had noticed that obscenely huge and towering billboards had crept both higher and nearer to the apartment's windows, though he'd once been guaranteed that by signing the lease he'd decisively risen beyond their reach. Now, in his dreams, the apartment had expanded, its floor extending on all sides from his tiny oasis of furnishings as if it were in fact the surface of an abandoned planet or moon, while the walls had dropped away, leaving him starkly surrounded on all sides by the tremendous billboards. These had now become the functional walls of his apartment, and yet as familiar as this should have made the billboards, he found himself enthralled with their unexpectedly overripe color, their fractal complexity, and, though this should have been impossible due to the static nature of the medium, their absorbing narrative implications, which seemed richer by far than the events of his own daily existence. In fact, Kent couldn't take his eyes off them. Somehow this came as no surprise.

CHEW BUBBLE GUM AND KICK ASS AT THE SAME TIME

Vantage and Strike, digging in an alley's refuse to make a nest for sleeping off their latest bender, found to their surprise a cardboard box full of apparently unused sunglasses. The box, though buried beneath mounds of rubbish, seemed placed carefully, as if hidden. Sunglasses, however, were hardly an object of particular value in a city ruled by eternal night and regular power failures, one so frequently lit only by the flares of burning vehicles.

Yet Vantage and Strike were curious and tried the glasses on. The result was revelatory, or consisted of hallucination disguised as revelation, or else in some manner illuminated the zone where the distinction between hallucination and revelation broke down permanently, or at least as long as one wore the glasses. The sunglasses seemed to render the world transparent of disguises. Businessmen were revealed, for the most part, as lizards, surprising no one. Commercial media exposed itself as a set of mind controls, as barren and direct as commands to *Eat*, *Consume*, *Obey*, *Reproduce*, and *Remain Asleep*. Yawn. The most fascinating, for Vantage and Strike, were the billboards: those they'd altered, and those they'd not yet reached, the ones on mile-high stilts or fenced in by armed sentry towers. They showed pictures, more vivid than the world itself, of the city sprawled and stretched in blazing noon, the streets empty apart from a few crouched figures or fugitive market stalls, the desert gaping between buildings that had once stood side by side. Then again they revealed the endless traffic jam, a huddled nightmare of smog and population. The billboards had become the last opportunity for the concurrent cities to sense one another: that one bereft in solar flares, the other choked with occupants straining to unreachable off-ramps, this one savagely wrecked in moonshade. The divergence of the three was a lie, or so the sunglasses and the billboards seemed to claim.

Vantage and Strike each poked out one lens so they could observe their city all ways at once, reality, dream, and illusion in strobe simultaneity, a trick that quit giving them pounding headaches just a few days after they first tried it. No doubt this was not the use the glasses' manufacturer had intended, but the view was fucking outstanding that way.

—artist's catalog, 2011

I rescinded my boycott on art crit just once for this ranting rave for Todd James, who is a kind of brother to me (and to my brother). Todd's paintings catch what I'd wish stories like This Shape We're In *or* Amnesia Moon *to look like if they'd been paintings—the wall art I wasn't, finally, talented enough to create myself.*

Todd James

Blood Sea, 2007, Todd James

The territory of Todd James's singularly enraged and expulsive outpouring of protest images may be generally that marked out by Goya, George Grosz, and Ben Shahn, but the neighborhood of his line's garrulous cynical squirming splendor, as well as his vernacular idiom of cartoon outrage, recycled advertising castoff, and corrupted child's scrawl is, unmistakably, a bit closer to home: Peter Saul, R. Crumb, Ralph Bakshi, Philip Guston, Red Grooms, and the notebook drawings of Claes Oldenburg. Of course it's also got a hot-wired lineage to the unruly mob of neighborhoods Todd James and I grew up in: '70s New York City in chaotic overripe decline, its streets explosive with native font which seemed to turn the place into a Joycean stream-of-consciousness doodle, as if the urban undermind's brainwaves were making themselves not only visible but into calligraphic floral or animal logos and brand names for mysterious products not available on any shelf in our tired cultural supermarket. In fact, James here gives fresh evidence of the continuity between the graffiti impulse and the critically sanctified "mark-of-the-hand" tradition in midcentury American painting, raising the question of what a Pollock or Gorky might have done on the side of a moving train. James's blacks, his death-inky warplanes and aircraft carriers, have the chunky authority of a Franz Kline, but as in de Kooning's *Woman*—that mighty joke that American painting can never stop getting—where the maelstrom of abstraction conjures up a Marilyn Monroe seduction more vertiginous than anything Madison Avenue dared unveil, every seemingly innocent surrealist gesture in James desublimates itself before the dreamer can even awaken: Yes, that warplane is jacking off bloody semen over your cities; yes, Marvel Comics' Red Skull has appropriated Captain America's son's sailor suit and gone unpunished; yes, the latest interrogation outrages are being hosted by bikini models and cuddly chipmunk faces ready for Saturday-morning cartoon syndication or McDonaldland. This new work (again, like Goya, etc.) is by its nature literary, too: Allen Ginsberg, Henry Miller, or Norman Mailer would have recognized in James a kindred drinker at the American stream, intoxicated and exhausted and exhilarated again by the mysterious complicity and mayhem of our manifest destiny's fever dream. These paintings smash the distance between death and jokes, between ingenuous-idealist protest sympathies and indifferent "first-person-shooter" couch-potato apathy, and, finally, between the viewer and what he or she probably goes around trying not to know about the present state of things. Welcome to the orgy of the real, sensationally inappropriate and unembarrassed, as always.

—artist's catalog, 2009

Writing and the Neighbor Arts

My footing in the visual arts encourages me to treat each story or novel as an artifact in the making. Not to hang on the wall, okay, but still needing a plastic-formal agenda, whether hidden or on its sleeve, to justify getting first in and then out of my studio. *The Fortress of Solitude*, for instance, spatially mimicked the shape of a two-CD box set enshrining a soul group's career and breakup. This didn't need to matter or even be legible to anyone but me.

The same synesthesia infected my critical frameworks, when I began to have those. I first got hold of what Stanley Kubrick meant to me when I heard him referred to as an abstract expressionist. The only narratives that never interested me at all were open-ended serials or series television: no frame equaled no art. (They had only to announce that *Lost* would intentionally end after six seasons and my pulse quickened—there might be something happening there.) I never knew how to even begin taking journalistic hyperventilation about literary plagiarism seriously—wasn't the whole twentieth century a victory lap of collage, quotation, appropriation, from Picasso to Dada to Pop? Who hadn't gotten what memo?

Me, maybe. In the larger culture, journalism enclosed the world of book-writing, a prisoner art. Newspapermen on deadline curated this museum. The Books Section might seem a privilege, while other estates jostled for pages in Arts, but it inscribed a miserable proximity, critics working in the same medium—sort of—as creators. The problem with most writing about books was that this proximity, and the vanities it inspired, meant you couldn't joke that the stuff was "dancing about architecture." Only it was.

Live Nude Models

Be careful what you wish for; you may turn out already to have had it. That's to say, to have had it before you could make intelligible use of it, perhaps before you could get your synapses to parse it for what it was. By the time I was seventeen years old and had a girlfriend who would take her clothes off (there had been one at fifteen who, serially, entrancingly, wouldn't), I'd been envisioning women with their clothes off, ravishing them with the secret lidless eyeball of my brain, for at least five years. Though these were five long, aching years, which I took entirely personally at the time, I do realize how mundane such a confession must be. Is. There wasn't anything baroque or complicated in my pining visualizations, or the procedure by which I took their edge off, and it's surely the case that a savvy person glancing my way would guess I did pretty well nothing else at the time.

Here's what's unmundane: In that same span, through my rude, ripened, teen-prime years, there were *live nude models appearing nightly* in my home—women to whose unclad forms my ordinary, lidded eyeballs had regular access. My father painted them, upstairs in his studio. "Nightly" exaggerates, but through those years nudes were the main subject of his large oils on canvas, of which he painted dozens—sometimes from memory or from studies, but often with the body present before him—as well as generating many hundreds of nudes on paper or vinyl, in pencil, oil crayons, or gouache, or combinations of those mediums, nearly each and every one of which was done in the presence of what at eight or ten I would have still called "a naked lady" (or, rarely, but it bears mentioning, in the presence of a naked man).

Me, I opened the door. I walked through. My father's studio was part of our home. I did this, probably, beginning at twelve or thirteen, when I would have learned to refer to the naked ladies in question as "models," as in a mock-casual formulation like "We can hang out in the kitchen, my dad's up with one of his models" or the defensively sophisticated "Sure, I see the models with their clothes off, it's no big deal." I do recall forming sentences like these, just as I recall the slightly widened eyes of the models themselves, a few times, as they met the eyes of the would-be-jaded twelve-year-old who'd pushed through the door without knocking. I can also bring up a good portion of ambiance (visual aspects of which are confirmed by the paintings themselves): the musty throw rugs and scarred chairs and hand-carpentered easels and exposed-brick wall, the upright, bolted-iron wood-burning stove my father later installed; the jazz or blues or (less often) leftist news and culture gab of WBAI seeping from the cassette-playing boom box; the savor of brushes marinating in turpentine and tangy odor of the cake of Lava soap—the only brand, my father explained, that would gently strip oil paint from human skin—at the shallow porcelain sink; the bulletin board layered with valentines from my mother and with enigmatic newspaper clippings (the death of Karl Wallenda was one) that would inspire later work of my father's, etc. What I can't supply, despite the clamor I by now imagine I hear from my reader on this point, is account of any parent-child consultations on the topic of the models and how I was or wasn't supposed to feel about them. I can't supply these because, I'm fairly certain, they didn't occur. Nudity Is Fine, like Nixon Is a Vampire or Grown-ups Smoke Pot, was a truth floating in our house, the sort I gradually inferred was somewhat more true inside our doors than out.

I not only glimpsed the models. At twelve or thirteen I declared myself an apprentice artist and began to draw them myself. Not in the studio upstairs, in our own house. Or, well, rarely there. Mostly I went along with my dad on "drawing group" night, to the home of his artist friends Bob and Cynthia, a loft space on Atlantic Avenue with square footage enough for a model to stand encircled by seven or eight artists sitting with sketch pads braced on crossed legs or seated before small easels. Specifically, seven adult artists (though my father was their elder statesman, likely at least a decade older than any of the others) and one teenager. Young teenager. I began before high school—I know this for certain because there were nudes in the portfolio of sketches I used to win entry into the High School of Music & Art that year. I was a regular at drawing group for three years, I'd guess. By the time I was sixteen I was through hanging out with my dad, for a while at least. But for three years I soaked my eyeballs in live flesh—not even a kid who'd grown up at a nudist colony could have been invited to stare like I stared. After all, I was an artist.

No one balked at my presence. This was 1977, 1978. The models, so far as I can rely on these memory tendrils I'm chasing, were blasé. These were mostly art students themselves, settled into an easy if boring gig. Likely posing for a group of men and women together was more comfortable, generally, than making a private exhibition for a solitary male, and evenings at Bob and Cynthia's were convivial. The routine followed the lines of every life-drawing class since publication of Kimon Nico-laides's *The Natural Way to Draw* and probably long before it: a series of rapid-fire poses so the artists could loosen with gestural sketches, then five- or ten-minute poses, then a few held long enough for a study— also long enough that the model might pause to stretch or even don a robe and take a five-minute break before resuming. Between poses the artists wandered to see others' work, and I did this, too. Sometimes the models roamed, too, in their robes. Other times they were uninterested in the results. I worked with Cray-Pas or gray or colored pencil, or compressed charcoal and, less often, painted in watercolor and gouache. I was less patient than the adults—I was there learning patience as much as anything—and remember feeling "finished" with studies before the longer poses were done and then watching the clock. Apart from that lapse I worked in absorption, and as with all absorbing work since I recall precisely zero from the mental interior of the experience.

What I wasn't doing—I'd know—was mental slavering. The Tex Avery wolf of sexual voraciousness not only restrained his eyeballs from first swelling like dirigibles and then bursting like loaded cigars; he slept. Any account of the evolutionary "hardwiring" of lust is stuck, I guess, dismissing me now as an outlier, or just a liar. The super-extensive actuality of women's bodies before my eyes was either too much or too little for me to make masturbatory mincemeat of.

Both too much and too little: The scrutiny was too much, the context too little. I don't mean they weren't sexy bodies. I'd guess they were. But Jonathan-seeing-them wasn't sexy at all. Even as I recorded with my charcoal or crayon the halo of untrimmed pubic bush and the flesh-braid of mystery that it haloed, I attained a total non-purchase on those bodies as objects of desire. The palace of lust was a site under construction—that's what I was off doing at night or in the afternoons, fantasizing about girls I knew who'd never even show me their knees. Then I slavered plenty.

Did I, in my imaginings, substitute for my non-girlfriends' unconquerable forms the visual stuff I'd gleaned at drawing group? Nope. As much as a T-shirt's neckline or tube top's horizon might seem a cruel limit to my wondering gaze, I didn't want my imagination to supply the pink pebbly fact of aureole and nipple, like those I'd examined under bright light for hours at a time. It wasn't that I found real women's bodies unappetizing but that I didn't have any use for them in the absolute visual sphere within which I'd gained access. Much like a person who's disappointed or confused at seeing the face attached to the voice of a radio personality well known to their ears, and then realizes that no face would have seemed any more appropriate, I suspect I didn't really make mental nudie shots of girls my age. I didn't picture them undressed, I imagined undressing them and the situations in which such a thing would be imaginable. My eyeballs wanted to be fingertips. I was a romantic.

A romantic teenage boy, that is. My romance encompassed a craving for illicit glimpses, not due to a lack of visual information but as rehearsals of transgression and discovery. A craving for craving, especially in the social context of other teenage boys, that mass of horny romantics. But we're talking about a terrible low point in the history of teenage access to pornography: Everyone's dads had canceled their *Playboy* subscriptions in a feminist epiphany a few years before (that everyone's dad had once subscribed to *Playboy* was a golden myth; I trust it was halfway true), and the Internet was a millennium away. A friend and I were actually excited when we discovered a cache of back issues of *Sexology*, a black-and-white, crypto-scientific pulp magazine, in the plaster and lathe of a ruined brownstone on Wyckoff Street. Pity us. When a couple of snootily gorgeous older teenage girls suddenly moved into the upper duplex of a house on Dean Street, there was some talk among the block's boys about climbing a nearby tree for a leer, a notion as halcyon-suburban as anything in my childhood. But the London plane trees shading our block had no branches low enough to be climbable, had likely been selected precisely for their resistance to burglars. The point is, I was as thrilled to imagine glimpsing the sisters as any of the other schemers. I could very well have gone off to drawing group the evening of that same day, but made no mental conjugation between the desired object and the wasted abundance before me.

Only two uneasy memories bridge this gulf, between the eunuch-child who breezed through a world of live nude models and the hormonal disaster site I was the rest of the time. One glitch was the constant threat or promise that a drawing-group model would cancel at the last minute, since tradition had it that one of the circle would volunteer for duty instead. Two of the group's members were younger women—named, incredibly enough, Hazel and Laurel—for whom I harbored modest but definite boy-to-woman crushes, and with whom I may have managed even to be legibly flirtatious. If one evening a model had canceled and either Hazel or Laurel took her clothes off, I'd likely have been pitched headfirst into the chasm of my disassociation. I never faced this outcome. The only substitute model ever to volunteer on my watch was our host, the hairily cherubic Bobby Ramirez. But I would never forget what didn't happen, who didn't undress. You may choose to see this as evidence against my assertion that the scene was not a sexual one for me. I choose to see it as certifying proof of my capacity for fantasizing about clothed women who lingered in the periphery of my vision *at the exact instant* I ignored naked ones in the center of my vision.

The second slippage took place not at drawing group but in my room, with my friend Karl. We were fourteen. Karl and I usually drew super-hero comics together, but this afternoon, deep into the porn drought of the '70s, we drifted into trying to produce our own doodling fantasy females without the veil of a cape or utility belt. At one point Karl reached an impasse in his attempt to do justice to the naked lady in his mind's eye and let me analyze the problem. Yes, the nipples were too small, and placed too high, on the gargantuan breasts Karl had conjured. He'd also too much defaulted to the slim, squared-off frame of the supermen we'd been compulsively perfecting. "Do you mind?" I asked. Taking the drawing from Karl, I compacted and softened the torso and widened the hips, gave his fantasy volume and weight, splitting the difference between the unreal ratio and something more persuasive. He'd handed me a teenage boy's fantasy and I, a teenage boy, passed back a woman, even if one who'd need back surgery in the long run. Karl and I were both, I think, unnerved, and we never returned to this exact pursuit. Our next crack at DIY porn was retrograde and bawdy, a comic called "Super-Dick," with images that were barely better than stick figures.

Confessing for the first time my authorship of Super-Dick, I'm flabbergasted, not at the dereliction of parental authority that would traipse nude women past the gaze of a boy still excited to sketch with ballpoint pen a hieroglyphic cock-and-balls in cape and boots and have it catapult into the obliging hairy face of a villain named Pussy-Man, but at the Möbius strip of consciousness which enabled that boy to walk around believing himself a single person, instead of two, or a hundred. If I've bet my life's work on a suspicion that we live at least as much in our wishes and dreams, our constructions and projections, as we do in any real waking life the existence of which we can demonstrate by rapping it with our knuckles, perhaps my non-utilization of the live nude models helped me place the bet. How could I ever be astonished to see how we human animals slide into the vicarious at the faintest invitation, leaving vast flaming puddings of the Real uneaten? I did.

My last year at Music & Art a teacher booked a nude model for us to draw in an advanced drawing class, one consisting only of graduating seniors. By chance this was the last time I'd ever sketch from a nude model, though I couldn't have known it at the time. By implication this was a privilege we seniors had earned after four years of art school: to be treated like adults. Still, there was plenty of nervous joking in the days before, and when the moment came, the doors and windows were kept carefully shaded against eyes other than those of us in the class. Needless to say, I felt blasé for several reasons, not least my own recent sexual initiation. I'd also begun to reformat myself as a future writer, rather than an apprentice artist (at seventeen I'd already been an apprentice artist a long time), and everything to do with my final high-school semester felt beneath my serious attention.

Yet ironically, I'll never forget the model that day. I remember her body when I've forgotten the others—had forgotten them, usually, by the time I'd begun spraying fixative on my last drawing of them, before they'd finished dressing. I remember her not because she was either uncannily gorgeous or ugly, or because I experienced some disconcerting arousal, but for an eye-grabbing anatomical feature: the most protuberant clitoris I'd seen, or have since. This wasn't something I could have found the language to explain to my fellow students that day, if I wanted to (I didn't). The model showed no discomfort with her body. She posed, beneath vile fluorescent, and standing atop the wobbling, standard-issue New York Department of Education tables I'd been around my whole life, the four legs of which never seemed capable of reaching the floor simultaneously, and we thirty-odd teenagers drew her, the whole of us sober, respectfully hushed, a trace bored if you were me, but anyhow living up to the teacher's expectation. But I do remember thinking: I know and they don't. (The boys, that would be who I meant.) I remember thinking: They'll think they're *all* that way.

On a Photograph of My Father

Geoff Brooks, circa 1975

The picture floats. Someone took it in the '70s, the white backdrop gives no clue. My dad owned that wide-lapel trench coat for fifteen or twenty years, typical thrifty child of the Depression. (He probably tried to give it to me at some point.) The beard's trim narrows the time frame slightly, that slightly rakish full goatee. So often later he wouldn't have bothered to shave his jaw to shape it. Put this in the early '70s. Somehow it floated into my collection of paper trinkets, ferried off to college, then to California for a decade. The only copy. By the time I showed it to my father, last week, he hadn't seen the photograph for thirty-odd years. He couldn't be sure of the photographer, guessing at three friends with comically overlapping names—Bobby Ramirez, Bob Brooks, Geoff Brooks. (I remember all three of them, beloved rascals from my parents' hippie posse.) He settled at last on Geoff Brooks, so that's the credit we'll give it. The picture was never framed nor mounted in an album, just survived shifted from file cabinet to cardboard box to file cabinet all this time. A scrap of Scotch tape on the left corner reminds me I had it taped up over a desk in Berkeley at some point. In a family that after my mother's death scattered itself and its memorabilia to far corners of the planet, and reassembles now sporadically and sloppily, the picture's a survivor. But I've lived with it for thirty years, gazed into its eyes as often, strange to say, as I have my father's living eyes.

And it shows Richard Lethem as I dream him, my idol. His midwestern kindness, prairie-gazer's soul, but come to the city, donning the beatnik garb, become the painter and poet and political activist he made himself, a man of the city. When I first knew my parents they were, paradoxically, just the two most exciting adults on the scene, part of a pantheon of artists and activists and students staying up late around the dinner table and often crashing afterward in the extra rooms of the house. My parents were both the two I had the best access to and the coolest to know, the hub of the wheel. I wasn't interested in childhood, I wanted to hang out with these guys. The picture shows my dad meeting the eyes of a member of his gang, both of them feeling their oats, knowing they were the leading edge of the world. I wanted him to look at me that way. He often did.

—*Granta*, 2010

Hazel

Oh, Hazel, you're making me crazy and lazy and hazy! Hazel, I think I love you! Hazel, you were the beginning of sex to me, a boy's love for an adult woman's mystery. I'm a little drunk on you, when I dim the lights and let the memories flood in . . . Hazel you are a Gypsy dancer . . . but let me try to explain.

My eyes are blue. Blue-gray. My father, a midwestern Quaker, has blue eyes. My Jewish mother had eyes that were something other. Brown, I would have said. My brother ended up with these eyes, too. *Hazel*, my parents both explained. This was important. Look for the green in the brown, the shimmer—that's Hazel. I tried, I looked. I pretended to see it, gazing into my mother's eyes, yes, sure, it's there—Hazel. They looked brown to me.

I associated this with a game of my mother's, another trick of gaze: She'd put her nose to mine so that our faces were too near to see in focus and say, with bullying enthusiasm, "See the owl! Do you see the owl? It's an owl, do you see it?" I never could see the owl. A blur, a cyclops, maybe a moth, but never an owl. I didn't know how to look for the owl. But I didn't know how to refuse: "Yes, I see the owl!" It was the same with Hazel. I saw and I didn't see. I saw the idea: something green in the brown, a richness, something Jewish and enviable and special, not mere brown eyes. The notion of Hazel balanced, in our family, against the specialness of blue eyes, it stood for everything that wasn't obvious in the sum of advantages or virtues between two parents. Hazel was my mother's beatnik Jewish side, her soulfulness. I granted it—I was in love with it! So Hazel was my first imaginary color, before Infrared, before Ultraviolet, and more sticky and stirring than either of those: Hazel is to Ultraviolet as Marijuana is to Cocaine, as Patchouli is to Obsession. My mother wore patchouli—it smelled Hazel.

My next Hazel was when I was fourteen or fifteen. My father is a painter, and I was following in his footsteps. He had a drawing group every Thursday night. I'd go and draw, sitting in the circle of artists, the one kid allowed. From the nude model. A mixed experience, a rich one. I was sneaking looks for hours at a time, in plain sight. This was the '70s. I demanded they treat me as an adult, and I was obliged. And there were two beautiful women, artists, who sat in the circle and drew from the model as well: Laurel and Hazel. Like the names of two rabbits. Laurel was blond and Hazel dark, no kidding. I loved them both, mad crushes. Again, an intoxicating mix, the nude before me, blinding my eyes, Hazel and Laurel my peers in the circle. The model would finish with a pose and you'd go around, murmuring approval of one another's drawings, pointing out flourishes. Crushes on your parents' female friends, when you're a hippie child, mash mothery feeling with earthy first stirrings of lust—you're not afraid of women's bodies, when you're a hippie child. That's got to be invented later, retroactively. I took showers outdoors with nudists, it was all good. Hazel was waiting for me, she was in store.

Then the Dylan song, of course, from *Planet Waves*. "Hazel." *Planet Waves* I'd put with *New Morning* and *Desire*, the three records of Dylan's most saturated with hippie aesthetics, the sexy Gypsy stuff, the handkerchief-on-the-head phase. "Hazel" is a ragged, tumbling song of lust, that Rick Danko organ sound: "You got something I want plenty of . . ." And from the same record, another lyric: "It was hotter than a crotch . . ." My mother loved Dylan, so it all folded together, the hot murk of Hazel, what I'd never seen but was ready to see, the green in the brown, Hazel, Dolores Haze-l, oh, I long for you still, you were the beaded, reeking initiation I never quite had, girls with potter's clay under their fingers, maybe, girls who when they danced spun in whirling skirts, and sex outdoors with bugs around and the sun in hazel eyes. And at night we'd see the owl, I was sure. Instead by the time I was ready it was an infrared or ultraviolet world, we danced with knock-kneed Elvis Costello jerks, sneering at Hazel, those grubby Deadhead girls in the next dorm, and made out with short-haired punks in cocaine fluorescent light. We reinvented body-fear, pale anomic anorexic sex-ambivalence. Hazel might be having all the fun, but she was shameful now, David Byrne had explained the problem perfectly. I pretended I'd never known her, and I hadn't—only trusted she'd be there, and detected the patchouli scent of her promise to me, the promise I failed to keep. Hazel, I never saw you.

—*Cabinet,* 2002

VI

9/11 AND BOOK TOUR

I'm eternally grateful to my past influences
But they will not free me
I am not diseased
All the people ask me
How I wrote Elastic Man

—The Fall, "How I Wrote Elastic Man"

I like hourglasses, maps, eighteenth-century typogra-
phy, etymologies, the taste of coffee, and Robert Louis
Stevenson's prose; he shares these preferences, but with a
vanity that turns them into the attributes of an actor.

—JORGE LUIS BORGES, "Borges and I"

Back to the slow train wreck of a self-reflexive public life. What in god's name are these two things—9/11 and book tour—doing in the same place? My fifth novel, Motherless Brooklyn, won a big award at the start of 2000, and my sixth, The Fortress of Solitude, best-sold in 2003. In between, something happened. Well, a few things. In the year before and the three after the terrorist attacks it was my luck to be granted the most and the pleasantest literary celebrity I could ever have imagined for myself, as a specifically "New York writer" (there'd be no reason for anyone to bother recalling I'd been a "Bay Area writer" before). I savored every part of this, even as I was bewildered at relinquishing lifelong preparations to be a neglected artist.

My response was obliging. I said yes to things for ten years. I'm still sorting through the results of that (specifically, by making this book). No complaints: Nobody told me to do anything. But the timing was such that among the first things nobody told me to do, only asked, was write and speak and be interviewed on the subject of the city after the attacks. It was a weird fate for someone whose brashest public pronouncements to that point had been to inform folks in the bar of the Radisson that they had more in common with Italo Calvino and Angela Carter and Don DeLillo than they knew, to the reward of pitying smiles.

Nine Failures of the Imagination

1. It began for me here, in the same room where I sit now, in Boerum Hill. It began as a non sequitur crackle of sunlight thunder, on a gorgeous morning after an evening of thunderstorms. I ignored the sound, took a shower instead, wondering about the sports page: Had Roger Clemens won his twentieth? The phone rang, and a friend asked, "Did you see it?" So I went to the window, and saw. In this part of Brooklyn the towers are the nearest bit of Manhattan, easily visible from upper stories or rooftops. Neighbors commute—excuse me, commuted—to them by walking across the Brooklyn Bridge. Both planes had arrived by the time I looked out the window. My under-caffeinated denial slid from the fact of it—*they're on fire, wow*—to tangential irritations, stuff I had to get done this week. I'd reenact this denial again and again in the next hours: the mind's raw disinclination to grant this new actuality, cognitive dissonance run riot. I'd entered—we'd all entered—a world containing a fresh category of phenomena: the *unimaginable fact*.

2. For the first forty hours of this war all I've done is shuttle between my apartment on Bergen Street, the homes of a few nearby friends, and the front-row seat provided by the Brooklyn Heights Promenade, a rim of park that looks out over the tip of Manhattan. All I've done, really, is try again and again to grasp the unimaginable fact. I've stared across

the river at the raw, unmediated plume, now black, now white, now gray, now black again. I've stared and stared and felt my mind slide from it again and again: unimaginable fact, confirmed by senses and testimony, confirmed by the procession of ash-bathed faces shambling through the neighborhood after crossing the bridge, confirmed by the television and yet granted no status by reeling, refusing mind. No status whatsoever. Turning from the plume to the television, I try again: Maybe CNN can sell it to me with their video loop, plane slicing cake of tower forever, the footage more ferociously lush and inevitable every time. I'll understand this fact soon, yes? No. No. Back to the Promenade, then, to contemplation of my lovely plume, Manhattan's inverted Fuji of roiling particles. And now back to the television.

3. *Am I willing?* Can I bear to narrate this into normality, forty hours after they crumbled and fell? To craft a story: *and then, and then, and then?* Will the words I'm spilling here seem fatuous or hysterical or naïve by the time they're read? Likely so. I'm failing and relieved to fail. I'm disgusted with myself for consenting to try. Speculation feels obscene. So does this self-indulgent self-castigation. Except there may be some slim value in offering to a rapidly toughening future some hint of the white noise of one human imagination failing, on what they're calling the day after, to yet meet the task at hand. The channel surf of denial and incomprehension: an extremely local report.

4. As a kid in this neighborhood it was a regular thing to walk to the Promenade to see the harbor and skyline. I'd go with my grandmother and she'd point out the statue, the ferry, Ellis, Governors. Later we stared from that perch as they assembled these erector-set-looking things, these twinned towers. Even then I was a New York purist, I preferred *old things*, and resented the dull Saltine boxes for dwarfing the Empire State. But they were mine anyway, I couldn't help it. Big Apple, Abe Beame, Bicentennial, World Trade Center, my cheesy '70s New York. A decade later, when I first married, I dragged a California bride to my city and we elevated to the roof of one of the buildings to exhilarate in the raw, dizzying wind of outer space. Yesterday, the erector set reappeared, just for a moment. Yesterday the same west-to-east wind

that once nearly whisked newlyweds from the rooftop blew pulverized tower across the river and into my mouth. I've eaten my towers.

5. Back to the Promenade, back. I've abandoned the television five, six times now to walk to the edge and widen my recalcitrant eyes and mind again at the plume. On the way up Henry Street I gather one of the crisped papers twinkling everywhere to the ground. A printout on old-style, tabbed computer paper. 7WTC 034: World Trade Center, building 7, thirty-fourth floor, I guess. Kirshenbaum, Joan. "For any report change complete this section and return to ops support, data centre." Joan Kirshenbaum, you contemporary Bartleby, if you're reading this I've got your scrap of paper.

6. Dear reader, two Sundays in the future: You know vastly more than I do about what I mean when I say war. Do you envy me, living in this *before*, this last shred of relative innocence? I hope not. I hope I ought to envy you, the wild sweet peace you enjoy, the simultaneous epiphany of universal human amity and accord, the melting of all world guns into memorial sculpture which took place on, say, September 16, the miracle that occurred in place of the carnage I'm dreading today. Oh, I hope I ought to envy you, I hope I'm a moron.

7. Reality check. As I write, sirens wheeling past my window. I'm two blocks from Atlantic Avenue and the city's largest Arabic neighborhood, which the cops have cordoned from traffic, anticipating and protecting against retaliatory chuckleheadedness. The radio's telling of another building fallen—you know, just another large, unmemorable office building in lower Manhattan crumbling to dust, not a big deal these days, it happens sometimes, relax—*It's not like the twin towers fell down!* The many, many things they're not telling us on the radio fall into two categories: things they're not telling us that we can pretty easily riddle out for ourselves like *we're picking up ears, we're picking up toes, god have mercy we're picking up penises and vaginas*; and things they're not telling us which we really can't fathom like for instance what the hell all these presently rushing sirens are rushing toward.

8. The Promenade yesterday was full of people, more than I've seen since the tall ships were in the harbor, and yet all absolutely still and silent. Each one of us came and stood, rooted at the spot where we first got the plume in full view. Every third or fourth mouth covered with a surgical mask, those without masks feeling just that tiny bit sorrier for ourselves, but then again not really caring. That vast communal silence. I was doing better there, standing with others, rightly gathered into a commonality, a field of eyes, with mouths emitting if anything only those slight, undramatized moans.

9. At the Promenade yesterday in the gathered silence and stillness of many minds looking through haze at an altered city one woman, seated on a bench, elbows on knees, calmly, effortlessly tilted her head and vomited. The splash heard in the silence. The head tilted just enough to avoid chin-dribble. Eyes never breaking from the task of gazing, gathering the new information.

—*The New York Times Magazine,* September 2001

Further Reports in a Dead Language

Thoughts that first ran through my head, all garbage now, like scorched paperwork over the harbor: *Wow, it's going to be hard to repair those tall buildings!* Couldn't Clinton just be president again? I mean really, that whole election thing was fun, but the real guy is alive, he's healthy, can't we just sort of slip him in there? *One of those buildings couldn't actually fall, could it? Could it?* There were people on those airplanes! We just watched a lot of people die! *Gore would be fine, just fine.* My breath stinks. Didn't brush my teeth. *The people on the floors above the fire. God.* The Pentagon, that's like the ultimate symbol of something: fortress, geometry. Somebody really hates geometry today. Penta-gone. *Traffic's going to be a drag.* There are people in the Pentagon. *There's really a LOT of people in the World Trade Center.* It only looked like a small plane because you can't credit the scale. It was a big plane. *It's still there, behind that cloud, it's an optical thing.* Only one tower, gosh, that's going to look weird! *I'd take George Senior. I'd take Nixon. I'd take a player piano, a balloon animal, a wind sock.* But no, this sophomore Virginia Woolf crap is a failure, another blasphemy, and a total waste, I can't go on with it, very sorry. Write that one yourself.

We'd abided so long in our shimmering impassive skins, sealed like airplanes ourselves, stationary airplanes: climate-controlled, with weather and pestilence and human frailty all sheltered inside. More than just the world's largest filing cabinets, my other and I were bodies undertaking a long consideration of space, ticking off earth rotations, swatting birds. When after so very long the new body entered mine I was accepting, more than I might have predicted. Though I shivered I tried to permit myself to learn what it had to teach me, this intersection of presences. Beside me was another struggle with the same knowledge: two brides, two grooms. But the marriages were brief. The lesson opaque. No, J. G. Ballard crap isn't going to do it, either, exaggerated empathy for the machines and buildings won't help anything, won't get me out of what I'm still trying not to feel.

I was invited to Turin, Italy, last spring for a citywide book festival. As I was driven from the airport to the hotel by my Italian hosts, I laughed at the billboards for the festival, which were visible everywhere in the city: They showed a face with eyes closed, pushed deep into the spine of an open book, as if to sniff or lick the joint of pages. "I guess that's the way to get Italians interested in books," I joked. "You have to suggest they're something to eat or fuck." Yesterday, here in Brooklyn, I walked into my local bookstore and talked with the owner, my friend Henry Zook. "People are reading," Henry said hopefully. When I asked what they were reading he said, "Nostradamus, and books about germs." Myself, I wanted to buy every book in the store and stack them into a windowless castle for myself, I wanted to stroke their papery bodies, I wanted, a little, to burn the store down. Language is metaphysics, and I hate metaphysics today. I hate the religious and philosophical lies which estrange me from the immediate life in favor of lost or imaginary kingdoms and gardens, in favor of paradisiacal or hellish afterlives, all lies. Today I want to eat and fuck.

—*Rolling Stone,* September 2001

To My Italian Friends

To my Italian friends,

In preparation for my visit to Mantua, which I'm anticipating with great pleasure, I find I'm asked again to speak on this question of how the world has changed since September 11. This isn't surprising—in my recent visits to Barcelona, London, Berlin, and Amsterdam I was greeted with this question, and related questions, time and time again. In fact, I'm grateful to be asked to write a few lines here, perhaps in the hopes of saying something which will satisfy my restless wish to eventually be asked a different question, one I'm better able to answer.

At the request of the *New York Times* I wrote a piece on September 12 and 13, a series of impressions, from my helpless window in Brooklyn, of the disaster that had fallen on our city. (The article was eventually cut in two, and the second portion of it was published in *Rolling Stone*.) The result was a pale scream of protest, nothing more—most of the novelists in New York were asked by one magazine or another to write something, and to me it seems our voices, at that moment, blended into one vast impotent scream. Still, I was proud to have written it, not for any illusion that it was illuminating or consoling for anyone else to read, but because the effort involved writing, doing my job. Like everyone else still alive in the city, my responsibility in the days following the disaster was to find a way to return to work, to reassert the collective reality of a city whose fragility had been revealed. To fail to resume work would have been to fail the community—the subway conductors had trains to pilot through the tunnels, the secretaries had to return to offices in buildings where bomb threats were being called in, in order to answer ringing telephones and copyedit legal documents, the Korean grocers had mangoes and papaya to set out for their Dominican and Puerto Rican customers. So, I sat in my house and did my feeble job, between bouts of self-pitying weeping. Since then I've been unable to speak on the subject directly with any intelligence, though I have stumbled through interviews all over Europe, against my own wish that a site of suffering be permitted a measure of silence, time, and even mystery.

I simply can't answer your question. I don't know anything you don't know. The experience a year ago, which will be with me forever, is nothing more than the wing of history's airplane grazing and tearing the scrim of unreality which had somehow still cloaked the world's ongoing disaster from our eyes. It seems distasteful to me that New York's suffering should be privileged as a revelation beyond a certain point, and that point was passed in October or November, at the very latest. Such naïveté, such historical amnesia, represents a thin trace of the impulse for reinvention which once fueled the American dream. But at this late date the American dream is only a kind of a cult or religion, and I'm not very fond of religions lately. Firemen who die like soldiers are tragic, even pathetically noble, but to exalt their deaths in the cause of belligerence is perverse and shameful, an inadequate parsing of the unexpected last line of the twentieth century's horror-poem. So don't ask how the world has changed—ask how I have changed. The answer is: I've changed *slightly*. I read my newspapers with increased horror and distrust, I regard the leaders of nations and movements with increased revulsion, I suffer increased shame at my own paralyzed inaction, and every day I give a quarter to the woman who sits on the corner of my block. The only question she asks—"Hey, do you have a quarter?"—is one to which I at least know an answer.

I look forward in September to being able to clasp your hands and kiss your cheeks, and to raise a glass of wine with you in consideration of what words can't reach.

All best,
Jonathan

—book festival program, Mantua, 2002

My Egyptian Cousin

I've never traveled farther from New York than western Europe; Saad Eddin Ibrahim is an advocate of democracy imprisoned in Egypt. But Saad and I are both outlying members of the same sprawling midwestern family: Saad is married to my first cousin Barbara. His name is in the news and on the op-ed pages these days, if you're looking out for it. A year ago, the *New York Times Magazine* ran a photo of Saad on its cover, in which he is seen peering from between the bars of his courtroom cage. But even such prominent items can be lost in the dispiriting muddle of Middle Eastern politics, so hard to keep in view amid yellow-alert warnings of poison-gas attacks, or alongside sniper headlines which further convince our fear-stupefied Western selves that anyone called Muhammad has a predisposition to run amok. Saad is a professor of sociology at the American University in Cairo and the founder and director of the Ibn Khaldun Center for Development Studies, which campaigns for a secular and democratic civil society in Egypt. Famous in Egypt for his controversial writing on minorities, and for his role as a presidential adviser and television commentator in the Sadat years, Saad came increasingly under attack in the official press during the Mubarak era. His defense of the persecuted Coptic Christians and his criticism of electoral corruption was, it seemed, tolerated because of his closeness to the Mubarak family—the president's wife and sons had been among his students. But Saad, like Falstaff, may have known his president too well and not well enough. When he publicly warned against the possibility of Mubarak grooming one of his sons to succeed him, he was arrested, as an object lesson to other would-be activists. Mubarak perhaps did not so much initiate this action as withdraw his protection, allowing reactionary elements, who had long been calling for Saad Eddin Ibrahim to be silenced, to do as they wished.

In July 2000, after raids on his home and on the Ibn Khaldun Center, Saad and twenty-seven of his students and colleagues were charged with accepting foreign funds for the purpose of defaming Egyptian society in a documentary film and a paper on election-rigging. The European Union, which supplied the funds in question, has since endorsed their use in four separate affidavits. The laws under which Saad was prosecuted were framed in an attempt to stem the flow of funds for subversive Islamist activities. He was tried before a special court set up after Sadat's assassination to deal with terrorists, but which is increasingly used to persecute homosexuals, members of religious minorities, and advocates of free speech. My cousin Barbara described the courtroom in a letter to me:

The scene can only be experienced, it is nearly impossible to describe: throngs of reporters blocking the line of vision between lawyers and the bench, cell phones going off every two minutes, lawyers dressed in "robes" that once were styled on British barristers', but now a tradition so long forgotten that glued-on cotton balls stand in for ermine ruffs. Janitors shuffle around in plastic flip-flops among years of cigarette butts asking us for baksheesh—during the proceedings—for "cleaning" the room. The defendants stand in an iron cage for the duration of the hearings, but the grill is so broken down that we can pass notes and coffee in to Saad at any time.

Five of Saad's students and colleagues were convicted along with him; most have now been freed having served nine months. Saad's captivity, though, still serves a purpose. I have tried to understand it this way: Imagine that the president of the United States, rather than ignoring the bee stings of a dissident leftist—Noam Chomsky, say, or Ralph Nader, perhaps Michael Moore—had him imprisoned. Astonishment would quickly give way to fear of speaking out. The incarceration of one person, the right person, can be an act of the most ruthless efficiency, chaotic kangaroo-court tableaux notwithstanding. So Saad, a sixty-seven-year-old scholar in failing health, faces six more years of imprisonment. An appeal hearing this month appears to be his last hope (short of a Mubarak pardon) of being spared.

My cousin Barbara spent her childhood in the Chicago suburb of Palatine and met Saad in 1967 when she was his student at DePauw University in Indiana; they were married in 1971 and moved to Cairo, where their two children grew up and where she is a director of research with the International Population Council. Her father—and mine—grew up on farms in Iowa and Missouri: Our grandfather was a traveling salesman who dealt in farm equipment and supplies. That she was able to make such a move may have something to do with the 1960s. Among the many international groups to send representatives to Washington, D.C., on October 25 for a Free Saad Eddin Ibrahim rally was the Duck, a group of Saad's former students and colleagues from DePauw, named for the Fluttering Duck—a coffeehouse, at the corner of Center Street and Vine in Greencastle, Indiana, where the lecturer and his midwestern acolytes used to hang out. In a recent e-mail circular, the Duck reminded members to send notes of protest to the Egyptian embassy, in order to help the Ibrahim family "to keep on keeping on."

I first met Saad sometime in the '60s, when I was five or six years old. I clearly remember him visiting our house in Brooklyn as early as 1971, and then more clearly still at Lethem family reunions held at various sites in Kansas, Arkansas, and Missouri on through the '70s. I understood his place in my life, and in my family, through a lens of "'60s consciousness" inherited from my parents. This inheritance was for me effortless and, until recently, unexamined. My mother was New York Jewish and, behind that, a mix of High German–assimilated and Polish-Russian shtetl; my father was midwestern-Protestant nothing, with distant Scots-English roots, and by the '70s had become a practicing Quaker, partly in protest against the Vietnam War. The real religion in our house, though, was a combination of art and protest and utopian internationalist sentiment. Through the Friends Service Committee and through our connection with the *Guardian*, a Communist newspaper, our family took in lodgers from all over the world— I remember particularly a Rwandan Tutsi and an Okinawan. Intermarriage, of any sort, was felt to be heroic, and Barbara, with her Egyptian family, seemed absolutely heroic. So did my fabled aunt Molly, the dark horse of my mother's family, who'd fled New York and married a Mexican, and then set up as a folk artist in Arizona. Even the midwestern Lethems were obsessed with their purported trace of Native American blood—my legendary great-great-grandfather, named Brown, was said to be half Oglala Sioux.

Also, I grew up in a Brooklyn neighborhood with more brown faces than white. So it was thrilling and consoling—not only righteous but intuitively right—that splashing around alongside us paler kids in the motel pool in Maryville, Missouri, during those '70s family reunions were my dark Egyptian cousins, Randa and Amir. And by the poolside, arguing politics with my World War II veteran uncles, and with my outspoken radical Jewish mother, was their growly, bearded, imperious, and quite lovable father, Saad. In fact, though we might by some current standards seem conceptually "opposed," we half-Jewish and half-Egyptian cousins were more like each other than we were like the many dozens of pure midwestern cousins surrounding us. We'd brought a new flavor to the Lethem family, a scent of the wider world, of cosmopolitan cities and oceans to a landlocked tribe. Though in New York City I made a very unconvincing Jew to other Jews—unobservant, un–bar mitzvahed, attending Quaker Sunday school—in Kansas I was hot currency. One of my cousins once walked me down a suburban street in Overland Park, Kansas, in order to brandish me on a mission of mercy: There was an adopted Jewish kid on the street, shy and ashamed at being the only Jew anyone in the neighborhood knew. He was perhaps seven or eight years old. I was proof that a kid like him could turn into a normal teenager: See, Jews are okay! Even Chris Lethem's got one in his family! I felt I was a token of a world improved by mongrelization. I was by that time enamored of Arthur C. Clarke, whose Stapledonian socialism thrummed just under the surface of his glossy futures. "We must not export our borders into space," he said. Those visions seemed to me then an obvious extension of my parents' hippie values. I remember once disconcerting my father by explaining, with the patronizing certainty of an adolescent lecturing an adult, that the chimera of nationalism would dissolve into a single planetary government within my lifetime, if not his. We were all going to intermarry and brownify and hold hands and honor our essential human cousinhood—weren't we?

Well, 2001 wasn't Clarke's year. I remember sitting with Saad twenty-five years earlier, watching the 1976 Olympics on a Missouri motel-room television. If at that time he had any inkling that the Islamist right, soon to slaughter Sadat, or the Reagan right, soon to slaughter FDR's and my parents' hopes for American society, were together going to keep the Fluttering Ducks among us in abeyance for another millennium or so, he didn't say anything to damage my own hopefulness. Certainly his outlook must have been more realistic than mine, or even my parents'. Still, it's unlikely he could have imagined the degree of slippage in his own culture—the extent to which the educated urban middle classes to which he and his students belong would be squeezed on either side by Islamic activism and what he has called the "Oriental despotism" of the "pharaonic" Mubarak regime.

In the immediate aftermath of the New York attacks Saad wrote a new postscript for the reissue of *Egypt, Islam, and Democracy*. Writing from his jail cell, he reminded us that, for Egyptians, September 11 has a relevant local precursor, one rarely mentioned in American discussions of the World Trade Center disaster—the attacks at the Temple of Luxor in 1997, in which Islamist militants killed sixty tourists, mostly Swiss, British, and Japanese, as well as a number of Egyptian guides. Saad describes what happened at Luxor as "the bitter harvest of the last decade." "It was like an earthquake: it was swift and devastating at the epicentre, but its economic and political aftershocks were longer and more pervasive." The terrorists "exposed the vulnerability of the state, the fragility of the economy and the soft underbelly of society." As New Yorkers must fear al-Qaida living next door, so must Egyptians. It isn't only the Lethems who would, given the chance, sooner be sunning themselves at a motel poolside.

—*London Review of Books,* December 2002

Writing this now in February 2011, in the weeks of lull after the Cairo revolution, I still can't know whether my small petition for confidence in the presence of a substantial secular civil conversation in the Arab world was prophetic or not. I hope so. Saad was freed in 2003, and worked in exile in Europe and America until a few days ago, when after Mubarak's resignation he returned to Cairo. Meanwhile, I recently heard from a man who'd been trying to locate his childhood suburban friend, so had Web-searched "Chris Lethem+Overland Park" and found himself on the London Review's *website. He wrote to say, "I was that one Jewish kid in Overland Park." Sometimes the Internet's nightmare of eternal return conjures something better and technotopian shivers run through my body like it is 1992 all over again.*

The next two attempt to rework 9/11 discomfort in a sidelong glance, sublimating the fact in speculation (something I'd do more extensively in Chronic City). They're the same piece in different guises, one more or less "fiction" ("Proximity People") the other "non" ("Cell Phones"). I like the fiction better, for its capacity to turn on itself, to eat its own voice. Here's the thing: I'd forgotten the existence of "Cell Phones" by the time I wrote "Proximity People." If I hadn't, I doubt I'd have felt free to try again.

Cell Phones

When I was a teenager I worked in a sandwich shop, the owner of which was peculiarly obsessed with formalities and protocol: methods of wrapping paper packages around prepared food, for instance, or of cleaning the blade and sheath of the mechanical slicer with a rag moving in a certain specified direction, or sequences of giving a customer change while their ten or twenty was still visible on the shelf of the cash register. He instilled in me an anal-Zen reverence for the observation of ritual in retail work, one which stayed with me long after I abandoned sandwich shops for used bookstores.

This shop owner insisted, as well, that we counterpersons observe a strict hierarchy as to the precedence of a real live customer, standing in front of us waiting to be served, over a caller on the telephone. Telephone customers, he explained, however preemptory and insistent, were to be considered as ghosts, nonentities, birds in the bush. They hadn't made the commitment to appear in person in the shop, and so weren't to be given any privileges to rival those customers who had. We shouldn't ever make someone standing before us wait while we dealt with a telephone order; we were always to put calls on hold. I suppose this was where my notion of the morality of proximity was first instilled.

Cell phones exaggerate this consideration. Compared to traditional (or should I call them *primitive*?) telephones, they break down space and time, the ordinary rules of access and proximity, to a bewildering degree. Like anyone, I'm annoyed at overhearing someone else's mobile-phone conversation in the close quarters of a train compartment or an airplane on the tarmac. I admit I find it satisfying when that overheard conversation is curtailed by instructions from the cockpit or by the train going into a tunnel. The cell-phone line out of the sealed quarters of a train or bus or airplane seems particularly unfair, a betrayal of the we're-all-in-this-together contract to share the discomfort, the temporary democracy, of mass transportation.

An airplane or train car is one of life's perfect traditional theaters, and we suffer its rupture by the Brechtian device of the mobile phone. The caller breaks the fourth wall, converting our humble story of togetherness into a metanarrative in which he is the controlling narrator. The cell-phone user has made irony of our sincere drama of grudging togetherness. As in a game of Prisoner's Dilemma, one person's opting out of behavior which reinforces solidarity makes everyone else want to bail out as well. The cell-phone user is like an airplane passenger who wears a parachute when nobody else has one. We wonder why he's entitled.

I've been reenvisioning my favorite filmic nightmares of transportation to include the mobile phone: movies like *The Poseidon Adventure*, or *Lifeboat*, or *The Taking of Pelham One Two Three*, or *Alive*. The John Ford Western *Stagecoach* is the paradigm for this genre: the disunified gathering of Reformed Prostitute, Cowardly Salesman, Drunken Doctor, Proper Pregnant Lady, Snide Gambler, Pretentious Banker, Rough Outlaw, Bumpkin Stagecoach Driver, etcetera, forced into temporary society by the marauding Indians on their tail. In my cellular version, the Salesman certainly calls out for a quick background check on John Wayne's Ringo Kid character. Meanwhile the Banker will have gotten in touch with his broker: "I want to divest from all stage-line and road-building holdings immediately. Put everything into bullets." And the Drunken Doctor no longer has to fight his urge for the bottle long enough to perform the delivery of the Proper Pregnant Lady's baby: She delivers the baby herself, out of sight of the men, while taking blow-by-blow instructions from a medical helpline. The introduction of a cell phone wrecks the traditional tale of a misfit microcosm banding together against external threat just as easily as it wrecks the banal solidarity of the daily commuter.

In the dire lifeboat of the real, however, things are not quite so simple. For if mobile phones offer a path out of the humble, every-day communities created by the close proximities of transportation, they've also recently proven to offer an eerie path into the privacies of the communally doomed. In September 2001 I was, as a New Yorker, asked to erase any stored messages in my voice mail, because the city-wide system had been strained by the families of World Trade Center victims all desperately saving last phone calls made from burning and collapsing buildings. The phone company wanted to find a way to preserve those messages, and their computer system was at a break-ing point. More famously, the calls made in and out of the fourth and final hijacked airplane were the key to creating a passionate and instan-taneous unity among those temporary heroes who are presumed to have smashed into the cockpit to bring the plane down, causing a crash which harmed only themselves and their attackers, sparing any target on the ground. Without knowledge of the larger situation they'd have remained as passive—and, perhaps, as distrustful of one another's theories or plans—as the four squabbling actors in Jean-Paul Sartre's *No Exit*. The image of their action, in turn, has become an irreducible evocation of fortitude and grace among strangers, too selfless to arouse any cynicism, though, alas, not too pure to appropriate for reprehen-sible politics.

Communication with the ground enabled those passengers to understand that they were seated in the larger stagecoach of history. Our *Poseidon*s and *Pelham*s and *Lifeboat*s are only, after all, poignant stand-ins for the whole world, for the vast continents of Bankers, Bumpkins, Prostitutes, Proper Ladies, Outlaws, and Drunk Doc-tors who must find ways to coexist. Yet if all men are brothers why does it still stir our annoyance when one of them opts to speak with those brothers-not-visible-at-this-precise-moment-in-space-and-time? Perhaps we're not ready to admit to the largest, the most global priori-ties, at least not until the choice is between crashing our airplane into a building full of others or an open field. Short of crisis, we prefer to keep our attention on local, visible, fleshly humans, not remote, theoretical, staticky ones. And so we neglect the ringing telephones from remotest precincts, unsure whether those passengers are even really in the same stagecoach as ours.

I wonder what it will feel like when the cellular phone is invented which can receive calls from the future? Will we choose to take the calls of those generations following us, whose needs we barely manage to acknowledge between our batterings away at the polar ice and the rain forest, or will we let them go through to voice mail? I suppose it will annoy me, the first time someone I'm speaking with puts me on hold to take a call from 3006. Shouldn't a call from a co-inhabitant of the same year be more important? What's that person from the future got over the immediacy of me? I suppose the answer will be that the person from the future has something to tell us. Perhaps a suggestion about where exactly we might want to crash this plane.

—BBC Radio, 2002

Proximity People

People who work at counters and make you wait while they answer the telephone, privileging the customer on the phone over the one right in front of their face, the one who made the trip, got out of bed, appeared in person. People who interrupt the phone call with the person who called first to use call-waiting to take the call from the person who called second. People who get to the counter and make the person waiting at the counter wait while they talk on their cell phone. People who glance at their e-mail when you're in the room. People who use handheld devices to glance at their e-mails while in your house. People who borrow your computer or handheld device in order to glance at their e-mails. People who answer e-mails from people they do not know with great alacrity and full capitalization and punctuation while replying slowly and with few if any capitals or punctuation marks to the e-mails of their devoted friends. People who unfriend their friends while friending their unfriends. People who do not acknowledge the person. Persons who are not personal.

People who visit parties and ignore their friends, do not *dance with the one that brung you*. People who have more time, more munificence, more courtesy, for strangers than for their friends. Children who love their uncles and aunts more than their father and mother, their cousins more than their siblings. People who have a picture of Jesus Christ or John F. Kennedy or Abraham Lincoln on their wall, as if Jesus Christ or John F. Kennedy or Abraham Lincoln was their relative. People who use the first names of celebrities. People who shorten the names of or create nicknames for those they don't know or barely know, in order to seem more familiar, especially in cases where people who are actually familiar with those named would never shorten their name or use a nickname. Rotisserie-baseball fans who never go to a baseball game or follow a "real" team. Married people who develop crushes on waitresses or bank tellers.

Those who speak to the invisible, the remote, those not present, while disfavoring the visible, the proximate, the present. Those concerning themselves with ghosts. Clergy of all types. People who wear pictures in lockets of grandparents they never knew, even as they disdain or neglect living uncles or aunts. People who construct family trees or visit genealogical websites but are brusque and rude to strangers on the subway. Those who adopt animals but not children. Eaters of fish but not pork.

People who concern themselves with the fate of slaves in distant capitals they have never visited and would never visit. People who read the International section before they read the Metro section, or never read the Metro section. People who read eagerly of discoveries of planets orbiting distant stars in unreachable galaxies. Anyone interested in SETI (the search for extraterrestrial intelligence). People who watch the Oscar telecast but don't go to movies. People who watch a telecast of celebrations in Times Square at midnight on New Year's Eve. Lip-synchers. Karaokeists.

People who read stories about imaginary people while real people stand before them unsung and unappreciated. People who read stories and experience real emotions while finding it difficult to feel real emotions when presented with the difficulties of their living friends. Science-fiction people. Historical reenactors. Pen pals. Those who fall in love remotely, projecting cherished values onto those distant from them, values that they never identify among those nearest to them. Constructors of time capsules. People who write in journals or diaries never intended to be read during their lifetimes. Anonymous authors. Anonymous donors. People who comment anonymously on the blogs of their friends. People who at parties glance over your shoulder while they speak with you, searching for a better option. Necrophiliacs.

Those studying foreign languages, especially dead languages. Students of Esperanto or Klingon. Those mourning the deaths of royalty. Those who love or hate anyone they've never met. Catholics drinking wine and eating wafer. Readers of secondary sources before primary sources. Archaeologists and anthropologists. Those cherishing extinct species. "Pay It Forward" people. Sexaholics. Doctors Without Borders. Mimes who follow people on the street.

People who use time machines to prevent the crucifixion of Jesus Christ or the Kennedy or Lincoln assassination but would not use time machines to apologize to those they personally disregarded in fourth or fifth grade. People from the future who use time machines to send lawyers from the future back into the past to place injunctions on the use of the resources of the present because of the effect of diminishing the resources available to those in the future, people who by some measures *do not yet exist*. Lawyers from the present who accept those from the future as their clients in class-action lawsuits against present-day people.

Lawyers for the unborn. Pro-lifers. Autograph hounds. Strangers who interfere in private arguments on the street. Fans. Ventriloquists. Ventriloquists on the radio. People who listen to podcasts while in the presence of others. Ham-radio operators. Stamp collectors, with their glue tabs and albums, adorers of the tenuous papery whisper of what comes from afar, soaking envelopes to reclaim canceled stamps, discarding the envelopes, ignoring the addresses, never noticing the names of the original recipients, *the persons for whom the letters were intended*, cherishing instead the postage.

Above all, writers.

—Granta, 2009

Repeating Myself

But questions about 9/11 weren't the only questions I answered. Pieces about 9/11 weren't the only commissions I took. I backed into a thousand remarks on dystopia, Brooklyn public schools, Tourette's syndrome, alphabetizing my record collection, John Wayne, and my top-ten or top-five neglected anything, including sandwiches. I turned out to be one of the garrulous ones, not something I'd necessarily have known in advance nor bothered to predict due to the aforementioned expectation of being neglected myself. The novelist Lawrence Shainberg, friend of Beckett and Mailer both, asked the Irishman his opinion of the Brooklynite, at which Beckett produced the typically pained epigram: "He's a bit . . . *copious* . . . for my taste." Some Beckett part of me endlessly muttered "copious," trying to interrupt my Mailerations on so many subjects, but was drowned out.

The subjects included, always, my books and myself. I'm a too-willing explainer, a penchant useful in a father of a toddler but embarrassing otherwise. "All I do is go around trapped in a bubble of regard," I said somewhere. "A book tour is a solipsistic nightmare." I spoke these words while on book tour, in a newspaper's offices. Even here, now, I'm explaining my explaining. "I don't know how to stop," Coltrane complained to Miles Davis, who replied, "Take the horn out of your mouth." My fascination at this anecdote suggests I don't know how to take the horn out of my mouth. I've given enough interviews that any striking notion I've ever managed aloud I've also paraphrased awkwardly a few dozen times, and contradicted outright another five or ten, a combination of my eagerness to tell in-person listeners what they want to hear and my discomfort at repeating myself, at least repeating myself exactly. Seeking variations—and to light up the jaded eyes of bored journalists—I've been variously flippant, morbid, and no doubt teeth-grindingly sincere on every topic ever pushed my way. The only approach I neglect is to bow out, to ignore a question or scratch an interview; I show up too often and say too much. The Internet acts as *Funes the Memorious*—a place where remarks go to never die. It's scattered with my blurry paraphrases, like twelfth-generation photocopies, of things I said a bit better five or twenty years earlier.

Maybe newcomers could just forage and assemble whichever interview replies they prefer. Eager to find me swearing allegiance to metafiction or Brooklyn, or disavowing these same things? It wouldn't be much trouble. Your Lethem may be more interesting to you than mine, perhaps even to me.

This piece, commissioned for an anthology of writers' book-tour humilia-
tions, was slight but opened a door. Breaking a taboo against acknowledg-
ing my curiosity about my public avatar, it made a tiny step toward this
book.

Bowels of Compassion

Book-touring, in the United States, is a slog. The process is much less romantic, so much less a coronation, than some might imagine. It's churlish to complain about the effort of one's publisher to bring a book to the light of an audience, and I won't complain here: I'll book-tour again this year, and I'll see many friends—booksellers, interviewers, and my publisher's remote operatives—acquired in earlier rounds. But the net effect is a slog through a morass of Sartrean repetitions. I begin tours cheerfully and end them as a zombie, hoping not to be ungracious in any number of dazed moments.

I think of my escorts. Not the type found in ads in the back of weekly newspapers, but "literary escorts," those local sprites schlepping writers in and out of airports, hotel lobbies, radio stations, and bookstores. Escorts are not the cause of mortification but the witnesses to it. They're the human link, the local flavor. I think of my escort in Minnesota, who drove a battered Toyota, its dashboard decorated with gopher skulls and dried branches of herb, and who escorted authors to support finishing an epic, book-length poem on the subject of road-kill. I remember my Vietnam-vet escort in Kansas City, bravely limping with his cane around the car to open my side door. I remember others and love them all.

I think of the radio. The radio is, for me, the void. A tour consists of waking at five, breakfasting in the airport, landing in a new city, and dropping one's bags in a hotel room, then being whisked to a radio station to make a nine or ten a.m. talk show, where a jaded local host who's read only a summary of your book and mispronounces your name will ask you questions about your mother and father and whether you know anyone really famous. Later that night you'll see local friends, you'll read aloud to live humans who've put aside part of their lives to come and see you stand at a podium. If you're lucky you'll have a nap in your hotel, you'll be treated to an elaborate meal—sometimes a good one—and you'll have time to figure out which city you're in. But not before you've been put on the radio. When you're talking on the radio you've had a flight and a coffee in a paper cup and a crumb of something. You've had time to empty your bladder—but only your bladder. Then you reply to questions asked by someone uninterested in the answers, into the whispery microphones of a padded booth. Your listeners, if they exist, are invisible, distant, and likely missed your name even if it was pronounced correctly. The radio is the void where you stare into your own soul on book tour and find nothing staring you back.

Once, a particular escort in a particular city came together with the radio experience in a way which was not so much mortifying as edifyingly humbling. She was a big, rowdy, middle-aged blonde who had been, some years before, the lead anchorperson on the local news. She'd also obviously been stunningly beautiful in her youth. She reminded me, immediately and delightfully, of Gena Rowlands in the Cassavetes film *Opening Night*—a character modeled, in turn, on Bette Davis in *All About Eve*. That is to say, a *real star*, made insecure by age. What I couldn't know was that her new job as escort—and I was evidently one of her very first authors—consisted, by design or accident, of a beautiful cure.

We stopped at two or three radio stations that day, and one television station. It happened at the first stop and every stop to follow: She was received as a returning comet. From the receptionists, to the producers, to the technicians, to the interviewers themselves, all were in awe that she'd swept in—and I was a token at her side, a negligible presence. How good she looked! How they missed her! What a bimbo they'd replaced her with! How shocking that she'd been cut from the air just for aging—nobody in this business had any respect anymore for the true giants! By dint of my tour itinerary, prepared months before and thousands of miles away in an office in Manhattan, this titan of local media made her return tour of local outlets. They fell over themselves. Here was true fame, a face they'd gazed at five evenings a week for ten years. I might have been Rushdie, I might have been Roth, I might have been T. S. Eliot, it wouldn't have mattered. She managed her courtiers graciously, and spoke forgivingly of the betrayal. "Oh, that's just this business . . . nothing personal . . ."

You out there: faceless army, tuned to morning talk. I know you're there. I've got something to tell you. Those authors you hear at nine or ten in the morning, speaking so tenderly or ragefully of their childhood or broken marriage, or meticulously defending their book against this or that possible misunderstanding, or answering unexpected questions about their hair color or their pets, or explaining why no one will ever know the final truth about what resides in the human heart, you *must know* this: They are holding in a bowel movement.

—*Mortification*, 2004

Stops

On Those Things My New Novel Forgot to Be About, Maybe

For me, there's a weird, unfathomable gulf—I almost wrote *gulp*—between the completion of a novel and its publication. Some days this duration feels interminable, as though the book has voyaged out like some spacecraft on a research mission, populated by forgotten losers like the ones in John Carpenter's *Dark Star*, a craft cut loose by those who launched the thing and now grown irretrievable, bent by space and time into something distorted and not worth guiding home. Then there are other days, where the book might be a pitch that's left your hand too soon, now burning toward home plate, whether to be met by a catcher's mitt or the sweet part of the bat you can't possibly know. Hopeless to regret it once you feel it slipping past your fingertips. Just watch. (That's the gulp.) The weirdness is in that interlude where the book has quit belonging to you but doesn't belong to anyone else yet, hasn't been inscribed in all its rightness and wrongness by the scatter-shot embrace and disdain of the world. It's a version of Schrödinger's cat, unchangeably neither dead nor alive in its box.

Sometimes, in that interlude, I find myself going over the collage of notes, the scraps of inspiration or non sequitur that I gathered up and clung to when there wasn't yet anything else to believe in. I don't outline books, or make systematic notes, nor draw up charts or character sketches, but I do accumulate shards of utterances, like a ransom note or early punk-rock flyer. That's to say, I glue shit together and stare at it, wishing for my book. I like glue. Once I start writing, I barely ever glance at the Frankenstein-scrapbook thing again. I don't need to. Whatever I've written is a thousand percent more useful than what I'd imagined I'd write. Still, it can be strange afterward to recall the book I imagined before the real one came along to blot it out.

Here's an item from Reuter's, headlined GERMANY: IMPOSSIBLE TO LOVE THE LITTLE GUY? NOT QUITE. "The Berlin Zoo came to the defense of a 3-month old polar bear cub named Knut, rejecting claims by animal rights campaigners that he should be killed by lethal injection because he has become too dependent on humans. The cub's fate has gripped the capital since his birth in December, when he and his twin brother were rejected by their mother, a former circus bear." Everything in this clipping fills me with awe, and now a certain ache of longing: How could I have failed to get Knut into my book? I should have written of nothing else. "A former circus bear"—what did Knut's mother see in her cubs that repulsed her, or was she afraid that if she loved them they'd become circus bears as well? Was she clownish or acrobatic, did she come to love the greasepaint and the roar of the crowd? And then there's the superb certainties of those activists, as fierce as any fundamentalist religion. "The hand-rearing had condemned the cub to a dysfunctional life," according to Frank Albrecht, the lead activist. I can't keep from wondering if Albrecht's mother was a circus performer as well. Even the Berlin Zoo—I've wandered past its stink myself, thinking of David Bowie and U2, amazed by the German teenagers who panhandle and deal drugs outside the Zoo station of the Berlin subway.

What book did I think I was going to write?

Here's a sentence from Adam Phillips's essay "Nuisance Value," in which he's attempting to paraphrase George Orwell's *Down and Out in Paris and London*: "Criminals, Orwell seems to imply in the book, are the people we punish for being a nuisance; artists are the people we reward for being a nuisance; successful businessmen are criminals disguised as artists." I could read that sentence a thousand times and not understand what it means, and yet it seems to explain every secret thing I've always suspected about contemporary existence, about our individual fates under the condition of "late capitalism" (or whatever our reality should be called); the sentence is like a John Ashbery poem to me in that way. I wanted to write a whole novel based on the sentence, but did I manage it? Maybe that's what I liked about the Reuter's wire piece about Knut: It seemed like it already *was* a novel based on the Adam Phillips sentence. The activists judged Knut to be a nuisance, not bear enough: He'd been reduced to criminal or homeless status by his dependency. Knut was Down and Out. The Zoo, defending him, elevated him to the status of an artist, an unprecedented, mongrel creation that while useless, and perhaps even dysfunctional, provided more than adequate "nuisance value." The clipping had after all also mentioned that "The zoo is braced for crowds." Money changes everything.

"Perhaps such secrets, the secrets of everyone, were only expressed when the person laboriously dragged them into the light of the world, imposed them on the world, and made them part of the world's experience. Without this effort, the secret place was merely a dungeon in which the person perished; without this effort, indeed, the entire world would merely be an uninhabitable darkness." Those words are James Baldwin's, from *Another Country*, and I collaged them into my notes, too—retyped them, actually, as I've just done again—wanting my book, whatever it was going to be, to live up to their challenge, to drag some small thing out into the light, out of the dungeon. And then I made up some characters, and put them in a story, and hammered out a few thousand sentences, tried to mete out surprise and delight, and got stuck with that odd novelist's burden, of spending so much time with my stick figures that they seem painfully real and deliciously dear to me. But really, who knows whether I've done any of what I most wanted to do? My book is a starship drifting loose from orbit, a pitch whose trajectory was shaped by the palm and fingers of my hand but now subjects itself to the mysteries of the air, beyond my fingertips. It's a meal I cooked but can't taste myself. I want the reader to taste what I first tasted in those fragments and clippings, my pathetic laminated plan for the future, like the collage of scenes of middle-class family life the parolee James Caan shows off to Tuesday Weld in the heartbreaking first-date scene in Michael Mann's *Thief*. My hope is that once I began the carpentry of storytelling I still remembered to pry open the gaps where the light could flood in, where Knut might roam, even if Knut went unnamed.

The great actor and director John Cassavetes, discussing what he rated as a failed performance by a well-known actor in an acclaimed film he hated—Martin Sheen in *Apocalypse Now*—made a remark which haunts me in its implications: He said he thought Sheen might have been able to do something with the role, as badly written as he considered it to be, if as an actor he'd been allowed to insert some "stops" into the performance. What he meant by "stops," I believe, were simply gaps, or hesitations, actorly silences. Moments when thoughts left unexplored by the words themselves could be allowed to flood in. This possibility has always seemed to me a beautiful one, first for its craftsmanlike insight into the performer's art, but also in its suggestion that even a despised and oppressive text, a piece of junk like Cassavetes felt *Apocalypse Now* to be, might be worth this attempt at salvage. In other words, even a dishonest world might be worth trying to inhabit honestly. For isn't the actor's plight strangely like our own, or Knut's, dropped into a world scripted before we were born and against our wishes?

—Powell's Books Blog, 2009

Advertisements for Norman Mailer

Salvage from an Infatuation

1.

There once was a boy who fell in love with Norman Mailer, a writer who called himself "Aquarius." Call this boy Aquarius-Nul, then. The name suggested all utopian possibilities the boy had glimpsed, born in the middle of the '60s to avidly countercultural parents. Their world, which he'd taken for *the* world, was a show that was closing: the dawning of an Age, but no age to follow the dawning. This boy's own stories, when they came, painted his parents' tribe as a withered race of superheroes, Super Goat Men and Women, who'd at least been large once in their lives. Aquarius-Nul's uptight cohort sometimes seemed inclined not even to try, only to mock such attempts. (Aquarius-Nul was as uptight as any of them. Call him A-Nul, maybe.)

2.

When Aquarius-Nul, who favored outlaw or outcaste identities (the Beats, the science-fiction writers), glanced at the then-present Mount Rushmore of U.S. writing, made of the Big Jews and Updike, Mailer was the only alluring prospect. For the teenage Aquarius-Nul, a major American novelist bragging of interest in graffiti, underground film, marijuana, and space travel was irresistible. Even better, Mailer was

the only head on that Rushmore who nodded to the value of the outlaw or outcaste identities (the Beats, and science fiction). That Mailer
was further a Jew and a Brooklynite yet had shrugged off those legacy
subject matters made him, for Aquarius-Nul, who'd want to believe
he could do the same, too good to be true. In fact, others on Rushmore would sustain Aquarius-Nul's interest before long. But not before
Aquarius-Nul had burned through Mailer's whole shelf, sometimes in
delirious wonder, sometimes guiltily bored, and, strangely, often both
at once.

3.

Enough with "Aquarius-Nul." (How could Mailer have stood it, typing "Aquarius" or "the Prisoner" or "the reporter" or even "Mailer"
what must have been so many thousands of times, instead of settling
for "I"?) And why so much self-regarding throat-clearing before getting
to any journalistic subject—why put Aquarius-Nul in front of Mailer
himself? Helpless tribute, I suppose, to the all-time ego king. Yet let
this be my chance to say that Mailer's unfashionably preening brand
of self-consciousness seems to me to be crucial in the formation of
another, lately fashionable brand—the Eggers of *Heartbreaking Work*
or the Wallace of *A Supposedly Fun Thing*—which, inoculated with savage undercutting doubt, conceals the lineage.

4.

Challenged once by a friend to name a single immortal literary character from postwar fiction—someone to rival Sherlock Holmes or
Madame Bovary in terms of bleed-through to popular consciousness—
I blurted out, "Norman Mailer!" I was halfway serious. Mailer, running hard against his limits at inventing a new form of novel as large as
his ambition or claims, invented, by means of *Advertisements for Myself*
and the third-person narrator of his journalistic books, by his television appearances, wife-stabbing, and so forth, the character of the
public Mailer instead—and triumphed. "Mailer finally got around to
writing encyclopedic novels during a period when, as a novelist, he no
longer really mattered, when, in fact, novels no longer mattered as they
did during the modern era. For a time, Mailer managed to leverage this

anachronism into a journalistic career based on a residual novelistic promise."—Loren Glass, *Authors Inc.: Literary Celebrity in the Modern United States, 1880–1980*. Fair enough: That catches exactly what it felt like to be let down by *Ancient Evenings* or *Harlot's Ghost*. But for those of us to whom the novel matters as much as anything ever mattered to anyone, the episode of Mailer and "the novel" was a quarter-century drama of bluff and impotence just as good as the great white novel he couldn't harpoon. For wasn't it transparent to the utmost and from the start—in *Advertisements for Myself*—that Mailer couldn't pull it off? Well, I had the benefit of hindsight; who knows what I'd have expected from Mailer if I'd encountered the drama in real time. In hindsight, Mailer looked in the late '50s to have become a radar detector for the onset of the postmodern novel—as he had for the postmodern cultural condition generally—in his declared topics, his appetite to engulf every dissident impulse and the whole atmosphere of paranoia and revelation that saturated the '60s, though he delivered barely any fiction to reflect it, in his predictions in essays like "Superman Comes to the Supermarket"; in his self-annihilating advocacy of Burroughs's *Naked Lunch*; in his desperate, dashed-off forays in *Why Are We in Vietnam?* and *An American Dream*, and so on. The reason Mailer couldn't arrive at a satisfactory postmodern style (even as he saw his one firm achievement in *The Naked and the Dead* mummified by ironic treatments of his war by Heller, Vonnegut, and Pynchon) was because postmodernism *as an art practice* extended from modernism, to which Mailer had never authentically responded in the first place. This might have been Mailer's dirty secret: He was still back with James T. Farrell's *Studs Lonigan* in the soul of his aesthetics, even as the rest of his intelligence raced madly downfield, sometimes sprinting decades past his contemporaries.

5.

That said, I think *An American Dream* is pretty good.

6.

So, defend indefensible Mailer. I once promised, in another essay, to land on judgment, not hover: *Advertisements for Myself*, *The Armies of the Night*, the two campaign books, and, er, parts of *The Fight*, parts of

Of a Fire on the Moon, parts of *Cannibals and Christians*, parts of *The Deer Park*, parts of etc. Parts, always parts. The novelist Darin Strauss, confessing his Mailer-thing to me when I confessed mine, said, "Other writers are inconsistent book to book, but Mailer's inconsistent within books, sometimes even within paragraphs . . ." I wonder: Does anyone credit Mailer this postmodern way, as a purveyor of fragments, a centrifuge of sentences? Mailer's false accents—Texas, Patrician, boxer-tough—are like Orson Welles's false noses. If only he'd landed, in the end, on a jeu d'esprit like *F for Fake* instead of the dreadful parade of King Tut, Oswald, Jesus, and Hitler . . .

7.

Joan Didion, 1979: "It is a largely unremarked fact about Mailer that he is a great and obsessed stylist, a writer to whom the shape of the sentence is the story." Conrad Knickerbocker, 1965: "Mailer has evolved a rhetoric that moves far beyond his original naturalistic endowments. His words always hinge on the event, but he gives perspective to events with a kinetic poetry that turns the huge losses of his characters into, strangely, gains of a kind." Knickerbocker again: "It's such a vulnerable book. What wrenching innocence, what cool nerve, to write melodrama in the Age of Herzog!" Cynthia Buchanan, 1972: "We read him not for moon talk, not for mayor talk, not for marches or wars on women, but because he is 'our genius' . . . He is medium and metaphor; he is infinitely vulnerable." Reading reviews of Mailer's books pre-'80s, you glimpse the world that's been lost (on both sides of the conversation). And twice comes that completely disarming and accurate judgment, that Mailer was above all "*vulnerable*." Sticking to Mailer's reviews pre-'80s, you wouldn't know that Mailer was fatally out of fashion.

8.

But no. With my lifelong habit of attaching like a remora-fish to interesting readers older than myself, and now, in the profession of mentoring writers much younger, I feel uniquely well vantaged to make the sad judgment that Mailer is as much on the skids as the world of referents in his work is evaporating. If nearly anyone above a certain age surely holds a set of opinions on Mailer—had taken the task of

understanding him, and not too quickly, as an appointment of their
literary citizenship, even if a weary one—it was as certain that anyone
below a certain age, even the most talented and alert of my students,
take Mailer's toxic preposterousness, and obsolescence, for granted. All
the pomp of Mailer's recent funeral rites, the endless tributes, felt like
an era tucking itself in for the long night, rather than the graduation of
Mailer's best writing from the burden of his person. I suspect we saw
the ark of Mailer's work being pushed out to sea with the corpse aboard,
not a moment too soon for a status quo for whom it still, fifty years on,
conveyed fear of disarrangement.

9.

If, as in the Isaiah Berlin formulation, "the fox knows many little things,
but the hedgehog knows one big thing," then Mailer's gift and curse
was to have been a hedgehog trapped inside an exploding fox. What the
hedgehog knew was that the uncanny symbolic life of our imagination
resolutely steered the outward action of the legible world, no matter
how much we might legislate it out of existence or deny its relevance
in one realm or another. This hedgehog thought had two tenets: First,
that in any realm of collective experience or action the pressure of the
denied myths would invariably make themselves crucial. Second, and
paradoxically, that in the life of a given individual the nourishment
and cultivation of the realm of the symbolic, the self's own intangible
dream stuff, was no small responsibility but a tender and delicate affair,
endlessly at risk of betrayal or abandonment. Fair enough. The difficulty was that the fox in Mailer wanted to detonate this hedgehog
of insight, like a grenade's shrapnel, into five decades of culture, into
McCarthyism, Vietnam, feminism, Gore Vidal, Madonna, Bret Easton
Ellis, ensuring himself a dozen frags for every decent kill.

10.

". . . the increasing anxiety of American life comes from the covert guilt
that abundance and equality remain utterly separated, and we have
reached the point where socialism is not only morally demanding but
unconsciously obvious—obvious enough to flood with anxiety the
psyches of those millions who know and yet do nothing." That's Mailer

in 1953. Socialism as "unconsciously obvious"! The implication, that Marx's work could only be fulfilled in Freud's, and vice versa, sounds to me like nothing so much as Slavoj Zizek, the hipster-provocateur of contemporary political theory.

11.

I lived for a time in Canada, and found myself fascinated by the slavish pride of a culture basking in a self-recriminating joke. "A lobsterman turned his back on three catches in an uncovered bucket. A bystander worried the lobsters would escape, but the lobsterman waved him off, saying, 'No problem, these are Canadian lobsters. If one reaches the top the others will pull him back in.'" Yet who, lately, seeing how transparent the Internet-comments culture has made our vast leveling rage, our chortling conformism and anti-intellectualism, our scapegoat-readiness, could keep from thinking: "We're all Canadian lobsters on this bus." If Mailer's grievance, as stated in *Advertisements*, was "The Shits Are Killing Us," then perhaps my grievance is along the lines of "We Have Met the Shits and They Is Us." By temperament or generational necessity (or both), I find myself again and again compelled by questions of collective culpability in conspiracies of amnesia and distraction, and by the vicarious waste of our best attention to ourselves and the others beside us. Likely anyone would agree that for three decades Norman Mailer took up too damn much room. Lately I've wondered whether, if another Norman Mailer came along, there'd be any room for him to take up at all.

White Elephant and Termite Postures in the Life of the Twenty-first-Century Novelist

Manny Farber's "White Elephant Art vs. Termite Art" is a characteristi-cally thrilling rhetorical gesture from a critic I adore and who bewil-ders me (by disliking movies I adore). "The three sins of white elephant art (1) frame the action with an all-over pattern, (2) install every event, character, situation in a frieze of continuities, and (3) treat every inch of the screen and film as a potential area for prizewinning creativity." Whereas: "A peculiar fact about termite-tapeworm-fungus-moss art is that it goes always forward eating its own boundaries, and, likely as not, leaves nothing in its path other than the signs of eager, industrious, unkempt activity." Farber locates an instance of what he calls "one of the good termite performances" in John Wayne in John Ford's *The Man Who Shot Liberty Valance*, a film which otherwise annoys the critic: "Wayne's acting is infected by a kind of hoboish spirit, sitting back on its haunches doing a bitter-amused counterpoint to the pale, neutral film life around him." Then Farber generalizes: "The best examples of termite art appear in places other than films, where the spotlight of culture is nowhere in evidence, so that the craftsmen can be ornery, wasteful, stubbornly self-involved, doing go-for-broke art and not car-ing what comes of it." His examples range from newspaper columns to detective novels by Chandler and Ross Macdonald to, weirdly, "the TV debating of William Buckley" (I guess you had to be there).

Once Farber's termite-elephant paradigm crawled into my ear, it never burrowed out the other side. I find it shaping my responses to nearly anything. For instance, the New York Mets outfield: Carlos Beltran a White Elephant ballplayer, Angel Pagan a Termite. This is nonsense, of course, in terms of the outcome of the ball game: Whether Beltran or Pagan hits a home run, it counts the same. Similarly, if a John Irving novel alters your frame of reference, it counts as much as if the alteration is performed by, say, Charles Willeford, or Patricia Highsmith. Certainly Termite vs. Elephant needs to mean something deeper than Underpaid vs. Overpaid, or Underrated vs. Overrated, or it means nothing at all (and it's unlikely John Wayne was underpaid for gnawing at the edges of Ford's film). Yet the situation complicates in the feedback loop of an audience's projections: Are Pagan's options on the field of play freer than Beltran's? Can he do more, as a result of Termite-affect?

Well, the juncture where this became personal should be obvious. Six books into avowed Termitism, somewhere between accepting an award for *Motherless Brooklyn* and the putting across of *The Fortress of Solitude*, I clambered into a White Elephant suit, the standard costume which, it looks to me, novelists of a certain "stature" are largely required to wear if they are to appear in public at all. (The other option, the infinitely seductive Invisible Elephant, anointed with silence-exile-cunning, may or may not be authentically available to anyone besides Pynchon and DeLillo anymore.) Please understand: I clambered in willingly. It's a rare and coveted thing, an invitation to don that costume.

A writer like me—well, me, specifically—had gone through an alternate-reality rehearsal for White Elephant Ops: On European book tour, France especially, where the instant a novelist of any type disembarks he or she's taken as a cultural ambassador on par with Susan Sontag—when this first happened to me, trust me, no one in the United States was asking the fresh-faced author of *As She Climbed Across the Table*, one barely untethered from the sales counter of Moe's Books, his opinion on Roth's chances of a Nobel, or Clinton's Kosovo policy. Did I explain to French or Germans that no one in America would flatter me with such questions? No. I weighed in. One silly morning in Turin I woke to a large headline in an Italian newspaper: A leading U.S. novelist had denounced Colin Powell, and he was I.

But in those days I had only to board the airplane back to JFK to regain termite freedom.

The splendor and disaster of elephant privileges were vivid to me before I tasted them myself: the peculiar immobility that made figures like Bellow, Heller, and Styron seem so dull before I'd read them (and then been sometimes surprised); the Ken Kesey escape act, which seemed to render him pitiable; the blowing-it-up-from-within of Joyce Carol Oates's helpless overproductivity, which enraged people; the defiant enmeshing disaster of Mailer's talking back to the problem, and his decades of faux-termite nonfiction, filmmaking, etc., before collapsing back into unwieldy-elephant-supreme; the woeful invisible-elephantism of Salinger; and so forth, leading up to the Agonies of Franzen.

There were so many things, apparently, you couldn't or shouldn't do once you'd written a novel that succeeded in the "big" way (or even one that tried to—success being, always, in the eye of the beholder, unless your sales stacked to the moon, which mine didn't). The worst of both worlds: The old high-modernist Authority of the role was in savage decline, yet White Elephants still seemed obliged to blunder around acting Authoritative, scorning opportunities for playfulness and distraction, never-apologizing-never-explaining (let alone replying to critics), stiffening in an encaustic of self-regard while waiting for the right young termite-wannabe-elephant to begin popping away with an elephant gun. Borges, in "Doctor Brodie's Report," describes the behavior of a certain tribe toward its elected king:

> Immediately upon his elevation he is gelded, blinded with a fiery stick, and his hands and feet are cut off, so that the world will not distract him from wisdom ... If there is a war, the witch doctors take him from the cavern, exhibit him to the tribe to spur the warriors' courage, sling him over their shoulders, and carry him as though a banner or talisman into the fiercest part of the battle. When this occurs, the king generally dies within seconds under the stones hurled at him by the Apemen.

But I exaggerate.

Anyway, I thought, my silly feelings about the bogus prerogatives invested in my role would be fun to explain, as part of the job of debunking bogus prerogatives—something to which I felt devoted, in a general way. I figured I'd had practice disappointing expectations before, for instance, by not wanting to follow my detective characters into sequel Conrad Metcalf or Lionel Essrog adventures. But those were termite-disappointments. (Termites migrated by Farber's definition, chewing the bounds of their own commitments.) An elephant's maneuvers, I found, were overdetermined. And there are elephant cops. Any caprice is taken as a dereliction of the novelist's mission of grinding downfield with the stolid, earnest, edifying-redemptive football of "the novel," a mission deemed crucial in a values-flattened, superficial, ironized culture. Of course, this takes for granted that we're a values-flattened, superficial, ironized culture, one starved for stolid, earnest, edifying stuff. I don't. My guess is that the not-too-secret secret of our times is that, behind a few self-congratulatory tokens of decadence and irony, an elephantine utilitarianism and conformism grinds at the center of our culture and its response to art and artists.

So I've teased, haplessly, at disqualifying my own elephant function. Extracurricular engagements and deliberate "minor works" at least freshened my own sense of possibility, but none were really provocative enough to do more than lengthen the wait for the "next major novel." The fact is that I waited, too, since my feeling for major novels is sincere and I'm proud and even amazed that people expect them from me. My bridges were left only half-burned, to the consternation of bystanders on both shores. But since my aesthetic methodology often involves splitting differences, it was natural for my career postures, once I realized I'd have to have some of those, to follow suit. This book is loaded with evidence of what termite moves you can still try to bust in an elephant suit. The sad fact is that a perfectly natural gesture of termitic appetite, like writing song lyrics for your friends in rock bands, may, coming from the perceived-elephant quadrant, resemble a gallery exhibition of Sylvester Stallone's oil paintings.

Out of my mingled termite-elephant fate, I learned two things that really mattered.

One: Distrust self-authorizing perma-termites. This goes with my critique of the sentimental auto-marginalizing of (beloved) zones like science fiction, or Brooklyn. If my reservations about the collective ethos of Internet culture can be pinned to one description, it's this: Internet culture flatters itself with the delusion of an infinitely renewable termite's license, a permanent oppositional status pardoning all guerrilla actions. One day any termite wakes up to find it is, if not an elephant, then certainly the biggest termite in the room. And with a trunk and ears. (Honesty about one's own power is an ethical prerequisite.)

Two: We're thrust onstage holding scripts—and I don't just mean "novelists." This is the Cassavetes insight I mentioned in "Stops," and which gave form to much of *Chronic City* (as major a novel as I've managed): What counts is what freedom you can taste, and what love you can offer, from inside the role you've been handed. But your script exists.

VII

Dylan, Brown, and Others

The incomplete is often more effective than completeness, espe-
cially in the case of eulogy: the aim of which requires precisely an
enticing incompleteness as an irrational element which presents
to the hearer's imagination the illusion of a dazzling sea and
obscures the coast on the other side, that is to say the limitations of
the object to be eulogized, as though in a fog. When one refers to
the known merits of a man and does so in detail and at length, it
always gives rise to the suspicion that these are his only merits . . .

—FRIEDRICH NIETZSCHE, *Human, All Too Human*

I was afraid to write about music for a long time. I felt the obvious reluctance to try what seemed destined to fail but also wondered if I wanted to see my writing brain colonize an area of such sheer joy. I suppose my reader's appetite for music writing made it inevitable that I'd shrug off the reservations. Once I did, my subject, typically, turned out to be the joy and *the reservations.*

Joy first.

The Genius of James Brown

1. The James Brown Statue

In Augusta, Georgia, in May of this year, they put up a bronze statue of James Brown, the Godfather of Soul, in the middle of Broad Street. In June, during a visit to meet James Brown and observe him recording parts of his new album in an Augusta studio, I went and had a look at it. The James Brown Statue is an odd one in several ways. For one, it is odd to see a statue standing not on a pedestal but flat on its feet on the ground. This was done at James Brown's request, reportedly. The premise being: man of the people. The result, however: somewhat fake-looking statue. Another difficulty is that the statue is grinning. Members of James Brown's band, present while he was photographed for reference by the statue's sculptor, told me of their attempts to get James Brown to quit smiling for the photographs. A statue shouldn't grin, they told him. Yet James Brown refused to do other than grin. It is the grin of a man who has succeeded, and as the proposed statue struck him as a measure of his success, he determined that it would measure him grinning. (Though in any of his many hundreds of compelling in-concert and backstage photographs James Brown scowls, squints, grits his teeth, performs facial expressions conveying detachment, ambivalence, dismay, aggression, and so on, in any publicity image— any posed photograph, say, taken alongside a president or mayor, or alongside some other showbiz legend, say, Aretha Franklin—James

Brown says "cheese." By James Brown the Augusta statue must have been deemed, essentially, publicity. Never apologize, never explain, and never let them see you without the rictus.) Otherwise, the statue is admirable: flowing bronze cape, helmetlike bronze hair perhaps not so much harder than the actual hair it depicts, and vintage bronze microphone with its base tipped, as if to make a kind of dance partner with James Brown, who is not shown in a dancing pose but nonetheless appears lithe, pert, ready.

Still, as with postage stamps, statues of the living seem somehow disconcerting. And very few statues are located at quite such weighty symbolic crossroads as this one. The statue's back is to what was in 1991 renamed James Brown Boulevard, which cuts from Broad Street for a mile, deep into the neighborhood where James Brown was raised from age six, by his aunts, in a Twiggs Street house that was a den of what James Brown himself calls "gambling, moonshine liquor, and prostitution." The neighborhood around Twiggs is still devastatingly sunk in poverty's ruin. The shocking depths of deprivation from which James Brown excavated himself are still intact, frozen in time, almost like a statue. A photographer would be hard-pressed to snap a view in this neighborhood that couldn't, apart from the make of the cars, slip neatly into Walker Evans's portfolio of Appalachian scenes from *Let Us Now Praise Famous Men*. Except, of course, that everyone in Augusta's Appalachia is black.

So the James Brown Statue may seem to have walked on its flat bronze feet the mile from Twiggs to Broad, to which it keeps its back, reserving its grin for the gentle folk on and across Broad Street, the side that gives way to the river—the white neighborhoods to which James Brown, as a shoeshine boy, hustler, juvenile delinquent, possibly even as a teenage pimp, directed his ambition and guile. Policemen regularly chased James Brown the length of that mile, back toward Twiggs—he tells stories of diving into a watery gutter, barely more than a trench, and hiding underwater with an upraised reed for breathing while the policemen rumbled past—and once the chase was over, he'd creep again toward Broad, where the lights and music were, where the action was, where Augusta's stationed soldiers with their monthly-paycheck binges were to be found. Eventually the city of Augusta jailed the teenager, sentenced him to eight-to-sixteen for four counts of breaking and entering. When he attained an early release, with the support of the family of his friend and future bandmate Bobby Byrd, it was on the condition that he never return to Augusta. Deep into the '60s, years past "Papa's Got a Brand New Bag," James Brown had to apply for special permits to bring his band to perform in Augusta; he essentially had been exiled from the city for having the audacity to transverse that mile from Twiggs to Broad. Now his statue stands at the end of the mile, facing away. Grinning. Resolving nothing. James Brown, you see, may in fact be less a statue than any human being who ever lived. James Brown is kinetic; an idea, a problem, a genre, a concept, a method— anything, really, but a statue.

2. The James Brown Show

This we know: The James Brown Show begins without James Brown. James Brown, a man who is also an idea, a problem, a method, etc., will have to be invoked or conjured, summoned from some other place. The rendezvous between James Brown and his audience—you—is not a simple thing. When the opening acts are done and the waiting is over, you will first be in the hands of James Brown's band. It is the band that begins the show. The band is there to help, to negotiate a space for you to encounter James Brown; they are there to, if you will, take you to the bridge. The band is itself the medium within which James Brown will be summoned, the terms under which he might be enticed into view. And this interval, before James Brown appears, is one in which it will be made certain you have no regrets or doubts, to measure your readiness and commitment.

The James Brown band takes the form, onstage, of an animated frieze or hieroglyphic, timeless in a very slightly seedy showbiz way, but happily so, rows of men in red tuxedos, jitterbugging in lockstep even as they miraculously conjure from instruments a perfect hurricane of music: a rumbling, undulating-insinuating (underneath), shimmery-peppery (up on top) braided-waveform of groove. The players seem jolly and astonished witnesses to their own virtuosity. They resemble humble, gracious ushers or porters, welcoming you to the enthrallingly physical, jubilant, encompassing noise that pours out of their instruments. It's as if they're merely widening for you a portal offering entry into some new world, a world as much kinetic, visual, and emotional as aural—for, in truth, a first encounter with the James

Brown Show can feel like a bodily passage, a deal your mind wasn't sure it was ready for your body to strike with these men and their instruments and the ludicrous, almost cruelly anticipatory drama of their attempt to beckon the star of the show into view. Yes, it's made unmistakable, in case you forgot, that this is merely a prelude, a throat-clearing, though the band has already rollicked through three or four recognizable numbers in succession; we're waiting for something. The name of the something is James Brown. You wish desperately for this man to appear, even if it is only to disappoint you (how could he live up to what you've yearned for; how could he live up to his own hype or hits; how could he live up to his own band, which just sounds *so great*?). You indeed fear, despite all sense, that something is somehow wrong: Perhaps he's sick or reluctant, perhaps there's been a mistake. There is no James Brown, it was merely a rumor. Thankfully, someone has told you what to do: You chant, gladly, "James Brown! James Brown!" A natty little man with a pompadour comes onstage and with a booming, familiar voice asks you if you Are Ready for Star Time, and you find yourself confessing that you Are.

How did you get here? Perhaps, like Nelson George, it was on the A train, heading to the Apollo Theater in the company of your mother, in 1967. Perhaps, like David Gates, it was in Boston, in 1968, the day after Martin Luther King was shot, for a concert broadcast live on television on an emergency basis, in order to quell the expected riots, a now-signal moment in the James Brown Legend. Possibly, like Peter Guralnick, you visited the Providence Arena in 1965, a wondering fan. Or maybe you're Fred Wesley, in 1967, seeing the James Brown Show for the first time at the Orlando Sports Arena in Florida, because Pee Wee Ellis, James Brown's then-arranger, has called you on the telephone and persuaded you to consider taking a gig playing in this band, a gig you're considering, despite your background in jazz and your impression that James Brown's music is silly pop, because you need the dough. Or perhaps you're me, which would mean that with your childhood friend Luke you've taken a Greyhound bus out of Boston in 1986, the summer of the first shuttle disaster, halfway up Cape Cod, to see the James Brown Show at the Hyannis Port Melody Tent.

In any event, you were there when He was summoned. You were there when He answered the call. To be in the audience when James Brown commences the James Brown Show is to have felt oneself engulfed in a feast of adoration and astonishment, a ritual invoca-tion, one comparable, I'd imagine, to certain ceremonies known to the Mayan peoples, wherein a human person is radiantly costumed and then beheld in lieu of the appearance of a Sun God upon the earth. For to see James Brown dance and sing, to see him lead his mighty band with the merest glances and tiny flickers of signal from his hands; to see him offer himself to his audience to be adored and enraptured and ravished; to watch him tremble and suffer as he tears his screams and moans of lust, glory, and regret from his sweat-drenched body—and is, thereupon, in an act of seeming mercy, draped in the cape of his infirmity; to then see him recover and thrive—shrugging free of the cape—as he basks in the healing regard of an audience now melded into a single passionate body by the stroking and thrumming of his ceaseless cavalcade of impossibly danceable smash number-one hits, is not to *see*: It is to *behold*.

Myself, I count it as a life marker: I first beheld the James Brown Show at the age of twenty-two. Again at twenty-eight, in San Francisco. And again this year, my forty-first.

Some testimony: "For moments he seemed motionless at center stage. Then Brown was moving. He cruised along the Apollo stage on a cushion of air, his black shoes skating rapidly. When he fell to his knees, microphone cradled in his hands, I was frightened. Was he sick? Did he have a headache? I turned to ask my mother what was bothering James Brown, but she was too busy smiling and bopping to the music to notice me" (Nelson George). "Because of King's assassination I was apprehen-sive about going, fearing trouble. For better or worse, though, all of what had happened was just blown away and forgotten the moment he hit the stage. Everything got swallowed" (David Gates). "This was the greatest theater I had ever seen, or most likely ever would see. This was what all the 'happenings' and 'be-ins' that we attended looking for a new form of participatory drama could only grope for, this was a kind of magic that no theory or academic study could envision, let alone conjure up . . . James Brown was a figure whose legend only sug-gested his reality" (Guralnick). "The audience was completely fucked up, responding to any and everything that James or the band did. The encore was like a climax on top of an already all-consuming climax. I felt guilty for not having bought a ticket" (Fred Wesley, realizing he's not going to be able to devote his life, and his trombone, to bebop).

"The rather seemly midsummer Hyannis Port audience, though surely also completely fucked up in their way, remained in their chairs, allowing Luke and me to make our way unimpeded down to the lip of the Melody Tent's stage, where James Brown soon crawled and begged and squirmed to within a few feet of us" (Lethem).

The James Brown Show is both an *enactment*—an unlikely and astonishing conjuration in the present moment of an alternate reality, one that dissipates into the air and can never be recovered—and at the same time a *reenactment*: the ritual celebration of an enshrined historical victory, a battle won long ago, against forces difficult to name (funklessness?) yet whose vanquishing seems to have been so utterly crucial that it requires incessant restaging in a triumphalist ceremony. You think: *This has happened before, I just wasn't there.* The show exists on a continuum, the link between ebullient big-band "clown" jazz showmen like Cab Calloway and Louis Jordan and the pornographic parade of a full-bore Prince concert. It is a glimpse of another world, even if only one being routinely dwells there, and his name is James Brown. To have glimpsed him there, dwelling in his world, is a privilege. James Brown is not a statue, no. But the James Brown Show *is* a monument, one unveiled at selected intervals.

3. In the Studio with James Brown, Day One

James Brown lives in the suburbs of Augusta, so while he is recording an album he sleeps at home. He frequently exhorts his band to buy homes in Augusta, which they mostly refuse to do. Instead, they stay at the Ramada Inn. James Brown, when he is at home, routinely stays up all night watching the news and watching old Westerns—nothing but Westerns. He gets up late. For this reason a day in the recording studio with James Brown, like the James Brown Show, begins without James Brown.

Instead I find myself in the company of James Brown's longtime personal manager, Charles Bobbit, and his band, approximately fourteen people who I will soon in varying degrees get to know quite well, but who for now treat me genially, skeptically, shyly, but mostly obliviously. They've got work to do. They're working on the new James Brown record. At the moment they're laying down a track without him, because James Brown asked them to and because since they're waiting around they might as well do something—though they do this with a degree of helpless certainty that they are wasting their time. It is nearly always a useless occupation, if you are James Brown's band, to lay down a track while he is not present. Yet the band does it a lot, wasting time in this way, because their time is not their own. So they record. Today's effort is a version of "Hold On, I'm Comin'," the classic Sam and Dave song.

The setting is a pleasant modern recording studio in a bland corner of Augusta's suburbs, far from where the statue resides. The band occupies a large room, high-ceilinged, padded in black, with a windowed soundproof booth for the drummer's kit and folding chairs in a loose circle for the band, plus innumerable microphones and cables and amplifiers and pickups running across the floor. On the other side of a large window from this large chamber is a room full of control panels, operated by an incredibly patient man named Howard. It is into this room that James Brown and the band will intermittently retreat in order to listen to playback, to consider what they've recorded. Down the hall from these two rooms is a tiny suite with a kitchen (unused) and dining room with a table that seats seven or eight at a time (used constantly, for eating takeout).

The band is three guitarists and one bassist and three horn players and two percussionists—a drummer in the soundproof booth, and a conga player in the central room. They're led by Hollie Farris, a trim, fiftyish, white trumpeter with a blond mustache and the gentle, acutely midwestern demeanor of an accountant or middle manager, yet with the enduring humor of a lifelong sideman—a hipster's tolerance. Hollie now pushes the younger guitarists as they hone the changes in "Hold On, I'm Comin'." Howard is recording the whole band simultaneously; this method of recording "live in the studio" is no longer how things are generally done. Hollie also sings to mark the vocal line, in a faint but endearing voice.

One of the young guitarists, cheating slightly on the live-in-the-studio ethos, asks to be allowed to punch in his guitar solo. This is Damon Wood: thirtysomething, also blond, with long hair and a neat goatee. Damon, explaining why he screwed up the solo, teases Hollie for his singing: "I can't hear myself with Engelbert Humperdinck over there." Howard rewinds the tape and Damon reworks the solo, then endears himself to me with a fannish quiz for the other guitarists—

Keith, another white guy, but younger, and clean-cut, and Daryl Brown, a light-skinned, roly-poly black man who turns out to be James Brown's son. "What classic funk song am I quoting in this solo?" Damon asks. Nobody can name it, not that they seem to be trying too hard. "Lady Marmalade," Damon says.

"Well," says Hollie, speaking of the track, "we got one for him to come in and say, 'That's terrible.'"

Keith, with a trace of disobedience in his eyes, asks if they're going to put the horns in the track. Hollie shakes his head. "He might be less inclined to throw it out," Keith suggests. "Give it that big sound. If all he hears are those guitars he'll start picking it apart."

Hollie offers a wry smile. He doesn't want to. Hollie, I'll learn, has been James Brown's bandleader and arranger on and off since the mid-'70s.

It is at that moment that everything changes. Mr. Bobbit explains: "Mr. Brown is here."

When James Brown enters the recording studio, the recording studio becomes a stage. It is not merely that attention quickens in any room this human being inhabits. The phenomenon is more akin to a grade-school physics experiment involving iron filings and a magnet: Lines of force are now visible in the air, rearranged. The band, the hangers-on, the very oxygen, every trace particle is charged in its relation to the gravitational field of James Brown. We're all waiting for something to happen, and that waiting is itself a story, an emotional dynamic: We need something from this man, and he is likely to demand something of us, something we're uncertain we can fully deliver. The drama here is not, as in the James Brown Show, enacted in musical terms. Now it is a psychodrama, a theater of human behavior, one full of Beckett or Pinter pauses.

James Brown is dressed as if for a show, in a purple three-piece suit and red shirt with cuff links, highly polished shoes, and his impeccably coiffed helmet of hair. When we're introduced I spend a long moment trying to conjugate the reality of James Brown's face, one I've contemplated as an album-cover totem since I was thirteen or fourteen: that impossible slant of jaw and cheekbone, that pop-art slash of teeth, the unmistakable rage of impatience lurking in the eyes. It's a face drawn by Jack Kirby or Milton Caniff, that's for sure, a visage engineered for maximum impact at great distances, from back rows of auditoriums.

I find it, truthfully, terrifying to have that face examining mine in return, though fear is alleviated by the rapidity of the process: James Brown seems to have finished devouring the whole prospect of me by the time our brief handshake is concluded.

I'm also struck by the almost extraterrestrial quality of *otherness* incarnated in this human being. James Brown is, by his own count, seventy-two years old. Biographers have suggested that three or four years ought to be added to that total. It's also possible that given the circumstances of his birth, in a shack in the woods outside Barnwell, South Carolina, in an environment of poverty and exile so profound as to be almost unimaginable, James Brown has no idea how old he is. No matter: He's in his mid-seventies, yet encountering him now in person, it occurs to me that James Brown is kept under wraps for so long at the outset of his own show, and is viewed primarily at a distance, or mediated through recordings or films, in order to buffer the unprepared spectator from the awesome strangeness and intensity of his person. He simply has more energy than and is vibrating at a different rate from anyone I've ever met, young or old. With every preparation I've made, he's still terrifying.

Readying me for this moment, over breakfast at my hotel, Mr. Bobbit had said, with a shrug, "He'll either like you or not, right away. Nothing anyone can do about it." At the same breakfast, characterizing James Brown's extraordinary awareness and attentiveness, his superhuman degree of control over his environment, Mr. Bobbit used phrases like *three-hundred-and-sixty-degree vision*, and *memory of an elephant*, impressions I'll find confirmed in dozens of personal accounts by band members and, soon enough, by my own experience. Mr. Bobbit also offered me a three-word summation: "Perceptive. Psychic. Paranoid."

I don't get to know the verdict. James Brown sits, gesturing with his hand: It's time for playback. James Brown and Mr. Bobbit sit in the two comfortable leather chairs, while the band is bunched around the room, either on their feet or seated in folding metal chairs.

We listen, twice, to the take of "Hold On, I'm Comin'." James Brown lowers his head and closes his eyes. We're all completely silent. At last he mumbles faint praise: "Pretty good. Pretty good." Then, into the recording room. James Brown takes his place behind the mike, facing the band. We dwell now in an atmosphere of immanence, of ceremony, so tangible it's almost oppressive. James Brown is still contained within himself, muttering inaudibly, scratching his chin, fussing, barely coming out of himself. Abruptly he turns to me.

"You're very lucky, Mr. Rolling Stone. I don't ordinarily let anyone sit in on a session."

"I *feel* lucky," I say.

Fussing his way into place, James Brown decides he doesn't like the microphone. "I want one with no felt on it. Get me a *cheap* mike. I made all those hits on a cheap mike." The mike is swapped. He's still irked, turgid, turned inward. "Are we recording this?" he asks. The answer comes back: yes. "The one we throw out will be the best one," he admonishes, vaguely.

Now he explains to the band that they're not going to bother with the track they recorded before he arrived. Go figure: Hollie was right. "Sounds good," James Brown explains, "but it sounds *canned*. We got to get some James Brown in there." Here it is, the crux of the matter: He wasn't in the room, ipso facto, it isn't James Brown music. The problem is fundamentally one of ontology: In order for *James Brown* to occur, you need to be James Brown.

He begins reminiscing about a rehearsal they enjoyed the day before, in the rehearsal space at the Ramada. The Ramada's room provided a sound James Brown liked, and he encourages his band to believe they'll recapture it today: "Gonna bring that room in here."

Now that the gears are oiled, a constant stream of remarks and asides flows from James Brown's mouth. Many of these consist of basic statements of policy in regard to the matter of being James Brown, particularly in relationship to his band: "Be mean, but be the best." These statements mingle exhortations to excellence with justifications for his own treatment of the men he calls, alternately, "the cats" and "my family." Though discipline is his law, strife is not only likely but essential: "Any time a cat becomes a nuisance, that's the cat I'm gonna want." The matter of the rejected track is still on his mind: "Don't mean to degrade nobody. People do something they think is good. But you're gonna hear the difference. Get that hard sound." Frequently he dwells on the nature of the sound of which he is forever in pursuit: "Hard. Flat. Flat." One feels James Brown is forever chasing something, a pure hard-flat-jazz-funk he heard once in his dreams, and toward which all subsequent efforts have been pointed. This in turn leads to a reminiscence about Grover Washington Jr., who, apparently, recently presented

James Brown with a track James Brown didn't wish to sing on. "He should go play smooth jazz. We got something else going. James Brown jazz. Nothing smooth about it. If it gets smooth we gonna make it not smooth." Still musing on Grover Washington Jr.'s failings, he blurts: "Just jive." Then corrects himself, looking at me: "Just *things*. Instead of people. Understand?"

Throughout these ruminations James Brown's band stands at readiness, their fingers on strings or mouths a few short inches from reeds and mouthpieces, in complete silence, only sometimes nodding to acknowledge a remark of particular emphasis. A given monologue may persist for an hour, no matter: At the slightest drop-of-hand signal, these players are expected to be ready. There's nothing new in this. The Hardest Working Man in Show Business is one of the legendary hard-asses: His bands have always been the Hardest Working Men in Show Business, the longest-rehearsed, the most fiercely disciplined, the most worn-out and abused. Fuckups, I'll learn, will be cold-shouldered, possibly punished with small monetary fines, occasionally humiliated by a tirade. James Brown's punitive anger is not at all a certainty: It is precisely his inconsistency, his unpredictability, that keeps the organization on its toes—or rather, keeps them gripping the floor with their toenails. These men have been systematically indoctrinated into what begins to seem to me less even a military- or cult-style obedience than a purely Pavlovian situation, one of *reaction* and *survival*, of instincts groomed and curtailed. Their motives for remaining in such a situation? That, I'll need more time to study.

"I'm an old man," James Brown says. "All I can do is love everybody. But I'm still going to be a tough boss. I'm still going to give them hell. I got a family here. I tried to meet everybody's parents." At this, he suddenly squints at Damon, the guitarist, and says, "I don't know your people." Permission has apparently been granted to reply, and Damon corrects him. "Yes, you met them in Las Vegas. Just briefly." Then James Brown points to his son, saying cryptically, "I don't know where this cat's coming from." Daryl dares a joke (which it dimly occurs to me was perhaps the point): "But you do know my people."

"That's what I'm talking about," says James Brown irritably. "Love." He poses a question, then answers it: "You go to the blood bank, what do you want? Human blood. Not baboon."

Throughout the afternoon, even as the band begins to record, these ruminations will continue, as though James Brown's mind is on permanent shuffle. Sometimes the subject is the nature of his art. "Jazz," he states simply at one point. Or he'll segue into a discourse on his relationship to hip-hop: "I'm the most sampled and stolen. What's mine is mine and what's yours is mine, too." At this, the band laughs. "I got a song about that," he tells me. "But I'm never gonna release it. Don't want a war with the rappers. If it wasn't good, they wouldn't steal it." Thinking of his influence on contemporary music, he mentions a song by Alicia Keys with a suspicious riff: "Sometimes you find yourself meeting yourself." Yet he's eager to make me know he's not slagging Keys: "I don't want to scrape nobody." Later, in a moment of seeming insecurity, dissatisfied with something in his own performance, he blurts: "The minute they put up that statue I was in trouble."

Much of the afternoon's spent working on an arrangement of a medley comprising another Sam and Dave song, "Soul Man," and one of James Brown's own most irresistible and enduring classics of the early '70s, "Soul Power." James Brown tinkers with the guitars, indicating the desired tones by wailing in imitation of a guitar, as well as by issuing what sound like expert commands: "Diminish. Raise nine. Flatten it." Of Damon's solo he requests: "Go psychedelic." It seems to be the nature of the guitarists—Keith, Damon, and Daryl—that they are the center of the band's sound, but also the source of considerable problems.

A horn player—a large, slightly hound-doggy saxophonist named Jeff Watkins—interjects. Raising his hand like a schoolboy, he suggests: "They might have it right, sir. They just didn't play it with conviction." To the guitarists, Jeff says, ever so gently, "Play it like you mean it."

They do, and James Brown listens and is persuaded.

"I'm wrong," the Godfather says, marveling. "*Play it like you mean it*—I like that, Jeff." James Brown's deadpan is perfect: It is as if he's never heard that particular phrase before.

Now he coaches his bass player, an aging, willowy, enigmatically silent black man named Fred Thomas, on the bass line: "Ding dong, ding dong." Again, he emphasizes: "Flat. Flat. Hard." Fred Thomas does his best to comply, though I can't hear any difference. James Brown turns to me, suddenly urgent, and introduces me to Fred. "It's all about Sex Machine," he says. "This man's on more hits than any other bass player in history." I nod. Of course, it will later occur to me that one of the most celebrated partnerships in James Brown's career was with the future Parliament-Funkadelic bassist Bootsy Collins—and anybody who cares at all about such things can tell you that Bootsy was the bass player on "Sex Machine." Fred Thomas was, in fact, Bootsy's replacement, which is to say he's been in the band since sometime in 1971. Good enough. But in this matter we've at least briefly entered what I will come to call the James Brown Zone of Confusion. James Brown now puts his arm around Fred Thomas. "We're both cancer survivors," he tells me gravely.

Now we come to an impasse: Howard, the engineer, stymied by the number of horn players James Brown wishes to record simultaneous with the rest of the band, protests: "I can rehearse sixteen people, but I can't record them." James Brown responds, with galactic irritation, "So we gotta do it canned? Can't do it live?" Howard sheepishly admits: "I can try a two-inch tape." James Brown: "Get it."

While Howard fusses with the two-inch tape, James Brown is possessed by an instant of Kabuki insecurity: "I'm recording myself out of a group." This brings a spontaneous response from several players, a collective murmur of sympathy and allegiance, most audibly saxophonist Jeff's "We're not going anywhere, sir." Reassured, James Brown paradoxically regales the band with another example of his imperious command, telling the story of a drummer, a man named Nat Kendrick, who left the room to go to the bathroom during the recording of "Night Train." James Brown, too impatient to wait, played the drum part himself, and the recording was completed by the time Nat Kendrick returned. "Go to the bathroom, you might not have a job." (Later, with James Brown gone from the room, Keith, stepping out for a bathroom break, makes a joke, one typical of the band's incorporation of James Brown's admonitory lectures into their private and ironic folklore: "I'm gonna pull a Nat Kendrick. Don't cut nothing without me.")

The two-inch tape is now in place, and James Brown and his band attack "Soul Man/Soul Power" once again. "It's about to be as good as it was yesterday," he says, reminding them again of the Ramada rehearsal. "We're not recording, we're just having fun." Indeed, everything suddenly seems to come together. "Soul Power" is an unbearably fierce groove when taken up, as it is now, by a James Brown who sings it as though he's never heard it before, with crazy urgency and rhythmic guile, his voice hopped up on the crest of the music like a surfer riding a curl. In a vocal improvisation, James Brown shouts in Gatling-gun time with the drums: "Food stamps! Welfare!"

This take sounds better by far than anything that's gone before it, and James Brown, seated on his stool at the microphone, looks half a century younger now. At the finish, he rushes from his stool directly to where I sit, and slaps me on my knee. "That was deep, Mr. Rolling Stone!" he exclaims, then dashes from the room. The band exhales a burst of withheld laughter the moment he's through the door. "Food stamps!" several of them cry out. "Never heard that before." His son Daryl says, "Damn, I almost dropped my guitar when he said that." They seem genuinely thrilled, and delighted now to have me here as a witness, and go rollicking out the door, into the room where James Brown, ever impatient, is already preparing to listen to playback. They've done it, cut a classic James Brown funk jam! Never mind that it is a classic that James Brown already cut in 1971!

The laughter and conversation cease as Howard is commanded to roll the tape. Midway through the first time he's heard the tape, James Brown's head sinks in weary dissatisfaction: Something's not right. When it ends, after a single beat of total silence, James Brown says soberly, "Let's do it again, a little slower." And so the band trudges back in, in dour obedient silence.

During the playback session, guitarist Keith leans in and whispers to me, "You've got to tell the truth about what goes on here. Nobody has any idea." I widen my eyes, sympathetic to his request. But what exactly does he mean?

4. The Time Traveler

Someday, someone will write a great biography of James Brown. It will by necessity, though, be more than a biography. It will be a history of half a century of the contradictions and tragedies embodied in the fate of African Americans in the new world; it will be a parable, even, of the contradictions of the individual in the capitalist society, portentous as that may sound. For James Brown is both a willing and conscious embodiment of his race, of its strivings toward self-respect in a racist world, and a consummate self-made man, an entrepreneur of the impossible. This is a man who, out of that shack in the woods of South Carolina and that whorehouse on Twiggs, mined for himself a career and a fortune and a legacy and a statue; who owned an airplane; who has employed hundreds; whose band begat dozens of famous and lucrative careers; whose samples provided, truly, the foundation for hip-hop; who had his photograph taken with presidents and whose endorsement was eagerly boasted of, first by Hubert Humphrey, then Richard Nixon; who was credited with keeping the city of Boston calm in the twenty-four hours after the assassination of Martin Luther King Jr.; a man who owned radio stations, controlling the very means of control in his industry; and who did all of this despite the fact that no likelihood except desolation, poverty, and incarceration might have seemed to exist.

He's also a martyr to those contradictions. That James Brown should succeed so absolutely and fail so utterly is the mystery. For, no matter his accomplishment and the will that drove it, he has no fortune. No plane. No radio stations. The ranch home that he so proudly bought for himself in a mostly white suburb of Augusta was claimed by the IRS in lieu of back taxes. Unlike those whose fame and money insulate them from scandal, James Brown has been beset: divorces, 911 calls, high-speed road chases ending in ludicrous arrests and jail sentences. This great exponent of black pride, of never dropping out of school, of making something of yourself, found his way, relatively late in life, to the illegal drugs not of glamour and decadence but of dereliction and street life, like PCP and crack cocaine. With their help, he nearly destroyed his reputation.

The shadow of his abuse of musicians and wives, disturbing as it may be, is covered in the larger shadow of his self-abuse, his torment and unrest, little as James Brown would ever admit to anything but the brash and single-minded confidence and pride he wishes to display. It is as though the cape act is a rehearsal onstage of the succor James Brown could never accept in his real life. It is as though, having come from being dressed in potato sacks for grade school and in the drab uniform of a prisoner to being the most spectacularly garbed individual this side of Beau Brummell or Liberace, James Brown found himself compelled also to be the Emperor with No Clothes. What his peculiar nakedness reveals is the full range of the torment of African American identity. Oblivious to racism, he was always also its utter victim; contemptuous of drugs, he was at their mercy. And the exposure of his bullying abuse of women might seem to have made squalid hypocrisy of his calls for universal love and self-respect.

For my part as a witness, if I could convey only one thing about James Brown it would be this: James Brown is, like Billy Pilgrim in Kurt Vonnegut's *Slaughterhouse Five*, a man unstuck in time. He's a time traveler, but unlike the H. G. Wellsian variety, he lacks any control over his migrations in time, which also seem to be circumscribed to the period of his own allotted life span. Indeed, it may be the case that James Brown is often confused as to what moment in time he occupies at any given moment.

Practically, this means two things. It means that sometime around 1958—approximately the year he began voyaging in time, if my theory is correct—James Brown began browsing through the decades ahead, '60s, '70s, '80s, and perhaps even into the '90s—and saw, or, more exactly, *heard* the future of music. This, if my theory is correct, explains the stubbornly revolutionary cast of his musical efforts from that time on, the way he seemed to be trying to impart an epiphany to which he alone had access, an epiphany to do with *rhythm*, and with the kinetic possibilities inherent but to that point barely noticed in the R&B and soul music around him. From the moment of "Night Train"—the track, oddly enough, during which Nat Kendrick went to the bathroom and James Brown had to play drums himself—onward, through one radically innovative track after another: "Out of Sight," "I Got You," "Papa's Got a Brand New Bag," "Cold Sweat," etc., James Brown seemed less a musician with an imperative either to entertain or to express his own emotional reality than one driven to push his musicians and listeners to the verge of a *sonic idea*, and then past that verge, until the moment when he became, more or less officially, the single-handed inventor of an entire genre of music called *funk*: "Sex Machine," "Super Bad," "Hot Pants," etc. That sonic idea has never been better expressed than by critic Robert Palmer: "The rhythmic elements *became* the song . . . Brown and his musicians began to treat every instrument and voice in the group as if it were a drum. The horns played single-note bursts that were often sprung against the downbeats. The bass lines were broken into choppy two- or three-note patterns . . . Brown's rhythm guitarist choked his guitar strings against the instrument's neck so hard that his playing began to sound like a jagged tin can being scraped with a pocket knife." Another way of thinking about this: James Brown seemed to hear in the interstices of soul and R&B—in the barked or howled vocal asides, in the brief single-chord jamming on the outros, in the drum breaks and guitar vamps—a potential for discarding the whole of the remainder of the music in favor of a radical expansion of these interstitial moments, these transitional glimpses of rhythm and fervor. James Brown was like a filmmaker who gets interested in the background scenery and fires the screenwriter and actors, except that instead of ending up with experimental films nobody wanted to watch, he forged a style of music so beguilingly futuristic that it made everything else—melody, lyrics, verse-chorus-verse—sound antique.

This time-traveler theory would best explain what is hardest to explain about James Brown, especially to younger listeners who live so entirely in a sonic world of James Brown's creation: That he made it all sound this way. That it sounded different before him. The more essential and encompassing a contribution of this kind, the more difficult to assess, in a fish-assessing-the-ocean sort of way. This time-traveler theory would explain, too, how in 1973, right at the moment when it might have seemed that the times had caught up, at last, with James Brown's sonic idea, that the torch of funk had been taken up and his precognitive capacities therefore exhausted, James Brown recorded a song, called "The Payback," which abruptly predicts the aural and social ambiance of late-'80s gangsta rap.

My theory also explains the opposite phenomenon, the one I so frequently witnessed in Augusta. If the man was able to see 2005 from the distance of 1958, he's also prone to reliving 1958—and 1967, and 1971, and 1985—now that 2005 has finally come around. We all dwell in the world James Brown saw so completely before we came along into it; James Brown, in turn, hasn't totally joined us here in the future he made. That's why it all remains so startlingly new to him, why, during one playback session, he turned to Mr. Bobbit and said, "Can I scream and moan? I sound so good I want to kiss myself!" He spoke the phrase as if for the first time, and that may be because for him it was essentially occurring to him for the first time, or, rather, that there is no first time: All his moments are one. James Brown, in this view, *is always conceiving the idea of being James Brown*, as if nobody, including himself, had thought of it until just now. At any given moment James Brown is presently reinventing funk, bringing his visionary idea home like a caveman dragging to his lair a mighty mastodon vanquished in the tundra. To record "Soul Power" in 2005, no matter how perverse a use of studio time it may seem to an outside observer, is equally as revelatory as to record it in 1971. James Brown, it turns out, is reinscribing the world.

This theory also neatly explains the James Brown Zone of Confusion: Fred Thomas as the bass player on "Sex Machine," and so on. It's hard, for a man of James Brown's helplessly visionary tendencies, to know what happened today, yesterday, or indeed, tomorrow. All accounts are, therefore, highly suspect. Nat Kendrick may in fact have gone to the bathroom during the recording of "Think" or "I'll Go Crazy." Nat Kendrick may not, indeed, have gone to the bathroom yet.

5. In the Studio with James Brown, Day Two

The faster James Brown thinks, the more fiercely his hipster's vernacular impacts upon itself, and the faster he talks, the more his dentures slip. So, though transcribing James Brown's monologues as they occur is my goal, much of what he says is, to my ears, total gibberish. As today's session begins, James Brown is recalling members of his band who've passed. "Clyde Stubblefield gone, Jimmy Nolen gone. What about the tall cat?" Hollie, apparently, knows who he means by "the tall cat," and replies, "Coleman? He's alive." This leads James Brown into the subject of health, primarily digestive health. He speaks of dysentery while on tour in third-world countries: "Doing number one and number two at the same time," and exhorts the band: "Maintain yourself." To me: "Olive oil. I always tell them, bring olive oil on the road." I don't ask what the olive oil is for. This reminds James Brown of the dangers of the road, generally, especially of exotic locations, which he begins to reel off: "Jakarta. Cameroon. Peru." He recalls: "We were in Communist Africa . . . at the end of the show there were baskets of money . . . protected by machine guns, though. Got confiscated for the government." He recalls the Zairian dictator Mobutu Sese Seko attempting to keep him and his band from departing when George Foreman's injury delayed the Foreman–Ali boxing match: "We got out. We got paid. One hundred grand." He tells of keeping one plane behind: "The cats is so backward they had the liquor on the plane and the instruments off. I told them to take the liquor off and put the instruments on, or we wasn't going nowhere." James Brown seems torn between bragging of munificence—painting himself as an "ambassador to the world" who paid his own way to Vietnam to entertain the troops—and bragging of his shrewdness in always getting paid in cash, even in circumstances of maximum corruption and intrigue: promoters dying mysteriously, funds shifted through Brussels.

Shrewdness wins, for the moment, as he switches to tales of his gambling prowess, though he seems initially most keen on Mr. Bobbit's confirming a time when he came within a digit of winning a million-dollar lottery. "Yes, sir, you almost hit that pot," agrees Bobbit. James Brown then tells of playing craps on the road. "I won enough from the Moonglows to buy myself a Cadillac. Them cats was so mad they stole my shoes. Wilson Pickett, all these guys, I look so clean, they don't think I can play. I was a street man even though I had a suit on." But his stake in being thought of as the luckiest man alive is compromised by an eagerness to divulge his secret: "shaved dice," which always came up the way he wanted them to. Just as abruptly, James Brown's reminiscences open to melancholy. "I did a commercial for the lottery and I haven't hit since." He muses on this, and it begins to seem, potentially, a metaphor for aging. "I lost the desire to play. I lost that." Later this day, I ask several members of the band whether James Brown is babbling for my benefit. Not at all, they explain. "He's making us ready for the road," Damon tells me, reminding me that on Monday James Brown and his band are heading to Europe for a month of shows. "He knows it's going to be hard. He wants us to remember we're a family."

When, what seems hours later, work at last begins for the day, it will be on two different fronts. First, James Brown records a ballad that trumpeter-and-arranger Hollie has written and arranged in his off-hours. The ballad, it turns out, has been lurking in the background for a while, with Mr. Bobbit and several band members gently inducing James Brown to give it a chance to be heard. Today James Brown has—impetuously, suddenly—decided to make use of it. Hollie, given this chance, hurriedly transposes the changes for the guitarists and hands out sheet music. The simple ballad is swiftly recorded.

James Brown then goes into a small booth, dons a pair of headphones, and in the space of about fifteen minutes, bashes his way through a vocal track on the second take. Audibly, James Brown is inventing the melody and arriving at decisions about deviations from that melody (syllables to emphasize, words to whisper or moan or shout, vowel sounds to repeat or stretch) simultaneously, as he goes along. With uncanny instincts married to outlandish impatience, he is able to produce a result not wholly unlistenable. Understand: This is a matter of genius, but an utterly wasteful variety of genius, and after we listen to the playback, and James Brown is out of range of the band's talk, Hollie and Keith agree that if James Brown were to regard the track he just recorded as a beginning—as a guide vocal to study and refine in some later vocal take—they might really have something. But they also seem resigned to the fact that James Brown considers his work on the track complete.

Next, James Brown writes a lyric to record over a long, rambling blues-funk track titled "Message to the World." For anyone who has ever wondered how James Brown writes a song, I have a sort of answer for you. First: He borrows Mr. Bobbit's bifocals. James Brown doesn't have glasses of his own, or left them at home, or something. Second: He borrows a pencil. Third: He sits, and writes, for about fifteen minutes. Then he puts himself behind the microphone. The result is a cascading rant not completely unlike his spoken monologues. Impossible to paraphrase, it meanders over subjects as disparate as his four marriages, Charles Barkley, Al Jarreau, a mixture of Georgia and Carolina identities he calls "Georgelina," the fact that he still knows Maceo Parker and that Fred Wesley doesn't live very far away either, Mr. Bobbit's superiority to him as a checkers player, the fact that he believes himself to have both Asian and Native American ancestry, and, most crucially, his appetite for corn on the cob and its role in his health: "I like corn, that's a regular thing with me. Gonna live a long time, live a little longer."

Afterward, we gather in our usual places for playback. Late in the eleven-minute song James Brown issues a universal religious salute: "Saalaam-Alechem-may-peace-be-unto-you, brother . . . believe in the Supreme Being!" As these words resound James Brown glances at me, and then abruptly commands Howard to roll the tape back to that point: There's something he wishes to punch in on the vocal. Hustling into the booth, when the tape arrives at the brief pause between "brother" and "believe," James Brown now wedges in a brief but hearty "Shalom!" (Incredibly, the additional syllables seem to fit rhythmically, as if something had been missing in that spot all along.) Reemerging, he points at me, and winks. "Shalom, Mr. Rolling Stone!" James Brown has pegged me as Jewish. So much for being invisible in this place. He has apparently tampered with the spontaneity of his own vocal, merely in order to appease what he imagines are my religious urgencies.

Indeed, he now fixates on me for a short while. During this same playback session, while deeply engaged in transcribing what I've heard around me, my head ducked to the screen of my PowerBook, I notice that James Brown has begun singing, a cappella, a portion of the song "Papa Was a Rolling Stone." I continue typing, even transcribing the lyrics of the song as he sings them: "Papa was a rolling stone / wherever he laid his hat was his home—" *Odd*, I think, *this isn't a James Brown song.* Then I hear the band's laughter and look up. James Brown is singing it directly at me, trying to gain my attention.

"Oh," I say, red-faced, as I look up at him. "Sorry. I forgot my new name."

"That's all right, Mr. Rolling Stone," says James Brown. "I was just *missing* you."

He begins bragging about the new song, about its relevance. "This is for the world. And the world is going to love it." The band, and Bobbit, and Danny Ray provide some low murmurs of approval. "The world could use it," he goes on. "It's out of gas. Needs filling up." More murmurs. "What you think, Mr. Rolling Stone?"

Unpersuaded by the song, I search for the simplest truth to tell. "I think I'm very lucky to be here, sir."

But today is also the day when I grow closer to the band. The musicians' wariness falls away when I agree, at Jeff's suggestion, to make a secret run for take-out barbecue. At the moment, James Brown is busy conducting the Bittersweets—his three female backup singers—in support vocals for Hollie's ballad. For hours none of the other musicians have so much as struck a note. As the afternoon drags into evening, it seems everyone (apart from James Brown) has begun to suffer hunger pangs. But the band is on call—in a state of mandatory readiness to begin playing at any moment—and nobody feels safe leaving to get food, despite the fact that the barbecue joint they have in mind is directly across the highway, in sight of the studio's doors, perhaps a two-minute drive at most.

I'm incredulous that James Brown's disciplinary statutes go to the extent of routine starvation, a classic brainwashing technique, though I don't mention this to the members of the band who are now covertly slipping me balled-up five-dollar bills so that I can buy them chopped-pork sandwiches. Even Fred Thomas—side man for three decades, bass player on more hits than any other, cancer survivor, and, unlike James Brown, a man who really does appear to be in his early seventies—is subject to the boycott on slipping out for a meal. This makes me a unique ally, simply for my freedom to borrow Keith's car keys and round up some eats. Saxophonist Jeff mentions that I shouldn't fail to treat myself to a regional specialty, a dish called "hash and rice" which, he claims, is available only within a fifty-mile radius of Augusta. When I return with the booty, dozens of the barbecue sandwiches, and they are unwrapped across the table in the small dining room, it is during the feasting that I begin to get stories from members of the band.

And this, in turn, leads to the unexpected confidences they'll share with me, later that night, back at the Ramada.

6. The Secret Life of the James Brown Band

Roosevelt Johnson, known always as R.J., sits with me and explains his role, a role he's occupied since he was nine, forty-two years ago: "Hold the coat." Excuse me? "Hold the coat, hold the coat." R.J. expands, then, on the basic principle of life in the James Brown entourage: You do one thing, you do it right, and you do it forever." It is the nature of traveling with James Brown that everyone treats him like a god: "The people that show up in every city, they all fall back into their old jobs, like they never stopped. The doormen stand by the door, the hairdressers start dressing his hair." R.J. is being modest, since his responsibilities have expanded to a performing role, as the second voice in a variety of James Brown's call-and-response numbers ("Soul Power," "Make It Funky," "Get Up, Get into It, Get Involved"), replacing the legendary founding member of the Famous Flames—James Brown's first band—Bobby Byrd. R.J. sounds uncannily like Byrd when he sings—or "raps"— Byrd's parts in the classic songs, and in concert R.J.'s ebullient turns often draw some of the mightiest cheers from the crowd, who nonetheless can have no idea who he is. Yet for him, his life is defined by his offstage work: "Someday I'm going to write a book about my life called 'Holding the Coat.'"

(Hearing this, Cynthia Moore, one of the Bittersweets, interrupts: "My book's gonna be called 'Take *Me* to the Bridge, I Want to Jump Off.'")

The greatest exemplar of the entourage phenomenon is, of course, Danny Ray, the little man with the pompadour and the voice familiar from so many decades of live introductions. ("There are seven wonders of the world, you are about to witness the eighth," etc.) Danny, from

Birmingham, Alabama, joined James Brown in the '50s, when they met at the Apollo Theater. He joined as a valet. And, though he has become nearly as recognizable a voice as James Brown himself, he is still a valet; indeed, his concern for the band's clothes obsesses Danny: He is the human incarnation of James Brown's lifelong concern with being immaculately dressed. Valet, and master of ceremonies, Danny is also the proprietor of "the cape routine"—i.e., he comes onstage to settle the cape over James Brown's shoulders when he collapses, and he receives the cape and takes it away when James Brown has shrugged free of it. (When Danny Ray was first introduced to me, it was as "the original capeman." Then, hurriedly, with a concern both for Danny's feelings and for an accurate historical record, the introducer whispered in my ear: "Actually, he's the *second* original capeman." Apparently, somewhere lost in time, is a first.)

R.J. and Danny Ray briefly allude to another responsibility that tends to devolve to valets: wrangling James Brown's irate girlfriends. Danny Ray cites a few vivid episodes: "Candace. Lisa. Heather. The one from Las Vegas that came to his house carrying a .357. She said, 'What is your intention?'" It is R.J. who finishes the story, laughing: "Brown said: My *intention* is for you to get on the plane, go back to Las Vegas. Get out of here."

Robert "Mousey" Thompson, James Brown's drummer, tells me: "I thought I'd last maybe three months. It was hard at first. Then I thought I'd last three years. Been thirteen years. I'd do anything for him. Touring is hard. I worry about him. If I thought his health was in danger I'd quit that day. Of course, if he heard me say that, he'd fire me."

Keith and Damon, the guitarists, ask me if I'd care to join them at a bar. We arrange to meet in Jeff's room at the Ramada. It is here that I learn Jeff's nickname: Sizzler. Sizzler is named for how frequently he "sizzles" a joint, and, sure enough, Jeff's room is a haze when I arrive to find Keith and Damon there, along with Mousey, and Hollie, and George "Spike" Nealy, the second percussionist. Here, safely distant from either James Brown's or Bobbit's ears, I'm regaled with the affectionate and mocking grievances of a lifer in James Brown's band. I think I'm beginning to understand what story it is Keith feels has never been told: the glorious absurdity of the band's servitude.

"We're supposed to follow these *hand signals*," Keith explains. "We've got to watch him every minute, you never know when he's going to change something up. But his hand is like an eagle's claw—he'll point with a curved finger, and it's like, do you mean *me*, or *him*? Because you're looking at me but you're pointing at him."

They take turns imitating James Brown's infuriating mimed commands to them during live shows. "It's like rock-paper-scissors," jokes Damon. Each of the band members, I gradually learn, has a spot-on James Brown impression available. Each has memorized favorite James Brown non sequiturs: "Sixteen of the American presidents were black," or the time he asked an audience for thirty seconds of silence for a fallen celebrity he called "John F.K." These men, it seems to me, are stymied by the impossibility of fathoming either their employer, this impossible master, or their own life choice: to remain his whim-whipped slaves. James Brown is both their idol and their jester, their tyrannical father and ludicrous child.

Jeff tells me of going on the David Letterman show for a three-minute spot. "We didn't discuss what we were doing until we got out there. Sound-checked a totally different song. I didn't know I was doing a solo on TV until he waved me out front."

Hollie, the longest-enduring among them there, says, "I don't think there's another band on the planet that can do what we do."

Damon adds: "I like to call it: Masters of the Impossible."

I ask whether James Brown has been jabbering particularly for my benefit. I regret the possibility that the past two days in the studio have been made more difficult for them because of my presence. "Listen," says Damon, "he's always performing. He'll chastise the band backstage for the benefit of a janitor passing by with a bucket."

Yet they hurry to make me understand their vast reverence and devotion—for you see, they're also the luckiest musicians on earth. Keith says, "Brown told us, *you got it made*. You cats are lucky, you're *made* now. Eleven years later I get it. The man hasn't had a hit for twenty years, but we'll work forever. We're going to the Hollywood Bowl, Buckingham Palace, the Apollo Theater, it never stops. We could work for a hundred years. You play with someone else you might have two good years, then sit for two years, wondering if anything's ever going to happen again. With James Brown you're always working. Because he's James Brown. It's like we're up there with Bugs Bunny, Mickey Mouse. There's no other comparison."

Damon says, "For me, it's just being onstage, waiting for those moments. He's a magic man. He's the only one who can make that party happen." The guitarists also tell of how James Brown has "bogarted" them onto this or that record. When someone wants a James Brown cameo, they ordinarily don't intend to hire James Brown's band, too. But knowing extra royalties from a hit can be precious to his sidemen, Brown snuck a chunk of his band onto the Black Eyed Peas' *Monkey Business*, when all the Peas were after was their boss's voice. Keith shares a cherished memory of being summarily inserted into the Dave Matthews Band and told to rearrange their version of a James Brown song the Godfather was to sit in on. Scamming gigs with James Brown makes these players feel like outlaws, too.

"Listen," says Jeff. "There's something we want you to hear." I've been corralled in Jeff's room for a purpose: the unveiling of the secret recordings of James Brown's band. The frustration these musicians feel at having no voice in composition or arrangement has taken its toll, a certain despair about the prospects for the present recording sessions. James Brown, they complain, just won't let his band *help* him. Yet these frustrations have, in turn, found an outlet.

Sizzler fires up his iTunes, connected to a pair of desktop speakers, and there, seated on a Ramada bedspread, I'm treated to an audio sample of What Could Be, if only James Brown would allow it. The songs are original funk tunes, composed variously by Damon, Mousey, Jeff, and Hollie, and recorded, under cover of darkness, in hotel rooms while the band travels, or while they assemble, as now, for official sessions. The songs, while lamed by the absence of James Brown on vocals, are tight, catchy, propulsive numbers, each with one foot in '70s funk and the other in a more contemporary style. They have the added benefit of being something new. In other words, they're not "Soul Power," but they're also not "Soul Power."

No one has dared tell James Brown that this music exists. He might fire them if he knew. In this, the band's wishful thinking tangles with their sense of protectiveness of the boss's feelings. For James Brown, it seems, has had so many important musicians outgrow his band— Bootsy, Maceo, Ellis, and Fred Wesley—that his passion for control has outstripped his curiosity about what his present roster might have to offer him. Anyone showing signs of a life of their own, musical or otherwise, tends to be the target of elaborate and vindictive humiliations. "It's abandonment issues," says Keith. "Has to do with being abandoned by his parents." Keith explains that James Brown is most eager, above all, to undermine the family lives of his band members; he'll deliberately schedule mandatory rehearsals to clash with weddings or funerals, forcing them to show allegiance to him instead. "He *always* screws with me if my wife is in the crowd," Keith tells me. "At the Apollo, first time she was going to see me play, he sat me down offstage, didn't let me go on." And each and every one of these members of the *James Brown family* is on his own when the shit hits the fan. The only mistake worse than stepping out of line is attempting to stand up for someone else who's being punished. Like Walmart, the one thing James Brown crushes most mercilessly is any hint of unionization.

All eyes go to Hollie. Hollie, after all, found a way to make James Brown aware of the ballad. If that could work, why not some of the secret funk? Hollie has certain privileges, due to his long tenure and his role as bandleader, which symbolically links him to the most influential members of the bands of the '60s and '70s: Ellis, Maceo, and Wesley. Even better, Hollie went away, to play with Steve Winwood for a number of years in the '80s, and then *came back*. Since James Brown is always bragging that everyone who leaves eventually *comes back*— a plain falsehood, in his band, or life, or anyone else's life, for that matter—Hollie's return is a vindication. Hollie, though, is a survivor perhaps precisely thanks to his lowered expectations. As the younger players urge him to attempt to mediate these secret recordings into official consideration—"*You* could do it, Hollie"—Hollie says little, only chuckles and rolls his eyes. The impression he gives is of someone who means to protect himself and his band during these sessions, and who believes the odds of improving the results of the sessions are not worth betting on.

The funniest of the secret recordings is a song called "Pimp Danny," which, unlike the others, consists not only of live instruments played directly into laptop computers but of samples of old James Brown records. The premise of "Pimp Danny" is that a certain master-slave relationship has been reversed: By pasting together various introductions to shows over the years, the band has created a track where Danny Ray takes the role of lead vocalist, saying things like: "I like to feel dynamite, I like to feel out of sight! I like to feel sexy-sexy-sexy!" The track isn't finished; the band is searching for what they are certain exists somewhere, a recording where James Brown introduces Danny

Ray, which they will then clip onto the front of the track, to complete the role reversal. "Pimp Danny" also samples the voice of Bobby Byrd, and a drumbeat from Clyde Stubblefield, one of the great drummers from James Brown's '6os band. In this way, "Pimp Danny" is not only a celebration of Danny Ray, who seems in many ways the band's talisman-in-servitude, but a yearning conflation of the legendary past eras of the band with its present incarnation. And there's a plan: Fred Wesley has promised to come to the studio tomorrow to record a few trombone solos, for old times' sake. (*Everyone comes back*.) The band wants to try to sneak Wesley back to the Ramada and have him add his horn to "Pimp Danny."

Many sizzles later, Keith and Damon and I have made it to the Soul Bar. They explain how this is the one establishment in all of Augusta that truly gives James Brown his props. Indeed, the bar is lined with gorgeous vintage James Brown posters and album jackets and memorabilia. (Much of this, Keith confesses, comes from his—Keith's—own collection; the bar is owned by a friend. Keith is beginning to strike me as the world's biggest James Brown fan.) "It's shameful," they explain to me. "If you're in Memphis, you can't get away from Elvis. Everything's Elvis glossies, Elvis salt-and-pepper shakers, whatever. Here there's nothing." The Soul Bar, which is packed with revelers, is playing loud rap, which spurs a brief rhapsody from Keith: "See, the thing about Brown, is his relevance sustains him. You hear a Chuck Berry song, a Jerry Lee Lewis song, it's an oldie. It's got no relevance. James Brown comes on, it's got relevance. Some rapper has a hit, it's got a little piece of him in it. He hears himself everywhere. His relevance sustains him." (I'm beginning uneasily to suspect Keith should be writing this piece, not me.) Damon says more about what they'd do if only they could seize control of the sessions: "James Brown should go out like Johnny Cash did. All that stuff about how he wishes he could record in the Ramada? Hell, we could do that tomorrow, if he'd let us use the computers." Keith says, "We're like a blade of grass trying to push up through the concrete."

Later Damon walks me back to the Ramada and, very gently, takes a little wind out of the "we could fix James Brown if only he'd let us" theory: "Look at how he got where he is. He always controlled everything himself. That's who he is. I mean, who has hundreds of Top 40 hits? Not me. You know how many thousands of people must have come around over the years with a song, thinking, 'Wouldn't that be cool, he'll hear my track and say *that's hot* and lay a vocal over it and we'll have a big hit'?"

7. I Sing of Myself

Now, to note that James Brown is *self-centered* or *egotistical* or *pleased with himself* is hardly an insight worth troubling over: It is the very first thing anyone might remark on, indeed, the only thing many people who believe they know nothing whatsoever about James Brown might respond if given his name in a word-association test:

> *Analyst: James Brown. Please say the first*
> *thing that comes to mind.*
> *Patient: I feel good!*
> *Analyst: Stay with that thought.*
> *Patient: Uh, just like I knew that I would?*

That James "I want to kiss myself" Brown dabbles in self-adulation hardly makes him unique in the history of art, though he scores points for unwavering fixity: James Brown knows no hesitation, no whisper of ambivalence, in his delight in his own person. His subjugation of his various bands' musical ambition to his own ego, to his all-encompassing need to claim as entirely an extension of his own genius every riff invented by anyone within his orbit, is, needless to say, a cause of much dispute. To put it simply: The James Brown sound, its historic sequence of innovations, depends on a whole series of collaborators and contributors, none of whom have been adequately acknowledged or compensated.

Yet the more I contemplated the band's odd solicitude toward James Brown's ogreish demands, their protectiveness and eagerness to soothe (James Brown: "I'm recording myself out of a band." Band: "We're not going anywhere, sir."), the more completely I became persuaded of Keith's viewpoint: that James Brown is reenacting an elemental trauma, the abandonment by his parents into a world of almost feral instability and terror. One doesn't have to look far. His 1986 autobiography, *James Brown*, bears the dedication "For the child deprived of being able to grow up and say 'Momma' and 'Daddy' and have both of them come put their arms around him."

This is a child who ate "salad we found in the woods" in his first years, a child who was sent home from school—in the rural South—for "insufficient clothes" (i.e., potato sacks). This is a teenager who was nearly electrocuted by a pair of white men who whimsically invited him to touch a car battery they were fooling with. This is a man who, during his incarceration in the '80s, long after he'd drowned his nightmare of "insufficient clothes" in velvet and fur and leather and jeweled cuff links, *was found to be hiding tens of thousands of dollars in cash in his prison cell*, an expression of a certainty that society was merely a thin fiction covering a harsh jungle of desolation and violence, and if James Brown wasn't looking out for James Brown, no one was.

His, then, is a solipsism born of necessity. When it most mattered, there was nobody to jump up and kiss James Brown *except* himself. His "family" is therefore a trickle-up structure, practically a musical Ponzi scheme, and anyone willing to give him their best is going to be taken for as long a ride as he can take them on. Gamble with James Brown and he will throw the shaved dice, until, like the Moonglows and Wilson Pickett, you are forced to understand that you are dealing with a *street man*. And as much as in the cases of Duke Ellington or Orson Welles, James Brown's ability to catalyze and absorb the efforts of his collaborators *is* a healthy portion of his genius.

And discipline is good for the child, after all. When James Brown sings, as he does, of corporal punishment—"Mama come here quick, bring me that lickin' stick," or "Papa didn't cuss, he didn't raise a whole lot of fuss / but when we did wrong, Papa beat the hell out of us"—it is with admiration and pride. Though his band consents to call itself his *family*, the structure bears at least an equal resemblance to jail—which is where James Brown was more likely to have absorbed his definitive notions of authority. So when his musicians begin to bristle under his hand, they find themselves savaged for their "betrayals"—for daring, that is, to risk subjecting James Brown to further experience of abandonment. This explains what I encountered in Augusta: The band James Brown has gathered in 2005 is the vanishing endpoint of his long struggle with Byrd, Maceo, Bootsy, Pee Wee, Wesley, and all the others: a band more inclined to coddle his terror than to attempt to push him to some new musical accomplishment, however tempting it might be.

James Brown is in his mid-seventies, for crying out loud. What more do you want from him? After all, his trauma, and its result—frantic creative striving, and fearsome, bullying ego and will—are not so terribly unique. What's *really* special about James Brown is how undisguised, how ungentrified he remains, has always remained. Most anyone else from his point of origin would long since be living in Beverly Hills, just as his peers in the R&B and soul genres of the '50s and '60s smoothed down their rough edges and negotiated a truce; either went Motown, meeting the needs of a white audience for safe, approachable music, or else went jazzily uptown, like Ray Charles. Whereas James Brown, astonishingly, returned to Augusta, site of his torment, and persistently left the backwoods-shack, backwoods-church, Twiggs Street–whorehouse edges of his music raw and on view. His trauma, his confusion, his desperation—those are worn on the outside of his art, on the outside of his shivering and crawling and pleading onstage. James Brown, you see, is not only the kid from Twiggs Street who wouldn't go away. He's the one who wouldn't pretend he wasn't from Twiggs Street.

8. In the Studio with James Brown, Day Three

Today is Fred Wesley day, and everyone's excited. The studio is more populous than before: For unclear reasons, today is also family day. James Brown's wife, Tomi Rae Brown, a singer who is a part of the band's live act, has brought along their five-year-old son, James Brown Jr. Then appears James Brown's thirty-one-year-old daughter, Deanna, a local radio talk-show host. Deanna has, variously, sued her father for royalties on songs she claimed to have helped write when she was six years old and attempted to commit her father into a mental institution; lately they're on better terms. Also on the scene is another son, whose name I don't catch, a shy man, who appears to be in his early fifties, and with two sons of his own in attendance—James Brown's grandsons, older than James Brown Jr.

These different versions of "family," with all their tangible contradictions, mingle politely, deferentially with one another in the overcrowded playback room, where James Brown and Fred Wesley are seated next to each other in the leather chairs. Fred Wesley, his red T-shirt stretched over his full belly, is a figure of doughy charisma and droll warmth, teasing and joshing with the children and with the room full of musicians eager to greet him. His eyes, though, register wariness or confusion, as though he's trying to fathom what is expected of him here, a little as though he fears he may have wandered into a trap.

James Brown, startlingly, has abandoned his three-piece suits today for an entirely different look: black cowboy hat, black sleeveless top, snakeskin boots, and wraparound shades. What we have here is the *Payback* James Brown, a dangerous man to cross. I wonder whether this is for Wesley's benefit, or whether James Brown just woke up on the Miles Davis side of bed this morning. James Brown is giving Fred Wesley a listen to "Message to the World," plainly hoping to please him. Fred Wesley nods along. The two of them slap hands when the song comes to James Brown's references to Maceo and to Fred Wesley. The smile James Brown shows now is by far the warmest and most genuine I've seen from him.

Next James Brown commands Howard to play an instrumental track for Wesley, a shuffle that James Brown calls "Ancestors." Fred Wesley listens closely to "Ancestors" once through and then says simply: "That makes all the sense in the world, Mr. Brown. Thank you very much." He fetches his trombone, in order to lay a long solo over the shuffle. I gather that, once again, a track is to be unceremoniously slammed together before my eyes.

The entire band, as well as the many family members, linger to gaze through the sound room's long glass window at Fred Wesley as he plays. He makes a rollicking figure there, his red T-shirt and gleaming trombone spotlit in the otherwise darkened studio. The band members I've come to know seem both exhilarated and tired; these long sequences of not-playing are wearing on them, but Fred Wesley is a genuine inspiration. Hollie, meanwhile, is troubling over the track's changes, trying to anticipate the next crisis: "Ask him if he wants me to transpose that keyboard, just so he'll be in D."

Wesley concludes and reenters the playback room. Next, James Brown enters the studio, in order to lay a "rap" over the top of the track. The moment the boss leaves for the soundproof chamber, the band members laugh with admiring pleasure: "Damn, Fred, you come in here and just start blowing, man!" They're thrilled at his on-the-spot facility. "Just went with those changes, never heard them before. I told him, 'it goes up a half octave'—bam."

Fred laughs back: "What could I do, damn. Shuffle in F!"

Now we listen as James Brown begins what he calls "rapping," a verbal improv no one seems to want to call a sheer defacement of Fred Wesley's solo. The spontaneous lyrics go more or less like this: "Fred

Wesley. Ain't nothing but a blessing. A blessing, doggone it. Get on up. Lean back. Pick it up. Shake it up, yeah. Make your booty jump. Clap your hands. Make your booty jump. Dance. Ra-a-aise your hands. Get funky. Get dirty. Dirty dancin'. Shake your boo-tay. Shake you boo-boo-boo-boo-tay. Plenty tuchas. Plenty tuchas. Mucho. Mucho grande. Shake your big booty. Mucho grande. Big booty. Cool-a. TUCHAS!" On delivering this last exclamation, an exhilarated James Brown rushes from behind the glass and, rather horrifyingly, in a whole room full of colleagues and intimates, points directly at me and says, "Tuchas! You got that, Rolling Stone?"

I say, "That'll go right into the piece, sir."

James Brown then makes a shape in the air and says, "South American boo-tay." We all laugh at the helpless insanity of it, at the electricity of his delight. "Jewish boo-tay," he says. "Jewish boys and Latina girls get up to a lot of trouble!"

Unfortunately, James Brown demands that we listen to "Ancestors" five times in a row—which we do, as usual, in a state of silent reverence, heads nodding at each end to the track. James Brown makes a "tuchas" joke every time the song resolves on that word, as if surprised to find it there. Then, heart-crushingly, he asks for a playback of "Message to the World"—the eleven-minute rant. A few band members have gradually crept out, but most sit in a trance through all the replays. I try not to dwell too much on the deserts of repetition these human souls have tolerated.

Next we listen to Hollie's ballad, recorded the day before. James Brown tells his wife the ballad's lyric is dedicated to her (the innocuous sentiments are along the lines of "If you're not happy, I'm not happy, either"). At this James Brown's wife gets nervous, and in a quiet moment I overhear her asking Damon exactly what it says.

"For me?" she asks again.

In irritation, James Brown says, "For *all* wives." This seems to put an end to the subject.

Afterward, in front of us all, James Brown's wife urges him to consider breaking from his work for a snack. His blood-sugar level, I learn, has been a problem. "I put a banana in the fridge for you," she says. This information displeases James Brown intensely, and the two begin a brief, awkward verbal tussle.

Mr. Bobbit leans in to me and whispers, "A rolling stone gathers no moss." Taking the hint, I go and join Wesley and the band, most of whom have tiptoed out of the playback room and are hanging out in the kitchen.

There, an ebullient Fred Wesley is teasing a rapt circle of admiring musicians for having the audacity to kvetch about how hard the James Brown of 2005 rehearses his band. "Y'all don't know *nothing* about no *eight-hour* rehearsal," he tells them. "Y'all don't got a clue. Y'all don't know about going to Los Angeles, nice bright sunshine, sitting there in a dark little studio for eight hours, all those beautiful women, all the things we could do, stuck rehearsing a song we've been playing for fifty years, going 'Dun dun dun' instead of 'dun dun doo.'"

Seizing their chance, the cats confide in Wesley about "Pimp Danny," and how they hope he will contribute a solo. "So is that why I'm here?" Fred Wesley replies warily, as if sensing a conspiracy of some kind. "I'll play trombone on anything," he explains to me. Though he's hoping to drive back to Atlanta tonight, he promises that if they get free of the sessions early enough he'll drop by the Ramada and join in the fun. "You know the story about the two-hundred-dollar whore? Guy says he's only got fifty dollars, she says that's all right, I'll fuck you anyway. 'Cause she just likes to fuck. That's me: I like to play."

The mood, in James Brown's absence, is giddy. R.J. joins us and pokes a little fun at Wesley for showing up for a session in a T-shirt, a choice that apparently would have been regarded as an infraction, back in the day. Cynthia ribs R.J. in turn, saying: "*His* T-shirt don't say 'Ray Charles' on it." She explains: "R.J. got thrown out for wearing a Ray Charles T-shirt." Fred Wesley says, "Hell, *I'd* have thrown you out for wearing a Ray Charles shirt around the boss." Then, abruptly, Wesley's expression takes on the appearance of a caged animal, as though he's been reminded of days gladly left behind. He makes a joke of it, saying, "This ain't some trick to get me to go to Europe, is it? I don't care what anyone's saying, I ain't going. Y'all can say hello to all them madams, mademoiselles, fräuleins, and señoritas for me, 'cause I *ain't* going."

Suddenly Mr. Bobbit has arrived with a vast delivery of take-out food: several gallon buckets of Kentucky Fried Chicken, assorted sides, and a few boxes of doughnuts, too. These are spread on the table, and James Brown emerges from the playback room and joins us. The blood-sugar issue, it appears, is to be addressed, and not by the banana in the fridge. Mrs. James Brown and James Brown Jr. are now nowhere to be seen.

James Brown, still in his black hat and shades, fills a plate with chicken and plunks himself down between me and Wesley. "You gotta talk to this guy," he says, indicating Fred Wesley. "That's twenty percent of your story, right there."

Fred Wesley demurs. "People always try to tell me that, but I'm always saying, there couldn't be nothing without the Man. It all comes through him. You need someone who thinks *unbounded*. I used to be contained within the diatonic scale. He'd tell me something and I'd say, 'It can't be written down, so it can't be played.' He'd say, 'Play it, don't write it down.' It took me years to understand. Now *I'm* a teacher."

(Alternately, from Wesley's memoir: "The whole James Brown show depended on having someone with musical knowledge remember the show, the individual parts, and the individual songs, then relay these verbally or in print to the other musicians. James Brown could not do it himself. He spoke in grunts, and la-di-das, and he needed musicians to translate that language into music and actual songs in order to create an actual show." I contrast these quotes not to accuse Fred Wesley of hypocrisy but because they so beautifully capture the paradox I found everywhere in these men's feelings for their leader, and my own: The Charlatan is a Visionary, the Visionary is a Charlatan.)

James Brown and Keith begin reminiscing, plainly for Fred Wesley's sake, about having to teach the Black Eyed Peas' bass player how to play a James Brown bass line. Usher's people, too, needed a tutorial. James Brown and Keith laugh at how slow others are to get it: the guitarist who said, "That's the wrong chord," and James Brown's reply: "How can it be wrong, when it's never been played before?"

The next quarter hour or so, eating chicken side by side, is easily the most intimate of my moments in James Brown's company. Whether energized by Fred Wesley's presence or by his wife's absence or by the chicken and corn and conversation, James Brown seems to enclose me in his sphere for a while, a sensation I'll treasure. I can't, however, detail what was said. Not because it's too cherished for me to share but because, as James Brown speaks frantically and continually to me through mouthfuls of food, I simply can't understand a word. James Brown eats quickly, as if fearful the food will be taken from him. I notice, too, that Mr. Bobbit has fried chicken and a frosted doughnut together on the same plate. Perhaps he, in turn, is afraid James Brown will finish his chicken and eat all the dessert.

Following this five o'clock lunch break, James Brown leads the Bittersweets in some more insert vocal arrangements, leaving the band and Fred Wesley sitting on their hands. Though James Brown's energy is phenomenal, as the evening drags toward seven the general belief is that nothing further will be accomplished here today. Jeff says, wonderingly, "I never even took my horn out of my case today. Checked my e-mail, smoked a twist, ate some Kentucky Fried Chicken." Yet it is on this cue, seemingly as if he has gleaned the risk of mutiny, that James Brown sends the Bittersweets home and calls instead for the band—the whole band.

James Brown's mood has turned again. He's so determined he's almost enraged. "Got to be ready," he chastises while they assemble. James Brown has decided he wants to play his organ, but snaps at Howard and snaps at Jeff as the amplifier cables get tangled and, briefly, unplugged. He also castigates Fred Thomas, who he claimed has missed a cue: "You want to play bass? Then play." Next he rages at Mousey, who, trapped in a separate booth, can't watch the hand signals. James Brown actually steps in and briefly plays the drums for Mousey, ostensibly showing him how it's done—shades of Nat Kendrick! The silence in the room, during these attacks, is suffocating. I can't help thinking of the present band's embarrassment in front of Fred Wesley, and of Fred Wesley's embarrassment in front of the present band. Here's living proof of every complaint they've wished to register with me.

The tinkering preparations and ritual outbursts at last conclude. James Brown takes his place behind the keyboard, looking ferocious in his shades and sleeveless top. He leads the band through an endlessly complicated big-band jazz-funk piece, which, after three or four false starts, he runs for a perhaps fifteen-minute take, long enough for him to request, by hand signals, two Fred Wesley trombone solos and a bass solo from Fred Thomas, and to give forth three organ solos himself. During his own solos—his famously atonal and abstract keyboard work is truly worthy of Sun Ra or Daniel Johnston—James Brown looks fixated, and again appears to have shed thirty years. At the end of his last solo he directs the horns to finish, and laughs sharply. "Takes a lot of concentration!" He turns to me and slaps me five. Fred Wesley turns to the ashen Fred Thomas and, perhaps trying to put a chipper face on what they've been through, says, "Playing that bebop, damn."

(Again, from Wesley's memoir: "Mr. Brown would sometimes come to the gig early and have what we call a 'jam,' where we would have to join in with his fooling around on the organ. This was painful for anyone who had ever thought of playing jazz. James Brown's organ playing was just good enough to fool the untrained ear, and so bad that it made real musicians sick on the stomach . . . after we got accustomed to the jams and saw the looks on his face when he played, the real pain got to be trying to keep from busting out in uncontrollable laughter.")

That night, a portion of the band gathers to lick its wounds in Jeff's room at the Ramada. Fred Wesley was, needless to say, detained at the studio too long to return to the hotel with them, so the "Pimp Danny" solo will have to wait for another opportunity. I ask about the long jazz song they recorded at the finish, fishing for some impressions of James Brown's rabid outbursts but not wishing to press too hard. The song, I tell them, was somehow familiar to me.

"That's some old number he's made us play a million times," Keith tells me. "That's just him wasting our time."

I ask if it is in fact some standard. Jeff says, "Yeah, I think it is based on something. We've been playing his version for so long, I can't remember what it is. Hollie, what does he call that?"

"He always just calls it 'Basic Brown,'" says Hollie, listlessly. None of them can recall the actual source melody, buried under the James Brown arrangements. Later, humming it for a knowledgeable friend, I'll learn it's the Harold Arlen–Johnny Mercer chestnut "Blues in the Night," recorded by everyone from Doris Day to Louis Armstrong to Van Morrison. The fact that these veteran musicians can no longer retrieve it from their own context is a perfect example of the James Brown Zone of Confusion. For them, "Blues in the Night" has become "Basic Brown"—the color of their world.

Jeff, one of the primary victims, tries to put the day in context. "Hey, we had good James Brown for four days. I'll take it. He was tired toward the end. But he just wanted to set up his toy soldiers one more time and go—" To make his analogy vivid Jeff sweeps his arm violently, as if clearing a table stacked with dishes, and makes a crashing noise with his voice.

Keith explains to me how little they were surprised. "We could tell it was a bad day first thing—by the way he was dressed."

9. Gateshead

I rendezvous with the band in England ten days later, for a performance in Gateshead. The musicians seem mildly amused to see me in this distant place, as though the week of touring and the Atlantic Ocean between this week and last have made my arrival in their dressing rooms a reunion. See? *Everybody comes back*. The doormen stand by the door, the hairdressers start dressing hair, and Mr. Rolling Stone starts asking questions.

The players are in another kind of survival mode now, keeping themselves healthy under punishing travel conditions, while trying to stay in the mood to put on The Show. Donning their red tuxedos, the guitarists point out details they can guess will amuse me. "Danny Ray had jackets made without pockets," says Damon. "He doesn't want to see any lines. So I don't have any place to put my picks onstage." I obligingly examine his tux—sure enough, no pockets. Damon explains that he has no recourse but to stack a supply of picks on an amp, where they invariably vibrate off, onto the floor.

The guitarists play James Brown songs in the dressing room. When "Talkin' Loud and Sayin' Nothing" comes on Keith's iTunes, Daryl says, proudly, "This is my song." I ask what he means and he tells of being present as a child for that session. Keith, sensing my interest in his archival material, displays on his laptop a video clip of James Brown at the Apollo in 1971. All three guitarists lean in to study it. "See his hand signal," Damon says. Keith explains: "This band was brand new. This is one of Fred Thomas's first gigs. He wasn't fucking with them yet. He was just trying to get through the show."

I ask them how the tour's been to this point. Damon, while not critical of the previous week's shows, says, "He needs to warm up on tour, too. Think of all the bits he has to remember. If he screws up, you notice." Damon recalls for me a night when the floor was slick and James Brown missed his first move, and as a result "lost confidence." Lost confidence? I try not to say: *But he's JAMES BROWN!* It is somehow true that despite my days in his presence, my tabulation of his foibles, nothing has eroded my certainty that James Brown should be beyond ordinary mortal deficits of confidence. And with this thought I discover that a shift has occurred inside me. I wish for the show tonight to be a triumphant one, not for myself, or even for the sake of the band, but so that James Brown himself will be happy.

I'm wanting to take care of him, too.

It's as if I've joined the family.

Bumbling along with the red-costumed tribe in the tunnel to the stage, I find myself suddenly included in a group prayer—hands held in a circle, heads lowered, hushed words spoken in the spirit of the same wish I've just acknowledged privately to myself: that a generous deity might grant them and Mr. Brown a good night. I still haven't seen Mr. Brown himself. Now I can hear the sound of the crowd stirring, boiling with anticipation at what they are about to see. As the players filter onstage into their accustomed positions, bright and proud in their red tuxes, to an immense roar of acclaim from the Gatesheadians, I settle into a spot in the wings, beside Danny Ray.

When the band hits its first notes and the room begins to ride the music, a metamorphosis occurs, a transmutation of the air of expectation in this Midlands crowd. They've been relieved of the first layer of their disbelief that James Brown has really come to Gateshead: At the very least, James Brown's Sound has arrived. I realize—as if for the first time, despite the fact that I've crossed the ocean for no other purpose—that I'm about to see the James Brown Show. After the band's long overture, Danny Ray, every impeccable tiny inch of him, pops onstage. The crowd hesitates. I suspect some percentage of them actually wonder: "Is it *him*? Has James Brown shrunken to this size?" The moment Danny Ray speaks, though, they are spared this confusion. "Give yourselves a big round of applause!" says Danny Ray, inviting the Gatesheadians to feel smug just for having gotten themselves into this situation. Then Danny Ray says, "Now comes Star Time!" and the roof comes off. Under Danny Ray's instruction the crowd rises to its feet. They begin to chant their hero's name.

When James Brown is awarded to them, the people of Gateshead are the happiest people on earth, and I am one of them. Never mind that I now know to watch for the scissors-paper-rocks hand signals, I am nevertheless swept up in the deliverance of James Brown to his audience. The sun god has strode across a new threshold, the alien visitor has unveiled himself to another gathering of humans. I see, too, how James Brown's presence animates his family: Keith, fingers moving automatically on frets, smiling helplessly when James Brown calls out his name. Fred Thomas bopping on a platform with his white beard, an abiding sentinel of funk. Hollie, the invisible man, now stepping up for a trumpet solo. Damon, who during Tomi Rae's rendition of "Hold On, I'm Comin'" can be heard to slip a reference to "Lady Marmalade" into his guitar solo.

This night James Brown gets the cape routine out of the way early, the way Alfred Hitchcock in his later films got his cameo out of the way in the first ten minutes or so, to spare his audience the distraction of waiting for it to appear. It turns out I've chosen to stand in a spot right over the hidden cape, and Danny Ray is forced to nudge me aside in order to fetch it. James Brown refuses the cape almost instantly, and Danny Ray stoically returns it to its place, seeming a little skeptical, a little disappointed, as if decades later he really still believes his task is to usher James Brown offstage at that moment, at last to give the man a rest.

The show builds to the slow showstopper, "It's a Man's, Man's, Man's, Man's World." The moment when James Brown's voice breaks across those horn riffs is one of the greatest in pop music, and the crowd, already in a fever, further erupts. James Brown's voice, it occurs to me, is hornlike—but not like a musical instrument, like an actual animal's horn. His voice is clawlike, fanglike, tusklike. When they cap the ballad by starting "Sex Machine," it is a climax on top of a climax. The crowd screams in joy when James Brown dances even a little (and these days, it is mostly a little). Perhaps, I think, we are all in his family. We want him to be happy. We want him alive. When the James Brown Show comes to your town—when it comes to Gateshead, U.K., in 2005, as when it came to the Apollo Theater in 1961, as when it came to Atlanta or Oklahoma City or Indianapolis, anytime—life has admitted its potential to be astounding, if only for as long as The Show lasts. Now that James Brown is old we want this to go on occurring for as long as possible. We almost don't wish to allow ourselves to think this, but the James Brown Show is a precious thing that may someday vanish from the earth.

Now James Brown has paused the music for a monologue about love. He points into the balconies to the left and right of him. "I love you and you and you up there," he says. "Almost as much as I love myself." He asks the audience to do the corniest thing: to turn and tell the person on your left that you love them. Because it is James Brown who asks, the audience obliges. While he is demonstrating the turn to the left, turning expressively in what is nearly a curtsy to Hollie and the other horns, James Brown spots me there, standing in the wings. *Everyone comes back*. The smile he gives me is as natural as that he gave Fred Wesley, it is nothing like the grin of a statue, and if it is to be my own last moment with James Brown, it is a fine one. I feel good.

—*Rolling Stone*, 2005

People Who Died

The summer of 1980 I was sixteen and unpersuasively cool. I listened to the Ramones, and clung to a thin claim of "having been there"— meaning CBGB, which let you in without an ID. But I meant to be a writer, and had begun favoring Talking Heads and Elvis Costello, music which buffered emotionality in layers of cleverness and metaphor, in postures of alienation. I spent a lot of afternoons at my desk, writing stuff that wasn't any good. One such day that summer the DJ on WNEW came on and announced a new single, a debut—"by a New York poet turned rock 'n' roller" was the way the he set it up. While the DJ rambled I had time to sneer in advance—this would probably be some flowery singer-songwriter, at best about as tough as Billy Joel. Then the DJ dropped the needle on "People Who Died" by Jim Carroll, which, by the end of one snarling, anguished chorus, had wrecked the walls of my pretensions. The song was a ticking bomb of rage at loss— "they were all my friends, and they died!" Carroll moans, as astonished that he's found a voice to report it as he is at the gruesome fact of death itself. Though I'd have to learn the lesson a thousand times again, Carroll's channeled beatnik vulnerability, shrouded in a punk rage which was still, that summer, an undeniable thing, was the first rebuke to my foolish hope that being a "writer" or an "artist" could mean skirting my emotions. No, it would always mean ramming straight into them— Carroll had put me on notice.

The DJ let it finish, then played it immediately again: He, and I, were that impressed. I still am. Nothing else of Carroll's has had that impact on me, but it hardly matters, because "People Who Died" is breaking me open still, and there's only room for so many songs like that in your life, even if Carroll had somehow managed a career that kept that song's impossible promise. Punk—or pop, or life—isn't always about keeping the promises you make, but daring to make them in the first place. Despite knowing what's at stake. Maybe even making them *because* you know what's at stake. That's what "People Who Died" knew that I didn't, that summer afternoon, and why it broke my heart twice quickly in succession, before I'd completely understood it could be broken—and why the song goes on breaking it now that I've learned.

—*GQ*, 2002

Only now do I realize this piece was an unconscious memorial to a book Paul Williams described to me several times before suffering the brain injury (falling from a bicycle) that meant he'd never write it. Paul's unwritten book, his masterpiece, was called The Beauty of the Singer.

The Fly in the Ointment

There's something about a voice that's personal, not unlike the particular odor or shape of a given human body. After all, that's pretty much what voice is: Summoned through belly, hammered into form by the throat, given propulsion by bellows of lungs, teased into final form by tongue and lips, a vocal is a kind of audible kiss, a blurted confession, a *soul-burp* you really can't keep from issuing as you make your way through the material world. How helplessly candid! How appalling! And because expressivity is the only standard, the low-chops approach forged by touchstone figures like Bob Dylan and Jim Morrison and Jonathan Richman helps define rock-and-roll singing, which is both egalitarian ("Anyone can do this!") and Dionysian ("But only if you're crazy with passion!") in its premises. Nor are genius-technical-liabilities solely a male province—I'm looking at you, Patti Smith, Chan Marshall, Tina Turner.

But, contrary to anything you've heard, the ability to actually carry a tune is in no regard a disability in becoming a rock-and-roll singer, only a mild disadvantage. As proponents of Aretha Franklin, Van Morrison, Jeff Buckley, and P. J. Harvey will attest, virtuosity can be gotten around. Meanwhile, nothing in the vocal limitations of a Lou Reed guarantees a "Pale Blue Eyes" result every time out, any more than singing as half terrible as Tom Waits guarantees a "Downtown Train." This sad truth several million forgettable spoken-whined-mumbled-intoned "indie-style" vocals (a few committed by Lou Reed himself) make incontestable.

Now, putting my own cards on the table: For me Bob Dylan and Patti Smith, just to mention two, are superb singers by any measure I could ever care about—expressivity, surprise, soul, grain, interpretive wit, angle of vision. Those two folks, a handful of others: Their soul-burps are, for me, *the soul-burps of the Gods*. The beauty of the singer's voice touches us in a place that's as personal as the place from which that voice has issued. If one of the weird things about singers is the ecstasy of surrender they inspire—that "Madness of Crowds" associated with voices like Elvis, Om Kalsoum, Teddy Pendergrass, etc., but is also present in intimate situations, as when a listener first communes with Jeff Buckley's "Lilac Wine" or Joni Mitchell's "Amelia" alone on headphones in the dark—another weird thing is the debunking response a singer can arouse once we've recovered our senses. It's as if they've fooled us into loving them, diddled our hardwiring, located a vulnerability we thought we'd long ago armored over. Falling in love with a singer is like being a teenager every time it happens.

Singers *are* tricksters. Sometimes we'll wonder if they're more like movie actors than musicians per se—we'll decide that the "real" R.E.M. is embodied by Buck, Berry, and Mills, not that kooky front man Stipe, or the "real" Rolling Stones is Richards-Wood-Watts-Wyman, rather than that irritating capitalist Jagger. But beware—go down this route and soon you'll find yourself wondering how the Doors sound sans "Mr. Mojo Risin'," or imagining someone can better put across Dylan's gnarly syllables than Dylan himself. Firm evidence is on the table against both those lines of inquiry. In truth, so often what makes a band like the Stones or R.E.M. (or the band Dylan transformed from the Hawks into the Band) so truly unique and powerful is in how the instrumentalists rise to the challenge of creating a home for the vocalists' less-than-purely-musical approach to a song: the braggadocio or mumbling, the spoken asides or too many syllables crowded into a line that destroys traditional rhythm or measure, those movie-star flourishes that compel us to adore and resent the singer at once.

The funny thing about this imposter-anxiety is that it infects singers themselves, to the extent that certain well-known vocalists have been known to decorate themselves onstage with a carefully unplugged guitar (I know of a couple). And it certainly explains the "rockist" bias in favor of singers who are also the writers of the songs they sing. If a vocal performance that tenderizes our hearts is a high-wire walk, an act breathtaking and preposterous at once, we can reassure ourselves that Neil Young or Gillian Welch or Joe Strummer have at least dug the foundations for the poles and strung the wire themselves. Singers reliant on existing or made-to-fit material like Janis Joplin, Rod Stewart, Whitney Houston—or, for that matter, a band's pure vocal instrument, like Roger Daltrey—might just be birds alighting on someone else's wire. Listening to singers who are like magnificent animals wandering through a karaoke machine, we may derive a certain thrill from wondering if they find the same meaning in the lyrics they're putting across that the lyrics' writer intended, or any meaning at all—as opposed to dwelling in a realm of pure sound-as-emotion.

This points to what defines great singing in the rock and soul era: that some underlying tension exists in the space between singer and song. A bridge is being built across a void, and it's a bridge we're never sure the singer's going to manage to cross. The gulf may reside between vocal texture and the actual meaning of the words, or between the singer and band, musical genre, style of production, or the audience's expectations. In any case there's something beautifully uncomfortable at the root of the vocal style that defines the pop era. The simplest example comes at the moment of the style's inception, i.e., Elvis Presley: First listeners *thought that the white guy was a black guy.* It's not too much of an exaggeration to say that when Ed Sullivan's television show tossed this disjunction into everyone's living rooms, American culture was thrilled by it, but also a little deranged, in ways we haven't gotten over yet. If few vocal styles since have had the same revolutionary potential, it wasn't for want of trying. When the Doors experimented with how rock 'n' roll sounded fronted by sulky bombast, or the Ramones or Modern Lovers offered the sound of infantile twitching, a listener's first response may be to regard their approaches as a joke. Yet that joke is the sound of something changing in the way a song can make us feel. In the café where I write this, Morrissey just came over the speakers, and it's unmistakable that he came through the Doors Jim Morrison opened. Janis Joplin's voice howled in the wilderness for decades before Lucinda Williams came along to claim its tattered and glorious implications. In doing so, she deepened them.

The nature of the vocals in post-Elvis, post–Sam Cooke, post–Ray

Charles popular music is the same as the role of the instrumental solo-
ist in jazz. That's to say, if it isn't pushing against the boundaries of its
form, at least slightly, it isn't doing anything at all. Whether putting
across lines that happen to be written by the singer, or were concocted
in a Brill Building or Motown-type laboratory, or covering a song pulled
in from another genre, from the blues, or bluegrass, or a show tune, the
singer in rock, soul, and pop has to be doing something ineffable that
cuts against its given context. Etta James, Ray Davies, Mama Cass, Mark
Kozelek, Levi Stubbs Jr.: These singers might not all seem like protest
singers, but they are always singing "against" something—whether in
themselves, in the band that's backing them, in the world they've been
given to live in or the material they've been given to sing, or all at once.
We judge pre-rock singing by how perfectly the lyric is served. That's
the standard Frank Sinatra exemplifies. We judge popular vocals since
1956 by what the singer unearths that the song itself never quite could.
It explains why voices such as Joan Baez or Emmylou Harris or Billy
Joel never really seem to be singing in the contemporary idiom, no
matter how much they roughen up their material or accompaniment,
and why Elvis—or Dylan—is always rock, even singing "Blue Moon."
It also explains precisely why such virtuosic pipes as Aretha Franklin's
or Karen Carpenter's function in the new tradition. No lyric written by
themselves or anyone else could ever express what their voices needed
to, and they weren't going to wait for the instrumental solo, or for the
flourish of strings, to put it across for them. They got it into their voices,
and their voices got it out into the air, and from there it passed into our
bodies. How can we possibly thank them enough?

—*Rolling Stone*, 2008

Dancing About Architecture
or
Fifth Beatles

When I dance these days I don't bend so much at the knees as I used to. My knee bends are more Kabuki indications, representational rather than presentational, like Lou Reed's vocal range, like Muhammad Ali teasing a video crew with boasts of flurries of punches so fast you couldn't see them, even as he posed with his upraised fists completely still. My dancing, these days, enciphers in shorthand the drops and knee bends of my twenties, even as it is likely circumscribed by my excess of drops and knee bends in my twenties—these were moves that, once I'd learned them, I drove, so to speak, into the ground, and my knees reminisce of old dance floors in clubs in Berkeley and Oakland and San Francisco when I climb too many stairs, a sad involuntary pun on dancing about architecture.

Other ghosts rustle in my dancing these days, kinetic memory-routines, muscle-quotes of punk-rock-ironized glam kicks, Elvis Costello intentional-awkward heel-scoots and skids, a kind of sideways bunny hop and mechanical stop and restart that I appropriated from my friend Sari, and which always reminds me of the B-52's and a certain beer-swollen wooden-plank dormitory living-room floor in Vermont. From that same scene my dancing self still periodically retrieves a mimicry of the solitary, ecstatic dancing of a young poet named Reggie, who'd cascade his body side to side to the Psychedelic Furs and Donna Summer, propelled by his hurling arms, as if caught up on the shut-tle of a gigantic loom—for a while I could only want to dance exactly like Reggie, and the phantom still gains possession of me from time to time.

When I got to college I was already a dancer. In my freshman year of high school I seized that role for myself, first, and definitively, at a Manhattan loft party full of hip adults to which my father had brought me and my new girlfriend, my first girlfriend—and when the dance floor filled, not to be outdone by my father's friends, I began impulsively and spastically showing off in the midst of the dancers, finding my own ready dance-appropriating instinct available when I needed it to even begin. An image is still fresh in my mind of the shaved-bald black man in a dashiki whose technique I glommed, or tried to—he bent at the waist, snapped his fingers, and shook his bright dome as if in a self-amused trance. His obliviousness to our regard was what I wanted for myself, was what I wished to hijack on behalf of my own craven pursuit of regard. I began immediately shaking my head, not yet capable of observing the finer details, how that dancer's headshaking must surely have been driven by less ostentatious but completely authoritative movements through his feet and hips, zones I'd yet to learn to activate. Yet my ears were open, I wasn't deaf to the music, I know I experienced the bodily rapture-in-sound where all real dancing begins. Alas, I was trying to lead my dance with my head, as if trying to play a song's bass line on a pair of cymbals or a triangle. Somehow I made this my trademark, no one intervened to advise me otherwise, and so I built my dancing body from the headshake downward, like a Cheshire cat begun at the grin. At grown-up parties in Brooklyn hippie communes I gradually worked it out on this basis, to the sound track of *The Harder They Come* and to the Rolling Stones and to Marvin Gaye and to the first Devo record which I smuggled in and was allowed to play sometimes, earning in the process a nickname from my father's best friend, Roy: He called me the Headman.

As the Headman I became the mascot dancer of a band in my high school, three brothers and a bass player named Blake Sloane, a blue-eyed soul group who called themselves Miller, Miller, Miller and Sloane. Their "hit" song, "Funky Family," a Jackson Five–ish single, was the song to the tune of which the Headman laboriously discovered his body: I danced to it at high-school parties and alone in my room, wearing out several copies of the Miller brothers' parent-financed 45. I was or wanted to be Miller, Miller, Miller and Sloane's Fifth Beatle, the evidence of their groove, and so at our high school's auditorium but also at an opening slot at CBGB I danced in some area closer to the band than the rest of the audience of my schoolmates (who were as much their whole audience at CBGB as they were in our high-school auditorium), my vicariousness charted in real space. But I never pretended I was in the band—Miller, Miller, Miller and Sloane's perfect name spoke of the inalterable sense of their lineup.

The height of my dancing—the apogee—came at a club called Berkeley Square, in 1990 or '91 it would have been. I'd spent the day at home discovering something new I could do with words—this was when I was writing a novel called *As She Climbed Across the Table*, a book I associate with my learning to take command of my sentences, to make them dance the way I wanted them to—and afterward gone out dancing with some friends. In the middle of a strenuous sequence of songs Prince's "Kiss" appeared, and in letting that song take me over, course through my body like a drug, with my dancing perhaps perfectly poised between savvy intention and callow frenzy, my knees and my head and what lay between all about as limber and aligned as my savvy and callow and frenzied sentences had been earlier that day, I found myself pretty sure that I was dancing, say, just about as well as anyone ever had. In fact I had the thought at that moment that though my equal at sentence-writing might be somewhere roaming the earth (perhaps there might even be a few of them out there), and that the same could be said of my dancing—that I might not be the only dancer working at such a high level at this moment in the planet's history—certainly there was no one alive at this moment who had both written and danced the way I had today. And I'm still almost convinced that this was true.

Writing about music was famously derided by Frank Zappa as "dancing about architecture." The whole enterprise may seem precious, overwrought, stillborn. Pop music, archetypal by nature and disposable by design, is fated to slip through the writer's fingers. And yet some of us keep trying to get near the music with our words, like a dancer assuming some relationship to the music with his responsive body, even if the musicians never know about it. There's something pretentious about daring to get up on the dance floor in the first place, and something presumptuous, but those of us who do it take courage from the possibility that it is those very pretenses and presumptions that may bring us closer to the desired object, that in fact may give us, even if only briefly, something in common with the makers of the music themselves.

The terms "jazz" and "rock and roll," as a great man once pointed out, are only blues musicians' slang for fucking. The whole history of pop, that half century or more of intricate delirium, is, in other words, *a fucking joke*, but for me it is a joke I grew up inside, a joke that was also a daydream, a shaggy-dog story, a surrealist fable like *Alice in Wonderland* or *The Phantom Tollbooth*, depicting an alternate reality of jokes taken with scrupulous deadpan, a world I wanted to climb inside and flesh out with my own yearning, a realm between audience and band that seemed as sacred as both and perhaps more sacred than either one. In other words, it's a bloody miracle I didn't turn out a rock critic. I'm still not entirely sure how I evaded the honor. This disposable stuff I've ruined my life letting matter more than my ethical obligations to society at large, as well as my schoolwork and sometimes my relationships: I'm indulging now in the hope that this particular utopian daydream not only matters but is some viable model of a world.

When I was younger it was hard for me to keep the future and the past from collapsing—I mixed up astronauts and dinosaurs, for instance. It was hard for me, too, thanks to the bohemian demimonde in which I dwelled, the milieu of my parents and their friends, all of them with their astonishingly valuable and mistreated record collections, to believe that Bob Dylan and the Beatles were not about fifty or a hundred years old, as canonical as F. Scott Fitzgerald or Walt Whitman, as revered as Thomas Jefferson or Abraham Lincoln. The first time I learned human beings still lived—some of them my aunts and uncles—who thought of rock and roll as "that noise," I barked laughter, feeling slaphappy disbelief. The myths of the '60s seemed biblically ancient.

So the quest for the identity of the "Fifth Beatle," an allegory of authenticity as deep as a Zen koan, represented an attempt to understand the world into which I'd been born. It haunted me like a ghost of crime, a Ross Macdonald investigation, where the façade of the present life peels off to expose the wild truths of the past, the impostures—some brave, some shameful—on which our contemporary reality was founded. Who was "Murray the K"? What was payola? Do you mean to say someone had to be *paid* to play rock and roll on the radio, that the music bought its way into our hearts? This idea conflated easily with the idea of "the hook" itself, the sense that pop was a trick, a perverse revenge against the banality of daily life dreamed up collectively by ten or fifteen Delta bluesmen and a million or a hundred million screaming twelve-year-old girls. If a rock-and-roll song with a killer hook was like a drug or a virus, and payola a kind of hypodermic needle, made to penetrate a resistant culture, then we all lived in a world permanently drugged or psychedelically sick with fever. If so, I was happy to live on the drugged and feverish side of the catastrophe.

The Fifth Beatle candidates after Murray the K—Sutcliffe, Best, Epstein, Voorman, Preston—made a sequence of suspects who were also victims. They seemed to indict the magic circle of four for some wrongdoing, but also confirmed them in their status as iconic survivors: Probably no one else deserved to be a Beatle. I remember the day I learned Ringo's drumming was "bad." So bad Paul had done some of it for him. Then—I recall it as if it was the very next thing I learned, like geometry leading to algebra—I found in the writings of some great man the beautiful thought that Ringo's role was to be our surrogate in the band, the Beatle who was also a fan of the Beatles, in awe of the "real ones" from the nearest possible proximity. So maybe there was no fifth Beatle, maybe there wasn't even a fourth! George, too, was given a free ride in the other songwriters' wake (yet you also could sense he was stunted or thwarted or cheated). John claimed bitterly that he wrote the hook to "Taxman," George's "best" song, just as Ray Davies was quick to note he helped his brother with "Death of a Clown," Dave Davies's greatest hit. So the sham notion of a "democracy of talent" within these groups, with its analogous utopian implications for collective action, for a gestalt-mind as depicted in Theodore Sturgeon's *More Than Human*, could dissolve into sour cynicism. The presiding genius probably could have done just as well with any other supporting cast. Or the reverse: The solo careers in the band's wake could seem so thin that the magic must have been in the lucky conjunction of a bunch of ordinary blokes, raised above their station as much by history and our love as by any personal agency—if there wasn't a Beatles we'd have had to invent one, and we did. For evidence, listen to the Beatles' *Live at the Hollywood Bowl*—here's a music content to ride like a froth of sea foam atop a tsunami wave of adulation and yearning for itself. What were little-girl screams if not the essential heart of the Beatles' true sound, the human voice in a karaoke track consisting of the band itself? Dylan? Study reveals he was always just the guy who happened to be smart enough to steal Jon Pankake's record collection, not so much a musician as a music-writer's daydream run mad.

Our urge to expose the trick is bound up in our mad love at being tricked, a revenge of the seduced, and a projection of our vanity into the space between the singer and the song. Jim Morrison and Michael Stipe, unmusical jesters, posturing poets, charlatans—yet imagine their bands shorn of them, and maybe you're left with only forgettable garage-rock outfits, nobody Chuck Berry couldn't hustle up in time to play a quick gig and then steal back out of town. Another charlatan was James Brown. Musicians who shared his stages hasten to explain Brown was, alas, not a musician: the Godfather of Soul, a fake Beethoven propped up by his orchestra. This notion of James Brown as a presider over music he could never himself play articulates his role as bridge between clown-jazz maestros like Louis Jordan and Cab Calloway, and the rappers whose world James Brown willed into being: the scatting, grunting foreground presence against a landscape of sonic astonishments. The showman's exhortations to the band, and shouts of surprise at the virtuosity of the soloists, mark him as an MC or DJ who has inserted himself onstage, a figure of pure will, distinct from the audience in terms not so much musical as Nietzschean. To dare to take that vicarious role he'd better be able to dance like a motherfucker—dance, or scream, or suffer, or make us suffer, or even better, all of the above.

This, too, is where the figure of the punk from hell—the Iggy Pop or Sid Vicious whose authority derives from his ineptitude, spontaneity, and pain—can seem an allegory for the whole history of pop itself: three lousy chords and a leather jacket. All little more than a jazzman's joke taken too seriously. A real music would have some pride, and we, in turn, would have a proper reverence for its history, a proper sense of its distance from ourselves. Instead, our pop life seems at every possible turn surrounded by the figure of the pretender, by swimmers in the ocean of the vicarious: the maker of mix tapes who believes he is in some way to credit for the beauty of the music, and who is believed by his lover, the child stars and American Idols whose degraded and ludicrous projection guiltily thrills us, the lip-synchers and air guitarists and mirror stars, the one-shot bands, the garage bands, the party bands that luck into a contract, those of us who've kidded ourselves that our dancing or our writing, or both, makes us something like rock stars, somehow sized to slip into Wonderland—we Fifth Beatles, we happy fakes. This whole story really is a naked egalitarian dream, isn't it?

—EMP Pop Conference, *The Guardian,* 2007

Dylan Interview

"I don't really have a herd of astrologers telling me what's going to happen. I just make one move after the other, this leads to that." Is the voice familiar? I'm sitting in a Santa Monica seaside hotel suite, ignoring a tray of sliced pineapple and sugar-dusty cookies, while Bob Dylan sits across from my tape recorder, giving his best to my questions. The man before me is fitful in his chair, not impatient but keenly alive to the moment, and ready on a dime to make me laugh and to laugh himself. As others have described, the expressions on Dylan's face, in person, seem to compress and encompass versions of his persona across time, a sixty-five-year-old with a nineteen-year-old cavorting somewhere inside. Above all, though, it is the tones of his speaking voice that seem to kaleidoscope through time: here the yelp of the folk pup or the sarcastic rim-shot timing of the hounded hipster-idol, there the beguilement of the '70s sex symbol, then again—and always—the gravel of the elder statesman, that antediluvian bluesman's voice the young aspirant legendarily invoked at the very outset of his work and then ever so gradually aged into.

It's that voice, the voice of a rogue ageless in decrepitude, which grounds the paradox of the achievement of *Modern Times*, his thirty-first studio album. Are these our "modern times," or some ancient, silent-movie dream, a fugue in black and white? *Modern Times*, like *Love and Theft* and *Time Out of Mind* before it, seems to survey a broken world through the prism of a heart that's worn and worldly, yet decidedly unbroken itself. "I been sitting down studying the art of love / I think it will fit me like a glove," he declares in "Thunder on the Mountain," the opening song, a rollicking blues you've heard a million times before and yet which magically seems to announce still another "new" Dylan. "I feel like my soul is beginning to expand," the song declares. "Look into my heart and you will sort of understand."

What we do understand, if we're listening, is that we're three albums into a Dylan renaissance that's sounding more and more like a period to put beside any in his work. If, beginning with *Bringing It All Back Home*, Dylan garbed his amphetamine visions in the gloriously grungy clothes of the electric blues and early rock 'n' roll, the musical glories of these three records are grounded in a knowledge of the blues built from the *inside out*—a knowledge which includes the fact that the early blues and its players were stranger than any purist would have you know, hardly restricting themselves to twelve-bar laments, but featuring narrative recitations, spirituals, X-rated ditties, popular ballads, and more. Dylan offers us nourishment from the root cellar of American cultural life. For an amnesiac society, that's arguably as mind-expanding an offering as anything in his '60s work. And with each succeeding record Dylan's convergence with his muses grows more effortlessly natural.

How does he summon such an eternal authority? "I'd make this record no matter what was going on in the world," Dylan tells me. "I wrote these songs in, not a meditative state at all, but more like in a trancelike, hypnotic state. *This* is how I feel? Why do I *feel* like that? And who's the *me* that feels this way? I couldn't tell you that, either. But I know that those songs are just in my genes and I couldn't stop them comin' out." This isn't to say *Modern Times*, or Dylan, seems oblivious to the present moment. The record is littered—or should I say baited?—with glinting references to world events like 9/11 and Hurricane Katrina, though anyone seeking a moral, to paraphrase Mark Twain, should be shot. And, as if to startle the contemporary listener out of any delusion that Dylan's musical drift into pre-rock forms—blues, ragtime, rockabilly—is the mark of a nostalgist, "Thunder on the Mountain" also name-checks a certain contemporary singer: "I was thinking 'bout Alicia Keys, I couldn't keep from crying / While she was born in Hell's Kitchen I was livin' down the line." When I ask Dylan what Keys did "to get into your pantheon" he only chuckles at my precious question. "I remember seeing her on the Grammys. I think I was on the show with her, I didn't meet her or anything. But I said to myself, there's *nothing* about that girl I don't like."

Rather than analyzing lyrics, Dylan prefers to linger over the songs as artifacts of music, and describes the process of their making. As in other instances, stretching back to 1973's *Planet Waves*, 1978's *Street Legal*, and 2001's *Love and Theft*, the singer and performer known for his love-hate affair with the recording studio—"I don't like to make records," he tells me simply, "I do it reluctantly"—has cut his new album with his touring band. And Dylan himself is the record's producer, credited under the nom de studio "Jack Frost." "I didn't feel like I wanted to be overproduced anymore," he tells me. "I felt like I've always produced my own records anyway, except I just had someone there in the way. I feel like nobody's gonna know how I should sound except me anyway, nobody knows what they want out of players except *me*, nobody can tell a player what he's doing wrong, nobody can find a player who *can* play but he's *not* playing, like I can. I can do that in my sleep."

As ever, Dylan is circling, defining what he is first by what he isn't, by what he doesn't want, doesn't like, doesn't need, locating meaning by a process of elimination. This rhetorical strategy goes back at least as far as "It Ain't Me, Babe" and "All I Really Want to Do" ("I ain't looking to compete with you," etc.), and it still has plenty of real juice in it. When Dylan arrives at a positive assertion out of the wilderness of so much doubt, it takes on the force of a jubilant boast. "This is the best band I've ever been in, I've ever had, man for man. When you play with guys a hundred times a year you know what you can and can't do, what they're good at. Whether you want 'em there. It takes a long time to find a band of individual players. Most bands are gangs. Whether it's a metal group, or pop rock, whatever, you get that gang mentality. But for those of us who went back further, gangs were the mob. The gang was not what anybody aspired to. On this record I didn't have anybody to teach. I got guys now in my band, they can whip up anything, they surprise even me." Dylan's cadences take on the quality of an impromptu recitation, replete with internal rhyme schemes, such that when I later transcribe this tape I'll find myself tempted to set the words on the page in the form of a lyric. "I knew this time it wouldn't be *futile* writing something I really *love*, and thought dearly *of*, and then I'm in the studio and having it be beaten *up* and whacked around and come out with some kind of incoherent thing which didn't have any resonance. With that, I was *awake*. I felt freed up to do just about anything I pleased."

But getting the band of his dreams into the studio was only half the battle. "The records I used to listen to and still love, you can't make a record that sounds that way," he explains. It is as if having taken his new material down to the crossroads of the recording studio Dylan isn't wholly sure the deal struck with the devil there was worth it. "Brian Wilson, he made all his records with four tracks, but you couldn't make his records if you had a hundred tracks today. We all like records that are played on record players, but let's face it, those days are gon-n-n-e. You do the best you can, you fight that technology in all kinds of ways, but I don't know anybody who's made a record that sounds decent in the past twenty years, really. You listen to these modern records, they're atrocious, they have *sound* all over them. There's no definition of nothing, no vocal, no nothing, just like—static. Even these songs probably sounded ten times better in the studio when we recorded 'em. CDs are *small*. There's no stature to it. I remember when that Napster guy came up across, it was like everybody's gettin' music for free. I was like, well, why not? It ain't *worth* nothing anyway."

2.

Hearing the word "Napster" come from Bob Dylan's mouth, I venture, as a fan whose life has been enriched by recordings that have not enriched certain musicians and their record companies, a question about bootleg recordings. In my own wishful thinking *The Bootleg Series*, a sequence of superb archival retrospectives, sanctioned by Dylan and released by Columbia, represents an unspoken consent to the tradition of pirate scholarship—acknowledgment that Dylan's outtakes, alternate takes, rejected album tracks, and live performances are themselves a towering body of work that faithful listeners deserve to hear. As Michael Gray says in *The Bob Dylan Encyclopedia*, the first three-disc release of outtakes "could, of itself, establish Dylan's place as the pre-eminent songwriter and performer of the age and as one of the great artists of the 20th Century." On *Love and Theft*'s "Sugar Baby," the line "some of these bootleggers, they make pretty good stuff" was taken by some as a shout-out to this viewpoint. Today, at least, that line seems to have had only moonshine whiskey as its subject. "I still don't like bootleg records. There was a period of time when people were just bootlegging anything on me because there was nobody ever in charge of the recording sessions. All my stuff was being bootlegged high and low, far and wide. They were never intended to be released, but every-body was buying them. So my record company said, Well, everybody else is buying these records, we might as well put them out." But Dylan can't possibly be sorry that the world has had the benefit of hearing, for instance, "Blind Willie McTell"—an outtake from 1985's *Infidels* that has subsequently risen as high in most people's Dylan pantheon as a song can rise, and which he himself has played live since. Can he? "I started playing it live because I heard the Band doing it. Most likely it was a demo, probably showing the musicians how it should go. It was never developed fully, I never got around to completing it. There wouldn't have been any other reason for leaving it off the record. It's like taking a painting by Manet or Picasso—goin' to his house and lookin' at a half-finished painting and grabbing it and selling it to peo-ple who are 'Picasso fans.' The only fans I know I have are the people who I'm looking at when I play, night after night."

With possibly mutual relief, we turn to matters of live performance. Dylan and his favorite band ever are just a few days from undertaking another tour, one that will be well under way by the time *Modern Times* is released in late August. I've always wanted to ask: When a song sud-denly appears on a given evening's set list, retrieved from among the hundreds in his back catalog, is it because Dylan's been listening to his old records? "I don't listen to *any* of my records. When you're inside of it, all you're listening to is a *replica*. I don't know why somebody would look at the movies they make—you don't read your *books*, do you?" Point taken. He expands on the explanation he offered for "Blind Willie McTell": "Strangely enough, sometimes we'll hear a cover of a song and figure we can do it just as well. If somebody else thought so highly of it, why don't I? Some of these arrangements I just *take*. The Dead did a lot of my songs and we'd just take the whole arrangements because they did it better than me. Jerry Garcia could hear the song in all my bad recordings, the song that was buried there. So if I want to sing something different I just bring out one of them Dead records and see which one I wanna do. I *never* do that with my records." Speaking of which: "I've heard it said, you've probably heard it said, that all the arrangements change night after night. Well *that's* a bunch of bullshit, they don't know what they're talkin' about. The arrangements don't change night after night. The rhythmic structures are different, that's all. You can't change the arrangement night after night—it's *impossible*."

On the doorstep of another tour, Dylan points out that whether a song comes across for a given listener on a given night depends on where exactly they're sitting. "I can't stand to play arenas, but I do play 'em. But I know that's not where music's supposed to be. It's not meant to be heard in football stadiums, it's not 'Hey, how are you doin' tonight Cleveland?' Nobody gives a shit how you're doin' tonight in Cleveland." He grins and rolls his eyes, to let me know he knows he's teasing at Spinal Tap heresy. Then he plunges deeper. "They say, 'Dylan never talks.' What the hell is there to *say*? That's not the reason an artist is in front of people." The words seem brash, but his tone is nearly pleading. "An artist has come for a different purpose. Maybe a self-help group— maybe a Doctor Phil—would say, 'How you doin'?' I don't want to get harsh and say I don't care. You *do* care, you care in a *big way*, otherwise you wouldn't be there. But it's a different kind of *connection*. It's not a light thing." He considers further. "It's alive every night, or it feels alive every night." Pause. "It becomes *risky*. I mean, you risk your life to play music, if you're doing it in the right way." I ask about the minor-league baseball stadiums he's playing in the new tour's first swing: Do they provide the sound he's looking for? "Not really, not in the open air. The best sound you can get is an intimate club room, where you've got four walls and the sound just *bounces*. That's the way this music is meant to be heard." Then Dylan turns comedian again, the guy newly familiar to listeners of his XM satellite radio show, whose casual verbal riffs culminate in vaudeville one-liners. "I wouldn't want to play a *really* small room, like *ten* people. Unless it was, you know, *fifty thousand dollars a ticket* or something."

3.

Let me take a moment and reintroduce myself, your interviewer and guide here. I'm a forty-two-year-old moonlighting novelist, and a lifelong Dylan fan, but one who, it must be emphasized, *doesn't remember the '60s*. I'm no longer a young man, but I am young for the job I'm doing here. My parents were Dylan fans, and my first taste of his music came through their LPs—I settled on *Nashville Skyline* because it looked friendly. The first Dylan record I was able to respond to as new— to witness its arrival in stores and reception in magazines, and therefore to make my own—was 1979's *Slow Train Coming*. As a fan in my early twenties, I digested Dylan's catalog to that point and concluded that its panoply of styles and stances was *itself* the truest measure of his genius—call us the *Biograph* generation, if you like. In other words, the struggle to capture Dylan and his art like smoke in one particular bottle or another seemed laughable to me, a mistaken skirmish fought before it had become clear that mercurial responsiveness—anchored only by the existential commitment to the act of connection in the present moment—was the gift of freedom his songs had promised all along. To deny it to the man himself would be absurd.

By the time I required anything of Bob Dylan, it was the mid-'80s, and I merely required him to be *good*. Which, in the mid-'80s, Dylan kind of wasn't. I recall taking home *Empire Burlesque* and struggling to discern songwriting greatness under the glittery murk of Arthur Baker's production, a struggle I lost. The first time I saw Dylan in concert, it was in a baseball stadium in Oakland, with the Grateful Dead. By the time of 1988's *Down in the Groove*, the album's worst song might have seemed to describe my plight as fan: I was in love with the ugliest girl in the world. Nevertheless, '80s Dylan was *my* Dylan, and I bore down hard on what was there. Contrary to what you may have heard (from Dylan in *Chronicles*, among other detractors), there *was* water in that desert. From scattered tracks like "Ninety Miles an Hour (Down a Dead End Street)," "The Groom's Still Waiting at the Altar," and "Brownsville Girl," to cassette-tape miracles like "Lord Protect My Child" and "Foot of Pride" (both later to surface on *The Bootleg Series*), to a version of "San Francisco Bay Blues" I was lucky enough to catch live in Berkeley, to a blistering take on Sonny Boy Williamson's "Don't Start Me to Talkin'" on *Late Night with David Letterman*, the irony is not only that "bad" Dylan was often astonishingly good. It is that his then seemingly rudderless explorations of roots music sources can now be seen to point unerringly to the triumphs to come—I mean the triumphs of *now*. Not that Dylan himself would care to retrace those steps.

When I gushed about the Sonny Boy Williamson moment on Letterman, he gaped, plainly amazed, and said, "I played *that*?"

So the drama of *my* projected relationship to my hero, thin as it may seem to those steeped in the '60s or '70s listeners' sense of multiple betrayals—*He's gone Electric! Country-Domestic-Unavailable! Christian!*—was the one Dylan described to David Gates of *Newsweek* in 1997, and in the "Oh Mercy" chapter of his memoir, *Chronicles, Volume One*: the relocation and repossession of his voice and of his will to compose and perform, as enacted gradually through the '90s. Early in that decade it might have seemed he'd quit, or at least taken refuge or solace in the solo acoustic folk records he'd begun making in his garage: *Good as I Been to You* and *World Gone Wrong*. Live shows in what had become "The Never-Ending Tour" were stronger and stronger in those years, but new songs were scarce as hen's teeth.

Then came *Time Out of Mind*, an album as cohesive—and ample—as any he'd ever recorded. When that was followed by *Love and Theft*, and then *Chronicles*, on top of the accumulating impact of *The Bootleg Series*, a reasonable Dylan fan might conclude he was living in the best of all possible worlds. In fact, with the satellite radio show beaming into our homes—Dylan's promised to do fifty of the things!—Dylan can be said to have delivered more of his voice and his heart to his audience in the past decade than ever before, and more than anyone might have reasonably dared to hope for. "Well, isn't that funny," Dylan snorts when I mention the "myth of inaccessibility," "I've just seen that Rolling Stone Press published a book of interviews with me that's *that* big." He stretches out his hands to show me. "What happened to this inaccessibility? Isn't there a *dichotomy* there?" You know what, friends? He's right.

Yet it's awfully easy, taking the role of Dylan's interviewer, to feel oneself playing surrogate for an audience that has never quit holding their hero to an impossible standard: The more he offers, the more we want. The greatest artist of my lifetime *has* given me anything I could ever have thought to ask for, and yet here I sit, somehow brokering between him and the expectations neither of us can pretend don't exist. "If I've got any kind of attitude about me—or about what I do, what I perform, what I sing, on any level—my attitude is, Compare it to somebody *else*! Don't compare it to me. Are you going to compare Neil Young to Neil Young? Compare it to somebody else, compare it to

Beck—which I like—or whoever else is on his level. This record should be compared to the artists that are working on the same ground. I'll take it any way it comes, but compare it to that. That's what everybody's record should be, if they're really serious about what they're doing. Let's face it, you're either serious about what you're doing or you're not serious about what you're doing. And you can't mix the two. And life is short."

I can't help but wonder if he's lately been reconditioned by the success of the Scorsese documentary to feel again the vivid discomfort of his unwanted savior's role. "You know, everybody makes a big deal about the '60s. The '60s, it's like the Civil War days. But I mean, you're talking to a person who *owns* the '60s. Did I ever want to acquire the '60s? *No.* But I own the '60s—who's going to argue with me?" He charms me with another joke: "I'll give 'em to you if you want 'em. You can have 'em." For Dylan, as ever, what matters is the work, not in some archival sense but in its present life. "My old songs, they've got something—I agree, they've *got* something! I think my songs have been covered—maybe not as much as 'White Christmas,' or 'Stardust,' but there's a list of over five thousand recordings. That's a *lot* of people covering your songs, they must have *something*. If I was me, *I'd* cover my songs, too. A lot of these songs I wrote in 1961 and '62 and '64, and 1973, and 1985, I can still play a lot of those songs—well how many other artists made songs during that time? How many do you hear today? I love Marvin Gaye, I love all that stuff. But how often are you gonna hear 'What's Going On'? I mean, who *sings* it? Who sings 'Tracks of My Tears'? Where is *that* being sung tonight?"

He's still working to plumb the fullest truth in the matter of his adventures in the recording studio. "I've had a rough time recording. I've managed to come up with *songs*, but I've had a rough time recording. But maybe it should be that *way*. Because other stuff which *sounds* incredible, that can *move* you to tears—for all *those* who were knocked off our feet by listening to music from *yester*year, how many of those *songs* are really good? Or was it just the *record* that was great? Well, the record *was* great. The record was an *art* form. And you know, when all's said and done, maybe I was never *part* of that art form because my records really weren't artistic at all. They were just documentation. Maybe *bad* players playing *bad* changes, but still something coming through. And the *something* that's coming through, for me today, was to make it just as real. To show you how it's real." Dylan muses on the fate of art in posterity. "How many people can look at the *Mona Lisa*? You ever been there? I mean, maybe like *three people* can see it at once. And yet, how long has that painting been around? More people have seen that painting than have ever listened to, let's name somebody—I don't want to say Alicia Keys—say, Michael Jackson. More people have ever seen the *Mona Lisa* than ever listened to Michael Jackson. And only three people can see it at once. Talk about *impact*."

Conversation about painting leads to conversation about other forms. "That's what I like about books, there's no *noise* in it. Whatever you put on the page, it's like making a painting. Nobody can change it. Writing a book is the same way, it's written in *stone*—it might as well be! It's never gonna change. One's not gonna be different in tone than another, you're not gonna have to turn this one up louder to read it." Dylan savored the reception of *Chronicles*. "Most people who write about music, they have no idea what it feels like to play it. But with the book I wrote, I thought: The people who are writing reviews of this book, man, they know what the hell they're talking about. It spoils you. They know *how* to write a book, they know more about it than me. The reviews of this book, some of 'em almost made me cry—in a good way. I'd never felt that from a music critic, *ever*." While my private guess would have been that Dylan had satisfied the scribbling impulse (or as he says on *Modern Times*, "I've already confessed / no need to confess again"), in fact he seems to be deep into planning for a *Chronicles, Volume Two*. "I think I can go back to the *Blonde on Blonde* album—that's probably about as far back as I can go on the next book. Then I'll probably go forward. I thought of an interesting time. I made this record, *Under the Red Sky*, with Don Was, but at the same time I was also doing the *Wilburys* record. I don't know how it happened that I got into both albums at the same time. I worked with George and Jeff during the day—everything had to be done in one day, the track and the song had to be written in one day, and then I'd go down and see Don Was, and I felt like I was walking into a *wall*. He'd have a different band for me to play with every day, a lot of *all-stars*, for no particular purpose. Back then I wasn't bringing anything at *all* into the studio, I was completely disillusioned. I'd let someone else take control of it all and just come up with lyrics to the melody of the song. He'd say, 'What do you want to cut?'—well, I wouldn't have *anything* to cut, but I'd be so beat down from being up with the Wilburys that I'd just come up with some track, and everybody would fall in behind that track, oh my God." He laughs. "It was sort of contrary to the Wilburys scene, which was being done in a mansion up in the hills. Then I'd go down to these other sessions, and they were in this cavelike studio down in Hollywood, where I'd spend the rest of the night, and then try to get some sleep. Both projects suffered some. Too many people in the room, too many musicians, too many egos, ego-driven musicians that just wanted to play their thing and it definitely wasn't my cup of tea, but that's the record I'm going to feature." Now, this may be the place for me to mention that I rate side two of *Under the Red Sky* one of the hidden treasures of Dylan's catalog. The album's closer, a garrulous but mysterious jump-blues called "Cat's in the Well," wouldn't be at all out of place on *Love and Theft* or *Modern Times*. But as he's told me, Dylan doesn't listen to the records. And unlike me, he claims no familiarity with *The Bob Dylan Encyclopedia*. ("Those are not the circles I really move around in," he chuckles, when I ask. "That's not something that would overlap with my life.") But just as when he praises his current band as his absolute best—an evaluation supporters of Mike Bloomfield and Al Kooper, not to mention Garth Hudson and Rick Danko, et al., might take issue with—I've come to feel that Dylan's sweeping simplifications of his own journey's story are outstandingly healthy ones. Puncturing myths, boycotting analysis, and ignoring chronology are likely part of a long and lately quite successful campaign not to be incarcerated within his own legend. Dylan's greatest accomplishment since his '60s apotheosis may simply be that he has claimed his story as his own. (Think of him howling the first line of "Most Likely You'll Go Your Way (and I'll Go Mine)" upon his return to the stage during the 1973 tour: "You say you love me / and you're thinkin' of me, / but you know you could be *wroooonngg*!") I take our conversation today the way I took *Chronicles*, and the long journal-song "Highlands": as vivid and generous reports on the state of Bob Dylan and his feelings *in the present moment*.

In other words, never mind that I think *Under the Red Sky* is pretty good. After that early-'90s disillusionment, how did he decide to record *Time Out of Mind*? "They gave me another contract, which I didn't really want. I didn't want to record anymore, I didn't see any point to it, but lo and behold they made me an offer and it was hard to refuse. I'd worked with Lanois before, and I thought he might be able to bring that magic to this record. I thought, well, I'll give it a try. There must have been twelve, fifteen musicians in that room—four drummers notwithstanding. I really don't know how we got anything out of that." He pauses to consider the record's reception. Released just after a much publicized health scare, the doomy lyrics were widely taken as a musical wrestling match with the angel of death. "I mean, it was perceived as me being some chronic invalid, or crawling on bleeding knees. But that was never the case." I mention that some are already describing the new album as the third in a trilogy, beginning with *Time Out of Mind*. Dylan demurs: "*Time Out of Mind* was me getting back in and fighting my way out of the corner. But by the time I made *Love and Theft* I was *out* of the corner. On *this* record, I ain't *nowhere*, you can't find me anywhere, because I'm *way* gone from the corner." He still toys with the notion I've put before him. "I would think more of *Love and Theft* as the beginning of a trilogy, if there's going to be a trilogy." Then swiftly gives himself an out: "If I decide I want to go back into the studio."

In a day of circular talk we've circled back to the new record, and I venture to ask him again about certain motifs. *Modern Times* shades *Love and Theft*'s jocular, affectionate vibe into more ominous territory, the language of murder ballads and Edgar Allan Poe: foes and slaughter, haunted gardens and ghosts. Old blues and ballads are quoted liberally, like second nature. "I didn't feel limited this time, or I felt limited in the way that you *want* to narrow your scope down, you don't want to *muddle* things up, you want every line to be clear and every line to be purposeful. This is the way I feel someplace in me, in my *genealogy*—a lot of us don't have the murderous *instinct* but we wouldn't *mind* having the license to kill. I just let the lyrics go, and when I was singing them, they seemed to have an ancient presence." Dylan seems to feel he dwells in a body haunted like a house by his bardlike musical precursors. "Those songs are just in my genes and I couldn't stop them comin' out. In a reincarnative kind of way, maybe. The songs have got some kind of a *pedigree* to them. But that pedigree stuff, that only works so far. You can go back to the ten-hundreds, and people only had one name. Nobody's gonna tell you they're going to go back further than when people had one name." This reply puts an effective end to my connect-the-dots queries about his musical influences. I tell him that despite the talk of enemies, I found in the new record a generosity of spirit, even a sense of acceptance. He consents, barely. "Yeah. You got to accept it *yourself* before you can expect anybody else to accept it. And in the long run, it's merely a record. Lyrics go by quick."

4.

When all is said and done, Bob Dylan is keen that I understand where he's coming from, and for me to understand that I have to know what he saw in the artists who went before him. "If you think about all the artists that recorded in the '40s and the '30s, and in the '50s, you had big bands, sure, but they were the vision of one man—I mean, the Duke Ellington band was the vision of one man, the Louis Armstrong band, it was the individual voice of Louis Armstrong. And going into all the rhythm-and-blues stuff, and the rockabilly stuff, the stuff that trained me to do what I do, that was all *individually* based. That was what you heard—the individual crying in the wilderness. So that's kind of lost, too. I mean, who's the last individual performer that you can think of—Elton John, maybe? I'm talking about artists with the willpower not to conform to anybody's reality but their own. Patsy Cline and Billy Lee Riley. Plato and Socrates, Whitman and Emerson. Slim Harpo and Donald Trump. It's a lost art form. I don't know who else does it beside myself, to tell you the truth." Is he satisfied? "I always wanted to stop when I was on *top*. I didn't want to fade away. I didn't want to be a *has*-been, I wanted to be somebody who'd never be forgotten. I feel that one way or another, it's okay now, I've done what I wanted for myself." These remarks, it should be noted, are yet another occasion for laughter. "I see that I could stop touring at any time, but then, I don't really *feel* like it right now." Short of promising the third part of the trilogy in progress, this is good enough news for me. May the Never-Ending Tour never end. "I think I'm in my middle years *now*," Bob Dylan tells me. "I've got no retirement plans."

—*Rolling Stone*, 2006

Now, reservations. The next two pieces depend on the stunt of writing about why I can't deliver the piece I've been asked to write. That's to say, a form of special pleading, made on ethical grounds I (obviously) wouldn't want to have to get behind in any larger sense. These minor courtroom theatrics are embarrassing, but I like the outcome in both cases. "Open Letter to Stacy" preserves any number of outright errors regarding a band I'd really only heard, never learned even the first fact about, at the point when I wrote it. At least the piece had the cleverness not only to predict the errors but to claim them as its imperative. "Otis Redding's Lonely Hearts Club Band" goes further, casting moral doubt on the editorial commission I'd accepted, that of projecting future unrecorded music by dead musicians (the method, it happens, of my favorite rock-and-roll novel, Lewis Shiner's Glimpses). This piece, conflating the vicarious psyche of the "fan" with the dubious motives of a white person who yearns to supernaturally rescue a black singer from fate, but declines to do so, could be seen as The Fortress of Solitude in a grain of sand.

When a music writer riffs on his ambivalence toward an assignment, he or she is guilty of being influenced by Lester Bangs. I'll just add that the emotional ambiance of both pieces (and probably a few others I've written) sounds, to me, to extend from a single line spoken by Marlene Dietrich in Orson Welles's Touch of Evil: "What does it matter what you say about people?"

Open Letter to Stacy (The Go-Betweens)

Dear Stacy,

When the Go-Betweens got back together and recorded a new album, I entertained fantasies of writing something about it. My first thought was to pitch it to *Rolling Stone*. I'd written an essay for them recently, and for reasons too elaborate to go into here, I've lately resurrected dormant fantasies of being a "rock writer." The truth is, it'll never happen. I'm too paralyzed by reverence, both for the musicians and for writers like Greil Marcus and Lester Bangs, and conscious anyway that research and interviewing aren't really my strengths. Plus I suspect, or at least don't understand, my own motives. But my reasons for not pitching a Go-Betweens piece weren't only generic ones. They were strong and specific and they far outweighed the self-aggrandizing urge to announce myself in public as the Go-Betweens' biggest fan, or to meet the band. In a Dylanesque "my weariness amazes me" way I found myself compelled by my own resistance to writing or thinking about the Go-Betweens reunion—to even buying the new record— compelled to such a degree that I began to want to write about *that*.

Here, then, are the reasons why.

1. The Go-Betweens are my favorite band. I listened to them in two distinct periods in my life: in the mid-'80s, when they existed and when

I was living in California, and in the mid-late-'90s, when their entire messy, elusive catalog was reissued on CD for the first time. Their songs are characterized by a complexity and self-awareness I want to call literary—in fact I'll do that. Their songs are beautiful and strange and emotional, but a lot of rock and roll is like that. The Go-Betweens are also smart and hesitant and not obvious. Not so much rock and roll is like that. There are a lot of historical facts surrounding the production of these songs: the punk context (they began in the late '70s, couldn't play their instruments at first, etc.) and the fact that they're from Australia but took up residence in England. I care and I don't care. I just don't want to shift my attention from the enduring, rewarding confusion of being the songs' devoted listener.

2. I have notions about the people in the band which are probably false, but they matter to me. Robert Forster and Grant McLennan are the Lennon-McCartney team at the heart of the band: They both write songs, they write some together, and they both sing. The third original member was a drummer named Lindy, and she's not on the reunion record. In my mind the friendship between these three people is beautiful and complicated. In a rich, fascinating evolution over the course of the six "original" Go-Betweens records these three people welcomed four new members (and learned to play their instruments), but that triangle always felt to me like the band's emotional and musical core.

3. Triangle, a key word. Here comes my falsely private confession: I've always imagined that Robert Forster and Grant McLennan were each Lindy's boyfriend in turn, and that the difficulties and ambiguities of this long arrangement and disarrangement are the impenetrable knot at the core of the music, the mystery that keeps me coming back. I know that the rock-band love triangle is a Fleetwood Mac cliché, but glimpsed (if I'm right that I glimpsed it) through the prism of the Go-Betweens' sensibility, it felt profound to me. In the '80s, when the band existed, when I saw them play live, my own life was shaped by a long, devoted love triangle—one which persisted, though it was never static. I won't say anything more about this, except that if we three had

been a band our six albums would have sounded as different from one another as the Go-Betweens' did. And we would have been as unmistakably the same band playing each time.

4. In Berkeley I lived on Chestnut Street, three blocks from a homely rock club called Berkeley Square. Every poor, scraping-along act touring California would get stuck there for a night, and it was rarely a full house. For years of afternoons I'd sit at home writing with the radio tuned to KALX, the college radio station, and when they gave away tickets to shows at the Berkeley Square I'd call up and answer a trivia question and get my name on the list, then walk over a few hours later and see the show. I'm good at trivia. I saw the Proclaimers and the Violent Femmes and the Throwing Muses there, along with other bands whose names I've forgotten. I was once one of literally five people at Berkeley Square for a My Bloody Valentine show on a Tuesday—we stood at the lip of the stage and endured the harshest volume I've ever experienced. When the announcement came that the Go-Betweens—an Australian band, whose very existence seemed mythical—were coming to the Berkeley Square, I don't know whether I purchased or won my ticket, only that I wouldn't have missed it, you know, for the world. They played to about twenty-five or thirty people, a loosely packed herd of worshippers, but our worship couldn't console the Go-Betweens, not this night. They were at the end of a tour that must have been some kind of disaster, and twenty-five bookstore clerks in Berkeley weren't going to turn it around. The band had been arguing, I think, before the show even began, and Lindy, the drummer, the original Go-Between, had been drinking. Really drinking, so she was lurching and obvious and couldn't keep time. By the fourth or fifth song Robert and Grant were both glaring at her in turn, and expressly showing her their hands on the guitars to try to dictate the tempo. The violinist, another woman, wouldn't look at her. They were miserable. They made it through a song, argued again, and then Lindy stormed off, between the two singers, toward the bar. She weaved. At the bar she got something—another drink? Water? Carrying it she lurched back to the stage, and as she moved through the crowd she brushed me, a butt-against-lap swipe, the kind which happens late at night at crazy parties, when intentions are blurry. I know this seems ridiculous,

but it happened. She was taunting one or both of the men onstage by making physical contact with men in the audience, and in the small, loosely populated room it was apparent that it was having an effect, though what sort I wouldn't presume to say. The horrible intimacy, the unexpected access to the band's unhappiness, was wrenching. It was also terribly sexy—I learned something that night about how vivid a smashed woman can be.

5. Lindy, as I said, isn't on the new record. I bought it and took it home today, and I listened to the first three songs in the car before I started crying, for myself and who knows else, and took it off. "The Go-Betweens" are now Robert Forster and Grant McLennan and a bunch of names I don't recognize (they've also got the help of Sleater-Kinney, a good sign, probably, in a general sense). Now, forget love triangles for a minute, there's something I've always liked about Led Zeppelin's refusal to exist for even one minute after John Bonham's death. And I'd always felt the opposite about the Who—that they betrayed their audience by carrying on after Keith Moon. And that the saddest single fact about the Beatles' decline was that Paul McCartney played drums on some of the tracks on *The White Album*. Poor Ringo. I mean, songwriters come and go, but the drummer is the band. I'll certainly play this record, and I may come to like it, but I guess if I had to give you one reason why I'm not going to try to write about the Go-Betweens' reunion, it's that I'm carrying a torch for Lindy. Her name isn't even in the *thank-yous*. There's a story there, I know there is, and the thing is, having come as far as I have with the idea of the Go-Betweens standing in for so much I've felt and lost, I don't want to know it.

—Open Letters, 2001

Otis Redding's Lonely Hearts Club Band

Otis Redding's Lonely Hearts Club Band

1967: Otis Redding plays the Monterey Pop Festival and becomes the official favorite soul singer of the rock audience; Otis Redding retreats from live performance for two months, the longest such break of his career (!), during which time he writes, among other songs, "Dock of the Bay," and is reportedly obsessed with playing, repeatedly, the Beatles' *Sgt. Pepper's Lonely Hearts Club Band* LP; Otis Redding records "Dock of the Bay," the unexpected sound of which baffles and dismays his friends and advisers, as well as his record company, who oppose releasing the song (whistling on the song's outro, instead of vamp-singing—how could Otis lose touch with his most basic gifts? Where's the soul-singer's intensity? Where's the love object? Wherefore all this chipper melancholy, or jolly resignation, or whatever you wanna call it, in the place of pleading, desperation, cajolement, flirtation, all the stuff that makes "a soul number"? *What is this shit?*), despite Redding's repeated expressions of confidence at the commercial viability of what he sees as a creative breakthrough, and the first evidence of a new sound, a leap in his own expressive capacity comparable to that of the Beatles—"This is it," he says, "my first number-one record" ("Try a Little Tenderness" had reached number two); Otis Redding dies in a small plane crash on his way to a gig in Madison, Wisconsin; "Dock of the Bay" reaches number one on the soul and pop charts, though whether it does so out of inescapable intrinsic fatedness or as the result of morbid sentiment, who knows?

With a Little Help from My Friends

What little authority I bear in this matter is secondhand: My facts, and my quotations, all come straight out of Peter Guralnick's book *Sweet Soul Music*, or from Guralnick's commentary track on Criterion's *Otis at Monterey* DVD. Though Guralnick's not responsible for my projections—and a speculative piece of this sort is utterly mired in its author's projections—he is responsible for his own, which are pretty damn persuasive. Yeah, though I sway in the storm of my own raging losses, the displacement of which causes me to weep each time I contemplate the beauty of Otis Redding's music, his ambition and confidence and unbearable charisma, his very presence on this planet, in those months before his death, I am but a puppet made very much of Guralnick's notions and his (admittedly contradictory) reportage. I never saw Redding sing, I was three years old when he died, and I required an array of concepts gleaned by reading critics like Guralnick to understand Redding as a revolutionary artist, or "Dock of the Bay" as a revolutionary song, as opposed to a sweetly irresistible "oldie" taken as much for granted at its debut as it is in retrospect. Just for one instance, I never would have heard a trace of the Beatles in "Dock of the Bay" in a million years of listening. I'm adamant that this exoskeleton I walk inside be made visible.

Otis in the Sky with Storm Clouds

What are we going to have to do here to get this piece off the ground (ha ha): Have Otis survive his crash? Walk away unscathed? Or heed some time traveler's imperative and never board the plane? Then, either way, vow to waste no more time and dash into the studio to lay down his masterwork? Shit. I hate this stuff. Forget about the butterfly effect, what about all the human hours wasted reversing irreversible plane crashes? What if we could have *those* back—the hours of our pointless musings? Because the plane always goes down, we know this.

Getting Better

Thinking this way invites cognitive dissonance. More than that—thinking this way consists solely of cognitive dissonance and nothing else. And it has a delicious quality. That unbreachable gulf between the finished, epochal, four-disc-set accomplishments of the actual guy who died and the masochistic dwelling on what might have been, the fact that the actual guy believed he was *getting better*, was about to roll out the good stuff and really blow some minds. The simplest definition of cognitive dissonance I know is the Aesop's fable "The Fox and the Grapes": The grapes look good/I can't have the grapes. Then, dissonance's resolution: Those grapes are surely sour, so I didn't want them anyway. Can we believe in the album that my (Guralnick's) fable implies—an album as good as the triangulation between "a soul *Sgt. Pepper*" and "Dock of the Bay" and Otis Redding's confidence in his growing power implies? Do we *want* to?

Fixing a Whole

Would the end of Orson Welles's *The Magnificent Ambersons* be as good as the film implied in the desecrated ruins that exist? What about Sappho's poems—do we want them complete? "Dock of the Bay," thanks to Guralnick (and now, for you, my reader, thanks to me), may have gained in beauty as the cornerstone of some imagined masterwork—or perhaps as the entrance to a vanished new world. But the gain is the beauty of the fragment, so much dreamier than the whole.

She's Leaving Home

C'mon, do it with me (or *for* me, since I'm admittedly avoiding the imperative of this piece: to imagine it for you): thirteen songs as beautiful and diverse and delicate as the array on *Sgt. Pepper*. But in a "soul" vocabulary, whatever that is. Forget that *Pepper* isn't your favorite Beatles LP (I don't mind if it is, though). You know what it sounded like at the time. That album's meaning in terms of the previous history of pop (or rock, or whatever) is etched in its grooves, and when we resist it now, as we often do, we're resisting that notion of the masterwork which changes everything because we're so disappointed at the revolution's double failure—both in the rejection and the adoption of its revolutionary terms, even in the lives of its own fomenters. So, c'mon, stay with me here: Otis Redding's about to do the same thing for soul. There's no reason he couldn't have titled a song "She's Leaving Home," agreed? But what would it have *sounded* like? Maybe we're pushing into Brian Wilson breakdown territory here. Maybe "Dock of the Bay" is to the projected Redding album as "Good Vibrations" is to "Smile"—an unkeepable promise. Maybe we're speculating on a terrible compromise, some crap, some mush, some intolerable pretension, some horrible '70s bloated art-rock suite we'd never have forgiven Redding for. I keep flinching. Those grapes suck.

Being for the Benefit of Mr. White

The Love Crowd, that's what he called them, to their delighted faces, when he played at Monterey. He was nervous as shit, despite his confidence, at least that's what's been reported. He followed Jefferson Airplane and their light show (and can't you actually hear a little bit of the San Francisco sound in the electric guitar line in "Dock of the Bay," come to think of it? More that—or a trace of the Velvet Underground—than Beatles). This whole project has an uneasy foundation in aspirations to "crossover": the demolition of the chitlin-circuit segregated world of which Otis Redding was the current prince at the time he played Monterey and supposedly introduced so many deaf hippies to soul. And what is *Sgt. Pepper* if not the single whitest album in rock's history to that point, the one which left Keith Richards/Bob Dylan–esque race-mummery the furthest behind? What exactly are we pining for Redding to have done to soul, anyway?

Within You Without You

We're fooling with ghosts here, and we probably deserve to be punished. We're trading on a stock market of pop notions against a backdrop of real pain. We went into karmic default from the moment we took the needle off the record, quit communing in a bodily sense with the beauty and yearning of the voice of the dead man, and began reading and thinking and, worst, pretending that the history of the reception of the commodified recording of that voice has any spark in it worth kindling in speculation. Notice I'm saying "we." Because I don't want to be alone here.

When I'm Sixty-four

More practically, we're pretending we really want to meet the aging Otis Redding. You couldn't have been thinking we'd kill him off again right after getting our precious album—we're not that sick, are we? So we keep him alive after, and risk the embarrassment we associate with, uh, Little Richard, James Brown, Chuck Berry. Hell, Paul McCartney. Seeing the purity wrecked, along with the body. Not that I'd ever wish anyone dead to preserve their purity, no, no, I didn't mean that. God, this is getting ugly.

Lovely Rita

Back to that damn, elusive album. Isn't part of the half-kept promise of *Sgt. Pepper*—and "Dock of the Bay"—the chance of a pop music with a credible subject outside of romantic love? Now we're getting somewhere. And if both artifacts could be described (ungenerously) as monuments to the self-gratifying capacities of their male artists, my preference for "Dock of the Bay" over *Pepper* (admittedly, it's a lot easier to love the perfect fragment than the erratic whole) could be that "Dock of the Bay" doesn't bother patronizing women in passing while it makes its way to the real subject. I don't know what I want, but I do know what I never want: to hear a soul equivalent of "Lovely Rita," let alone "Eleanor Rigby." Soul's propensity for first-person stories, for righteous complicity over faux-objectivity, went a long way toward protecting it from glib two-dimensional portraiture.

Good Morning Good Morning

There are other times when I don't care about that album, I'm just dying to know what Otis Redding heard when he played *Pepper* over and over again. Did he sing along? Did he skip this song, or barely notice it, or was it one of his favorites? Did the rooster sounds make him laugh?

Otis Redding's Lonely Hearts Club Band (Reprise)

Perhaps the purloined-letter aspect of *Pepper*—the most obvious thing hardest to keep in mind—is the way this ostensible message from the future of music was mired in nostalgia. Nostalgia for various pre-rock-'n'-roll musics; nostalgia for the artifacts of the Beatles' parents' worlds; nostalgia for nostalgia; nostalgia, in the end, for itself—manifest on the spot, in the form of a reprise (which is nevertheless not a *conclusion*—see below). So, in its concern with lost worlds, it seemed to instantaneously wreck the new world it claimed to bring into being. In the wake, what we're certain to fall back on, after all, is comfort. So, in that sense, "Dock of the Bay" is as far as Otis had to go. Why not just play that song again?

A Day in the Life

Otis Redding was twenty-six years old in 1967. Given that I'm thirty-nine and have the audacity to wake up some mornings, drag the comb across my head, etc., and believe that my best work is still ahead of me, I don't really know how to measure the world it seems to me was lost. I only don't want to lie to you about it, make up a bunch of song titles, fake release dates, whatever. I'll just sit underneath those grapes until I can't stand it anymore.

—*Black Clock,* 2004

Rick James

Dwell long enough in pop culture's mind's eye and you'll be forgiven or forgotten; watershed glam-funk craftsman Rick James didn't live long enough to pull off either one. Television comedian Dave Chappelle's riotous send-up of the performer's addictions, abuses, and all-around sleaziness managed instead, in the year preceding James's death, to resurrect and thoroughly reinscribe the musician's self-inflicted image as a clownish amoral grotesque. Not quite pop music's Fatty Arbuckle—James's party indiscretions left no corpses, and after a prison term for the second of his convictions for sexual assault he drifted rather easily back into his recording career—neither did he parlay his romance with the crack pipe into a poignant image of repentance, à la Richard Pryor. And no matter how often he alluded to tastes for white or underage women, he was never as threatening a figure as, say, Jack Johnson, or even Chuck Berry. Not with that panda-bear posture, not with that childish leer. Instead, dogged by how perfectly the term "Super Freak" fit to the cartoon-pimp image he manufactured and then inhabited far too sincerely, James seemed merely icky, and silly.

What's lost behind the caricature is, well, only everything I'd like to suggest ought to be recalled about Rick James.

1. Despite an aura of heavy-lidded indolence that attached to his long, drug-addled slide from atop the pop charts, Rick James worked harder

than most, toiled at his trade, paid lavish dues: sixteen years' worth by the time of "Super Freak"'s overnight success in 1981. James might be the Pete Rose of funk; deprived of Sly Stone's or Prince's native genius, he scrapped his way to the top. Born (as James Johnson Jr.) in Buffalo, New York, in 1948, James was third of eight children raised on the wrong side of that hard-bitten town's tracks by a single mother, a Harlem nightclub dancer turned numbers-runner. Already bearing a rap sheet at fifteen, James ran away to the Naval Reserves, then went AWOL on being designated for Vietnam. In Toronto exile he formed the Mynah Birds, an integrated rock band which included a young Neil Young and a future member of Steppenwolf. On behalf of the band, James played his one card: Poppa may have been a rolling stone, but his uncle was also a Temptation—specifically Melvin Franklin, the bass-voiced anchor of the legendary singing group. So, the Mynah Birds were signed to Motown, but an irate manager tipped James's presence in Detroit to the military police. Motown shelved the demo tapes, and James spent a year in the brig for his desertion. Then came another decade's apprenticeship; songwriting and arranging for Motown, more demos, more forgotten bands in Detroit and London, and at last, in 1978, fourteen years after his first band, a breakthrough with the single "You and I," from his debut album. Nor did the effort diminish with success: Along with his own steady output, James was a tireless impresario who created hits for the Mary Jane Girls, Teena Marie, and Eddie Murphy. In collaborations on his own records James gave a leg up both to his elders, the Temptations and Smokey Robinson, and to some of the rappers who had yet to conquer the world. As much for his showmanship and his lunacy, James ought to be remembered for his ambition, his fluency, his professionalism. Among his colleagues and collaborators, he is.

2. While never an innovator at the level of James Brown, George Clinton, or Sly Stone, the sound that James concocted was sturdy, glossy, and irresistible. Reliant on magpie appropriations, particularly of the sounds of Clinton's band Funkadelic, James was a consolidator and synthesist, one who punched the funk's essence into a commercial sphere unknown to his rivals, who never forgave him for it (George Clinton mocked him as "Slick James"). By the time of his commercial and artistic triumph—the album *Street Songs*, which held both "Super

Freak" and "Give It to Me," his two mightiest singles—the mercurial and opportunistic James was calling his music "punk funk," which wasn't so far from the truth. "Super Freak," above all, was a confection full of vocal mannerisms and twitchy synthesizer hooks that suggested he'd been listening to Elvis Costello, Devo, and the Cars as closely as to his fellow funksters. The sound he fashioned, full of clean guitars, swirly keyboards, and pop hooks, blew open the door that Prince would walk through a year or two later. It also prefigures Rick Rubin's guitar-and-rap epiphanies with Run-DMC and the Beastie Boys, and the sound of Outkast. Not a bad legacy for the Pete Rose of funk.

3. "Super Freak" itself probably shouldn't be glossed over too lightly. Consider the lives that hook has lived! Has anyone who ever heard it not succumbed? Can't you bring it to mind in an instant, now? *Boing-boingy-bump, querburp, querburp!* As musical memes go, it's one of the immortals, one which transcended its first incarnation, in "Super Freak," to become the core of what's still (sorry, purists) the top-selling rap single of all time: MC Hammer's "You Can't Touch This." When Rick James first heard how whopping a slab of "Super Freak" the rapper had sampled—without James's knowledge, let alone his permission—he wasn't at all happy, though oceans of royalties soothed his pain. Hammer's hit won James his only Grammy, perhaps an appropriate irony for a musician dependent on borrowed riffs himself.

4. "Super Freak" notwithstanding, if I could free your mind of preconceptions I'd steer you elsewhere to contemplate Rick James's muddled legacy. Motown belatedly issued, as a bonus to a "Deluxe Edition" of *Street Songs*, a live disc of Rick James and his Stone City Band playing in Long Beach, California, at their very height, in 1981. Try, if you will, "Ghetto Life," which in this rendition is stripped of studio gloss, instead is nearly drowned in his fans' collective roar. Here's where the promise of "punk funk" is kept: These ragged, furious guitars, blended with James's ragged, furious voice, and ragged, furious lyrics, suggest a reconciliation of Bill Withers, perhaps, or Stevie Wonder, with the sonic insult of Gang of Four or the Fall. James sings:

One thing 'bout the ghetto
You don't have to hurry
It'll be there tomorrow
Sister don't you worry

Here, genuine pride and defiance are impossible to mistake. If Rick James had to turn from that place to a glamorous and then a loathsome self-erasure, we can at least recollect that he reached it once.

—*The New York Times Magazine*, 2004

an orchestra of light that was electric

an orchestra of light that was electric how fine a thing would that be? i'd been waiting for and envisioning one wondering what its name would be for all my twelve years and now here one was and its name was the name of the idea itself generic and why not since there could never be two such orchestras. in sublime stupidity i took this for music from the future messaged to me by the occult stations of top forty am radio which to my understanding no one on this earth listened to and which could only be tuned in at night. the instruments and voice stirred and twitched me at some native level. activated me like a robot programmed with feelings. do ya want my love and i did. power chords washed in strings, organized and sugared by a mathematics i couldn't enter only savor. i could detect the telephone line the music was a far heard thing crushed into nearby radios never as clear as i wanted. i sensed this might be commercial art surrealism slicked by madison avenue guilty and intoxicatingly sweet like a bottle of stolen kahlua but for me somehow idealized a livin' thing so that my guilt became the secret champion of its fragile science fictional yearning for a future music and defender of its indefensible glamour and finish. when i located some critic who tendered praise for their earliest records as an extension of the beatles' abandoned work i felt a whoosh of vindi-cation. and when they were lumped like coal in the irredeemable bin of pink floyd boston eagles steve miller that punk convicted of corporatism or worse of vichy collaboration with disco olivia neutron bomb i held out quiet certainty that their turned to stone mister blue sky candy bar compression kept faith with radio miracles and wasn't completely unrelated to the ramones reaching for spector's wall that unreachable epic shape as distant as kafka's castle. never had to speak this defense but kept quiet faith with shine a little love and i did and don't bring me down and i didn't. never had to worry about the songs i didn't like, just the ones i did and this robot candy love never moved closer and had to be resolved or moved further away and had to be renounced and now they live in my jubilant secret ipod and i can't get it out of my head.

—*Black Clock,* 2006

VIII

WORKING THE ROOM

The novel will be at your funeral.

—NORMAN MAILER

Once I'd written a few book reviews and literary introductions that I thought stood up as essays, and liking collections of these things by other writers, I started to imagine a collection of my own. I'd call it Working the Room, *an urbanist play on Updike's* Hugging the Shore, *but also embedding a reference to Mailer's notorious "Evaluations: Quick and Expensive Comments on the Talent in the Room." I loved the title so much I had to set it free, to Geoff Dyer. Now what would I call the collection?* Shugging the Whore? No. Anyway, once I'd written the Harper's essay I began planning this more centrifugal book instead.*

Bolaño's 2666

In Philip K. Dick's 1953 short story "The Preserving Machine," an impassioned inventor creates a device for "preserving" the canon of classical music—the sacred and, he fears, impermanent beauties of Schubert, Chopin, Beethoven, and so forth—by feeding it into a device which transforms the compositions into living creatures: birds, beetles, other animals resembling armadillos and porcupines. Outfitting the classic pieces in this manner, then setting them free, the inventor means to guarantee their persistence beyond the frailties of human commemoration, to give them a set of defenses adequate to their value. Alas, the musical-animals become disagreeable and violent, turn on one another, and, when the inventor attempts to reverse-engineer his creations in order to prove that the music has survived, reveal themselves as a barely recognizable cacophony, nothing like the originals. Or has the preserving machine revealed true essences—irregularities, ferocities—disguised within the classical pieces to begin with?

Dick's parable evokes the absurd yearning embedded in our reverence toward art, and the tragicomic paradoxes "masterpieces" embody in the human realm which brings them forth and gives them their only value. If we fear ourselves unworthy of the sublimities glimpsed at the summit of art, what relevance does such exalted stuff have to our grubby lives? Conversely, if on investigation such works, and their makers, are revealed as ordinary, subject to the same provisions and defects as the rest of what we've plopped onto the planet—all these cities, nations, languages, histories, etc.—then why get worked up in the first place? Perfect or, more likely, imperfect, we may suspect art of being useless in either case.

Literature is more susceptible to these doubts even than music or visual arts, which can at least play at abstract beauty. Novels and stories, even poems, are helplessly built from the imperfect stuff: language, history, grubby human incident, and dream. When so many accept as their inevitable subject the long odds the universe gives the aspirations of our species, degraded as it finds itself by the brutalities of animal instinct and time's remorseless toll, books may seem to disqualify themselves from grace: How could such losers cobble together anything particularly sublime?

The Chilean exile poet Roberto Bolaño, born in 1953, lived in Mexico, France, and Spain before his death in 2003, at fifty, from liver disease possibly aggravated by intoxicants. In a burst of invention now legendary in contemporary Spanish-language literature, and rapidly becoming so internationally, Bolaño in the last decade of his life, writing with the urgency of poverty and his failing health, constructed a remarkable body of stories and novels out of precisely such doubts: that literature, which he revered the way a penitent loves (and yet rails against) an elusive God, could meaningfully articulate the low truths he knew as rebel, exile, addict; that life, in all its gruesome splendor, could ever locate the literature it so desperately craves in order to feel itself known. Is a lifetime spent loving poems in a fallen world only a poor joke? Bolaño sprints into the teeth of his conundrum, violating one of the foremost writing-school injunctions, against writer-as-protagonist (in fact, Bolaño seems to make sport of violating nearly all of the foremost writing-school rules against dream sequences, against mirrors as symbols, against barely disguised nods to his acquaintances, etcetera). Again and again he peoples his singular fictions with novelists and poets, both aspiring and famous, both accomplished and hopeless, both politically oblivious and committedly extremist, whether right or left. By a marvelous sleight of hand writers are omnipresent in Bolaño's world, striding the stage as romantic heroes and feared as imperious villains, even as aesthetic assassins—yet they're also persistently marginal men, slipping between the cracks of time and geography, forever reclusive, vanished, erased. Bolaño's urgency infuses literature with life's whole freight: The ache of a writing-workshop aspirant embodies sexual longing, or dreams of political freedom from oppression, even the utopian fantasy of the eradication of violence, while a master-novelist's doubts in his works' chances in the game of posterity can stand for all human remorse at the burdens of personal life, or at the knowledge of the burdens of history.

In the literary culture of the United States Roberto Bolaño has become a talismanic figure seemingly overnight. The "overnight" is the result of the compressed sequence of the translation and publication of his books in English, capped by the galvanic appearance, last year, of *The Savage Detectives*, an eccentrically encompassing novel, both typical of Bolaño's work and explosively larger, which cast the short stories and novellas that had preceded it into English in a sensational new light. By bringing scents of a Latin American culture more fitful, pop savvy, and suspicious of earthy machismo than that which it succeeds, Bolaño has been taken as a kind of reset button on our deplorably sporadic appetite for international writing, standing in relation to the generation of García Márquez, Vargas Llosa, and Fuentes as, say, David Foster Wallace does to Mailer, Updike, and Roth. As with Wallace's *Infinite Jest*, in *The Savage Detectives* Bolaño delivered a genuine epic inoculated against grandiosity by humane irony, vernacular wit, and a hint of punk-rock self-effacement. Any suspicion that literary culture had rushed to sentimentalize an exotic figure of quasi-martyrdom was overwhelmed by the intimacy and humor of a voice that earned its breadth line by line, defying traditional fictional form with a torrential insouciance.

Well, hold on to your hats.

2666 is the permanently mysterious title of a Bolaño manuscript rescued from his desk after his passing, the primary effort of the last five years of his life. The book was published posthumously in Spanish in 2004 to tremendous acclaim, after what appears to have been a bit of dithering over Bolaño's final intentions—a small result of which is that its English translation (by Natasha Wimmer, the indefatigable translator of *The Savage Detectives*) has been bracketed by two faintly defensive statements justifying the book's present form. They needn't have bothered. *2666* is as consummate a performance as any nine-hundred-page novel dare hope to be: Bolaño won the race to the finish line in writing what he plainly intended, in his self-interrogating way, as a master statement. Indeed, he produced not only a supreme capstone to his own vaulting ambition but a landmark in what's possible for the novel as a form in our increasingly, and terrifyingly, post-national world. *The Savage Detectives* looks positively hermetic beside it.

2666 consists of five sections, each with autonomous life and form, sufficient that Bolaño evidently flirted with the notion of separate publication for the five parts. Indeed, two or three of these might be the equal of his masterpieces at novella length, *By Night in Chile* and *Distant Star*. In a comparison Bolaño openly solicits (the novel contains a series of unnecessary but totally charming defenses of its own formal strategies, and magnitude), these five long sequences interlock to form an astonishing whole, in the same manner that fruits, vegetables, meats, flowers, or books interlock in the unforgettable paintings of the Italian master Giuseppe Arcimboldo to form a human face.

As in Arcimboldo's paintings, 2666's individual elements are easily cataloged, while the composite result, though unmistakable, remains ominously implicit, conveying a power unattainable by more direct strategies. Parts one and five, the bookends—"The Part About the Critics" and "The Part About Archimboldi"—will be the most familiar to readers of Bolaño's other work. The "critics" are a group of four European academics, pedantically rapturous on the topic of their favorite writer, the mysterious German novelist Benno von Archimboldi. The four are glimpsed at a series of continental Archimboldi conferences; Bolaño never tires of cataloging how a passion for literature walks a razor's edge between catastrophic irrelevance and sublime calling. As the four become sexually and emotionally entangled, the puzzle of their devotion to a writer who declines their interest—declines, in fact, ever to appear—inches like a great Lovecraftian shadow over their lives.

Following dubious clues, three of the four chase a rumor of Archimboldi's present whereabouts to Mexico, to Santa Teresa, a squalid and sprawling border city, globalization's no-man's-land, in the Sonoran Desert. The section's disconcertingly abrupt ending will also be familiar to readers of the novellas: The academics never locate the German novelist, and, failing even to understand why the great German would exile himself to such a despondent place, find themselves standing at the edge of a metaphysical abyss. What lies below? Other voices will be needed to carry us forward. We meet, in part two, Amalfitano, another European wrecked on the shoals of the Mexican border city, an emigrant college professor raising a beautiful daughter whose mother has abandoned them, and who is beginning, seemingly, to lose his mind. Bolaño's genius is for weaving a blunt recitation of life's facts—his novels at times evoke biographies, case studies, police or government files—with digressive outbursts of lyricism as piercing as the disjunctions of writers like Denis Johnson, David Goodis, or, yes, Philip K. Dick, as well as the filmmaker David Lynch. Here, Amalfitano considers a letter from his absconded wife:

> In it Lola told him that she had a job cleaning big office buildings. It was a night job that started at ten and ended at four or five or six in the morning . . . For a second he thought it was all a lie, that Lola was working as an administrative assistant or secretary in some big company. Then he saw it clearly. He saw the vacuum cleaner parked between two rows of desks, saw the floor waxer like a cross between a mastiff and a pig sitting next to a plant, he saw an enormous window through which the lights of Paris blinked, he saw Lola in the cleaning company's smock, a worn blue smock, sitting writing the letter and maybe taking slow drags on a cigarette, he saw Lola's fingers, Lola's wrists, Lola's blank eyes, he saw another Lola reflected in the quicksilver of the window, floating weightless in the skies of Paris, like a trick photograph that isn't a trick, floating, floating pensively in the skies of Paris, weary, sending messages from the coldest, iciest realm of passion.

Bolaño has been compared to Borges for his bookishness, but from the evidence of a prose always immediate, spare, rapturous, and drifting, always cosmopolitan and enchanted, the Bolaño boom should be taken as immediate cause for a revival of the neglected master Julio Cortázar. (Cortázar's name appears in 2666, but then it may seem that *every* human name appears there, and that Bolaño's book is reading your mind as you read it.)

By the end of Amalfitano's section a reader remains, like the earlier critics, in possession of a paucity of real clues as to 2666's underlying "story," but suffused with dreadful implication. Amalfitano's daughter seems to be drifting into danger, and if we've been paying attention we'll have become concerned about intimations of a series of rape-murders in the Santa Teresa slums and foothills. What's more (if we've been reading flap copy or reviews), we'll have noted that "Santa Teresa" is a thin disguise over the real town of Cuidad Juárez, the site of a dismayingly underreported sequence of unsolved crimes against women, with a death toll that crept into the hundreds through the decade of the '90s. In the manner of James Ellroy, but with a greater check on both prurience and bathos, Bolaño has sunk the capital of his great book into a bottomless chasm of verifiable tragedy and injustice.

In the third section—"The Part About Fate"—this real-world material dawns into view in the course of a marvelously spare and pensive portrait of a black North American journalist, diverted to Santa Teresa to cover what turns out to be a pathetically lopsided boxing match between a black American boxer and a Mexican opponent. Before arriving in Mexico, though, the journalist visits Detroit to interview an ex–Black Panther turned motivational speaker named Barry Seaman, who delivers, for twelve pages, the greatest ranting monologue this side of Don DeLillo's Lenny Bruce routines in *Underworld*:

> He talked about the stars you see at night, say when you're driving from Des Moines to Lincoln on Route 80 and the car breaks down, the way they do, maybe it's the oil or the radiator, maybe it's a flat tire, and you get out and get the jack and the spare tire out of the trunk and change the tire, maybe half an hour at most, and when you're done you look up and see the sky full of stars. The Milky Way. He talked about star athletes. That's a different kind of star, he said, and he compared them to movie stars, though as he said, the life of an athlete is generally much shorter. A star athlete might last fifteen years at best whereas a movie star could go on for forty or fifty years if he or she started young. Meanwhile, any star you could see from the side of Route 80 . . . might have been dead for millions of years, and the traveler who gazed up at it would never know. It might be a live star or it might be a dead star. Sometimes, depending on your point of view, he said, it doesn't matter, since the stars you see at night exist in the realm of seeming. They are semblances, the same way dreams are semblances . . .

At last, and with the blunt power of a documentary compilation, comes part four, "The Part About the Crimes." Bolaño's massive structure may now be understood as a form of mercy: 2666 has been conceived as a resounding chamber, a receptacle adequate to the gravity—the weight and the force—of the human grief it will attempt to commemorate. (Perhaps 2666 is the year human memory will need to attain in order to bear 2666's knowledge.) If the word "unflinching" didn't exist I'd invent it to describe these nearly two hundred pages, yet Bolaño never completely abandons those reserves of lyricism and irony that make the sequence as transporting as it is grueling. The nearest comparison may be Haruki Murakami's shattering fugue on Chinese military atrocities in Mongolia, which sounds the moral depths in *The Wind-Up Bird Chronicle*. Like Murakami, Bolaño's method encapsulates and disgorges dream and fantasy, at no cost to the penetration of his realism.

By the time we return to matters of literature, and meet Archimboldi, a German World War II veteran and a characteristically culpable twentieth-century witness whose ambivalent watchfulness shades the Sonoran crimes, we've been shifted into a world so far beyond the imagining of the first section's "critics" that we're unsure whether to pity or envy them. Though Archimboldi's literary career is conjured with Bolaño's customary gestural fulsomeness, 2666 never presents so much as a scrap of the fictional master's fiction. Instead the titles of Archimboldi's books recur as a kind of pulse of implication, until the conjectured power of an unknown literature has insisted itself upon us like a disease, one that might just draw us down with the savagery of a murderer operating in a moonless desert.

A novel like 2666 is its own preserving machine, delivering itself into our hearts, sentence by questing, unassuming sentence; it also becomes a preserving machine for the lives its words fall upon like a forgiving rain, fictional characters and the secret selves hidden behind and enshrined within them: hapless academic critics and hapless Mexican boxer, the unavenged bodies deposited in shallow graves. By writing across the grain of his doubts as to what literature can do, how much it can discover or dare pronounce the names of our world's disasters, Bolaño has proven it can do anything, and for an instant, at least, given a name to the unnamable.

Now throw your hats in the air.

—*The New York Times Book Review*, 2008

Homely Doom Vibe

Who listens?

An irresistibly compact and annoying question, posed by George, the title character of the book in your hands. That question is like a pinprick of light in a dark surface: the only entrance you'll be offered. Better crawl through and see what's there.

How good does an author or a book have to be to be reintroduced? To be pulled back into print by the devotional efforts of editors and writers (all of us only readers, really, when it comes down to it), pulled back against the unceasing tide of new titles, how good? I'm here to tell you how very good Paula Fox is. It's hard to do more, though, than be a gnat buzzing at the outer surface of a lozenge, writing critically about an artifact as dense, distinctive, and self-contained as *Poor George*. If, however, the lozenge is somehow swallowed and absorbed, an essence seeps through the body, then lives on the surface like a new set of nerves. What I mean to say, as I try to decide what to tell you about *Poor George*, is that I'm lately wearing the book as a skin, one particularly tender to social loathing and self-loathing, to morbid confession disguised as chitchat, and, above all, to postures of self-willed innocence in human relations. Paula Fox writes with a crushing accuracy about these things, here and elsewhere. And if this isn't always a skin I'm completely eager to wear, perhaps I'm closer to understanding how a writer as great as Fox can linger for so long at a proximity from the acclaim and readership she deserves. There's no justice but maybe a certain inevitability, that a master of elucidating what's denied everywhere under the surface of human moments—and of measuring the texture of that insistent, howling denial—should find her own work denied, kept at bay at the edge of vision.

So who's this George who wants to know who listens? He's a schoolteacher, a husband, a Samaritan—a nobody. George might be trying and failing to father a child, and he might also have an Achilles' heel in the area of unexamined bisexual longing—likely there's a few longings, his own and those of his loved ones, which he'd be well advised to take a closer look at. But really, here's the key thing about poor George: Don't tell the guy, but *he's made of gorgeous sentences.* Sentences which are gorgeous because of how closely they listen. A vibrant writerly intelligence shines everywhere through the bars of George's prison—in fact the bars of his prison themselves might be said to be made up of the compressed and blinding sunlight of literary sensibility. Try, for instance:

"He had to convince Ernest of—of what? Convince him that much had gone before, that he had not sprung from sticks and stones to find himself on a dead planet thinly covered with sidewalks leading nowhere."

Or:

"When she is silent she is very silent, George thought, and found himself interested in her. She vomits speech, then retreats, like some mud dweller."

Or:

"In that empty landscape where only the two trees and the toppling uprights of the shed gave shelter, they had stumbled towards each other, falling into the prickly dust in a thick, graceless embrace, their faces straining against each other's shoulders like two swimmers racing desperately for opposite shores."

The question is, *who listens to sentences like these?* Not George. George only teeters at knowingness, then retreats. Not only is he not as smart as the sentences which form the bars of his prison but, disconcertingly, crucially, he's not as smart as the sentences he's given to speak. Fox grants him the acid wit accorded the rest of her characters, but his tongue knows more than he does, as he completes his numbed and persevering daily route through himself and his life. George watches his wife cry: "One large, luminous tear was on her cheek; dazzled by its brilliance, he watched it run under her chin and disappear. Perhaps, he thought, he was crazy. The weight . . . the weight of everything was stupefying." I'd venture that the weight George staggers under is the weight of how much everything is forced to mean when you've tried to deny the meaning of what actually is.

Now the buzzing gnat reminds me to inform you that *Poor George* is funny. Not "also funny" but essentially, vitally funny, in the perverse vein of Kafka and Flannery O'Connor. There are Diane Arbus photographs in prose here, as Fox offers her vision of bodies as poorly operated puppets:

"Four young men walked by. They were disparate in physical type but each face bore the same sullen inward look. They were thin, shaggy, book-carrying, slovenly, and their arms and legs appeared to have been glued on with little consideration for symmetry. 'I have seen the future and it walks,' George said. At that moment one of them turned and stared at Lila, at her prominent breasts. There was no expression on his face at all."

Here's another:

"The woman, red-haired and massive, was shaking a small boy whose head was encased in a transparent bubblelike helmet. On it was printed 'Space Scout.' From inside, the boy gazed out coolly like a fish. A blind Negro, his white cane poking out in front of him, hesitated and stopped. The woman shot a furious glance in his direction, then banged on the helmet with her knuckles."

Poor George was Fox's first published novel; *Desperate Characters*, now part of the pantheon, her second. I heard echoes: Ernest, the kid in *Poor George*, is a conflation of *Desperate Characters*' stray cat and the vandals who savage the country house, while *Poor George*'s Walling mimics Charlie Russel in *Characters*, each a hipster-irritant contrast to the uptight male lead. What *Poor George* does that *Desperate Characters* resists doing is explode. It feels like Fox tried it once each way, in her first two: tightening the screws in *Characters* and letting the wheels fall off in *Poor George*. The result is both more disorienting and more relieving, in the strict sense of tension released.

To my eye, the funny nightmare of its last sixty pages aligns *Poor George* with novels by Thomas Berger, Charles Webb, L. J. Davis, and Bruce Jay Friedman, all pretty much contemporary. Reminding me of all of them at once, it helped me get how '60s literary critics might try to label a certain vein of American fiction of the time—though the label they found, "black humor," was as inadequate as any a writer was ever compelled to reject. I'm not even sure why I bring it up, except that *Poor George* is of its time, richly so. And, that I miss a certain homely doom vibe which seemingly used to be more casually deployable, as in those novelists I've listed, and in films like Robert Altman's *Three Women* and Alan Rudolph's *Remember My Name*, and in Randy Newman's songs from the same period. Yet if it's amazing what can be recognized and forgotten (or denied), it's also amazing what can be restored, and Paula Fox has, I think, become the most encouraging revival from completely-out-of-print status since Dawn Powell. What I mean to say is, for yourself, not for me or Paula or George, read the book. Listen to it.

—Introduction for *Poor George*, 2001

Ambivalent Usurpations

Is there any stronger evidence of the anhedonia of our reading culture than that Thomas Berger's novels don't flood airport bookstalls? There is simply no better way to destroy an hour or three. I envy you your first encounter, if that is what it is, with *Meeting Evil*, or with Berger (and, yes, this is a fine place to start). This is one of Berger's most relentless and ingenious fictional "contraptions," as a praiseful reviewer once dubbed them, and now that it is in your hands—turn to chapter one and be shanghaied—it needs, as they say, no further introduction.

I'll give it one anyway, just for the chance to shout that Thomas Berger is one of America's three or four greatest living novelists. I emphasize *novelist*, for Berger's greatness resides in the depth and extensiveness of his commitment to and exploration of his chosen form. There's no writer more invested in and trusting of the means and materials of *fiction qua fiction*: scenes and sentences, chapters and paragraphs, and, above all, characters—their voices and introspections, their predicaments in fictional worlds. He's cultivated this investment to the exclusion of all forms of topicality or sociology, autobiographical appeals to readerly interest, superficial "innovations," or controversialism. Berger's too interested in the mysteries of narrative to bother with metafiction, yet his world does possess a certain rubbery pleasure in its own artifice. He doesn't bother to disguise fiction's proscenium arch—his "realism," such as it is, resides in his assiduous scrutiny of daily existence, at levels both psychological and ontological. Berger adores novels too much to play at their destruction, or to be embarrassed at his participation in a tradition.

Berger's commitment has another aspect: Apart from a scattering of short plays and stories, he's devoted himself entirely to the novel and eschewed side work like journalism, screenwriting, or teaching. Nor has he spent his capital pontificating, issuing manifestos, attending conferences, or granting more than a small handful of interviews. What this may have cost him in terms of journalistic ink, who knows? A few years ago I made the mistake, in writing an entry on Berger for a literary encyclopedia, of claiming that he'd fallen from a "critical and popular heyday" in the '60s. Berger wrote me to gently correct my error, explaining he'd never had a "heyday," dragging out the sales figures to prove it. No, Berger's hovered for fifty years in a middle distance, proof neither of the proposition that genius is always rewarded nor that it is universally overlooked. The paradoxical fate of a writer impossible to revive because he's never been sufficiently neglected is somehow quite suitably Bergerian.

In material terms, Berger's been unflinching in his dedication: twenty-two novels since his 1958 debut, *Crazy in Berlin*. His shelf, while unified both by his unmistakable gentle irony and his uncanny ear for musical collisions of high and low diction, effloresces in wild diversity: a quasi-Updikean quartet of novels following the life stages of a lumpen, angelic alter ego named Reinhart; a pair of shambolic historical-legendary epics, *Little Big Man* and *Arthur Rex* (the former, his best-known novel, now followed by a sequel); and a handful of loving demolitions of genre—the private-eye novel in *Who Is Teddy Villanova?*, utopian and dystopian fiction in *Nowhere* and *Regiment of Women*, fables of wish fulfillment in *Being Invisible* and *Changing the Past*. The remainder are harder to pigeonhole or typify, though all develop motifs of power, victimization, and guilt in human affairs, and all exhibit the curious capacity of his fictional situations to shift like a weather vane between farcical misunderstanding and ominous, sadomasochistic abuse. Many, including *Meeting Evil*, impinge on the material of the crime novel, or *policier*, though they never reproduce the tone typical of those genres. (Meanwhile, the audience that savors crime in fiction has overlooked Berger, much as the tropical explorers, in the famous *Mad* magazine cover illustration, are unaware, as they scrutinize the trees, that they are huddled in the concavity of an enormous footprint.)

These less-categorizable novels, with their nominally realist settings and full of human blundering ranging from adultery and murder to badly cooked meals, constitute the strongest argument for Berger's importance. The sequence I have in mind begins with the monumental *Killing Time*, Berger's fourth, which resembles a Jim Thompson novel rewritten by an American Flaubert. An inquiry into a beatific, existentially profound sociopath who regards himself as the enemy of time, it contains the first of a series of portraits of faintly malicious, hugely pragmatic cops. Berger's fascination with policemen—the guilt they inspire in introspective souls, the morbidity they indulge as a by-product of their mission, the mental ambiguity-filters they necessarily adopt—is matched only by Alfred Hitchcock's.

Next come *Sneaky People*, *Neighbors*, and *The Feud*. *Sneaky People* and *The Feud* are a pair of large-ensemble midwestern urban novels, full of fond reproductions of American vernacular speech in its vanished splendor, full of unsentimental cross-sections of turf mostly abdicated by American novelists after Booth Tarkington. *Neighbors* (Berger's favorite among his own books) inaugurates a masterful triumvirate of novels of menace—its companions are *The Houseguest* and the book you hold in your hands. Each makes a study of what I'd call *ambivalent usurpation*—uncanny scenarios wherein a terrifying struggle for power emerges from within a banal milieu. Each features a principal provocateur and a principal victim—but Berger is fascinated by the ways in which innocence and reserve are complicit with chaos and impulsivity. He makes a study of the malignancy of charisma, but of the torpor of reflection as well. In the words of Reinhart, "People use us as we ask them to: this is life's fundamental, and often the only, justice." This theme of ambivalent usurpation—exchanges of unspecified guilt and obligation between pairs of human "doubles"—resonates with motifs in works by artists as apparently disparate as Dostoyevsky, Harold Pinter, Patricia Highsmith, Orson Welles, and, again, Hitchcock. It's typical of Berger, however, that once his theme of doubleness has been established, rather than emphasize similarity between characters to a fatuous degree, he instead exercises his fascination with the fact that differing types *do* exist: However we might become ensnared by another, the lonely fact of self persists.

The paradoxical logic of Berger's scenes connects him above all to Franz Kafka. Eschewing ostentatiously dreamlike settings, *Shadows and Fog*–ian Eastern European atmosphere, or diction, Berger engages with Kafka's influence at a native level, grasping how the elder writer reconstructed fictional time and causality to align it with his emotional and philosophical reservations about human life. Berger's tone, like Kafka's, never oversells paranoia or despair. Instead, he explores the fallibility of the human effort to feel justified or consoled in the gaze of any other being, and the absurdity and heartbreak of the disparity between intention and act. The results are never dreamlike. Berger locates that part of our *waking* life which unfolds in the manner of Zeno's paradox, where it is possible only to fall agonizingly short in any effort to be understood or to do good. In doing so, he illuminates what it was that necessitated Kafka's exaggerations. And by splitting the difference halfway back to daylight—and setting his daylit persecutions among strip malls and suburban developments—he unnerves us even more deeply.

Berger offers further pleasures: droll wit, formal slyness, and the diction and vocabulary of a Henry James high on H. L. Mencken. He's as brilliant a student of American talk as Nabokov or DeLillo, and my favorites among his sentences often pivot on fragments of tabloid squawk elevated into odd majesty by their surrounding syntax. Indeed, to believe Berger's own (suspect) testimony, language is his *only* subject. Among his countless eloquent demurrals of discussion of the moral, philosophical, or psychological implications of his work, my favorite is one given to Brooks Landon, Berger's most essential critic: "I have never believed that I work in the service of secular rationalism (the man of good will, the sensible fellow, the social meliorist who believes the novel holds up a mirror to society, etc.). I am essentially a voyeur of copulating words."

Those demurrals reflect Berger's distrust of the shifting ground of language, and his horror of abstractions and false certainties, which preclude nearly any human gesture less immediate than the cooking by one person of a delicious meal for another. All else is laden with presumption at best, grim manipulation at worst: Every person is surely full of purposes, and Berger suspects his own as direly as anyone else's. ("Remember that you will understand my work best when you are at your most selfish," he has also told Landon.) The letters that I am so fortunate as to receive from Berger are full of enthusiasms: for character actors like Elisha Cook Jr. and Laird Cregar, for Superman comics, for Anthony Powell's *A Dance to the Music of Time*, for the novels of Barbara Pym, Marcel Proust, and Frank Norris, and as well for some but not all of the writers and filmmakers to whom I've presumed to compare him. Perhaps the feast of culture is another port in the storm of existence (to mix a metaphor), though Berger's main characters are never artists or writers, and those few creative types who do appear are usually ogres or bozos, if not both.

Landon has explored Berger's sustaining relationship to Nietzsche, whose notion of "slave" and "master" personalities presages Berger's interdependent victims and victimizers. Other critics point to Berger's engagement with existentialism of the type which was fashionable in postwar culture when he began writing. The murderers in *Killing Time* and *Meeting Evil*, so unalike in other ways, both reflect a fascination with existentialist rationales for motiveless murder, à la *Crime and Punishment*, and Camus's *The Stranger*, and Hitchcock's *Rope*. What's clear, too, is that in his novels of menace Berger is compelled by and attracted to his provocateur villains for their dynamism, and for their talent for testing the certainties of everyday life, the rote morals of policemen, etc. And yet, unlike the typical novelists of Berger's own generation, the Keseys and Kerouacs, and even the Updikes and Roths, the dissident against social complacency is *never* Berger's hero. What Berger resists in social rebellion is its resemblance to what it attacks: its self-validating smugness, its readiness to manipulate in its own cause, its cobbled-together moral jargon, its bottom-line disinterest in the mystery of daily existence, its poor listening skills.

Berger isn't an experimental writer in any of the usual senses of the word. But in his ferocious devotion to paradox and irony as investigatory tools, his fiction consists of an endless, irresolvable experiment into what can be translated out of the morass of lived human days into useful and entertaining stories—though Berger would likely argue that no story can be useful, and then jibe that no one was meant to be entertained beyond himself. Berger's uncertainty is his being and his implement. The uniquely vertiginous nature of a page of his fiction is testament to the daily experiment of his art.

In the Bergerian world, masks are often peeled away to reveal further masks, yet just as often what was mistaken for a mask turns out to be a face. No irony is conclusive enough not to give way to a deeper irony, and the deepest of all is the realization that first impressions are sometimes adequate, or that it is the rare quandary that is actually improved by sustained pondering. Fate is for the embracing: As a Berger policeman once wisely remarked, "Death can happen to anyone." No one, however grotesque or ill-mannered, is so remote from the human predicament that he is ineligible for the occasional epiphanic insight, yet no one, however saintly or patient, is likely to be able to make use of the insights at hand in the flurry of a practical transaction involving another person. Just when Bergerian loneliness seems ubiquitous, contact is unexpectedly made, and though Berger's sex scenes are often barren and harsh, his tender evocations of romantic yearning may be the least-appreciated aspect of his books. No grace can ever be earned, in Berger's world, but it does fall like precious rain here and there.

Meeting Evil is on the unmerciful side of his shelf, but odd, sunny moments break through—it wouldn't be Berger otherwise. It's also spare, in the manner of his late books (apart from the *Little Big Man* sequel). The structure, hard to discern on the first roller-coaster plunge through, is elegant and ironclad: In the first section John Felton is persecuted and harassed by the police, by bystanders, and by his wife; in the third section, he is abandoned by all of them. Richie's incursion is the only consistent note in his reality, and it is one of purest mayhem; the only person responsive to John is a madman. Between, in the book's second section, Berger delves into Richie's self-justifying viewpoint, in pages as lean and shocking as an X-ray of the brain of a shark. In those, we learn that the madman listens to John for the simplest reason: He likes him.

Berger is now seventy-eight years old. It's a rare privilege to witness a great novelist's arc beyond such an age, but Berger is unflagging, and it may not be too much to wish for several more novels. The recent books are gentler, more forgiving, and often serve as consolations of earlier sequences: *Orrie's Story* returned to the midwestern panoramas of *Sneaky People* and *The Feud*; the overlooked *Suspects* revisits the sincere and troubled policemen of *Killing Time* while excusing them from the duty of confronting an existential superman. And just as the fourth Reinhart novel, *Reinhart's Women*, sheltered that beset character from the historical strife of the first three books, his newest, *Best Friends*, may be seen as a gentle capstone to the three novels of menace which include *Meeting Evil*. In it, the twinned characters, usurper and usurpee (can you tell them apart?), meet not as strangers but as lifelong friends who uncover the strangeness hidden inside familiarity. But it is also a pining love story, and another Kafkaesque parable of shifting perspective, and more: Berger has insisted that *Best Friends* felt to him, in the writing, like nothing he'd ever done. As a novelist this brings my heart into my throat. I only hope that at his age I'll be not only working but working, in Berger's manner, without presumptions, without a safety net constructed of the good reviews gathered over a lifetime. Each time Berger writes he ventures out with only his style for courage.

As a favor to my friend I've avoided the word which has dogged his years on this planet: I have not called him *comic*. But I would fail here if I didn't report that his books have made me laugh harder, over *my* years on the planet, than any others on my shelves. I predict that you will laugh, too, and that you will find, as I have, that this laughter sustains itself even after the contemplation, inevitable after absorbing more than one or two of Berger's books, of the vast distress at the human plight that necessitated their writing. Berger isn't comic. He, like life, is merely, and hugely, fucking funny.

—Introduction for *Meeting Evil*, and *The Village Voice*, 2003

Rushmore Versus Abundance

> *Your true task, as a son, is to reproduce every one of the enormities*
> *touched upon in this manual, but in attenuated form . . . choose*
> *one of your most honored beliefs, such as the belief that your*
> *honors and awards have something to do with you, and abjure*
> *it . . . Fatherhood can be, if not conquered, at least "turned down"*
> *in this generation—by the combined efforts of all of us together.*
>
> —DONALD BARTHELME, "A Manual for Sons"

Grooming this chapter, I spotted myself wielding the formulation "one of America's three or four greatest living novelists" in the Berger piece, and the phrase "unceasing tide of new titles" in discussing Paula Fox's republication.

If these are received terms (and they are), what's being received? And who's on the receiving end?

Here's Mailer's worst legacy: the degree to which he reified the notion of a Rushmore frieze of "greatness," proceeding through Hemingway to himself. Not content to announce White Elephant Triumph as the only possible redemption for the claims of his ego, he declared it as the standard for a generation. Mailer-Bellow-Updike-Roth-ism was our reward. The paradigm, though discredited, inane, unwieldy, and obnoxious, is still fitted over the current life of literary culture at the drop of a certain type of long and moderately successful novel into the conversation. Let that book take a large prize, or be a best seller for a month or two, and Rushmore's under construction again—only who'll play Lincoln, Jefferson, and Roosevelt?

Rushmore is a founding-father dream, a religious myth, and worse: It's a lid on not-thinking. Screw Rushmore. Dismantle the graven image, Hemingway-Faulkner-Fitzgerald-Steinbeck begat Bellow-Mailer-Updike-Roth who begat the counterculture Rushmore of Heller-Kesey-Pynchon-Vonnegut who begat the shrinking-readership Rushmore of DeLillo-Coover-Barth who begat the humiliating post-stature-edition-and-just-pick-any-four-depending-on-who's-hot of Wallace-Moody-Chabon-Franzen-Eugenides-Powers-Vollman-or-even-sometimes-Lethem. (Dismantle it from inside, oh you my brothers! They only project our features on that stone to mock us for how deficient we appear there!)

The crime of Literary Rushmore, the one that anyone notices first, is that which ought to dissolve Rushmore forever in a bath of shame, but never does: The stone heads are white American men. There's never a Cather or Ellison or Baldwin or Oates or Ozick or Morrison on that mountain, no matter how unmistakably said person may have knocked one out of the ballpark that particular year, or decade, or century. There's the sole evidence you'd ever need that the Rushmore construction is ritual authoritarian enactment, not a description of any engaged reader's, or writer's, context. Such groupings consist not of an argument but of an incantation of power.

Coming of age as a reader, I took an instinctive, cool-hunter's pleasure in defying the Rushmores presented to me: Speak, to sixteen-year-old Lethem, the names "Heinlein, Clarke, Asimov" and he'd spit back "Clifford Simak"; to the twenty-six-year-old bookstore brat, try "Fitzgerald, Hemingway, Faulkner" and he'd reply "Nathanael West" or, to "Coover, Barth, etc.," "Gilbert Sorrentino." (An echo of my fetish for identifying Fifth Beatles.) At the peak of Mailer-Roth-Bellow-Updike dominance, it seemed incredible to care about the novel and not also be reading James Salter and Robert Stone and Richard Yates. In the same spirit, when I called someone like Berger "one of America's three or four greatest living novelists" I'd add (usually in my head, less often aloud) "with Steven Millhauser and Steve Erickson and Stephen Dixon."

And all of that, let me be the first to point out, is only to speak of other white American men (so many of them named Steve). If you actually open the menu of twentieth-century writing, as anyone with a real appetite must inevitably do, the idiocy of exclusion moves beyond the ethical crime of rendering other "discourses" invisible: It's aesthetic starvation. As a teenager I knew, with a defiance that resembled an identity politics, that Chandler, Highsmith, Dick, Delany, and Shirley Jackson had more to give than much of what I'd find on the library's respectable front shelves. Soon after, small-press brain explosions included Michael Brodsky and Harry Mathews, the equivalent of a Marvel Comics reader's discovery of the existence of R. Crumb and Gary Panter. Iris Murdoch, Dawn Powell, Ann Beattie, Katherine Dunn, and Christina Stead were thunderbolts of my catching-up-to-women in my twenties and thirties. This happened not through self-policing for a respectable show of diversity but from readerly hunger. At the risk of being obnoxious, it always struck me that literacy consisted precisely of this: having off-center preferences derived from a termite's reading plan.

James Baldwin's *Another Country* was the compass through my own racial-familial mire in *The Fortress of Solitude*, but nobody apart from me mentioned Baldwin's name, even after I begged. Rushmore writers were the only comparisons bestowed, apparently, even if just to say I hadn't clobbered my way, Mailerishly, into their bracket. Insidious, wearisome Rushmore ritual informs the white male American novelist, in interview upon interview, that he needs to think only about other white male American novelists, a bunch of his contemporaries who are—if he's lucky—constantly being asked about him.

Literary nationalism's another Rushmore lie. I guess the word "American," prefixed to anything, widens jaded eyes and shifts copies, but my reading life wasn't geopolitically orderly. Did I care that Lewis Carroll or Aesop were European when they lit my fuse? The first long novel I vanished inside was called *Nobody's Boy*, a translation of the classic *Sans Famille*, but did I, at ten, notice the French title in parentheses? Particularly in late-twentieth-century English, where Rushdie and Ishiguro and even the translated Murakami seemed as hot-wired to my own vocabularies and curiosities as anyone American or even living down the block, why should I consent to the dull imposition of the national context? It wasn't how I embarked to where I was headed, so why should it be where I arrived when I got there?

*Literary competition is not a zero-sum game with a single winner,
or even a ranked list of winners—that all-too-naïve image of
the canon in which, say, Shakespeare has first place and the gold
cup, followed by Chaucer with the silver, in second place, Milton
with the bronze, in third . . . The concept of literary quality is
an outgrowth of a conflictual process, not a consensual one. In
the enlarged democratic field, the nature of the conflict simply
becomes more complex. Even among the most serious pursuers of
the aesthetic, there is more than one goal; there is more than one
winner. Multiple qualities and multiple achievements are valued—
and have been valued throughout the history of the conflicting
practices of writing making up the larger field called the literary.*

—SAMUEL R. DELANY, "Emblems of Talent"

The arts are produced by overcrowding.

—WILLIAM EMPSON, *Some Versions of Pastoral*

*Washington Irving, in a little story called "The Mutability of
Literature," in his* Sketch Book, *wrote: "The inventions of paper
and the press have put an end to all restraints . . . the stream of
literature has expanded into a torrent—augmented into a river—
expanded into a sea . . . The world will inevitably be overstocked
with good books. It will soon be the employment of a lifetime
merely to learn their names." Lamenting the torrent of books is a
frequently-encountered modern trope (one of its greatest exponents
being Jonathan Swift). For 16th-to-19th century people of a certain
cast of mind, the printing press was what their latter-day fellow-
travelers call the MFA program: the Death of Literature.*

—MATTHEW BATTLES

*Pre-1985, we are victims of the availability heuristic—we've
no idea whether there was vastly more fabulous culture to be
created than we created because, of course, it was never created. A
function of classism, racism, sexism, capitalism, totalitarianism,
religion, and technology . . .*

—RICHARD NASH

The hiding-in-plain-sight aspect of Rushmoreism is the minimalist head count: "three or four," like Beatles or an outfield. This is the source of my lazy default to the received notion of an "unceasing tide of new titles"—the rote complaint that the floodgates are too wide. I want to chip at this part of Rushmore, too. Cognitive science has established how annoyed our brains are to be asked to count above five or six; supermarkets learn it's shrewd to make five premium mustards available, not twenty. And it's a standard trope of middle age to get grouchy at swarms of new, unrecognizable stuff: Forgivable, then, is the middle-aged author's lament of overpublication, which crops up routinely. I suppose it's forgivable, too, from young newcomers full of feral juice, motivated by terror that they'll arrive pre-drowned-out.

But why should our grasp of literary culture, in its current state of explosive abundance and range, be hostage to this hindbrain's coping impulse? What matters, in reading, is discernment and engagement, not the size of the field upon which those occur. It matters even less that the field be shrunken to assuage dumb anxieties that we're missing something worthwhile. (Trust me, we're missing something worthwhile.) How on earth can abundance damage anything for anyone, unless what's damaged is some critic's pining to control what shouldn't be controlled, or to circumscribe boundlessness?

Acknowledging abundance entails no surrender of standards. (That should go without saying, but in this era of bogus alarms about abdicated standards, doesn't.) Here's another view from snotty bookstore-clerkland: Every year there was a "literary" novel that was the novel read by the people who didn't read novels anymore, the people who hadn't been reading novels for years but hadn't yet admitted it to themselves. The memo would go out: X is the book that will stand in for caring about novels for another twelve months or so; read it and you've punched the clock, read it and your ass is covered. (I'm sure this phenomenon makes publishers very happy; I'm also sure it leads them to make some terrible decisions.) Some years the novel that occupied that role was a good one, some years, well, not so good. But there was nothing funnier to those of us at the bookstore who took novel-reading as seriously as life itself than talking with the customer who, in the past four years, had read only *Perfume*, *Love in the Time of Cholera*, and *Snow Falling on Cedars*, and who has now rushed anxiously to the purchase counter with *Smilla's Sense of Snow* gripped in his mitts. Such customers were always anxious, for trying not to be left out of something you are fundamentally out of is an anxious business. Will I like this book as much as those others? That's what this customer wanted to know. Is this the *right* book to read, *this* year?

But the answer was simple: Of course you'll like it. That book is guaranteed to blow your mind. Starve yourself of the experience of the novel and every novel's a feast, a revelation. Every novel is Cervantes.

Standards require not only the acknowledgment of abundance but the absorption of abundance. How can any honest reader, or critic, make abundance the enemy? It rules the past—sorry, but that's unfixable. I may die never having gotten to *Miss MacIntosh, My Darling* or *The Worm Ouroboros* or *An Armful of Warm Girl*, books that for twenty years or so I've had staring from my shelf, radiating the possibility they'd rewire my brain if I'd only squeeze them into my schedule. You may, if you hadn't heard of them before, die before seeing their titles mentioned a second time.

Demographics, and what Delany calls the "democratized field," determine that abundance will even more brazenly rule the future.

Time sorts.

Can we embrace both operations? Probably not, no more than we can either embrace mortality or get our heads around infinity. Carving three or four heads on Rushmore, or pounding out another dull list of the top-ten this-or-that, may be a kind of death-in-life, an attempt to freeze the chaos of abundance at a tolerable place. It is also a somewhat understandable flinching response to the prospect of perishing by dissolution.

But me, I'd sooner drown in a sea of books than die in space where I can hear only myself scream.

Outcastle

Ten and twenty years ago I used to play a minor parlor trick; I wonder if it would still work. When asked my favorite writer, I'd say "Shirley Jackson," counting on most questioners to say they'd never heard of her. At that I'd reply, with as much smugness as I could muster: "You've read her." When my interlocutor expressed skepticism, I'd describe "The Lottery"—still the most widely anthologized American short story of all time, I'd bet, and certainly the most controversial (and widely censored) story ever to debut in *The New Yorker*—counting the seconds to the inevitable widening of my victim's eyes: They'd not only read it, they could never forget it. I'd then happily take credit as a mind reader, though the trick was too easy by far. I don't think it ever failed.

Jackson is one of American fiction's impossible presences, too material to be called a phantom in literature's house, too in print to be "rediscovered." She's both perpetually underrated and persistently mischaracterized as a writer of upscale horror, when in truth a slim minority of her work has any element of the supernatural (Henry James wrote more ghost stories). While celebrated by reviewers through her career, she wasn't welcomed into any canon or school; she's been no major critic's fetish. Sterling in her craft, Jackson is prized by the writers who read her, yet it would be self-congratulatory to claim her as a writer's writer. Rather, Shirley Jackson has thrived, at publication and since, as a reader's writer. Her most famous works—"The Lottery" and *The*

Haunting of Hill House—are more famous than her name and have sunk into cultural memory as timeless artifacts, seeming older than they are, with the resonance of myth or archetype. The same aura of folkloric familiarity attaches to less-celebrated writing: the stories "Charles" and "One Ordinary Day, with Peanuts" (you've read one of these two tales, though you may not know it), and her last novel, *We Have Always Lived in the Castle*.

Though she teased at explanations of sorcery in both her life and her art (an early dust-jacket biography called her "a practicing amateur witch," and she seems never to have shaken the effects of this debatable publicity strategy), Jackson's great subject was precisely the opposite of paranormality. The relentless, undeniable core of her writing—her six completed novels and the twenty-odd fiercest of her stories—conveys a vast intimacy with everyday evil, with the pathological undertones of prosaic human configurations: a village, a family, a self. She disinterred the wickedness in normality, cataloging the ways conformity and repression tip into psychosis, persecution, and paranoia, into cruelty and its masochistic, injury-cherishing twin. Like Alfred Hitchcock and Patricia Highsmith, Jackson's keynotes were complicity and denial, and the strange fluidity of guilt as it passes from one person to another. Her work provides an encyclopedia of such states and has the capacity to instill a sensation of collusion in her readers, whether they like it or not. This reached a pitch, of course, in outraged reactions to "The Lottery": the bags of hate mail denouncing the story as "nauseating," "perverted," and "vicious"; the canceled subscriptions; the warnings to Jackson never to visit Canada.

Having announced her theme—Jackson's first novel, *The Road Through the Wall*, finished just prior to "The Lottery," is a coruscating exposé of suburban wickedness—Jackson devoted herself to burrowing deeper inside the feelings that appalled her, to exploring them from within. Jackson's biographer, Judy Oppenheimer, tells how in the last part of Jackson's too-brief life the author succumbed almost entirely to crippling doubt and fear, and in particular to a squalid, unreasonable agoraphobia—a horrible parody of the full-time homemaker's role she'd assumed both in her life and in her cheery, proto–Erma Bombeckian best sellers *Life Among the Savages* and *Raising Demons*. However painful her final decade, though, her work enlarges as it descends, from the sly authority of "The Lottery" into moral ambiguity, emotional unease, and self-examination. The novels and stories grow steadily more eccentric and subjective, and funnier, climaxing in *We Have Always Lived in the Castle*, which I think is her masterpiece.

"The Lottery" and *Castle* are intertwined by the motif of small-town New England persecution; the town, in both instances, is pretty well recognizable as North Bennington, Vermont. Jackson lived there most of her adult life, the faculty wife of literary critic Stanley Edgar Hyman, who taught at nearby Bennington College. Jackson was in many senses already two people when she arrived in Vermont. The first was a fearful ugly duckling, cowed by the severity of her upbringing by a suburban mother obsessed with propriety. This half of Jackson was a character she brought brilliantly to life in her stories and novels from the beginning: the shy girl, whose identity slips all to easily from its foundations. The other half of Jackson was the expulsive iconoclast, brought out of her shell by the marriage to Hyman—himself a garrulous egoist, typical of his generation of Jewish '50s New York intellectuals—and by the visceral shock of mothering a quartet of noisy, demanding babies. This was the Shirley Jackson whom the town feared, resented, and, depending on whose version you believe, occasionally persecuted. For it was her fate, as an eccentric newcomer in a staid, insular village, to absorb the reflexive anti-Semitism and anti-intellectualism felt by the townspeople toward the college. The hostility of the villagers helped shape Jackson's art, a process that eventually redoubled, so that the latter fed the former. After the succès de scandale of "The Lottery" a legend arose in town, almost certainly false, that Jackson had been pelted with stones by schoolchildren one day, then gone home and written the story. (Full disclosure: I lived in North Bennington for a few years in the early '80s, and some of the local figures Jackson had contended with twenty years before were still hanging around the town square where the legendary lottery took place.)

In *Castle*, Jackson revisits persecution with force and a certain amount of glee, decanting it from the realm of objective social critique into personal fable. In a strategy she'd been perfecting since the very start of her writing, that of splitting her aspects among several characters in the same story, Jackson delegates the halves of her psyche into two odd, damaged sisters: the older Constance Blackwood, hypersensitive and afraid, unable to leave the house; and the younger Merricat Blackwood, a willful demon prankster attuned to nature, to the rhythm of the seasons, and to death, and the clear culprit in the unsolved crime of having poisoned all the remaining members of the Blackwood family (apart from Uncle Julian).

The three survivors—Constance, Merricat, and the frail and daft Uncle Julian—dwell together in their grand house at the town's periphery, rehearsing past trauma and fending off change and self-knowledge. Constance cooks and cleans in a time-struck ritual observance of the missing family's existence, while Merricat makes her magical forays into the woods and her embattled shopping trips into the center of town, there to contend with the creepy mockery of the village children, who propagate the family history of poisoning as a singsong schoolyard legend. Uncle Julian, dependent on Constance's care, putters at a manuscript, a family history, in an attempt to make sense of the rupture that has so depopulated his little world. Julian's a reader's surrogate, framing questions ("Why was the arsenic not put into the rarebit?") and offering thematic speculations ("My niece is not hard-hearted; besides, she thought at the time that I was among them and although I deserve to die—we all do, do we not?—I hardly think that my niece is the one to point it out.") that frame our curiosity about the events that Merricat, our narrator, seems so eager to dismiss.

Merricat's voice—ingenuous, defiant, and razor-alert—is the book's triumph, and the river along which this little fable of merry disintegration flows. Despite declaring her eighteen years in the first paragraph, Merricat feels younger, her voice a cousin to Frankie's in Carson McCullers's *The Member of the Wedding*, or Mattie's in Charles Portis's *True Grit*: an archetype of the feral, pre-sexual tomboy. Merricat is far more disturbing, though, precisely for being a grown woman; what's sublimated in her won't be resolved by adolescence. Indeed, typically for Jackson, sexuality is barely present in the book and, needless to say, sexuality is therefore everywhere in its absence.

The story is a frieze disturbed. Merricat has stilled her family, nailed them like a book to a tree, forever to be unread. When Cousin Charles arrives, transparently in search of the Blackwoods' hidden fortune (though like everything else in the book, the money's a purloined letter, secreted in full view), he brings a ripple of disturbance that his cynical mission doesn't fully account for. Uncle Julian leads us to the brink of speculation when he mentions their ages: Cousin Charles is thirty-two, and Constance is twenty-eight. No one—certainly least of all Merricat—will say that Constance is a kind of Emily Dickinson, drowning sexual yearning in her meticulous housework, and in sheltering her damaged uncle and dangerous sister, but certainly that is the risk that Charles truly represents: the male principle. (Uncle Julian is definitively emasculated, possibly gay—certainly it was his harmlessness that permitted his survival of the poisoning.)

Merricat, an exponent of sympathetic magic, attacks this risk of nature taking its course by confronting it with nature's raw, prehuman elements: first by scattering soil and leaves in Charles's bed, and then by starting a fire: better to incinerate the female stronghold than allow it to be invaded. It's a cinch to excavate a Freudian subtext in the scene of the firemen arriving at the house ("the men stepping across our doorsill, dragging their hoses, bringing filth and confusion and danger into our house," "the big men pushing in," "the dark men going in and out of our front door")—just as easy as to do the same with the prose of Henry James. From the Oppenheimer biography we know Jackson objected very strictly to this sort of interpretation, as James surely would have, and as we likely ought to on their behalf. The point isn't that this material *isn't* embedded in Jackson's narrative; the point is that its embedding is in the nature of an instinctive allusiveness and complexity, forming one layer among many, and that to trumpet such an interpretation as a master key to material so nuanced would be to betray the full operation of its ambiguity. Sex is hardly the only sublimated subject here. Consider that great American taboo, class status: In "The Lottery" undertones of class contempt were coolly objectified; in *Castle* the imperious, eccentric Blackwoods are conscious of their snobbery toward the village, and conscious, too, how the persecution they suffer confirms their elevated self-image.

This double confession of culpability is typical of the snares in Jackson's design: For many of her characters, to revel in injury is a form of exultation, and to suffer exile from drably conformist groups—or families—is not only an implicit moral victory but a form of bohemian one-upmanship as well: We have always lived in the (out)castle, and we wouldn't want it any other way. Jackson, a famous mother and a tormented daughter, also encoded in her novel an unresolved argument about child-rearing. When at the height of her crisis Merricat retreats to the summerhouse and imaginatively repopulates the family table with her murdered parents, they indulge her: "Mary Katherine should have anything she wants, my dear. Our most loved daughter must have anything she likes . . . Mary Katherine is never to be punished . . . Mary Katherine must be guarded and cherished. Thomas, give your sister your dinner; she would like more to eat . . . bow all your heads to our adored Mary Katherine."

The terror of the scene is intricate, for we suspect these fantasies are as much re-creations as revisions of past reality. Elsewhere Uncle Julian muses aloud about whether Merricat has been too utterly adored to develop a conscience. The motif links *Castle* to the midcentury's crypto-feminist wave of child-as-devil tales like *The Bad Seed* and *Rosemary's Baby*, and to the sister-horror film *Whatever Happened to Baby Jane?* But Jackson's book is *The Bad Seed* as rewritten by Pinter or Beckett—indeed, Jackson's vision of human life as a squatter's inheritance in a diminishing castle recalls the before-and-after of the two acts of *Happy Days*, where Beckett's Winnie, first buried up to her waist, and then to her neck, boasts: "This is what I find so wonderful. The way man adapts himself. To changing conditions." As Constance and Merricat's world shrinks it grows more defiantly self-possessed, and as threatening elements are purged their castle gains in representative accuracy as a model of the (dual) self. When at last the villagers repent of their cruelty and begin gifting the castle's doorstep with cooked meals and baked goods, the situation mirrors that of Merricat's play-acting in the summerhouse—only this time the offerings laid at her feet are real, not imaginary. The world has obliged and placed a crown on Merricat's head. Her empire is stasis.

—Introduction for *We Have Always Lived in the Castle*, 2006

Thursday

How do you autopsy a somersault? G. K. Chesterton's *The Man Who Was Thursday: A Nightmare* is one of the great stunts ever performed in literary space, one still unfurling anytime you glance at it, as perfectly fresh and eloquent as a Buster Keaton pratfall. The book constructs its own absolute and preposterous terms in the manner found most often in certain children's books, *Alice in Wonderland*, or *The Phantom Tollbooth*, or Russell Hoban's *The Mouse and His Child*. Like those books, it offers the possibility of being about everything and nothing at once, and vanishes at the end with the air of a dream. Like them it begs to be reread.

Description is appropriately impossible, except by a series of exclusions. Kingsley Amis called *Thursday* "not quite a political bad dream, nor a metaphysical thriller, nor a cosmic joke in the form of a spy novel, but it has something of all three." To that I'd add: not quite a roman noir, nor a simplistic religious allegory, nor—despite Chesterton's subtitle—a nightmare. It's much too complete and legible to be a nightmare, and, really, too happy—yet far too personal and strange to parse as an allegory of Chesterton's Catholicism. For a while it does resemble a kind of Dickensian noir, but the stakes are all wrong. A noir exalts sex and money, and no two things could be further off Chesterton's radar. Here, villain and MacGuffin are combined in one being in the monstrous and godlike figure of Sunday, the president of the Anarchist

Council. If *Thursday*'s a version of *The Maltese Falcon*, it's one in which Sydney Greenstreet is encrusted head-to-toe in precious rubies and disguised with black enamel, to then steal away with the booty of himself.

Of course, there aren't really characters in *Thursday*, not any more than there are characters in Lewis Carroll, or in a drawing by M. C. Escher, or in John Lennon's "I Am the Walrus." This is definitely an "I-am-you-and-you-are-me-and-we-are-all-together, joo joo ga joob" sort of world. But there are *characterizations*, and those are dashed off with a breezy, almost distracted assurance: Gabriel Syme, the insouciant and mild poet-policeman, feels wonderfully individual from his opposite number, the soapbox orator and sole true anarchist, the blazing and Blakean Lucian Gregory. Nevertheless, the reader understands instantly that the two are essentially Chesterton's two natures, given form as philosophical sprites and pitted against each other. Chesterton loved argument, and his arguers are lovers, or at least twinned souls.

The real characters are the ideas. Chesterton's nutty novelistic agenda is really quite simple: to expose moral relativism and parlor nihilism for the devils he believes them to be. This wouldn't be interesting at all, though, if he didn't also show such passion for giving the devil his due. He animates the forces of chaos and anarchy with every ounce of imaginative verve and rhetorical force in his body. You know he's been tempted by these things; you feel it in how adoringly he loathes them. President Sunday, that huge gorgon of darkness, induces horror and desolation in Chesterton's heroes, but they're also drawn to him as toward a black sun.

The book begins with Syme and Gregory in an open-air debate in the London suburb of Saffron Park, bathed in a glow of sunset which establishes the surrealistically oversaturated descriptive atmosphere once and for all: "All the heaven seemed covered with a quite vivid and palpable plumage; you could only say that the sky was full of feathers, and of feathers that almost brushed the face." Right at the start the book threatens to be all charming talk—and I do mean charming: Chesterton's is sophistry you'd listen to forever. The two poets debate art and anarchy and the fate of the world and insult each other like a couple of affectionate spin doctors on cable television, working themselves up to the point where they've just *got* to hurry off together to a pub. Sort of like college. It's then, though, that things get beautifully weird. The table they've seated themselves at slowly begins to rotate, until it corkscrews into an underground passage. There, Gregory explains, a secret anarchist cell will gather that very evening to elect a new Thursday to the Great Anarchist Counsel of all Europe, which has seven members, each named for a day of the week.

That kicks off the most spectacular sequence of bluff-calling in literature: Gregory calling Syme's bluffs, Syme calling Gregory's in return, and most of all Chesterton calling his own imaginative and ontological bluffs until he reaches the highest levels of straight-faced improbability. The invention is breathless, and so's our man Syme, as he dodges and twists through ominous breakfasts, freak snowstorms, battles on beaches and in forests, shadowy pursuits by relentless, street-stalking figures, and a sword battle conducted in a time trial with an approaching locomotive and against an opponent who never bleeds. The garish cast of spies and policemen trade places with innocuous ease, and the conversation is always somehow droll and hysterically doomy at once. The trick to Chesterton is that he takes himself and his notions at face value, only every face is a mask with another mask underneath. It's been pointed out again and again that Chesterton advances his arguments, as well as his stories, by the use of paradox. What's less frequently noted is his furious use of *velocity*. The book has the compression of a three-minute Warner Brothers epic like *Duck Amuck*.

Because of his fondness for paradox, and for the stark and shuddering sense of aloneness in an indifferent universe which tends to come over Gabriel Syme every third page or so, *Thursday*'s been much compared to the novels of Kafka. C. S. Lewis was the first to make this identification, and I can understand why it stuck, but the comparison's viable only if taken as another Chestertonian inversion: Chesterton's the anti-Kafka, really. He may tease you for a while with the possibility of never reaching the Castle, but his conclusion—not to give anything away, I hope—is that it's impossible not to reach the Castle, because you've been inside it the entire time. The only question left is whether there *is* an outside to the Castle. Lucian Gregory would claim so, but I doubt Chesterton would be likely to agree with him. Kafka himself read Chesterton and detected the humming engine of optimism at the book's core, saying, "He is so gay, one might almost believe he had found God." Gay's an excellent word. The books trills with Chesterton's happiness. The miracle—assuming you believe in miracles—is that it's never smug. Chesterton is so thrilled by his acrobatic stroll along the razor's edge of nihilism that he earns his sunniness anew on every page.

Why not put *The Man Who Was Thursday* in its real context? The book was published in England in the same year as Kenneth Grahame's *The Wind in the Willows* and Joseph Conrad's *The Secret Agent*, and in some ways it describes a perfect midpoint between the two better-known books. The pre–Great War London full of revolutionaries with bombs in their coats and young men drunk on radical philosophies that Conrad and Chesterton describe is eerily identical, and confirms an element of realism in *Thursday* it would otherwise be easy to overlook. The Conrad feels more culturally prescient because he cast his book as a tragedy—and because his terrorists drew real blood—but it's the same early whiff of twentieth-century horrors both writers have tasted in the air. Seen from the other perspective, Chesterton's young men are seduced to anarchism much as Mr. Toad in *The Wind in the Willows* is seduced away from a quiet life by the riverside by the obnoxious craze for motorcars. That is to say, in both *Thursday* and *Willows* the damage is reversible, the genie may be put back in the bottle. Motorcars might be renounced, and weasels and stoats driven from Toad Hall. Once the real weasels ran amok in Europe a bit later, it became hard to imagine anyone as serious as Chesterton writing such a reassuring book except as an act of nostalgia.

Antidote to Conrad, or *The Wind in the Willows* for grown-ups, have your pick. Either way, this really is one of the great books of reassurance and consolation—maybe one of the only great books of reassurance and consolation. As John Carey writes, "Usually we feel superior to innocence, associating it with stupidity. But in Chesterton's case that will not work. If you think yourself cleverer than him, the odds are about ten million to one that you are wrong." Chesterton subtitles *Thursday* "A Nightmare" and prefaces it with a poem to his friend Edmund Clerihew Bentley, which suggests he feels he's finally tackled a certain morbid part of himself, as if in writing *Thursday* he'd confronted a specter out of his mad, bad, dangerous, and gloomy youth: "This is a tale of these old fears / Even of those emptied hells, / And none but you shall understand / The true thing that it tells." Yet the book is cheering because it feels, like the poem, retrospective: You sense Chesterton's long since put the possibilities of despair and suicide—even doubt—firmly out of reach by the time of writing. His giddy and paranoiac soufflé is evidence, finally, of a man making grotesque and hilarious faces in the mirror, freaking himself out completely, then turning to his desk and diligently, elaborately, and brilliantly explaining the faces away.

—Introduction for *The Man Who Was Thursday*, 2001

My Disappointment Critic

*The job of the regular daily, weekly, or even monthly critic
resembles the work of the serious intermittent critic, who writes
only when he is asked to or genuinely moved to, in limited ways
and for only a limited period of time . . . What usually happens
is that (the staff critic) writes for some time at his highest level:
reporting and characterizing accurately . . . and producing insights,
and allusions, which, if they are not downright brilliant, are
apposite . . . What happens after a longer time is that he settles
down. The simple truth—this is okay, this is not okay, this is vile,
this resembles that, this is good indeed, this is unspeakable—is not
a day's work for a thinking adult. Some critics go shrill. Others go
stale. A lot go simultaneously shrill and stale. A few critics, writing
quietly and well, bring something extra into their work . . . Some
staff critics quit and choose to work flat out again, on other
interests and in intermittent pieces. By far the most common
tendency, however, is to stay put and simply to inflate, to pretend
that each day's text is after all a crisis . . .*

—RENATA ADLER, "The Perils of Pauline"

*As Bloom has settled into this second career, so his old virtues
have gradually fallen from him. An extraordinary amount
of the work of the last decade is luxurious with padding and
superfluity; there is hardly a book of his that would not have been
better off as an essay. He is not a critic anymore, but a populist*

appreciator . . . Above all, for Bloom, writers must be ranked,
and the greatness of the very greatest asserted again and again.
Moreover, all great writers are essentially alike.

—JAMES WOOD

The house of fiction, as Henry James once said, has "not one
window, but a million," and hence no single aperture gives access
to what James called "the need of the individual vision and the
pressure of the individual will." Different novelists look to different
models. Fielding, Sterne, and Stendhal set the pattern for the
ironic or self-conscious novel, flaunting its own narrative devices.
Balzac became the great exemplar of the social novel, as Scott and
Manzoni did for the historical novel. Tolstoy's deceptive simplicity
transformed style into a transparent window on the real. Kafka's
metaphorical novels and stories turned fiction into fable or parable.
Each of these writers depends on exact circumstantial detail, but
the strength of their fiction comes not from the phrase, the sentence,
the metaphor, as critics like Wood would have it, but from how
they actualize larger units of scene and theme, plot and character.
It can be misleading to approach fiction primarily through its
language, a technique better suited to the study of poetry . . .

—MORRIS DICKSTEIN

Everyone speaks of the "negative capability" of the artist, of his
ability to lose what self he has in the many selves, the great of the
world. Such a quality is, surely, the first that a critic should have;
yet who speaks of the negative capability of the critic? How often
are we able to observe it?

—RANDALL JARRELL, "Poets, Critics, and Readers"

What happened is this: I wrote a book (*The Fortress of Solitude*) and
James Wood reviewed it. What happened next: I wrote James Wood
a long, intemperate letter. (Not an open letter.) And he wrote a curt
postcard in reply. Eight years later, I haven't quit thinking about it.
Why? The review, though bearing a few darts ("Depthless Brooklyn,"
"squandered," "before our disappointed eyes"), wasn't the worst I'd
had. Wasn't horrible. (As my uncle Fred would have said, "I know from
horrible.") Why, I hear you moan in your sheets, why in the thick of

this Ecstasy Party you've thrown for yourself, violate every contract of dignity and decency, why embarrass us and yourself, sulking over an eight-year-old mixed review? Conversely, why not, if I'd wished to flog Wood's shortcomings, pick a review of someone else, make respectable defense of a fallen comrade? The answer is simple: In no other instance could I grasp so completely what Wood was doing.

Also, I had expectations. (That fatal state.) I felt, despite any warnings I should have heeded, that to be reviewed at last by the most consequential and galvanizing critical voice, the most apparently gifted close reader of our time, would be a sort of graduation day, even if I'd be destined to take some licks. Taking some, I'd join a hallowed list. I mean this: I'd have taken a much worse evaluation from Wood than I got, if it had seemed precise and upstanding. I wanted to learn something about my work. Instead I learned about Wood. The letdown startled me. I hadn't realized until Wood was off my pedestal that I'd built one. That I'd sunk stock in the myth of a great critic. Was this how Rushdie or DeLillo felt—not savaged, in fact, but harassed, by a knight only they could tell was armorless?

As it happened, I wandered into this encounter a self-appointed expert in the matter of expecting—a lot? too much?—and being disappointed. I'd written a cycle of personal essays called *The Disappointment Artist*, its subject, precisely, the crisis of being so fraught with preemptory feelings in approaching a thing—a book, a movie, another person—that the thing itself is hardly encountered. So was I too ready to see Wood in my own framework, a version of "the narcissism of minor difference"? Or did it make me specially qualified to demand of Wood what I'd demanded of myself: that in the critical mode I sort out self and subject, even if they always again intermixed, at least long enough to spare the pouring-on of inapt disappointment?

James Wood, in 4,200 painstaking words, couldn't bring himself to mention that my characters found a magic ring that allowed them flight and invisibility. This, the sole distinguishing feature that put the book aside from those you'd otherwise compare it to (Henry Roth, say). The brute component of audacity, whether you felt it sank the book or exalted it or only made it odd. These fantastic events hinge the plot at several points, including the finale—you simply couldn't not mention this and have read the book at all.

Or rather, you couldn't unless you were Wood. He seemed content to round up the usual suspects: italics, redundant clauses, and an American kind of "realism" he routinely deplores. Perhaps Wood's agenda edged him into bad faith on the particulars of the pages before him. A critic ostensibly concerned with formal matters, Wood failed to register the formal discontinuity I'd presented him, that of a book which wrenches its own "realism"—*mimeticism* is the word I prefer—into crisis by insisting on uncanny events. The result, it seemed to me, was a review that was erudite, descriptively meticulous, jive. I doubt Wood's ever glanced back at the piece. But I'd like to think that if he did, he'd be embarrassed.

Strangely enough, another misrepresentation, made passingly, stuck worse in my craw. Wood complained of the book's protagonist: "We never see him thinking an abstract thought, or reading a book . . . or thinking about God and the meaning of life, or growing up in any of the conventional mental ways of the teenage Bildungsroman." Now this, friends, is how you send an author scurrying back to his own pages, to be certain he isn't going mad. I wasn't. My huffy, bruised, two-page letter to Wood detailed the fifteen or twenty most obvious, most unmissable instances of my primary character's *reading*: Dr. Seuss, Maurice Sendak, Lewis Carroll, Tolkien, Robert Heinlein, *Mad* magazine, as well as endless scenes of looking at comic books. Never mind his obsessive parsing of LP liner notes, or first-person narration which included moments like: "I read Peter Guralnick and Charlie Gillett and Greg Shaw . . ." That my novel took as one of its key subjects the seduction, and risk, of reading the lives around you as if they were an epic cartoon or frieze, not something in which you were yourself implicated, I couldn't demand Wood observe. But not reading? This enraged me.*

"The conventional mental ways of the teenage Bildungsroman." Here, fobbed off in one casual phrase, may be the crux: *the conventional*

---

*As for "thinking about God," was there ever a more naked instance of a critic yearning for a book other than that on his desk? Can Wood's own negative capability not reach the possibility that in some life dramas "God" never made it to the audition, let alone failed to get onstage? Pity me if you like, but I can't remember even considering believing in either God or Santa Claus. The debunking was accomplished preemptively, preconsciously. Hence, not a subject in my Bildungsroman. Sorry!

mental. Wood is too committed a reader not to have registered what he (apparently) can't bear to credit: the growth of a sensibility through literacy in visual culture, in vernacular and commercial culture, in the culture of music writing and children's lit, in graffiti and street lore. What's at stake isn't a matter of "alternate" or "parallel" literacies, since these others aren't really separate. They interpenetrate and, ultimately, demand familiarity with the Bloomian sort of core-canonical literacy. (I couldn't have written my character's growth into snobbery without *Portrait of a Lady* and *Great Expectations* at my back, but James and Dickens were simply not where I boarded the bus.)

What's at stake is the matter of *unsanctioned* journeys into the life of culture. And I don't believe anyone sanctions any other person's journey into the life of culture. This is the point where I need to confess that my attention to James Wood, in the years since sending my letter, has been as cursory as it was before that uncomfortable passage (uncomfortable for me; I doubt my letter ruffled his feathers). Earlier I'd been content to sustain a cloudy image of a persuasive new critic who made people excited and nervous by passionately attacking novels that people (including myself) passionately believed in; now I found myself content to revise that in favor of an impression of an unpersuasive critic whose air of erudite amplitude veiled—barely—a punitive parochialism. It didn't make me want to read him, so I'm not qualified to make any great pronouncements. I've only glanced, over these years, and it may be that my confirmation bias is in play when I do. Here's what I see in my glances. When Wood praises, he mentions a writer's higher education, and their overt high-literary influences, a lot. He likes things with certain provenances; I suppose that liking, which makes some people uneasy, is exactly what made me enraged. When he pans, his tone is often passive-aggressive, couched in weariness, even woundedness. Just beneath lies a ferocity which seems to wish to restore order to a disordered world.

Not that any God had me in mind, but if you'd designed a critic to aggravate me you couldn't have done better. About books I'm Quakerish, believing every creature eligible to commune face-to-face with the Light; he's a high priest, handing down sacred mysteries. To one who pines for a borderless literary universe, he looks like a border cop, checking IDs. The irony of Wood's criticisms of Bloom is that Wood's own "narcissism of minor difference" looks unmistakable: Wood is a critic whose better angels are at the mercy of his essentialist impulses.

His postcard to me? I've lost it, but can give a reliable paraphrase, since after my outpouring, rather than address what I'd said, Wood spared me just one or two arched-eyebrow lines. It was as though my effort bore an odor of ingratitude. "I'm sorry you felt that way," he wrote, more or less. "I liked the book so much more than any of your other work." His tone, it seemed to me, that of an aristocrat who never *really* expected those below him to understand the function of the social order. He's not angry, he's disappointed. Well, that makes two of us.

On Bad Faith

My original letter to Wood included the suggestion that he was "in bad faith." This, the confidante who vetted the letter wanted to challenge. He knew Wood and didn't believe that was "the explanation" (though he couldn't propose an alternative). But maybe it was a bridge too far. Reading the above, written eight years after, I see I've reached for the same term. What does it mean to me?

I'm not actually trying to read James Wood's mind, or to change it now. Whether Wood consciously or unconsciously betrayed a standard he recognizes, or could be made to recognize, doesn't interest me. His *piece* is in bad faith. The instant it was published, with its blanketing tone of ruminative mastery, and yet with all it elides or mischaracterizes, it was so—period. It was in bad faith with my novel, and, I'd say, with novels, an enterprise to which Wood believes himself devoted, a belief I'd have no basis for challenging. So let's call this "resultant bad faith," a term which spares us the tedium and rage of guessing at the interior lives of those with whom we more than disagree.

The American Vicarious

Miss Lonelyhearts and *The Day of the Locust*

1.

Halfway through *Miss Lonelyhearts*, Nathanael West's eponymous protagonist blurts out:

> Perhaps I can make you understand. Let's start from the beginning. A man is hired to give advice to the readers of a newspaper. The job is a circulation stunt and the whole staff considers it a joke. He welcomes the job, for it might lead to a gossip column, and anyway he's tired of being a leg man. He too considers the job a joke, but after several months at it, the joke begins to escape him. He sees that the majority of the letters are profoundly humble pleas for moral and spiritual advice, that they are inarticulate expressions of genuine suffering. He also discovers that his correspondents take him seriously. For the first time in his life, he is forced to examine the values by which he lives. This examination shows him that he is the victim of the joke and not its perpetrator.

The passage, so disconcertingly clean and direct that it could remind you of a Hollywood screenwriter's treatment (that mercenary form in which West would come to specialize, a few years later), perhaps represents the book West suspects he ought to have written, or the book he suspects his reader thinks he ought to have written. That's to say, a coherently tragic narrative grounded, under an urbane, lightly hard-boiled surface, in comprehensible "values." The story this paragraph suggests is the sort that might have been nicely handled by a novelist like Horace McCoy, whose *They Shoot Horses, Don't They?* could be considered a temperamental cousin to West's, its metaphor of the dance marathon forming a lucid indictment of the failure of popular imagination to encompass the Great Depression's dismantling of the American dream.

Certainly this embodies a part of West's intention. *Lonelyhearts* was inspired by glimpses of real letters written to a real advice columnist, and is set in a persuasively scoured and desperate early-'30s Manhattan, rendered with the scalpel precision that was West's prose standard. And though his books have taken on a timeless value, one measure of his singular value is as a uniquely placed, and uniquely gifted, historical witness, a bridge between literary eras. His was a sensibility that extended the Paris-expatriate, surrealist-drunken sophistication of '20s literary culture to the material and milieu of Steinbeck, Tom Kromer, Edward Dahlberg, Daniel Fuchs, and other '30s writers (some explicitly tagged as "proletarian")—that is, to poverty's social depredations, with all the accompanying lowered sights, vicarious daydreams, and susceptibility to cults, fads, and games of chance.

Yet hardly anything in this context prepares us as a reader for a plunge into the nihilistic, hysterical, grotesque-poetic frieze that is the fifty-eight-page "novel" we know as *Miss Lonelyhearts*. For what that inadequate synopsis implies ("for the first time in his life, he is forced to examine the values") is an approach to depicting fictional characters that is precisely the approach West couldn't ratify: psychologically rounded, possessed of adequate reserves of self-possession, and capable of making and recognizing a traditional "mistake," of making a hero's progress through a typical plot, even if it is to be a tragic one. This isn't West's way. The journalist known to us only as "Miss Lonelyhearts," like his antagonist-editor Shrike, indeed, like every human creature he encounters (including those "profoundly humble" authors of the advice-seeking letters), is a species of chimera, in many ways a mystery to him- or herself. If West's characters are human, it is only unfortunately so: trapped in a grossly prominent physical form, a creature lusting and suffering in bewildering simultaneity. As far as their "values," or *personalities*, these are glimpsed only fleetingly against a screaming sky full of borrowed and inadequate languages and attitudes—commercial, religious, existentialist, therapeutic, criminal.

West's characters mostly don't engage in conversation. In its place they toss blocks of rhetoric, of elegant mockery or despair, at one another like George Herriman's Ignatz Mouse chucking a brick at Krazy Kat's head. (In *Lonelyhearts* it isn't only the letters but nearly all the characters' speeches to which it is impossible to make reply.) The comparison of the form of *Lonelyhearts* to a comic strip isn't mine but West's, who intuited that for all his grounding in Dostoyevsky and T. S. Eliot, he needed to find some version of vernacular form to embody his insight that "violence in America is idiomatic." The novel's short, sardonically titled chapters persistently end in morbid slapstick and cumulatively take on a slanted, compacted quality, like crashed cars exhibited bumper-to-bumper. Dislodged on the very first page from traditional identification with the travails of *Lonelyhearts*'s protagonist—on one side by the horrific chorus of the advice-seeking letters themselves, on the other by the preemptive mockery of Shrike— the reader finds any possibility of redemptive self-pity brilliantly undermined. (A critic explained—or complained: "Violence is not only West's subject, it is his method.") West's masterpiece is a merci- lessly unsympathetic novel on the theme of sympathy.

2.

New York is vertical, Los Angeles horizontal, as well as three thou- sand miles farther from any grounding in European historical con- sciousness. The difference between West's New York novel and *The Day of the Locust*, his Hollywood apocalypse, mimics these differences of cultural geography and form. *Lonelyhearts* is defined by stairwells and elevator shafts and basement speakeasies, *Locust* by the littering of a fundamentally desert landscape with arbitrary architectural mon- strosities, with random and flimsy quotations of different building styles, whether for use as temporary movie sets or (barely more per- manent) dwellings. Lizards scurry across this ground, and in place of *Lonelyhearts*'s claustrophobic compression, *Locust*'s savage attention flits from character to character, leaving more oxygen and sunlight between the comically lumpen human operators—though eventu- ally they'll crowd together and swarm this landscape like lemmings. Acutely conscious of the double-edged myths of Progress and Manifest Destiny (the diffident Jew Nathan Wallenstein Weinstein converted himself to the imperially urbane "Nathanael West" because, he joked, he'd heard Horace Greeley's call to "Go West, young man"), West explicitly defines Los Angeles as the place where the American (egalitarian) dream has ended up, first to replicate itself in the synesthetic cartoons of the motion picture industry, and then, under the exposing glare of sunlight, to die.

Of course it is also six years deeper into the Depression, and no one in *Locust* would bother, as does Shrike in *Lonelyhearts*, to puncture unattainable fantasies of luxurious bohemian escape. The inadvertent Californians in *Locust* have made their last migration, and in this zone of shoddy historical facsimiles history itself seems to have ground to an end. The aspiring painter Tod Hackett, the book's best hope of a reader surrogate (and West's best shot at such a thing, in any of the books), a protagonist-watcher who dares both to dream of love and to attempt an artistic encapsulation of what's before him, can only plan a canvas depicting the gleeful burning of Los Angeles by its cheated inhabitants—in destruction, they might make it their own. West shows the film industry from its margins, the lame cast-off vaudevillians and extras, the aspirants and showbiz parents, grasping intuitively that these figures articulate the brief continuum between manufacturing and merchandising bogus dreams, and lining up to buy them. The pathetically wishful movie scenarios dreamed up by the wannabe-starlet Faye Greener, Tod Hackett's tormenting love object, are hardly less viable than the sorts of films that West himself ended up dashing off during his facile stints as a studio writer—the point seems to be not simply that anyone could dream such stuff up but that everyone did, simultaneously. Most were buyers, not sellers. West's diagnosis of the American vicarious anticipates both reality television (where Andy Warhol's quip about everyone gaining fifteen minutes of fame became a drab processional) and the overturning of the "death tax" (where politicians aroused a righteous populist indignation in favor of the inheritance of fortunes, just on the chance every American would acquire their rightful own). West wouldn't have wondered *what's the matter with Kansas*, and he knew the problem wasn't limited to Kansas, or Los Angeles, or the '30s. In 1967 Gilbert Sorrentino discerned *The Day of The Locust*'s prediction of Ronald Reagan's future presidency, and this book, a sun-blazed Polaroid of its moment, seems permanently oracular.

3.

West's ultimate subject is the challenge (the low odds, he might insist) of negotiating between on the one hand the ground-zero imperatives and agonies of the body, and on the other the commoditized rhetorics of persuasion, fear, envy, guilt, acquisition, and sacrifice (those voices that George Saunders has nicknamed "The Braindead Megaphone" of late capitalism) in hopes of locating an intimate ground of operation from which an authentic loving gesture might effectively be launched. That he identified this challenge as a baseline twentieth-century American dilemma as early as he did granted him a superb relevance to the future of American literature—the ongoing future, I'd say. In the weeks while I've been rereading West, the unfolding of a global financial collapse has many speaking of a "second Great Depression," the public mechanics of which will certainly be subject to the same forces of transference, denial, and fantasy that West made his obsessive motifs. Last month in suburban Long Island, on the day nicknamed "Black Friday" for its hopes of pushing retail accounts into the black of profit, a tide of bargain-fevered shoppers trampled to death a retail clerk attempting to manage their entry into his store. The newspaper business has almost dissolved beneath a willful tide of "authentic" voices demanding to be heard; its response is nearly as neurotic as Miss Lonelyhearts's. Which of West's contemporaries can we imagine weighing in intelligibly on blogging, or viral marketing? (Picture Ernest Hemingway's blank stare—and he lived a quarter-century longer than West—or F. Scott Fitzgerald in a fetal position.) By applying the magpie aesthetics of surrealism and T. S. Eliot to the "American Grain," by delving into the popular culture and emerging not with surrender or refusal but with an acid-drenched, double-edged critique, West became the great precursor to Heller, Pynchon, Philip K. Dick, Colson Whitehead, and so much else, probably including Bob Dylan's "Desolation Row." West died, with his wife, in an automobile collision while returning to Los Angeles from a hunting trip in Mexico. His biographer, Jay Martin, gives evidence of the many books West had sketched out to write after *Locust*; the greatest phantom-limb oeuvre in American fiction.

—*The Believer*, 2009

IX

THE MAD BROOKLYNITE

He's broken our hearts yet again.

—*The Brooklyn Paper,* 2011

I suppose I'm ambivalent about Brooklyn, in a can't-take-it, can't-leave-it way. Periodically I "pull a geographical," to use the addict's terminology. Yet the witness protection program has never protected me from my own long witnessing.

Ruckus Flatbush

The Manhattan Bridge is spring-loaded and cars tilt off like bad pinballs aimed with deranged precision at the Williamsburg Dentist's Bunker Tower and then score, lighting it up with a honking buzz that makes you need your braces tightened again—rubber-band my jaw and start over. Junior's a Tang wedding cake permanently on fire, smoke and scorch wreathing from the upper banquet-hall windows. A guy with teeth the size of manhole covers bites into a cheesecake and pastrami on latkes triple-decker and a chunk of translucent pastrami fat falls sizzling off the curb melting the black tar and causing a swerving wreck between a block-long mafioso stretch limo and a Philip Guston garbage truck with a real dead cat strapped to its grille. Three siblings in identical bowl cuts emerge blinking from the Department of Health, each with freshly fitted Medicare spectacles, identical plastic frames, three Swifty Lazars in Moe haircuts. Mom tugs them across and they get stranded like ducklings on the median line. The wind smashes the hands of the tower's clock off line like Dr. Seuss fingers, today is Pluterday, twenty-five o'clock on Ruckus Flatbush!

May not be a crack in everything but there surely is in Brooklyn and you're falling in, scrabbling fingers finding no purchase, help somebody I got wedged in Butt Flash Avenue!

Serial killer's picking off the end of the line at the DMV renewal window and nobody notices.

Harry M. Octopus Institute of Practically Nothing Anyhow. One Year Certificate. One flight up.

WE FIX U GOOD.

Third Degree, Fourth Degree, Butt Flash Extension. South Pockmark Avenue. Corner of Pock and Butt.

Eight-foot-tall man in a perfect Malcolm X suit selling whole leopard skins and persimmon oil and cobra-venom incense and a table of books by some conspiracy wrangler named Napoleon Fung gets hungry for a Jamaican meat patty wrapped in spice bread. Wrap that in a slice of pizza and cough out a chicken bone you didn't even know was in there. Drumstick bones in an accumulating heap teeter down the subway portal. The city bus skids off Butt Flash, onto Full Time, doomed pedestrians swept in its Soylent Green people-catcher depositing them in a jumble onto the Albeit Squalor Mall escalators, going up!

Never Street, Jape Street, Doubtful Place, Murder Avenue. Stifle, between Bums and Hurt.

Soar into space or use Googlemaps to make sense of this place, read the smashed black orbs of sidewalk gum like an aerial map of disease vectors, urban dismay, or merely the exhausted moment when the wrung-out blob of xylitol spills from your lips. Chew Ennui! Rise higher, now sight the workmen's gloves scattered in the gutters with their fat smashed canvas fingers resembling popped corn. Were their hands lopped off? Higher, now a distribution of church spires confesses the forgotten plots of acreage and silence, Brooklyn a planet of towns, plow it up and start over. Dime Savings Bank was a fieldstone to begin with, biggest ever. Shifted it out of Manfred Von Bergen's farm. Metrotech a meteorite, fell in the '70s, they started scraping out windows. Plane crashed on Schumer's Horn in '81, folks were living in it the next day. Yo Mama included!

Turn left on Tightwad. Place you want is on Living Stoned. Off Smear. Talk to a guy I know. You don't even have to say my name, he'll know I know you. No, you'll know when you see him. All taken care of. You talk he talks all talk no trouble. Cash only! No checks!

This place don't look like much but it's legendary and nearly historical. They kept slaves on Doubtful Place, so I heard. Black ones. I remember when they tore down that theater. They had to close down Grim Ugly Plaza because a tidal wave of rats ran east. Hey, don't take my word for it. You could look it up or alternately go fuck yourself.

The Aggravated Antic.

Pathetic Street.

Dude snatched a purse and they chased him all the way down Hurt to Why Cough. Dude lived in the Why Cough Garbage.

Guy crawls blinking out of the Lost Isolation Rail Road terminal with a blue Dodgers cap on his head with the visor ripped off, sort of like a Dodgers beanie or yarmulke. White beard down to his scabby knees, covering his crotch, maybe this guy's Rip Van Brooklyn! Nothing covering his ass, though. Hey, Rip, get some pants! That's no Fertile Crescent!

This Times Plaza? Rip asks the nearest passerby.

Thefuckkeryu tokkinbout?

Where is my pawnshop where is my newsstand what's that weird rectangle building full o' gizmos this is not my beautiful intersection go fuck yerself where you been sleeping all this time, old freak? Time don't stand still! Get some pants and cover yer ass!

You ain't seen nothin' yet!

To the Moon, Alice!

Fuggeddabouddit, Gofuckkalamppost, Musteatapileofshit, Welcome to Brooklyn!

Rip Van Calamity creeps for cover into the Doray Tavern ("Where Good Friends Meet"), a bar like a black hole, daylight bent and broken at its threshold, full of Mohawk ghosts, guys that fell off in-progress skyscrapers chasing a falling half a ham sandwich and ending up embedded to their sternums in Manhattan concrete sidewalks. Here at the Doray they paint the whiskey black. Not the bottles, the whiskey. The ghosts pour shots and chaser down their neck holes and welcome Rip with a hearty hoist of a glass. His kind of people, and he theirs.

Used to work in the then I worked in the that was when I lived in the before all the then after I worked in the then I used to sleep in the before they filled in the hole in the I used to be able to hide in the catch a few zzz's in there sometimes before they filled it all in.

Fuggeddabouddit, Fuggedda, Fugget.

I already Fuggot.

Problem with people these days money. Problem with money these days people. People with money these days problem. People with problem these money days.

The higher you go there you are.
To the moon and all I got was this goddamn parking lot.
Beautiful shadows everywhere.
You like it so much, you live there!

—*Brooklyn Was Mine*, 2008

Crunch Rolls

Cap'n Crunch rolls into the station at seven-thirty on a Tuesday, causing a little ripple of excitement and recognition among the morning commuters, the wet-haired Wall Street guys and the bleary homeless folks just waking up and dragging their bedrolls and the secretaries with their fingers marking a page in a mass-market paperback and the domestics, mostly island ladies, headed in the other direction to take care of the young babies and, most of all, the high-school kids, headed uptown to LaGuardia or Bronx Science or out to Aviation in Long Island City, jostling each other in their knapsacks and then jaws dropping as Cap makes his brash debut. A lot of these kids might have communed with Cap once already today (a few of the Wall Street guys did this, too), scraping their gums on his oaty squares, flooding their milk and their bloodstreams with his sugar—but here the dude is in the flesh! Cap's looking a little crazy, a little freaky around the edges, like maybe he's been up all night in some club, but it's him all right. A subway platform is an involuntary oasis of community, everyone studiously ignoring everyone else, but this explosion of paint and vibrancy and meaning where they were expecting only a grimy machine goes like ecstatic lightning through the population here—we who smile are smiling partly at one another and partly at the fact that the others don't smile, don't bow to a contemporary deity like Cap'n Crunch the way we do—what's the matter with them, don't they have a *television* in their house?

The photographs in this book unveil graffiti's origins in tribalism, cave painting, and cargo cult. Figures morphing in and out of font describe the alphabet's own provenance in hieroglyph and pictogram (never more obvious than in the case of the ultimate common denominator of this convergence, *The Saint* logo), and simultaneously points the way to the alphabet's inevitable future as insignia, decal, emblem: These twenty-six letters we use so routinely were never going to sit still, not when they were loaded up with so much mythological garbage and magic, how could we have ever expected them to? No, they were destined to leap into the sky, onto our walls and our transport, screaming with occult notions and inscrutable claims of identity. These words and names we brandish so unthinkingly were pictures all along—and like most pictures, they were pictures of *people*. Not just ordinary people, but gods and ghosts and heroes, mocking nightmare clowns, idols of cool, figures of sex, superstition, and commerce. And the easy quotations of comic books and cartoons and advertising are indigenous evidence of the universal practice of sampling and mashup, the unquestioning privilege the artist claims over *all* the languages, verbal and visual, that float through his or her mindscape, indifferent to the claims of the proprietors of intellectual property. What's delivered so often by the creators here, with the immediacy typical of the pop impulse, is the slick and chaotic vocabulary of commercial culture decanted brilliantly into folk idiom, on the spot, in the dark, on the fly. The figures roll into your mind like a train into a station, with a squeal and a groan of metal on metal. And then the doors open.

—Introduction to *Mascots & Mugs: The Characters and Cartoons of Subway Graffiti*, 2007

Children with Hangovers

The children with hangovers are taking out the garbage. I watch from above as they lurch out of the basement apartment. Their garbage is in brown paper sacks, the kind you have to request to be given anymore at the grocery checkout, and the paper sacks are rotten and soggy, splitting like tomatoes. The children with hangovers stagger out cradling the sacks, hoping to keep them from bursting before reaching the curb. They slump them in a heap in the street, coming away with fingers stained with salad dressing and coffee grounds. Then they turn back to the apartment, squinting groggily in the morning sun. It is early for the children with hangovers.

The man next door stands out on the curb, beside his neatly knotted green plastic garbage bags, scowling at the children with hangovers. I am sure he can hear the bass thrum of their music through his walls, as I can hear it up here on the top floor of the house, pulsing clear through the apartment between. I am sure that, like me, the man next door does not understand how the children with hangovers can keep it up.

The man next door has five flagpoles. He displays three at all times, an ordinary flag, a rattlesnake coiled above the words DON'T TREAD ON ME, and a POW/MIA flag, with crossed sabers on a black field—prisoner of war, missing in action. On the fourth pole he shows a flag for every season, an Easter flag, with pink stripes and bunnies for stars, a scary black-and-orange Halloween flag, a Valentine's flag, a Thanksgiving flag, and so forth. The fifth pole is always bare, ready for some crisis or affiliation not yet born.

The recycling trucks come before the garbage trucks but no one has left anything for the recycling men, not the man next door or the children with hangovers or the man in the apartment between, or me.

The postwoman comes next, and as always she comes up the stoop and pushes a single fat bundle of mail, bound with a rubber band, through my slot. Then, as she has done lately, she goes down the stoop and rings the bell for the basement apartment. Though she's left all the mail for the house upstairs she rings the bell of the children with hangovers and when they come to the door the postwoman goes inside.

Often when I go down to sort out the mail I run into the man who lives in the apartment between, just as he is coming in from his night shift driving a taxi in the city. He drives all night and early morning and returns to sleep through the late mornings and afternoons and early evenings, and then he awakens again near nightfall. I hear his alarm clock buzz at eight or nine. Then he begins drinking and cursing and readying himself for his shift, which begins after midnight. He continues to drink in the taxicab as well and by the time he returns in the mornings he is usually looking as bad as the children with hangovers, or worse. When I run into him in the hall I offer him his mail, and then his hands are too full, with his bottle and his pistol which he keeps under his seat while he drives his cab. He asks me to hold his pistol while he looks at the mail I've handed him, then finds his keys and unlocks his apartment door. Once his door is opened he reclaims his pistol and goes inside. The mail for the children with hangovers I bring upstairs into my apartment.

I live in fear of hailing a cab one night in the city and finding that my driver is the man from the apartment between.

I never see the postwoman leave the basement apartment but she must at some point go and resume her rounds. I just never see her go.

This evening the children with hangovers build a bonfire in the backyard. Perhaps this is why their bags of garbage are so exclusively oily and damp. They have been hoarding their paper and cardboard for the bonfire. The bonfire is many feet around and grows to a quite impressive height. I can see magazines burning, centerfolds, glossy paper the color of flesh wrinkling in the blaze. Soon I see they have begun stacking broken chairs and shelving and other items, plastic and

THE ECSTASY OF INFLUENCE

ceramic vessels from their kitchen, onto the fire. The children with hangovers dance laughing in a circle around the fire, with bottles in their hands. They light cigars and smoke them as they dance and sing around the fire. The postwoman is there with them in the yard, dancing, too. I don't know whether she's been in their apartment all day or whether she came back.

I hope she has not burned the mail.

The alarm clock of the man in the apartment between buzzes while I am looking out the back window at the tower of flame, which rises well above the heads of the children with hangovers now.

The mail for the children with hangovers is all collection notices and credit card offers and I sort through it, making two piles: collection notices, credit card offers. I have two large piles. The only mail the children with hangovers will accept are the free gifts which sometimes arrive, videotapes or CDs or CD-ROMs which I bring downstairs and leave at their door.

The children with hangovers have never invited me inside.

I think the children with hangovers are fucking the postwoman.

The garbage has not been picked up from the front curb. Today may be an obscure garbage holiday, a patriotic or religious civic occasion nobody can keep track of, not even the man next door.

The smoke from the bonfire curls through my back windows, so I shut them.

The children with hangovers have begun giving out my phone number when bill collectors call. I handle these calls for them, explaining just as well as I can, trying to spare any misunderstanding.

The collectors rant and fume on the line. I am patient with them, hearing them out, soothing them exactly as one would an infant. This sometimes takes hours, but I've decided it's the least I can do.

—*Lit*, 2003

L. J. Davis

This can only be entirely personal for me, I have no way around it. Not least because in considering the matter of "the Brownstoners"—those straggling individuals and families, nearly all of them white, who, by laying claim in the '60s to a few of the aging and tattered row houses in the neighborhoods on the periphery of downtown Brooklyn, set the groundwork for the disaster and triumph of Brooklyn's slow-motion gentrification, so full of social implications and ethical paradoxes, and trailing any number of morbid and comic life situations not unlike those depicted in L. J. Davis's three novels of Brooklyn—I am considering the matters of my own life. My parents *were* Brownstoners, and the complexly uncomfortable facts in the case, discernible behind Davis's Brooklyn novels and also behind Paula Fox's *Desperate Characters* and Thomas Glynn's *The Building*, are the facts of my childhood. These were the facts I eventually excavated in a long novel called *The Fortress of Solitude*, but yet which no matter how deeply I dig, I will never completely demystify.

Not least, but not only. Writing about Davis's *A Meaningful Life* is personal for me because L. J. Davis was my first writer, and by that I mean not in the sense of Lewis Carroll or L. Frank Baum, who were among the first writers I read, but that he was my first captive specimen. L.J. and his family lived on the next block (he still lives in the neighborhood, and so do I), and I was best friends with his son Jeremy. When I first conceived the wish to be a writer, the thought was pretty easily completed by the phrase: *like Jeremy's dad.* I liked what I saw. L.J. sat at the back end of an open, high-ceilinged parlor floor devoted to book-shelves. (That I alphabetize my books now is probably attributable to the fact that his were alphabetized.) His desk was massive—I think it had to be, to support the weight of his manual typewriter, which I recall as a piece of epic ironwork wreckage, something you'd seen driven around on the back of a flatbed truck in search of a vacant lot where it might be safely abandoned. In that office, when Jeremy and I weren't shooed away, I was introduced to the existence of the books of Thomas Berger, Charles Webb, Leonard Michaels, and Kingsley Amis ("I was happy to be called Brooklyn's Kingsley Amis," L.J. once told me, "until I had the misfortune of being introduced to Kingsley Amis"), and to Leonard Cohen's *New Skin for the Old Ceremony* LP. These are all tastes I've retained, and the flavor of which seem relevant now to the pleasure I take in L.J.'s novels—rightly relevant, it seems to me, though I could never defy the associative force of childhood memory.

So *A Meaningful Life*, along with the true literary thrill it offers on rereading, provides for me a shudder of recognition, or a whole series of shudders. In three of L.J. Davis's four novels, young men who can only be described as sick, chronically ill with self-knowledge of their preju-dices and reservations, find their ambivalent fates manifest in scenes of brownstone renovation in downtown Brooklyn, where the joists and pillars of the grand and tempting old houses are too often rotten to the core. More even than Fox's great novel, close to the bone though it cuts, *this* reproduces the world I dawned into when my parents moved to Dean Street. The dystopian reality of late '60s and early '70s outer-borough New York City can be difficult to grant at this distance; these streets, though rich with human lives, were collectively damned by the city as subhuman, crossed off the list. Firehouses and police sta-tions refused to answer calls, whether out of fear, indifference, or both. As L.J. told me once, most simply: "Anyone who chose to move to the neighborhood was in some way crazy. I know I was." The precarious-ness of this existence—morally, sociologically, financially—was never exactly permissible, outside of L.J.'s books, to name, or at least not with such nihilistic glee.

L.J., refusing to blur the paradoxes of racial and class misunder-standing in idealist sentiment, was "un-PC" before there was such a thing. By being so, he turned some of his neighbors against him, exem-plifying a loneliness he, from the evidence of his books, already felt as an innate life condition. That he also chose with his wife to adopt two black daughters to raise in his brownstone alongside their two white sons is a fact that still stirs me in its strangeness and beauty. I remember thinking even as a teenager that L.J. had made his home a kind of allegory of the neighborhood, perhaps partly in order that he might refuse to stand above or apart from it. Then again, with characteristic dryness (unforgivable in the eyes of some local parents), L.J. once awarded a friend of mine and Jeremy's the Dickensian nickname "Muggable Tim," and recommended we avoid walking the streets with him. When after thirty-odd years of personal shame at such stuff I finally managed to open my mouth in *The Fortress of Solitude*, I had L.J. to thank.

L.J., with Berger and Webb and Bruce Jay Friedman and a few others, found himself cast, by contemporary critics, as a black humorist, though most writers associated with that label disavowed it. Many, like L.J., were critical darlings who bumped to the lower rungs of the midlist; if a concocted literary "movement" doesn't sell books, what good is it? In any event, these writers could be called sons of Nathanael West, but, unlike West, unburdened of the formal pressure of modernist aesthetics. In L.J.'s case, he appears to have tempered his West with a jigger of P. G. Wodehouse. "I *like* slapstick," L.J. recently told me, as if guiltlessly confessing a murder.

L.J.'s family home also gave evidence of a fanatical interest in world history, which had been Davis's major at Stanford. He and Jeremy shared a fondness for antique lead toy soldiers, for John Huston's adaptation of Kipling's *The Man Who Would Be King*, for scrupulously realistic board-game re-creations of European wars, and for the Flashman novels of George MacDonald Fraser. Born in Seattle but raised in Idaho, L.J. explained in a typically caustic autobiographical statement (written for the jacket of his first novel, *Whence All But He Had Fled*):

> There is something about Boise, its isolation and its inbreeding and its density, that fosters a specialized kind of hatred of parent for child and child for parent. I think the West, the concept of the heroic West, has a great deal to do with it. The pioneers are closer than they are in other places . . . It has something to do with the great good place found. The second generation agrees almost by default with the first, and the third can think of nothing but going away. Going away is not easy. Its goal out there is specific: San Francisco, and San Francisco is 642 miles away.

The Americanist context, its grand themes of Manifest Destiny and Manifest Disappointment, are terrifically relevant to *A Meaningful Life*, the most severe of L.J.'s Brooklyn novels. It's precisely the undertow of pioneer failure that gives the book its oxygen and reach, and which makes it more than a brilliant complaint or comic-existentialist howl in the night. By his description of his hero Lowell Lake's failing attempt to pen a novel of "the founding and settlement of Boise, Idaho," and by other near-subliminal touches (Lake suffers his premarital jitters at Donner Pass), we see Lake's disastrous reverse-pilgrimage into Brooklyn, the easy destruction of his tissue-paper WASP idealizations upon immersion in the racial boiling pot of the inner city, in terms of an American incapacity or unwillingness to meet the true implications of its founding promises, made to itself and to the future. Every arrival aimed at some golden San Francisco of the mind falls leadenly short, landing in a Boise of regret and loathing. In this, Davis's America opens unexpectedly into Kafka's unattainable Castle, and the Zeno's paradox chances of breaching its doors.

> "Do you realize I'm the first member of my family to cross this thing in a hundred years?" said Lowell as they bridged the Mississippi at Saint Louis. His emotions were strange and sinking, but not precise enough to put a name to.
>
> "Big deal," said his wife.
>
> They came to New York at night, hurtling through a hellish New Jersey landscape the likes of which Lowell had never dreamed existed, a chaos of roadways and exits, none of which made any sense, surrounded by smoke and flashes and dark hulking masses and pillars of real fire a thousand feet high, enveloped in a stench like dog's breath and dead goldfish.

In Davis's helpless vision, West collapses into East, the American future into the bloodstained European colonial past. Plus the contractor you hired just wrenched out and demolished the irreplaceable Carrara marble mantelpiece, without asking.

—Introduction for *A Meaningful Life*, 2009

Agee's Brooklyn

I want to try and sing back at *Brooklyn Is*, James Agee's song of Brooklyn, this astonishing secret text which like the heart of the borough itself throbs in raw shambolic splendor, never completely discovered, impossible to mistake. Agee is such a loving, explosive, and mournful singer; his prose aims the methods of Walt Whitman like a loving bullet toward the next century, brings that greatest singer of American identity smash up against the midcentury's grubby, boundless polyglot accumulation of successive immigrant hordes, and predicts the outer-borough songs to come, the ones that could only have been written by immigrant sons and daughters themselves—Malamud, Fuchs, Paley, Gornick, Marshall—though Agee, much like Whitman, can seem to encompass and predict any author who ever tried to touch Brooklyn since: Henry Miller, Paula Fox, myself. Agee's breath and voice come cresting at us out of the past, yet keenly modern and engaged in every syllable with the tides of the past that rush under the craft of his words—Agee can seem to be surfing the past, always in danger of being swallowed by the high punishing curl of time, always somehow riding atop it instead. Yet if he's a singer he's also a painter, brushstroking with his language the sun-bleached brownstone façades of Slope and Heights and Hill, the shingles and stucco of Flatbush and Greenpoint, the graffiti and commercial signage left like clues for future archaeologists—the brush of his prose is as fond and melancholy as Mark

Rothko's in his subway paintings or Philip Guston's in his street scenes, before both painters sank their feelings for the city in abstraction. He writes as though drunk on matters of space and geometry and distance, always seeing the life of the city whole and in microscopic miniature at once, and persistently smashing together architecture and emotion, conveying in the grain of a "scornful cornice" or a "blasted mansion" or a "half-made park with the odd pubescent nudity of all new public efforts" or "drawn breathing shades" or an "asphaltic shingle" (his neologism suggesting "asthmatic," "exalted," "Sephardic," and who knows what else) his sense that the archipelago of islands settled by the mad invaders of this continent and the refugees who followed, and the nature of the buildings and the streets and the signs the arrivistes constructed everywhere upon these New York islands, are in every way implicated in the experience of any given life lived even temporarily within their bounds, including his own. The shape of the land, in other words—and of the houses and trees and roadways, and the subways now running underneath them—has, in Agee's view, subdued and civilized and corrupted those who had arrived to subdue and civilize and corrupt this place; they made it strange and were made strange by it in turn. Agee tackles head-on Brooklyn's doubleness, the paradox of the borough's weird preening inferiority complex at its proximity to Manhattan and its simultaneous bovine oblivious hugeness, its indifference to attempts at definition—including Agee's own. He nevertheless made himself so open, such a portal for collective presence, that he truly can seem to have managed to allude to every icon of the place, every glorious shred of ruined culture a Brooklynite might ever flatter himself thinking only he'd cherished, and to have mentioned every talismanic name, Ex-Lax, Adelphi, DeKalb, finding vital concrete poetry in the enigma of the names, stitching time together, speaking to every Brooklyn dweller, past or future. In my own instance, Agee paints at one point a devastating cameo of Brooklyn Heights gentility and insularity (subtitled: *the dusk of the Gods*); reporting his snobbish host's fear, that "Negroes" and "Syrians" are "within two blocks of us"; those same "Syrians" now own great swaths of the neighborhood in question, which truly belongs more to them than to any other constituency (and where is the great novel of Arab American immigrant life on Atlantic Avenue?); they are, in fact, the landlords of the apartment on Bergen Street in which I sit writing this today—so it may seem that Agee is at my shoulder. The essay's prose is, at last, more than tidal, it's cyclonic, as the narrative rises up on the swirling imaged-junked cone of Agee's prophetic style to see the borough and its people whole, diving through parlor windows or into movie-theater seats or along a quiet Sunday street to sweep up another handful of lives in a few sprung, compacted sentences and sweep on. To end at the zoo, a perfect symbol of Agee's ultimate insinuation: that all this mad paving and dressing up and scribbling on walls (or on pages) and pouring tea from china cups is still finally nothing more than a vision of the natural world—that all our cultural outcroppings, chaotic and placid alike, are just evidence of our peculiar animal activities, and that Brooklyn is only a particularly dense and dreamy version of the zoo that is all human life, an enclosure where any number of not terribly imaginative or visionary individuals can collectively realize a great visionary mass result, a kind of vast art installation made by instinctive, consolation-seeking animals, merely by living their beautiful, ordinary, mad lives in adjacency to one another.

—Introduction for *Brooklyn Is*, 2005

Breakfast at Brelreck's

Under the shadow of the Williamsburg Savings Bank tower small, faintly visible men brave streams of traffic at the intersection of Atlantic and Flatbush avenues. Brooklyn's two great streets arrive in good spirits there and are demoralized, having unexpectedly tangled with the more prosaic Fourth Avenue, which points toward but never reaches the sea, being interrupted by a cemetery. Fourth Avenue, strewn with oil-stained automobile-repair shops, destroys the human imagination, this is widely known. What's less known is that it is also too much for Flatbush and Atlantic.

These nearly microscopic men in hats and coats scurry among an archipelago of desolate street corners, flattened brick-littered lots, a traffic island with a newspaper stand, and the Long Island Rail Road terminal, the only evidence for which above the ground is a pipe-and-plywood scaffold layered with decades of torn posterings.

A truck corners Fourth and humps over the curb beside a cigar store. A small boy runs from the traffic island, ducking behind the men crossing: From the newsstand he's stolen a comic book, *Blue Beetle #1*. The Blue Beetle is a Charlton Comic, drawn by Steve Ditko, Marvel's outcast. The men hasten, the avenues moan. The men are assembling for a late breakfast at a counter inside the bowels of the terminal. Some recognize one another. Others merely sense a kinship of worn shoes and pen-inky fingertips, an ache in the left quadrant of the rib cage, a dislike for a certain barber, a sister's son in the army, circles drawn in newspapers around telephone extensions never dialed.

A sign painted in fifteen-foot-high letters on pink brick asks HAVE YOU HAD ANY LATELY? CLAMS, STEAMERS.

A pawnshop features a variety of typewriters, trumpets, and wristwatches, plus one bassoon.

Two Chinese joints, No Pork Restaurant and Fu King Food Shop. Both serve from behind bulletproof glass.

Nobody can say what's sold at Samuel J. Underberg's, but with that signage he's made sure they won't forget his name.

Down inside the station against a backdrop of rusty squeals and staticky timetable announcements the men sit at the coffee-shop counter and fold their newspapers, lick their fingers, frown. The counter's built into a corner of the station behind the ticket desk. The glass door which might shield it from the rumblings and oil smoke is tied open with a frayed white rope; hung from the rope's a sign at least twenty years old showing a steaming cup and the single word OPEN. The sign behind the counter formed of movable red plastic letters with teeth which press into grooves in a green felt background says egg sandwich 39¢, egg and cheese 49¢, tuna 39¢, english 5¢, coffee tea 19¢, juice 15¢, juice tomato 19¢. Nobody's ordered tea or juice tomato in a thousand years and counting.

The men all wear hats which featured originally a tiny peacock's feather, now missing. The exception is one small man in a brown suit with frayed cuffs and a stained collar. He wears a blue cap with a B on it, a baseball cap with the bill missing so it resembles a beanie or yarmulke. When the talk starts it is always this man in the blue cap who starts it. The others have arrayed themselves at the counter around him according to their tolerance.

"Mighty Brelreck's," says the man in the blue cap now, his tone heavily sarcastic.

No one replies.

"Like sunflowers we turn our heads toward the radiance of Brelreck's urn," says the man in the cap. "Like sunflowers it is a *fershlunken* miracle we are still on our feet."

"Writing poetry?" says another man without turning his head.

"Reading, not writing," says the man in the cap. "It still occurs in certain quarters."

This bait goes untaken. Coffee is slurped in quiet concentration, as though the world's turning depends on certain metabolic balances being achieved at this counter deep beneath the pavement.

A woman bursts in—if a woman entered Brelreck's on tiptoe she'd be bursting. This one's a thin Negro lady with short hair barretted in certain places, wearing a windbreaker and a skirt and sandals. Her nails are painted a blue not unresembling that of the beanielike cap. She speaks with urgency to anyone listening.

"How do you get to Kennedy airport?"

A man in an ordinary hat answers. "Car or train?"

"I'm walking."

"That's a long way."

"Just tell me."

They're all going to be involved, they can just feel it. "You don't understand, lady," says another man. "That's however many miles. You can't walk."

"I walked here."

"From where?"

"Myrtle."

"A trifle, here from Myrtle. You're talking that twenty times over."

"Tell me, please."

Shrugs all around.

The Brelreck's man leans in and says, "Want a coffee?"

"Sit, sister, have coffee."

"Yeah, we'll treat you. You gotta consider this in depth."

The woman sits between the primary advice-giver with the ordinary hat and the man with the cap. The man with the cap leans in now and says, "Idlewild." Anyone can sense his pleasure in the syllables.

The woman stares at him like he's naked.

"Formerly Idlewild, now named for our late president. The name's already a relic, I see it in your eyes."

Shrugs and eye-rolling all around.

"You know where you're sitting?" says the man with the cap.

Woman shakes her head, takes a first sip.

"The last Brelreck's remaining. You might not care, but Brelreck's once had the city like this." He shakes a gripped hand. "One hundred and thirty outlets including the observation deck of the Empire State, of which you've surely heard. Brelreck's had a roasting plant on Avenue D you could smell in Sunnyside, and a plantation in Cuba. You from Cuba perchance?"

"No."

"Ah." He waits, but nothing's coming. "Well, so where was I? Brelreck's, of course—mighty Brelreck's." He shoots a look at the Brelreck's man, who turns in disgust.

"That's right," says the man in the blue cap. "It's nothing to be proud of. What happened to Brelreck's, you ask? My fine lady, they overreached." The grasping hand now shoots out, trembles on the brink of some unseen goal, retreats. "Went head to head with Chock Full o'Nuts. You don't need me to tell you how that came out. Today we're noshing in the ghost of a thing, madam, not a thing itself."

"You really walking to Kennedy?" says the man in the ordinary hat. He and the others have had time now to get their minds around it. Why shouldn't she if she wants to is the general drift.

She nods.

"You just go straight out Atlantic, all the way."

Another guy leans in. "But we're talking a long way. You never knew a street was so long as this."

"You'll think you're crazy," says another. "It just goes. Don't give up."

"A lot of the stores out that direction have yellow signs," adds a guy who usually doesn't say anything.

Everyone looks.

"Sue me," he says, holding out his hands like now they shouldn't wonder why he never talks. "I don't know the reason. Maybe somebody had a special on yellow once."

They all let this sink in, with annoyance.

"Anyway," says the man with the ordinary hat. "You get all the way out there the end of Atlantic, you gotta take a hard right at something called the Grand Concourse."

"Grand Concourse even have a walkway?" someone raises.

A bunch of guys wave it off. She's become like a horse they've bet on. They all want to see it done. "She'll walk underneath," someone says.

"There's one more thing you should know," says the man in the blue cap.

The woman stares at him, puts down her cup.

"This place, it's more than just Brelreck's that drew you here."

"Not now," says another guy. But it's hopeless.

"Aboveground around here, Flatbush and Atlantic, you notice how for blocks everything's flattened out? All those empty lots?"

Woman makes the error of nodding, not that there's any alternative.

"It's no accident this place looks like that. Few grasp or understand this was meant to be the new Ebbets Field. They got as far as picking out the site and knocking it all down. Could have been a Fenway, a Wrigley. Something beautiful. Then the Dodgers—whoosh—Los Angeles."

Somebody stage-whispers, "Get going, lady, it's okay. You'll be here all day."

The woman looks at the Brelreck's man, her eyes asking if the coffee was really gratis. He nods.

"Forget Los Alamos," says the man in the cap, his voice rising. "Forget the Bikini Islands. This is ground zero right here."

The woman is nearly out the door. Some guys are more gentlemen than others, they tip their newspapers slightly in farewell.

"We're dwelling here inside the scar from Brooklyn's ripped-out heart or possibly lungs!" the man in the cap screams. "The vital organs!"

The place has no echo, the scream dies in the air. The woman is gone. The man in the ordinary hat jerks his head at the Brelreck's man for more coffee. Newspapers are being wrinkled in serious consideration. Someone, we're not saying who, has got a streak of egg on his lapel—wouldn't happen if the schmuck would cook the yolk all the way like he was asked. The man in the blue cap snorts, scratches his nose, tries to settle.

"The vital organs," he mutters.

They've heard it before.

Above, a truck has busted an axle and sags at the triangle's curb, halting traffic on Fourth for miles. The woman exploits the tie-up to cross against the lights, and hurries down Atlantic. She sees a kid on a bicycle, waves him to a stop. He spins his pedal backward while she forms her question.

"How do you get to Kennedy airport?"

(thanks to Lukas Jaeger)
—*Konundrum Engine Literary Review*,
and liner notes for The Maggies' CD
Breakfast at Brelreck's, 2000

The Mad Brooklynite

I first spoke with the Mad Brooklynite on the Bergen Street platform, where we'd both stepped off the G train to wait for an F train, to take us deeper into the borough. The Brooklynite was a small man in a brown suit with frayed cuffs and a stained collar. He wore a blue cap with a B on it, in a typography I associated with the departed Brooklyn Dodgers. The bill of the cap was missing, reducing it to a sort of Dodgers beanie or yarmulke. "Do you have the time?" he asked. I did, and I told it to him. It was a quarter past three. "In Manhattan the train stations have clocks," he said. "Apparently we're a secondary class here in Brooklyn; our business could never be so important, and our need for the time of day is thus insignificant as well." I offered a nod, and a slight smile. His point was striking—why were there fewer clocks in the Brooklyn stations? What was being expressed? The Brooklynite changed the subject. "Did you know the G train is the only train in the entire subway which never enters the island of Manhattan?" I shook my head. "The sorriest train in the system," he continued. "It suffers from low self-esteem. Perhaps it should be allowed to change its route one day a year and enter Manhattan, just so it could taste the honor." I smiled to make him know I understood his sarcasm. "But that raises an ontological issue," he said, surprising me. "If a G train goes into Manhattan can it truly be regarded anymore as a G train? Perhaps its exclusion from the island is an intrinsic property." I shrugged; I couldn't know. "Here's another: the *Village Voice*," said the Brooklynite. "In Manhattan it's given out free; in Brooklyn we pay a dollar and a quarter. Our attention is less valuable to their advertisers, I suppose. Perhaps if we had clocks in our stations and knew the time of day we'd be more efficient, and hence more likely to generate enough disposable income to afford Pilates instructors and phone sex." I felt I could argue with the Brooklynite's logic, but I didn't choose to do so. The F train arrived, and we boarded. I shuffled away from the Brooklynite, found a seat, and began reading my newspaper. The Brooklynite stood by the doors. After the Carroll Street station the F line becomes elevated, and as we rose into the sunlight the Brooklynite turned to me and beckoned with a crooked finger. "Come, look." Helpless to refuse, I stood and joined him at the doors. "Consider the Williamsburg Savings Bank tower," he said. "Our sole skyscraper. Such a bare skyline, with just that blunt, homely phallus. Manhattan's a porcupine, a formation in crystal, a piece of electronic circuitry. Brooklyn's a bare crotch with a lonely erection. I'd be shocked if it didn't someday wilt in shame." I chuckled, but the Brooklynite only scowled more deeply. "Full of dentists, too," he said. "And empty offices. They rent for three or four hundred dollars a month. I know a plumber who rents one just to store his tools." He grew introspective. "My own dentist kept offices there, so long ago. Dr. Theodore Schemella. He's surely passed. I wore braces as a child; I would ascend to his office, where he would tighten the bonds on my teeth with great effort. I recall his elbows trembling, like an arm-wrestler's." We passed over the Gowanus Canal, Brooklyn's armpit; it went unremarked. "This trestle is unnecessarily high, don't you think?" asked the Brooklynite after a brief silence. It was true: I'd never considered it, but the F train does rise an unaccountable distance from the ground there, as it moves toward Park Slope. "A terrific view of Manhattan," he said sadly. "That's the only justification. The rise here ensures we consider the island as we retreat to our hovels. It splays Brooklyn out like a grubby body beneath us, Manhattan like the banners of heaven in the distance. They want to rub our noses in it once more, before we fall again into darkness." The Brooklynite grabbed my arm.

—*McSweeney's*, 1998

X

WHAT REMAINS OF MY PLAN

I'm like a doctor and it's an emergency room. And I'm the emergency.

—PHILIP ROTH

Forgiveness means giving up all hope for a better past.

—LILY TOMLIN

Micropsia

Twenty-five years before self-diagnosis, the waking dream; I think I was eight when it came. I lay on the cool tile of the bedroom I shared with my brother, in the desert of hours after lights-out, having meant to go into my parents' room and ask for a glass of water. Instead I fell, incapacitated by the sensation I'm now able to give the name *micropsia*. The room was dark apart from a night-light, and what illumination leaked in from the hall. I imagine I heard my own heartbeat.

I was afraid but also transfixed. Rather than cry out I lay still, tracing the mental contours of the extraordinary hallucination. My body, vast and ponderous, a felled redwood on the forest floor, a Sphinx poised on a beach. My consciousness, shrunken to gnat-size, a speck, or pinprick of light, contemplating the vast body from a great helpless distance. Any notion that this speck of will could operate the mountain range of body was banished. My fingers and toes were far-off peninsulas, unseeable over the planetary curve of my body, impossible to command. The hallucination was visual, but also kinesthetic; I felt the swollen acreage of my outline loom even with my eyes shut.

That wasn't all. The sensation had a narrative hook, a built-in epiphany still arriving. As I contemplated the persistence of my body I understood that, however, distended and transformed, *it* was *I*, too. I might not be able to operate my carcass in this state—who could move a mountain?—but I could inhabit its dimensions. I wasn't limited to that feeble speck I'd been a moment before. Or, rather, the speck was free to roam now over the vast surfaces of the bodyscape, to survey the limits where the mass met the tile, journey to those distant fingers. When the sensation receded and I regained use of my limbs I returned to bed, self-enraptured. My secret was something intense enough to fell me but, however irrational, it seemed to me if I could defeat my fear it would become a kind of power. I kept the secret.

The hallucination returned maybe twenty times through my childhood, but was never again so rich and complete, so possessing. Usually it came at night, though on certain lonely sun-splashed afternoons I'd lie on the floor in that same spot and induce the thing, invite it back. I named my mountainous body: the lion. The dwindled observer: the speck. I savored these trippy fugues. When they dimmed and grew infrequent, I mourned. The perspectival shift, from speck to lion, was a tiny mental orgasm, or an allegory of the mushrooming potential of awareness. When I spoke of it to children or adults no one recognized or confirmed *lion-and-speck*. Others' confusion confirmed my thing as private and unquantifiable, an involuntary philosophical song of the body. That suited me. I loved knowing the lion and the speck, was proud I'd banished my fear of knowing them, and associated them with what was deep and unique in me, what I'd least want to lose.

I lost them. By college I'd stopped making those mysterious detours. As the lion and the speck left my world I made one gesture of curation, an odd, opaque poem I submitted to a writing class. "I must recall the keys of my quality," I wrote, "or else become the point as opposed to the lion." My teacher, who was pretty hard on me generally, scribbled on the sheet that he didn't understand the poem and that it might be my best. I wasn't a poet. The poem was placed in a folder and forgotten. The texture of the experience was forgotten, too, and then the fact of it. There was no context for the memory, no prompt. The only thing that had ever reminded me of my hallucination was itself.

Ten years passed without thinking of it once, until one day I read a novelist's description of a boy's bedtime terrors: "Suddenly it was as if he were looking through the wrong end of a telescope: his own feet looked tiny, tapering with the distance, the toy soldier nearly imperceptible in his faraway hand. A fascinating change of perspective, making him feel like a giant of geological proportions—" The syndrome in the book had a name, micropsia. The novelist hadn't made it up. I was joined abruptly to my eight-year-old self. This déjà vu that wasn't brought me nearer to the lion and the speck than since before writing my dirgelike poem. The whole intensity of that paralyzing first episode returned.

The passage in the novel restored the strange milky jewel of micropsia to my possession and robbed me of it forever. I should be grateful. I might have stumbled across my poem and recollected my lonely wonder. More likely not. But the lion and the speck were now overwritten by banal micropsia, a symptom known to frighten children but considered harmless. Testimony, then, to the extinguishing force of names. The child acquiring a language is a being climbing forever out of the skin of the world, into a matrix of myths and symbols. What dreams Kaspar Hauser must have known.

My only revenge has been to become a collector of literary micropsia, committed by those who never were robbed. It typically hides in books I loved before I discovered it lurking there, Swift's *Gulliver*, Barthelme's *Dead Father*, Clarke's *Rendezvous with Rama*. From Cortázar's *Around the Day in Eighty Worlds*: "But it so happens that the man-child is not a gentleman but a cronopio who does not understand very well the system of vanishing lines that either creates a satisfactory perspective on circumstances or, like a badly done collage, produces a scale inconsistent with these circumstances, an ant too big for a palace . . . I know this from experience: sometimes I am larger than the horse I ride and sometimes I fall into one of my shoes . . ." From Stead's *The Man Who Loved Children*: "She fell asleep really and woke up shrieking, dreaming another old nightmare that she often tried to describe to them, 'Hard-soft, hard-soft,' a dream without sight or name, which her hands dreamed by themselves, swelling and shriveling, hard-soft . . ."

—1998/2011

Zeppelin Parable

Everybody knows "The Caravan Barks and the Dogs Move On." Fewer know "The Zeppelin Sails and the Dogs Sniff the Gas Nozzles." This is how it goes:

The potential zeppelin is in the field, lying sagged and helpless along the grass, a membrane painted with gay colors, struggling to assert itself, expecting to fly, unable yet.

The dogs are kept at bay in the parking lot in anticipation of the great moment. They pick boogers, call their spouses on cell phones, solve crossword puzzles, crack puns, speculate, lap from water bowls, etcetera. In this they resemble the irascible poker-playing reporters killing time as they wait for the execution of the convicted murderer in *His Girl Friday*.

The gas flows from the pipes, which are laid in long sections of hose and fitted with nozzles. The nozzles connect to the inflow nodules of the vast baggy zeppelin.

The gas comes from underground, from purportedly "great deep secret sources." The gas would certainly stay underground unless it had a zeppelin to fill, because the gas is by nature bashful, deferential, conflicted.

Slowly the zeppelin inflates, taking succor and inspiration from the munificence of the gas.

Lift Is Achieved.

Ropes Are Loosened.

Hoses Disconnected from Valves.

Many Shouts.

Hurry, it's in the air!

No one can pinpoint the moment the bag becomes truly a zeppelin, thanks to the gas, but after so long a wait, a water-boiling interlude, this phase transition in fact seems to elude even the closest watcher: suddenly. Now there is much to do. We all adore the zeppelin when it sails, do we not? We are all ready to have our hearts broken.

The dogs are loosed and rush baying onto the field.

The zeppelin is unbound from earth now, unfixed, a thing of the sky and beyond. It wants to go to outer space—not as a rocket would but by drifting, by departing this world with our amazed and yearning eyeballs in gentle tow.

There could never be enough of this.

If only X were here to see it!

The dogs have joined us now where we stand under the zeppelin's fuzzy shadow, the zeppelin soaring so gradually, yet now already beginning to depart the field, to incline for the mountains, there to be lost in the higher air—

Look!

Great god, look! It's the mother ship!

Look!

But the dogs have their noses to the ground. They're chasing traces, sniffing hoses, rooting for nozzles.

No, dogs, that's beside the point! The gas was only to fill the zeppelin—please, look, before it is too late.

One dog whines, finding a nozzle, and rolls over it in his excitement. Others come growling and grumbling, wanting a piece of the action. He's got a good one! This dog can really detect a strong whiff of gas, a tendril left behind in the quick disconnection of nozzle from socket.

Yummy, the dogs all say. Nasty, yummy gas. Gotta gotta get me some of that.

No, look in the air! we shout.

It's so beautiful!

Too late, gone. They missed it.

The Zeppelin Sails and the Dogs Sniff the Gas Nozzles.

'Twas ever thus.

Hey, man, these dogs don't even LIKE zeppelins! They like gas.

Cut 'em some slack.

Yeah, what were we thinking?

—*McSweeney's*, 2004

What Remains of My Plan

There's something embarrassing about knowing what you know, after a while. On certain days it can all seem to plunge into either the category of that which never needed explaining in the first place or that which you're astounded to realize you've never even begun making clear. Heads nodding in agreement are usually also falling asleep, but just when you think you're the last one awake in the room, admonishing the snoring, your head jerks upward on your stiffening neck, and you see the crowd has tiptoed out not wishing to disturb. The lecture was your dream of lecturing. In it, you tested precepts unimportant to anyone but yourself. On those days it is a relief the room is vacant.

When Thomas Berger was asked why he wrote, he said, "Because it isn't there." Bernard Malamud's answer to the same question: "I'd be too moved to say." Somewhere between climbing Berger's imaginary mountain and, like Malamud, recording a grievance against inexpressibility, that's where my answer lies. It's probably typical of me that I solve the question by looking to the right and left of me for Berger's and Malamud's assistance, but then again there was nobody asking the question but myself in the first place, so I needed some company.

"Writing is a lonely business" is both a dull myth and a material fact of the profession, one I happen to be temperamentally suited to endure but which doesn't gratify my sense of what it's *for*. I began writing in order to arrive into the company of those whose company meant more to me than any other: the world of the books I'd found on shelves and begun to assemble on my own, and the people who'd written them, and the readers who cared as much as I did, if those existed. Humans are social animals, but I'd been socialized to ghosts, arrangements of sentences on pages, and needed urgently to be audible to them. People could come afterward. They would, wouldn't they? Sometimes I think I relied on that too much. But it's too late to demote the ghosts I gave first seating at my table. Some pretty fine human beings have indulged my error, over the years.

My friend Maureen, a professor of philosophy, once told me of the moment she recognized her vocation. It was when she heard philosophical work analogized as the task of creating an area of descriptive illumination against the backdrop of a sea of infinite dark. To work to clarify even a tiny area of night, to infill it with philosophical light, was all one could hope for, a life's honorable work. Yet the emphasis she'd heard, the emphasis that moved her to commitment, wasn't that of acknowledging the brave lonely smallness of a single philosophical enterprise. It was that the context for the effort's meaning was the proximity, however faint or distant, of other small zones of illumination. The work that had gone before and would come after. The work going on adjacent and simultaneously, all around.

Among the things I'm embarrassed to know, finally and after all, is that the conversation never really got better than the talk in the bar of the Radisson. Elsewhere the drinks were more expensive, but I've never been great at appreciating expensive drinks. The model proposed by the science-fiction field, unsustainable for me, alas, was of a coherent ongoing collective action, engaged in by a cadre of living writers and the only-very-recently dead. We were always to reinscribe and honor the whole history of the field every time we jotted a line. If, in the bar of the Radisson, I often wanted to scream, "You fools, don't you see, it's every man for himself?," ever since exiting that inoperative utopia I've been shouting, "You fools, don't you understand, we're all in this together?" That shout is this book.

Even more embarrassing to realize I know, the best action may be not in the bar of the Radisson but in the scorned conference room, where a panel discussion is playing to a packed house, where the most helplessly committed audience any artist could ever dream existed is currently being taken for granted, around the clock. Here and there—

not only at the science-fiction convention but on a book-tour stop in a medium-size city—the secret readers of the world are made visible, not the aspiring writers or even the Amazon reviewers jockeying in that tiny social arena, but the naked minds complicating themselves by extended submission to a machine of words that some other human, possibly you, threw together. How marvelous that anyone should want to do such a thing and then announce themselves in public! It really is strange for all concerned, most of all for the writers, who if they are honest have, usually, nothing to add to, but every probability of accidentally subtracting from, whatever it was they managed to put across. Yet in my gratitude I go around accepting your gratitude, and then, when I'm asked questions I open my mouth and words fly out, every time.

The truth is, nothing about what I do qualifies me to weigh in on this and that, and it is probably only dangerous that my practiced employment of the tool of language makes my personal opinions decant from my brain so readily. For they are only a person's opinions. When I make a remark about politics my qualification is that I'm a citizen, like you, not that I'm a novelist. When I make a remark about culture—about a song or a film or even a book—my qualification is that I'm a fan. I knew a crack addict once who explained to me that before he smoked crack, or took any drug, he drank beer. No matter how glamorously vile, illegal, and destructive others might consider crack to be, he personally saw beer as his baseline situation. Well, before I wrote, and in between each of the times that I wrote, I was a reader, and surely after I have quit or been rendered incapable of writing I'll be a reader still. That's my beer.

What's a novelist? I remove myself from human traffic to sit in a room alone and make up stories about human traffic that doesn't exist. For my living I climb into and then punch my way out of the paper bag of my solipsism on a daily basis—and on the days I don't manage to punch my way out there is no coach who blows a whistle and tells me to remove myself from the field in favor of a better-rested substitute ("Where's your Negative Capability today, son?"). Among other things, this is nice work if you can get it. The loneliness is overrated, especially if a bookshelf is near, and mine is.

When I was fifteen, I for the first time handed over a book to its author for an autograph—it was Anthony Burgess. I still drag my books out and have them autographed by the people who wrote them, not only in order to someday put my grandchildren through rocket-pilot school but because the sorcery of the connection between those lumpy and endearing human animals and the flights of language and invention that sometimes fly out of their fingers still astounds me. And because having had my own books pressed into my hands for a signature has never stopped seeming like the only certain thing I had to offer the people who've troubled to exit their homes to view me. Yes, I am the person who made that weird thought go into your head. Yes, I'm as flabbergasted as you are, really. Thank you.

Nietzsche: "The thinker or artist whose better self has fled into his works feels an almost malicious joy when he sees his body and spirit slowly broken into and destroyed by time; it is as if he were in a corner, watching a thief at work on his safe, all the while knowing that it is empty and that all his treasures have been rescued."

Memorial

Well, the first thing to admit
Is that it isn't dead yet. Or never lived.
It was a memorial to itself all along.
My creature stands, a wicker man,
Built of postures weathered into timber.
Interior shelves jammed, paraphernalia
Wreathed in dust webs, yet of
Sporadic use. So I don't tear it down.
Besides, I'm fascinated. He looks
Like me, but was never me.
I've slept inside a night or two
But lately camp a little farther West.
Squatters use it as much as I do.
At certain hours, chimps of rage
Mount candles in the eyes.
I've heard them dancing at its feet, the fools.

Imogen is our friend's daughter, and our friend.
More important, today she is our babysitter.
She loves stupid jokes and baking,
Talks like a born writer, but quips,
"I could never be a writer—too many words."

Imogen's young, sure, but our baby is dew,
And looks on Imogen as a savant, a titan.
Who knew Imogen was out there? Why complain if
They keep bringing them along like hotcakes?
(The baby has no cynicism. Imogen's, if it exists,
Is made of green saplings, bent into a kooky cup,
Hidden in the woods. Maybe she wears it like a crown.)

A dark tribe, prey to fair invaders,
Hosted their blond lords for a season, until
Some local flu, to which the tribesmen were inured,
Chopped them down like trees.
Then, seeing how the foreigners had favored their dead,
The tribe buried the blonds
In a gated plot, on a high hill,
Each in a box, and marked with stone.
Then maintained the scene for generations,
Memorial to—you know—*what can happen.*
Their own dead the natives dispatched
In mounds of sand on a sloped beach,
To wash to sea, as tradition ordained.

"I'll write a poem," I joked,
Teasing my golem into view.
Nothing makes him grunt like a poem.
(I learned I was no poet sophomore year.)
But what shock, to see how decrepit
That figure had become. By night
My camp had drifted West, farther
Than I'd imagined I'd go. Or than he'd imagined.
He doesn't have much imagination!
Who would restock those shelves? Or use
The binoculars? Could my memorial be made
A scarecrow on shoals, a warning? Likely not.
He may not be visible to anyone else.

—*Guilt & Pleasure,* 2008

Things to Remember

1. I remember hearing once (I don't remember where) that memory honors no point of origin, has no interest in or indeed any capacity for making a pure return to the site of its inception. No, instead each memory is only a photocopy of the previous memory. Memory, ventriloquist but no dummy, loves the path of least resistance. We trash the original and start again with the last version, like a nervous troupe of actors working from a script in endless revision, always basing our performance on the most recent draft. And, to keep our performances coherent, burning every available scrap of the previous edition. We have no recourse to the author or to any of the author's sources, no document or evidence, no mountain to pilgrimage backward toward. Glance back and the mountain is gone. Better not to glance, so you may imagine you feel its massiveness at your back. The only document is our revision, these freshly inked onionskin sheets clutched in our trembling grasp, current for the moment, but no more final than the previous sheaf, quite equally eligible to be discarded. Memory is a rehearsal for a show that never goes on.

2. No wonder dreams are fatal and must be systematically forgotten. The memory of a dream is every bit as tangible as any other memory. As tangible as those based on some dim receding occurrence or

encounter, a moment, an undream. The memory of a dream is stronger, in a way, because it knows it is a fiction.

3. I remember that when I was a child forgetting enraged me. It seemed a conspiracy enacted by others. My own memory was perfect, and I doubted anyone else was honest when they claimed to have forgotten. How awfully convenient for them. They could call themselves forgetters but I called them liars. After a few years I was forced to consider a substitute hypothesis, seeing that the forgetters, who were everyone, so often seemed in good faith. Their dispute with the obvious permanence of memory was a weakness begging indulgence. The ritual fiction of forgetting was the only way they could tolerate themselves, the only method for getting through their days. I was stronger than anyone I knew, but not in the way I'd first imagined. They believed they forgot, and I, alien among them, would be forced to pretend to believe them as well, in order to form an adequate tolerance of the sole universal religion, the one in which I found myself enrolled anywhere I encountered another consciousness, another conscience. And yet the power of faith is that it enlists disbelievers by pretense. Masks, as always, melt into the face. I forgot that forgetting was a falsehood, began to believe the ritual not only necessary but involuntary. The moment I experienced forgetting I forgave them all instantaneously, even as I joined their cult. I have never forgotten, however, my original suspicions.

4. We make lists of things we want to remember, and then we lose the lists. My life is a tattered assemblage of abandoned calendars, misplaced agendas, water-damaged address books with names blurred, family trees I've never managed to hold coherently in mind, third cousins unrecalled named for third uncles unmet, files of papers I've misplaced or never look into, schoolwork praised by teachers with faces I can't bring to mind. I once found a packet of love letters from a woman I couldn't recall. A list of mummified sentiments as useless as a grocery receipt. Our memories may be tomb-worlds, after all, a place to spare others having to dwell. Whereas the one thing I am sure I can remember about your eyes is that each time I see them they'll be eyes I could never have forgotten. We list things in order to cross them off,

to relegate them with relief to the kingdom of amnesia. So leave me off your lists.

5. What if we are only, after all, a kind of mortal list, a countdown? Human consciousness may be time's attempt to remember itself. It is possible we are only things to remember. The enumerated lives, the names of those gone, our letters and maps and charts, a mnemonic device for otherwise uncountable eons, a way to give a hint of flavor to the void. Yet time most likely found it unbearable to remember itself entirely. A glance in that direction was all that was needed. How attendantly can we care to notice ourselves slipping away, how eager should we be to remember forgetting, and being forgotten? So, mercifully, we're not falling down on the only job we're given, because our job is double, we're markers and erasers. (I'll never get over my delight at discovering the erasable marker, with which on a smooth surface one may endlessly draw and redraw a day's agenda, as if each day's was different from another's: *1. Remember. 2. Lunch break. 3. Forget.*) We're here as much to forget as to remember, that's what it means to punch the clock. To forget on time's behalf. How could time hope to be forgotten without us?

—*Tar*, 2008

Acknowledgments

Eric Simonoff, Bill Thomas, Sonny Mehta, Devin McKinney, Kevin Dettmar, John Hilgart, Shelley Jackson, Brian Berger, Franklin Bruno, Herman Ottsirkel, Jaime Clarke, David Shields, Vivian Gornick, and Amy, Enabler.

And Sean Howe, Matthew Specktor, and Giles Harvey, each in their way co-author of these pages.